W9-DFI-688

Thank you for picking up
Haikyu!! volume 22! Working
on this series has kept me
so busy that I haven't been
able to get any exercise, but
I recently started swimming.
Cramming even just 30
minutes of swimming in every
day has me feeling so good that
my work is going smoother than
ever! Seems like it, anyway.

HARUICHI FURUDATE began his manga career when he was
25 years old with the one-shot Ousama Kid (King Kid), which
won an honorable mention for the 14th Jump Treasure
Newcomer Manga Prize. His first series, Kiben Gakuha, Yotsuya
Sensei no Kaidan (Philosophy School, Yotsuya Sensei's Ghost
Stories), was serialized in Weekly Shonen Jump in 2010.
In 2012, he began serializing Haikyu!! in Weekly Shonen Jump,
where it became his most popular work to date.

HAIKYU!!
VOLUME 22
SHONEN JUMP Manga Edition

Story and Art by
HARUICHI FURUDATE

Translation **1** **ADRIENNE BECK**
Touch-Up Art & Lettering **2** **ERIKA TERRIQUEZ**
Design **3** **JULIAN [JR] ROBINSON**
Editor **4** **MARLENE FIRST**

HAIKYU!! © 2012 by Haruichi Furudate
All rights reserved.
First published in Japan in 2012 by SHUEISHA Inc., Tokyo.
English translation rights arranged by SHUEISHA Inc.

The stories, characters and incidents mentioned
in this publication are entirely fictional.

No portion of this book may be reproduced or transmitted
in any form or by any means without written permission
from the copyright holders.

Printed in the U.S.A.

Published by VIZ Media, LLC
P.O. Box 77010
San Francisco, CA 94107

10 9 8 7 6 5 4 3 2 1
First printing, April 2018

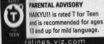
PARENTAL ADVISORY
HAIKYU!! is rated T for Teen
and is recommended for ages
13 and up for mild language.
ratings.viz.com

www.shonenjump.com

www.viz.com

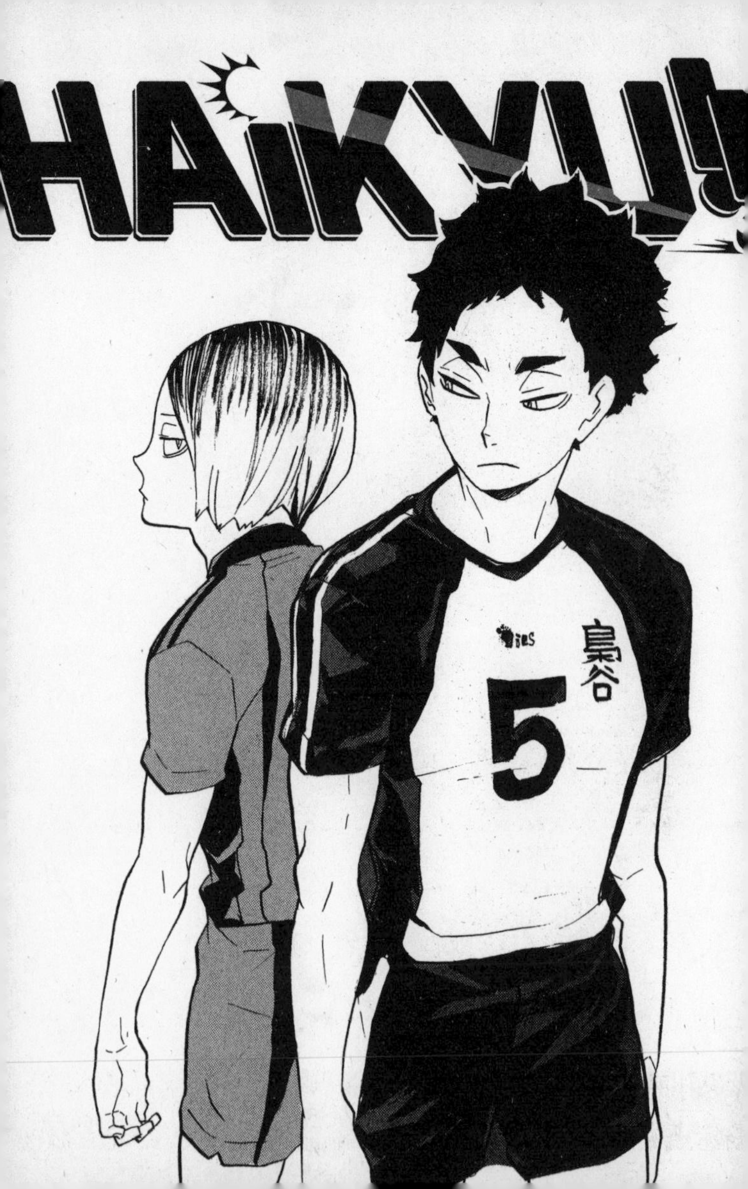
HAIKYU!!
梟谷
5

Karasuno High School Volleyball Club

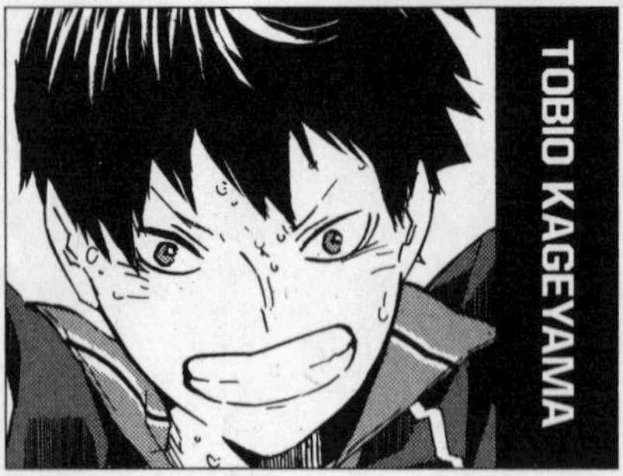
TOBIO KAGEYAMA

1ST YEAR / SETTER

His instincts and athletic talent are so good that he's like a "king" who rules the court. Demanding and egocentric.

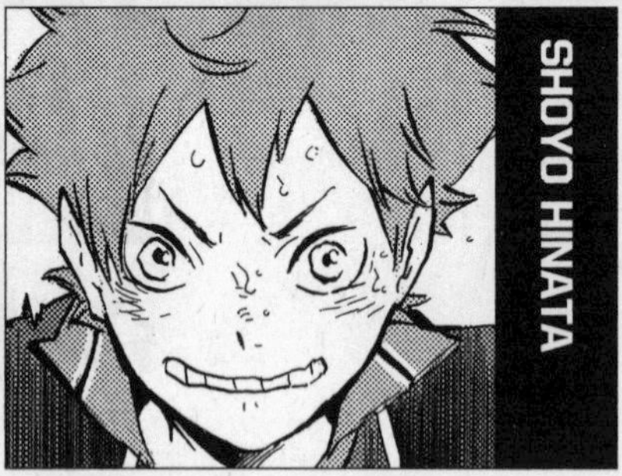
SHOYO HINATA

1ST YEAR / MIDDLE BLOCKER

Even though he doesn't have the best body type for volleyball, he is super athletic. Gets nervous easily.

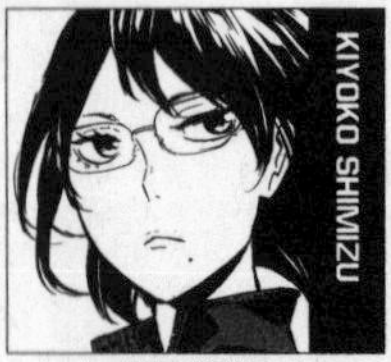
KIYOKO SHIMIZU

3RD YEAR
MANAGER

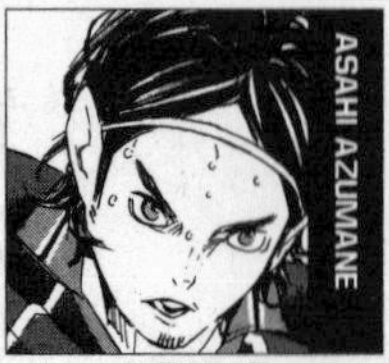
ASAHI AZUMANE

3RD YEAR
WING SPIKER

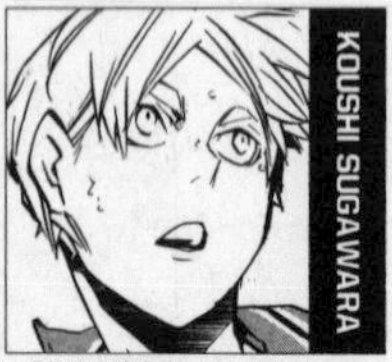
KOUSHI SUGAWARA

3RD YEAR (VICE CAPTAIN)
SETTER

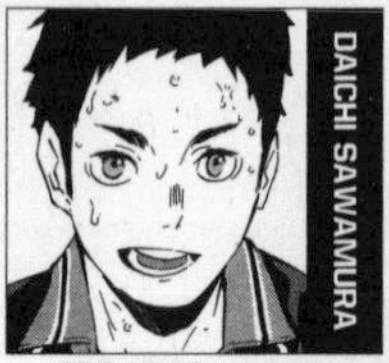
DAICHI SAWAMURA

3RD YEAR (CAPTAIN)
WING SPIKER

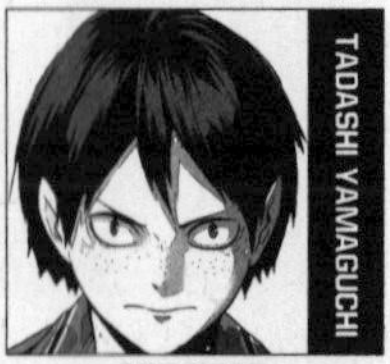
TADASHI YAMAGUCHI

1ST YEAR
MIDDLE BLOCKER

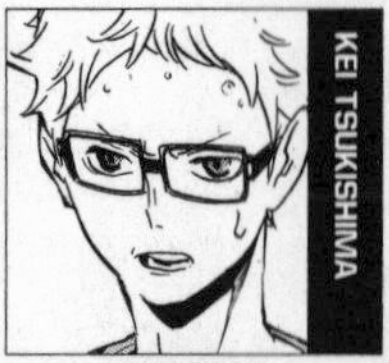
KEI TSUKISHIMA

1ST YEAR
MIDDLE BLOCKER

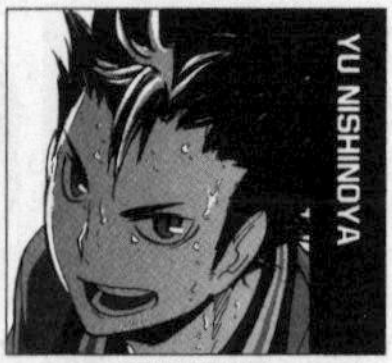
YU NISHINOYA

2ND YEAR
LIBERO

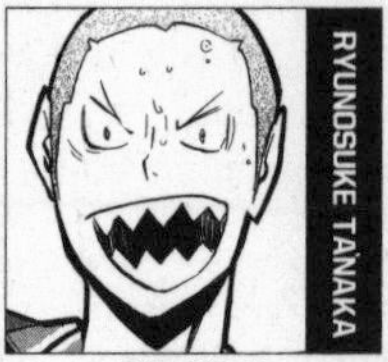
RYUNOSUKE TANAKA

2ND YEAR
WING SPIKER

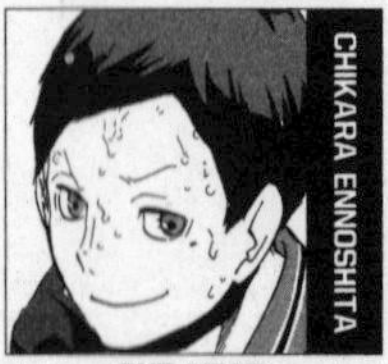
CHIKARA ENNOSHITA

2ND YEAR
WING SPIKER

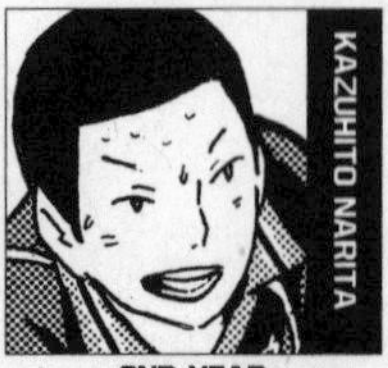
KAZUHITO NARITA

2ND YEAR
MIDDLE BLOCKER

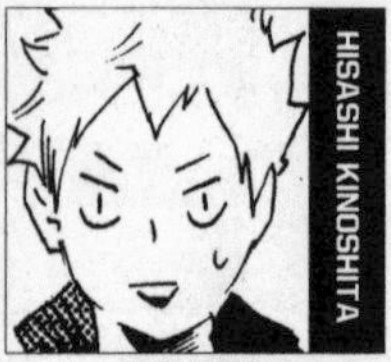
HISASHI KINOSHITA

2ND YEAR
WING SPIKER

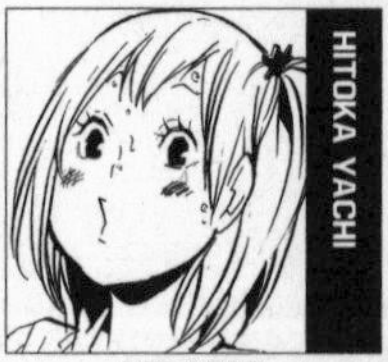
HITOKA YACHI

1ST YEAR
MANAGER

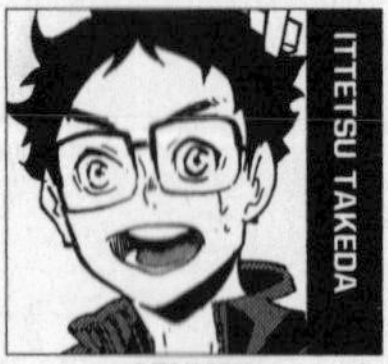
ITTETSU TAKEDA

ADVISER

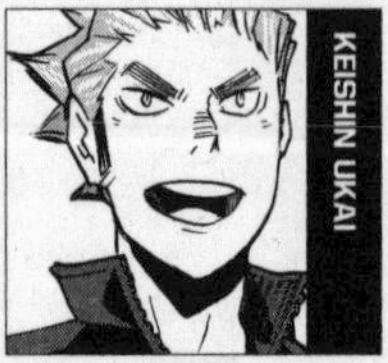
KEISHIN UKAI

COACH

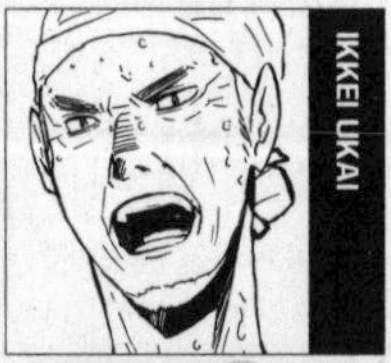
IKKEI UKAI

FORMER HEAD COACH

CHARACTERS

TOKYO AREA SPRING TOURNAMENT QUALIFIER TOURNAMENT ARC

Nekoma Volleyball Club

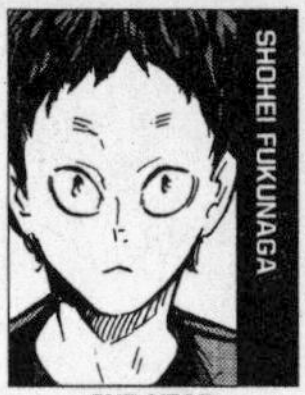
SHOHEI FUKUNAGA
2ND YEAR
WING SPIKER

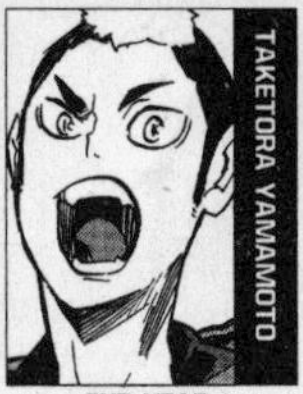
TAKETORA YAMAMOTO
2ND YEAR
WING SPIKER

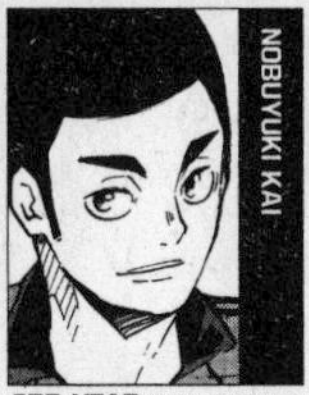
NOBUYUKI KAI
3RD YEAR (VICE CAPTAIN)
WING SPIKER

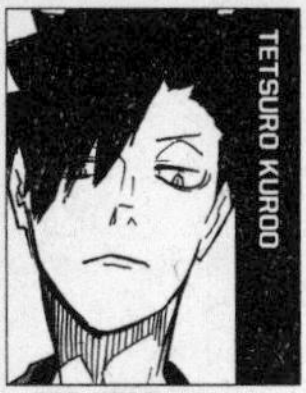
TETSURO KUROO
3RD YEAR (CAPTAIN)
MIDDLE BLOCKER

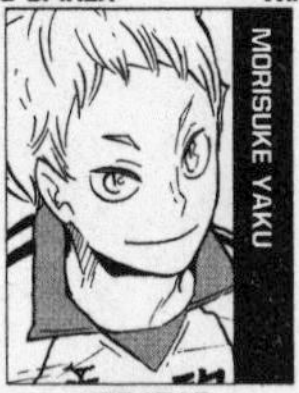
MORISUKE YAKU
3RD YEAR
LIBERO

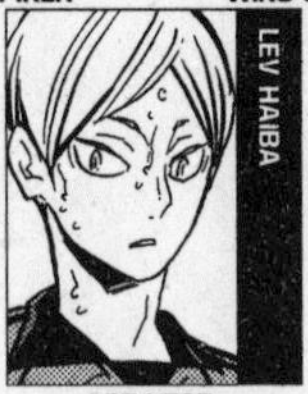
LEV HAIBA
1ST YEAR
MIDDLE BLOCKER

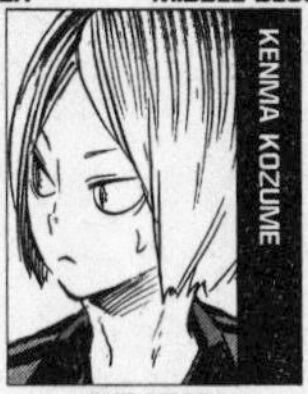
KENMA KOZUME
2ND YEAR
SETTER

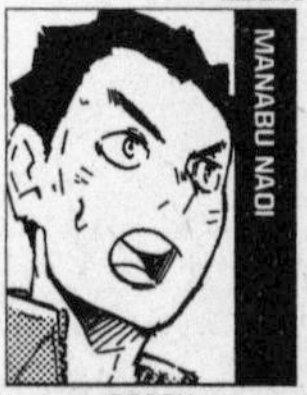
MANABU NAOI
COACH

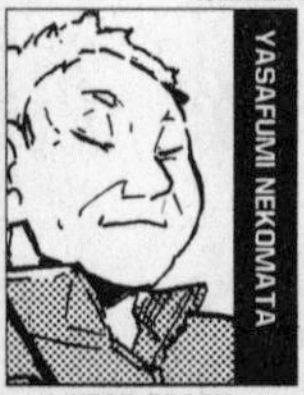
YASAFUMI NEKOMATA
HEAD COACH

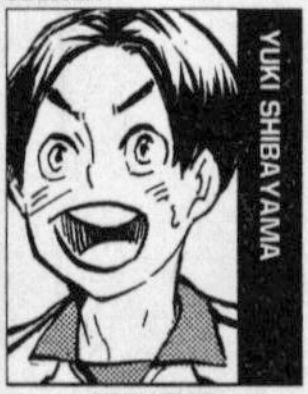
YUKI SHIBAYAMA
1ST YEAR
LIBERO

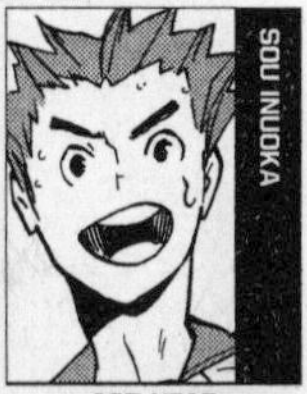
SOU INUOKA
1ST YEAR
MIDDLE BLOCKER

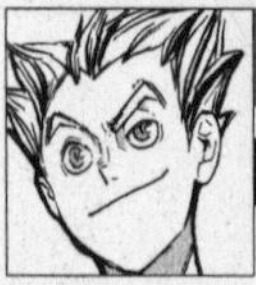

FUKURODANI ACADEMY VOLLEYBALL CLUB

KOTARO BOKUTO

3RD YEAR (CAPTAIN)
WING SPIKER

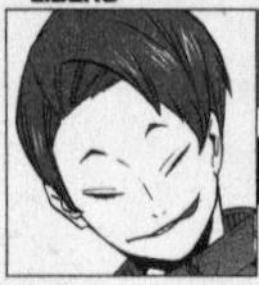

NOHEBI ACADEMY VOLLEYBALL CLUB

SUGURU DAISHO

3RD YEAR (CAPTAIN)
WING SPIKER

Ever since he saw the legendary player known as "the Little Giant" compete at the national volleyball finals, Shoyo Hinata has been aiming to be the best volleyball player ever! He decides to join the volleyball club at his middle school and gets to play in an official tournament during his third year. His team is crushed by a team led by volleyball prodigy Tobio Kageyama, also known as "the King of the Court." Swearing revenge on Kageyama, Hinata graduates middle school and enters Karasuno High School, the school where the Little Giant played. However, upon joining the club, he finds out that Kageyama is there too! The two of them bicker constantly, but they bring out the best in each other's talents and become a powerful combo. Karasuno has won their way to the finals of the Spring Tournament Qualifiers, where they face the perennial champions—Shiratorizawa! In the fifth and final set, Shiratorizawa has match point! But Tsukishima, who had been injured, is able to come back into the game. Though the team is running on fumes, Tsukishima picks their best rotation to set a trap for Ushijima. Shiratorizawa's super ace manages to avoid the trap, but Hinata unveils a new attack, giving Karasuno the point it needs to punch its ticket to nationals! Meanwhile, the Tokyo qualifier tournament is gearing up for its final rounds...

HAIKYU!!

22 LAND VS. AIR

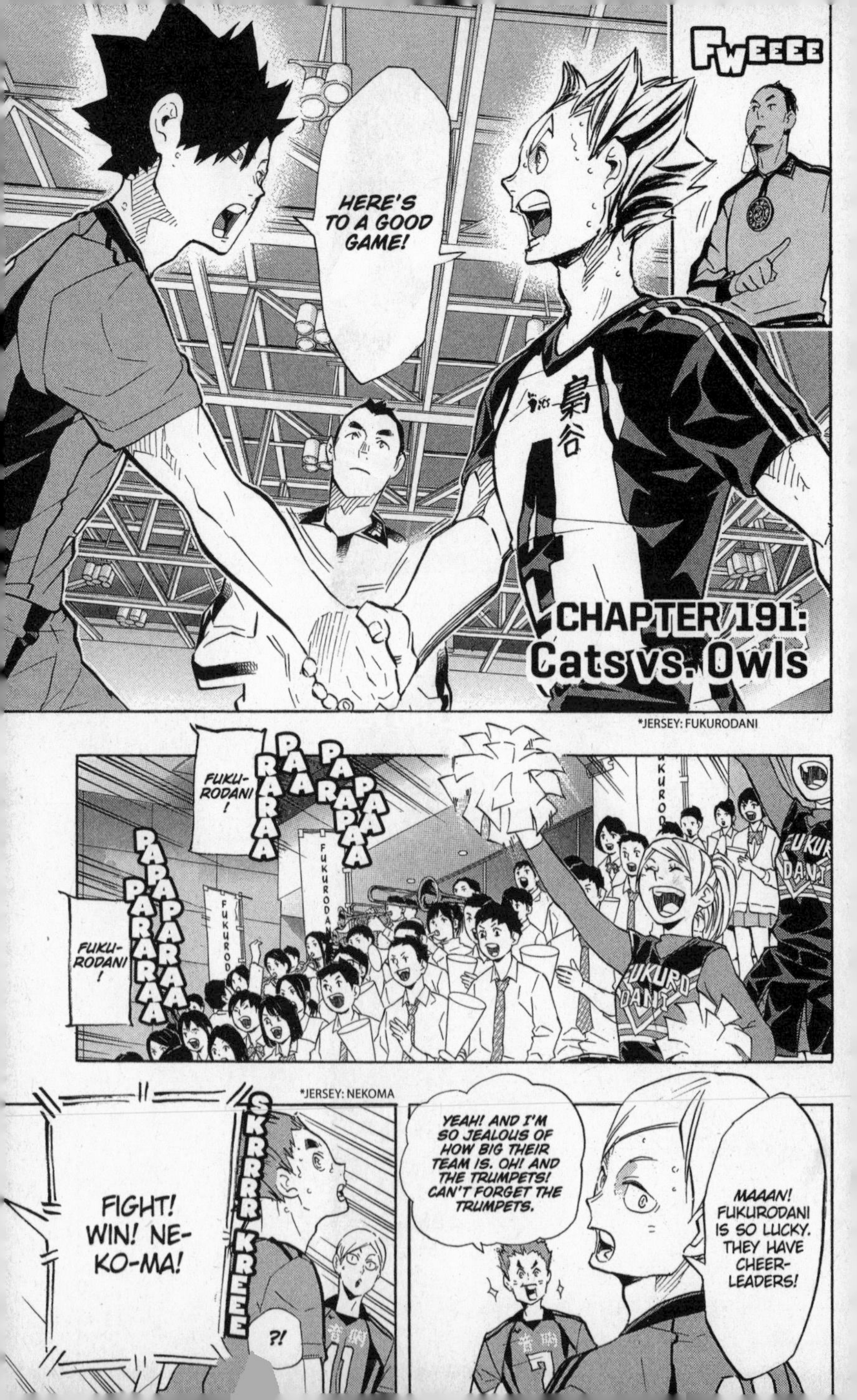
FWEEEE
HERE'S TO A GOOD GAME!
CHAPTER 191: Cats vs. Owls
*JERSEY: FUKURODANI
PARAPAPAA
PAA
PAA
RARAA
FUKURODANI!
FUKURODANI
FUKURODANI
FUKUROD
PAPAPARAA
PARARAA
FUKURODANI!
FUKURODANI
*JERSEY: NEKOMA
MAAAN! FUKURODANI IS SO LUCKY. THEY HAVE CHEERLEADERS!
YEAH! AND I'M SO JEALOUS OF HOW BIG THEIR TEAM IS. OH! AND THE TRUMPETS! CAN'T FORGET THE TRUMPETS.
SKRRRR KREEE
?!
FIGHT! WIN! NE-KO-MA!

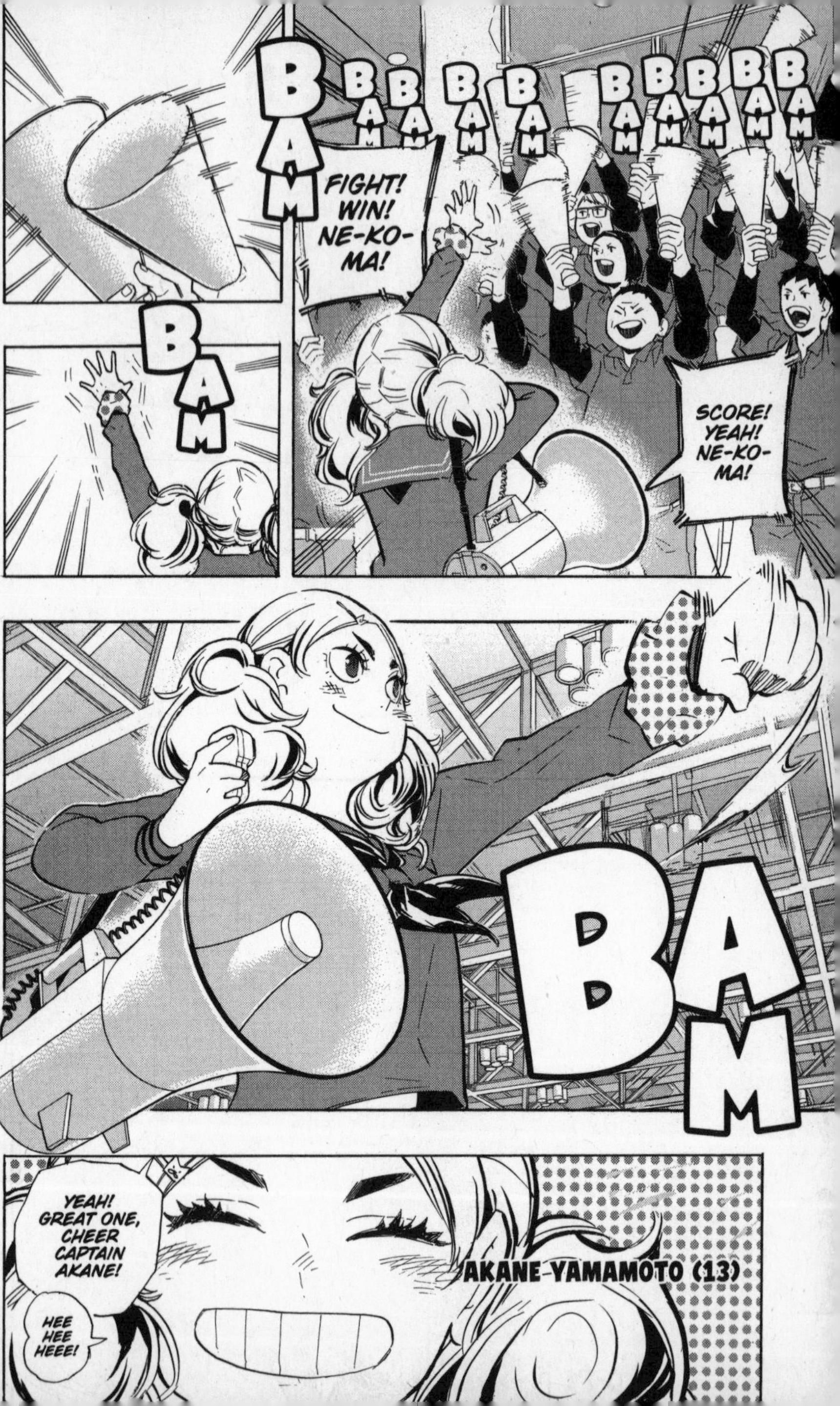
BAM
BAM
BAM
BAM
BAM
BAM
BAM
BAM
BAM
SCORE! YEAH! NE-KO-MA!
FIGHT! WIN! NE-KO-MA!
BAM
BAM
BAM
AKANE YAMAMOTO (13)
YEAH! GREAT ONE, CHEER CAPTAIN AKANE!
HEE HEE HEEE!

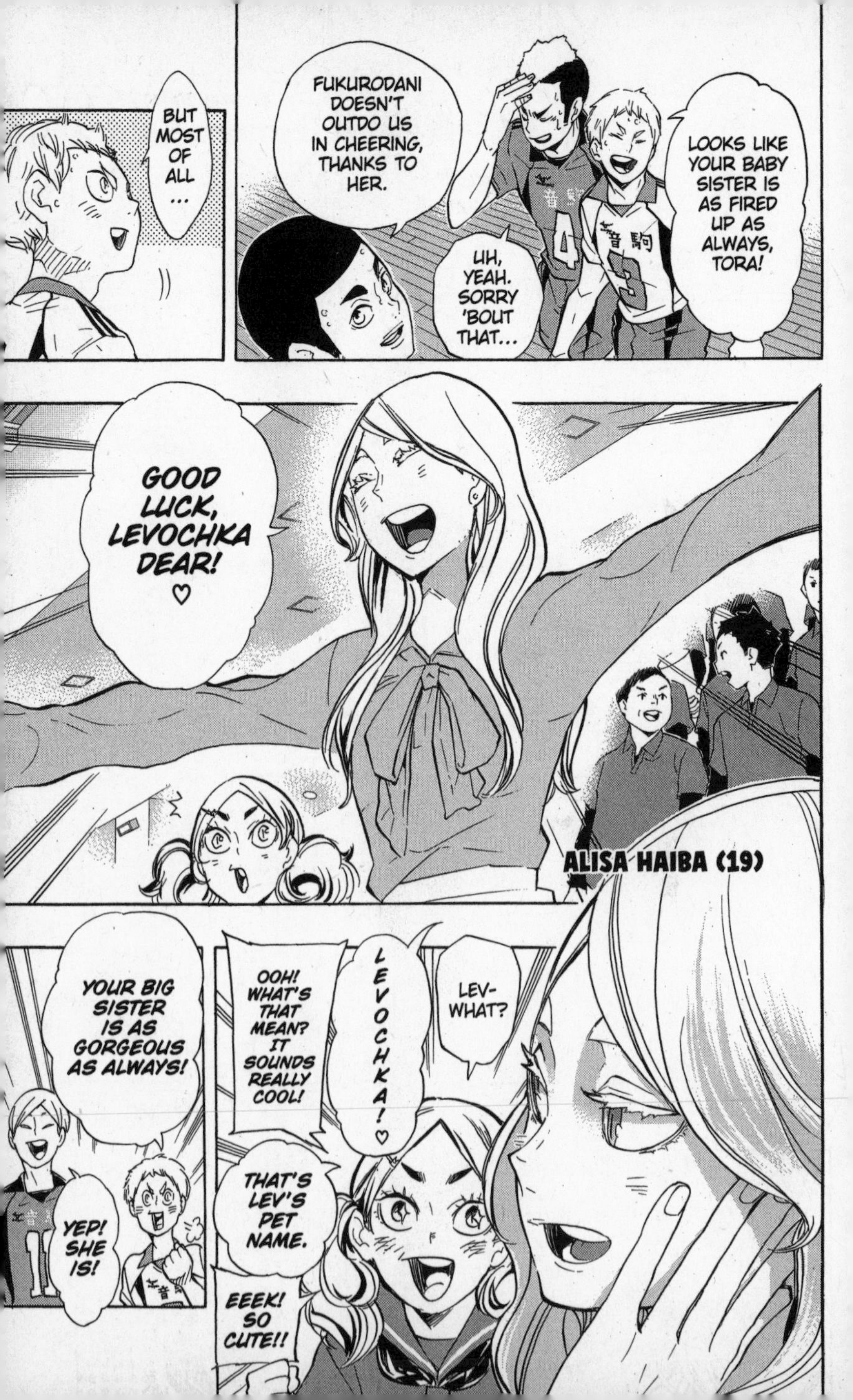
LOOKS LIKE YOUR BABY SISTER IS AS FIRED UP AS ALWAYS, TORA!
FUKURODANI DOESN'T OUTDO US IN CHEERING, THANKS TO HER.
UH, YEAH. SORRY 'BOUT THAT...
BUT MOST OF ALL...
GOOD LUCK, LEVOCHKA DEAR! ♡
ALISA HAIBA (19)
LEV-WHAT?
LEVOCHKA! ♡
OOH! WHAT'S THAT MEAN? IT SOUNDS REALLY COOL!
THAT'S LEV'S PET NAME.
EEEK! SO CUTE!!
YOUR BIG SISTER IS AS GORGEOUS AS ALWAYS!
YEP! SHE IS!

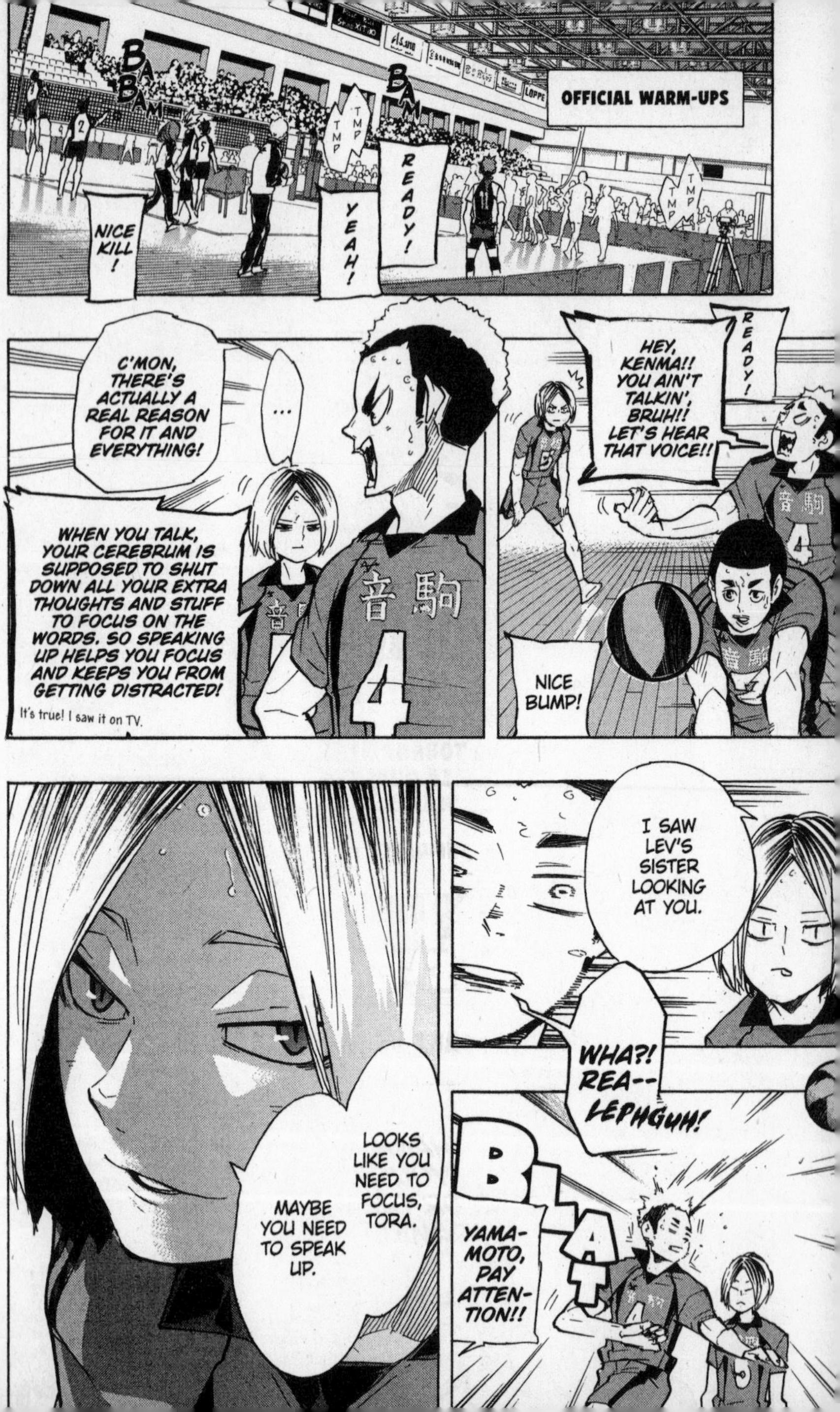
OFFICIAL WARM-UPS
TMP TMP
READY!
BAM
YEAH!
TMP TMP
BABAM
NICE KILL!
READY!
HEY, KENMA!! YOU AIN'T TALKIN', BRUH!! LET'S HEAR THAT VOICE!!
NICE BUMP!
C'MON, THERE'S ACTUALLY A REAL REASON FOR IT AND EVERYTHING!
...
WHEN YOU TALK, YOUR CEREBRUM IS SUPPOSED TO SHUT DOWN ALL YOUR EXTRA THOUGHTS AND STUFF TO FOCUS ON THE WORDS. SO SPEAKING UP HELPS YOU FOCUS AND KEEPS YOU FROM GETTING DISTRACTED!
It's true! I saw it on TV.
I SAW LEV'S SISTER LOOKING AT YOU.
WHA?! REA--LEPHGUH!
BLAT
YAMAMOTO, PAY ATTENTION!!
LOOKS LIKE YOU NEED TO FOCUS, TORA.
MAYBE YOU NEED TO SPEAK UP.

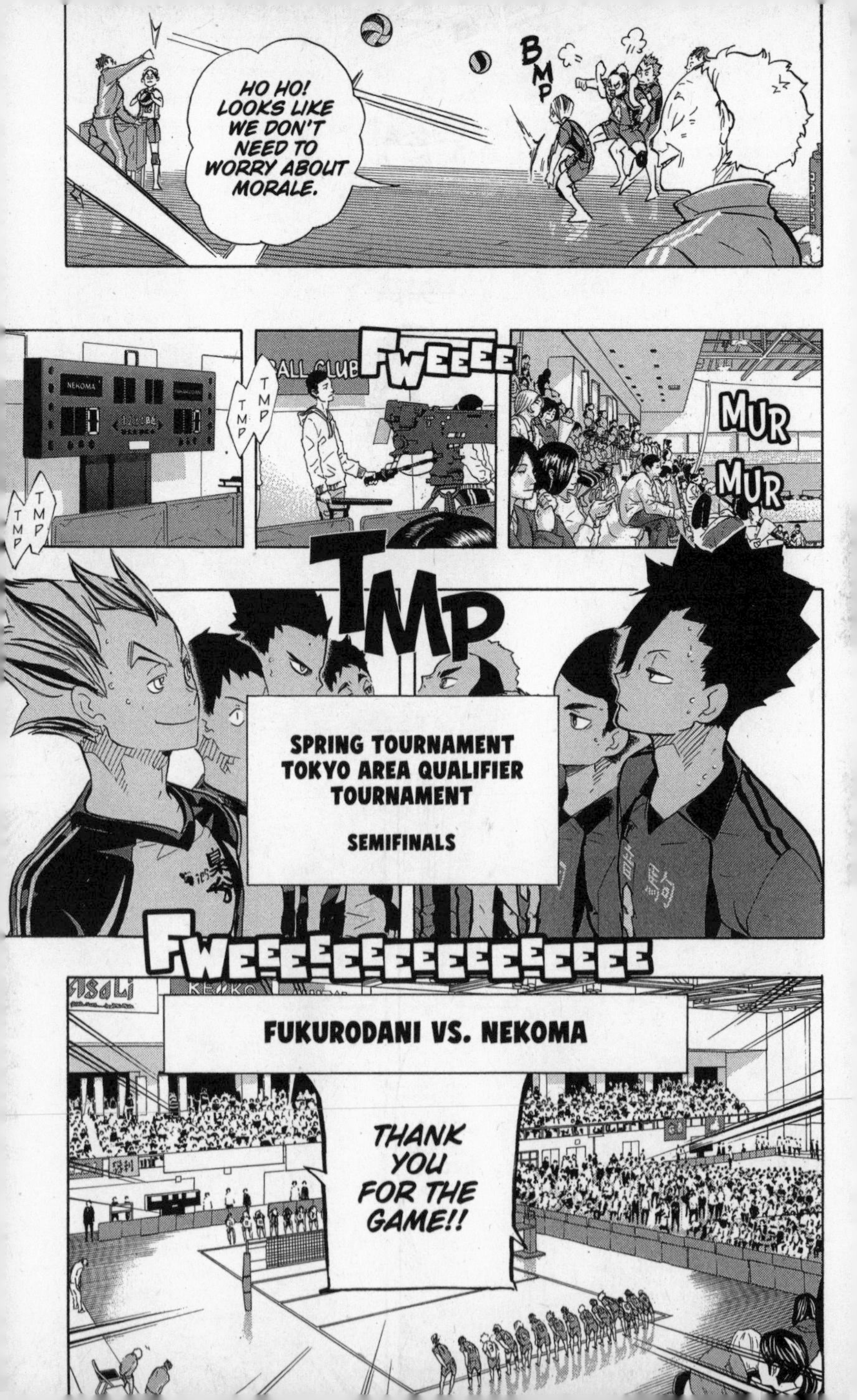
BMP
HO HO! LOOKS LIKE WE DON'T NEED TO WORRY ABOUT MORALE.
MUR
MUR
FWEEEE
TMP TMP
TMP TMP
NEKOMA
TMP
SPRING TOURNAMENT
TOKYO AREA QUALIFIER
TOURNAMENT
SEMIFINALS
FWEEEEEEEEEEEEE
FUKURODANI VS. NEKOMA
THANK YOU FOR THE GAME!!

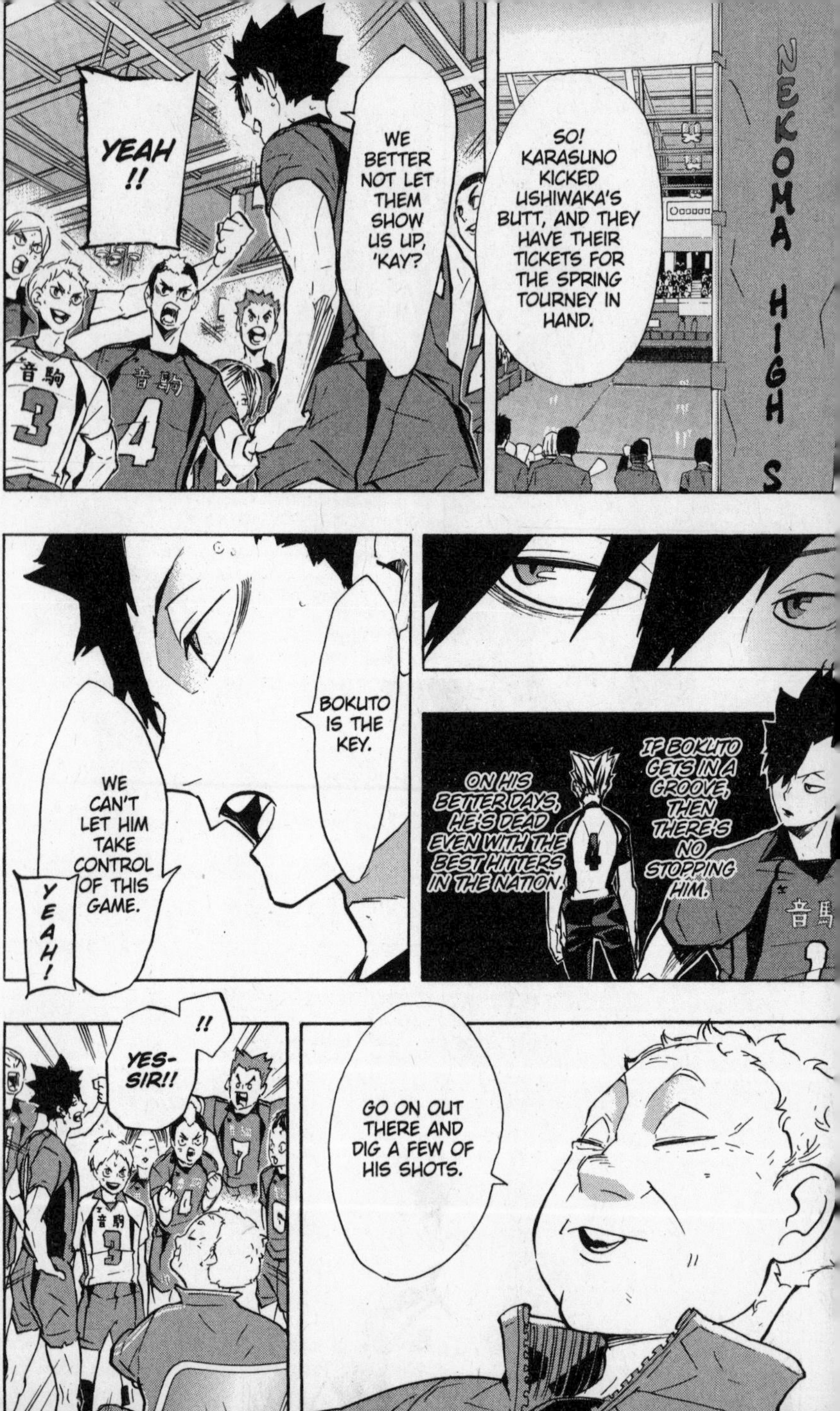
NEKOMA HIGH S
SO! KARASUNO KICKED USHIWAKA'S BUTT, AND THEY HAVE THEIR TICKETS FOR THE SPRING TOURNEY IN HAND.
WE BETTER NOT LET THEM SHOW US UP, 'KAY?
YEAH!!
IF BOKUTO GETS IN A GROOVE, THEN THERE'S NO STOPPING HIM.
ON HIS BETTER DAYS, HE'S DEAD EVEN WITH THE BEST HITTERS IN THE NATION.
BOKUTO IS THE KEY.
WE CAN'T LET HIM TAKE CONTROL OF THIS GAME.
YEAH!
GO ON OUT THERE AND DIG A FEW OF HIS SHOTS.
!!
YES-SIR!!

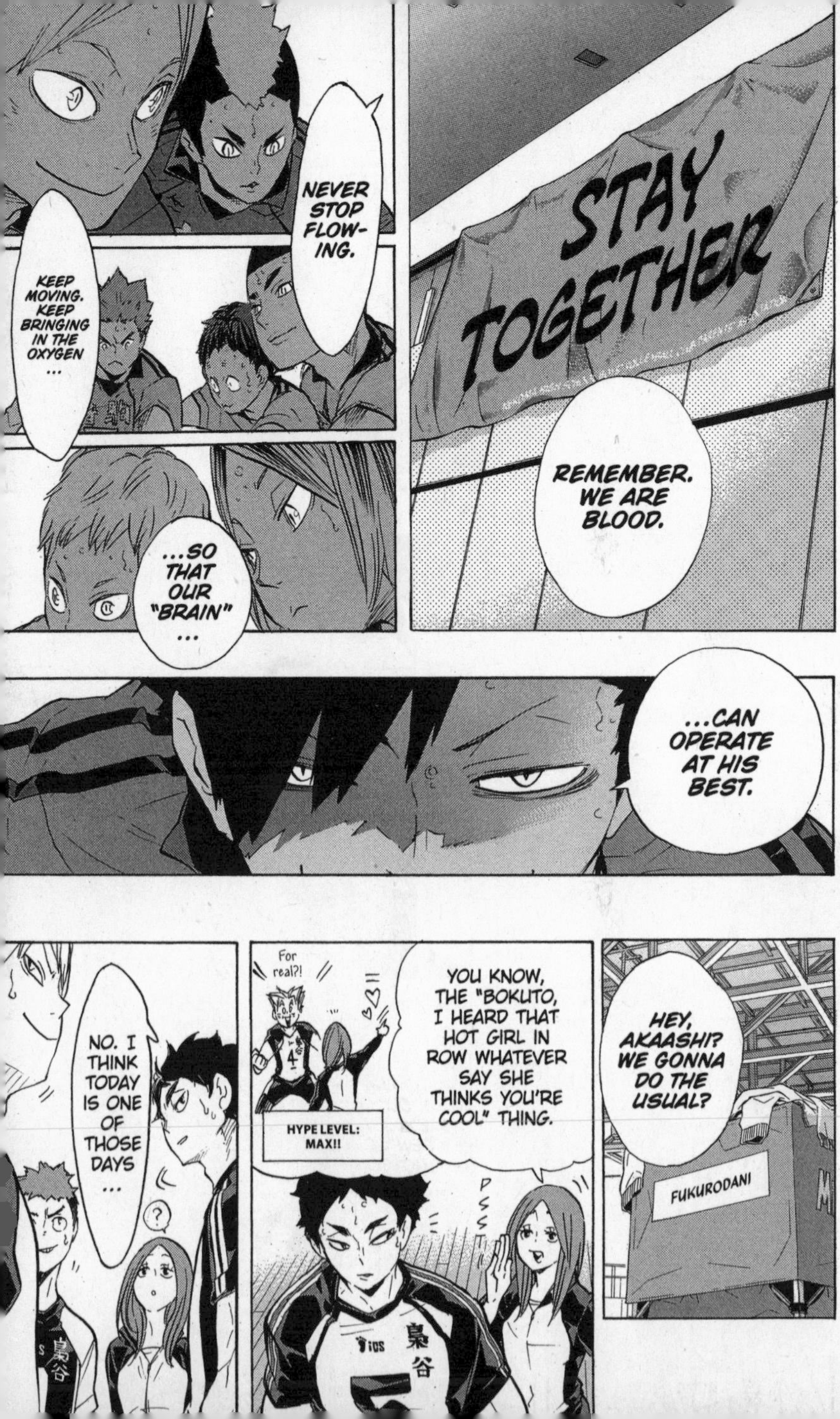
STAY TOGETHER
REMEMBER. WE ARE BLOOD.
NEVER STOP FLOW-ING.
KEEP MOVING. KEEP BRINGING IN THE OXYGEN...
...SO THAT OUR "BRAIN"...
...CAN OPERATE AT HIS BEST.
HEY, AKAASHI? WE GONNA DO THE USUAL?
FUKURODANI
YOU KNOW, THE "BOKUTO, I HEARD THAT HOT GIRL IN ROW WHATEVER SAY SHE THINKS YOU'RE COOL" THING.
For real?!
HYPE LEVEL: MAX!!
PSST
NO. I THINK TODAY IS ONE OF THOSE DAYS...

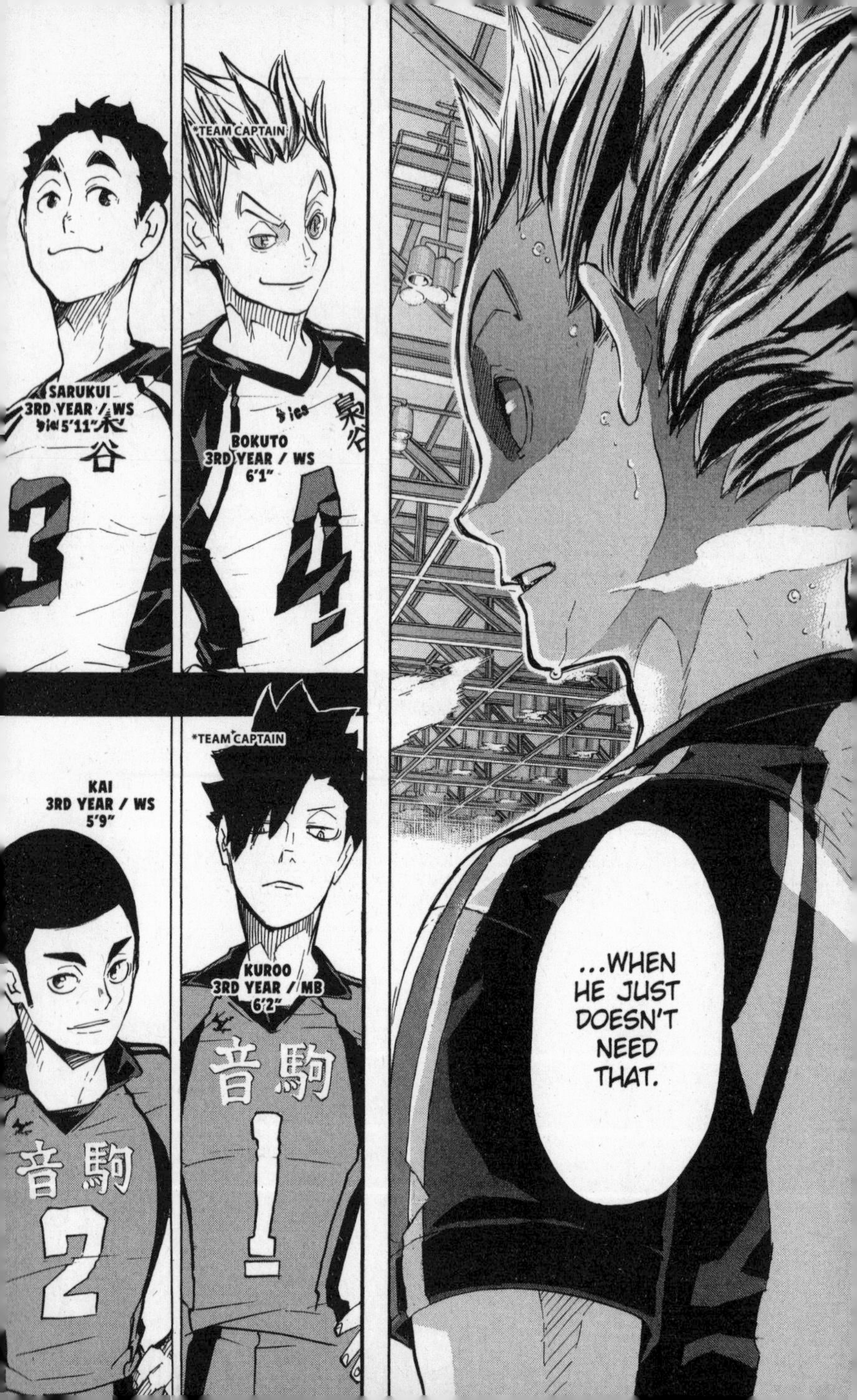
...WHEN HE JUST DOESN'T NEED THAT.
*TEAM CAPTAIN
BOKUTO
3RD YEAR / WS
6'1"
SARUKUI
3RD YEAR / WS
5'11"
*TEAM CAPTAIN
KUROO
3RD YEAR / MB
6'2"
音駒
KAI
3RD YEAR / WS
5'9"
音駒

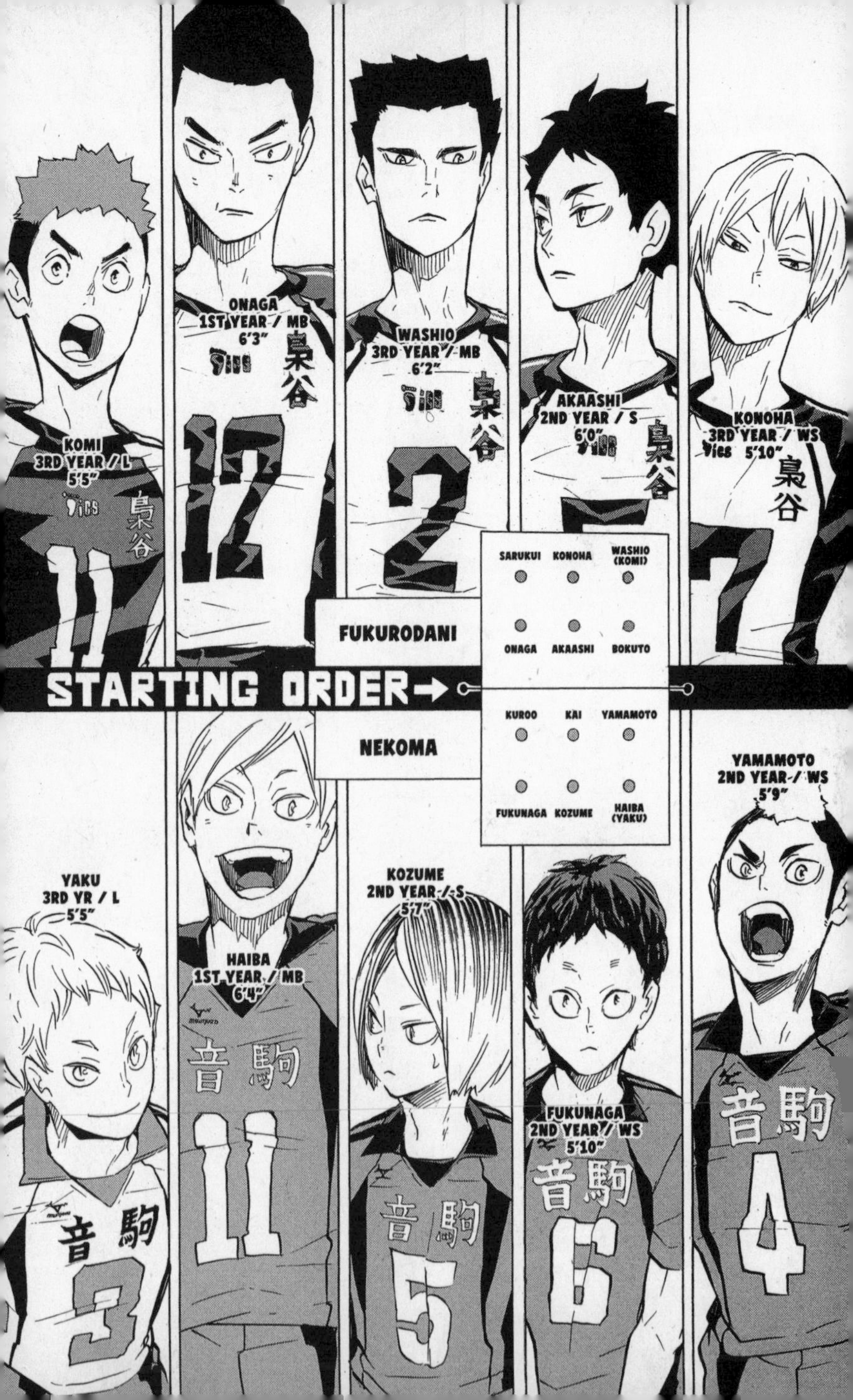
KONOHA
3RD YEAR / WS
5'10"
AKAASHI
2ND YEAR / S
6'0"
WASHIO
3RD YEAR / MB
6'2"
ONAGA
1ST YEAR / MB
6'3"
KOMI
3RD YEAR / L
5'5"
STARTING ORDER
FUKURODANI
SARUKUI KONOHA WASHIO (KOMI)
ONAGA AKAASHI BOKUTO
NEKOMA
KUROO KAI YAMAMOTO
FUKUNAGA KOZUME HAIBA (YAKU)
YAMAMOTO
2ND YEAR / WS
5'9"
FUKUNAGA
2ND YEAR / WS
5'10"
KOZUME
2ND YEAR / S
5'7"
HAIBA
1ST YEAR / MB
6'4"
YAKU
3RD YR / L
5'5"

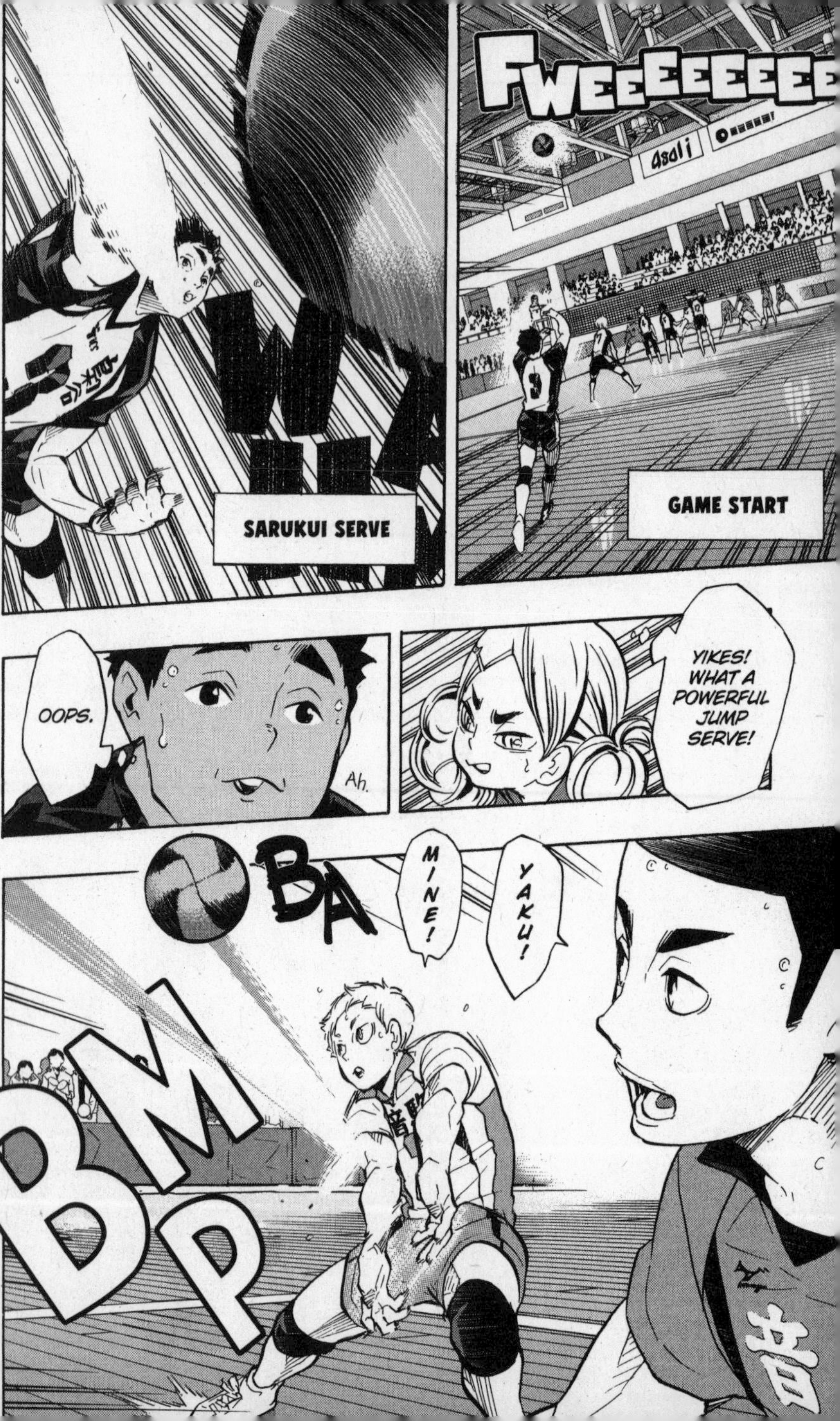
FWEEEEEEEE
GAME START
SARUKUI SERVE
YIKES! WHAT A POWERFUL JUMP SERVE!
OOPS.
Ah.
YAKU!
MINE!
BA
BMP

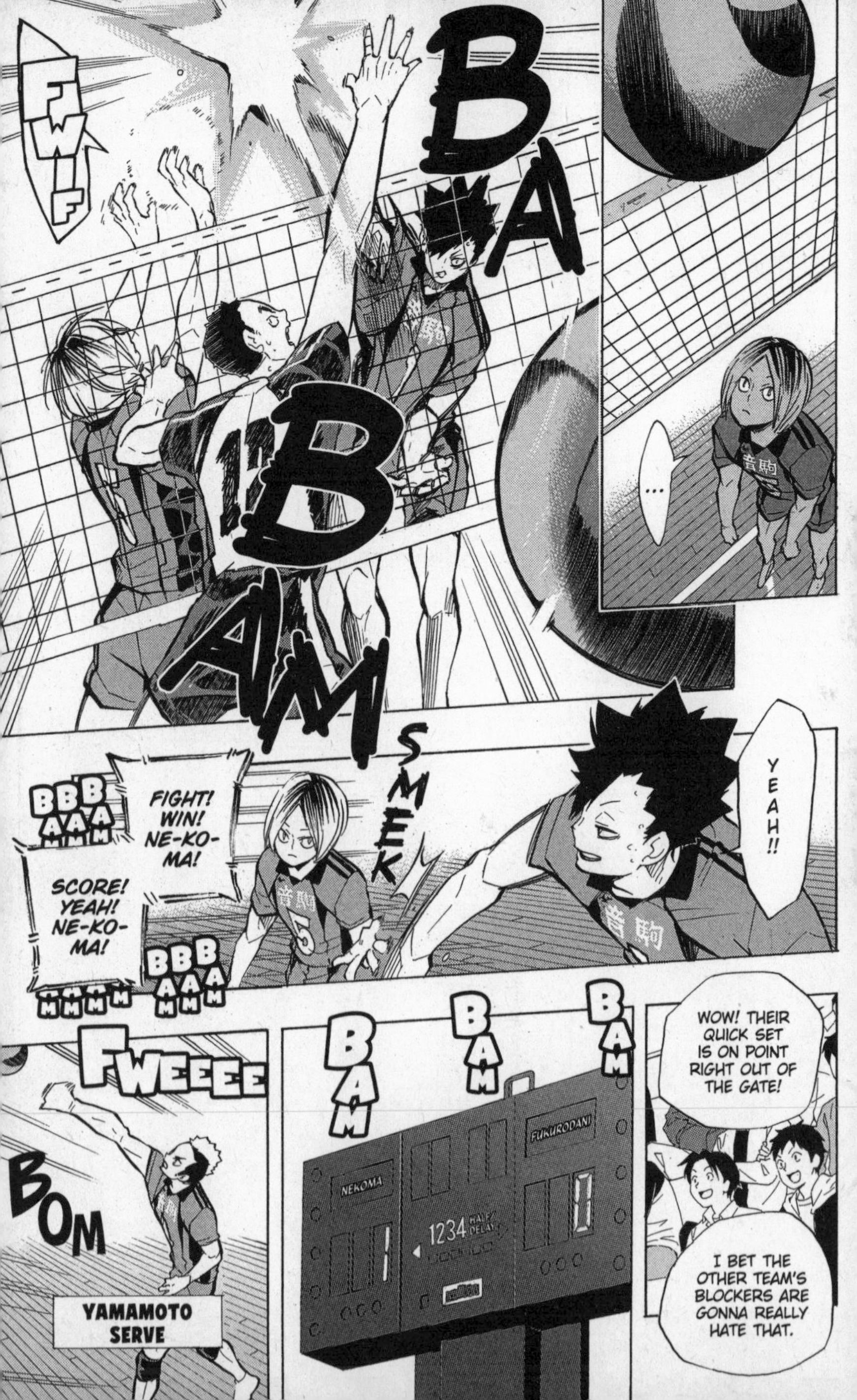
...
BA
FWIF
BAM
YEAH!!
SMEK
FIGHT! WIN! NE-KO-MA!
BBBAAAMMM
SCORE! YEAH! NE-KO-MA!
BBBAAAMMM
WOW! THEIR QUICK SET IS ON POINT RIGHT OUT OF THE GATE!
I BET THE OTHER TEAM'S BLOCKERS ARE GONNA REALLY HATE THAT.
BAM
BAM
BAM
FUKURODANI
NEKOMA
1234 HALF/DELAY
1
0
FWEEEE
BOM
YAMAMOTO SERVE

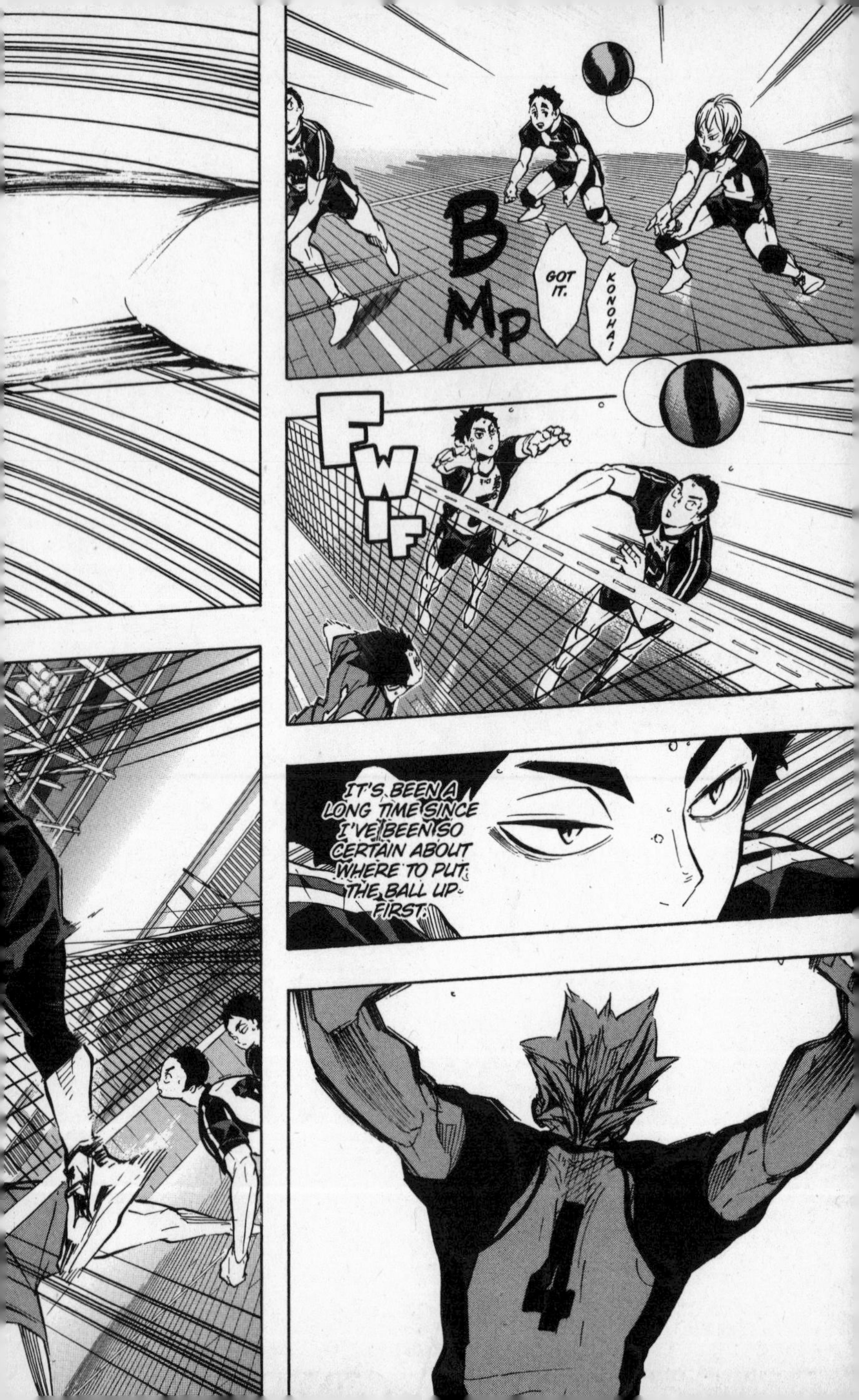
KONOHA!
GOT IT.
BMP
FWIF
IT'S BEEN A LONG TIME SINCE I'VE BEEN SO CERTAIN ABOUT WHERE TO PUT THE BALL UP FIRST.

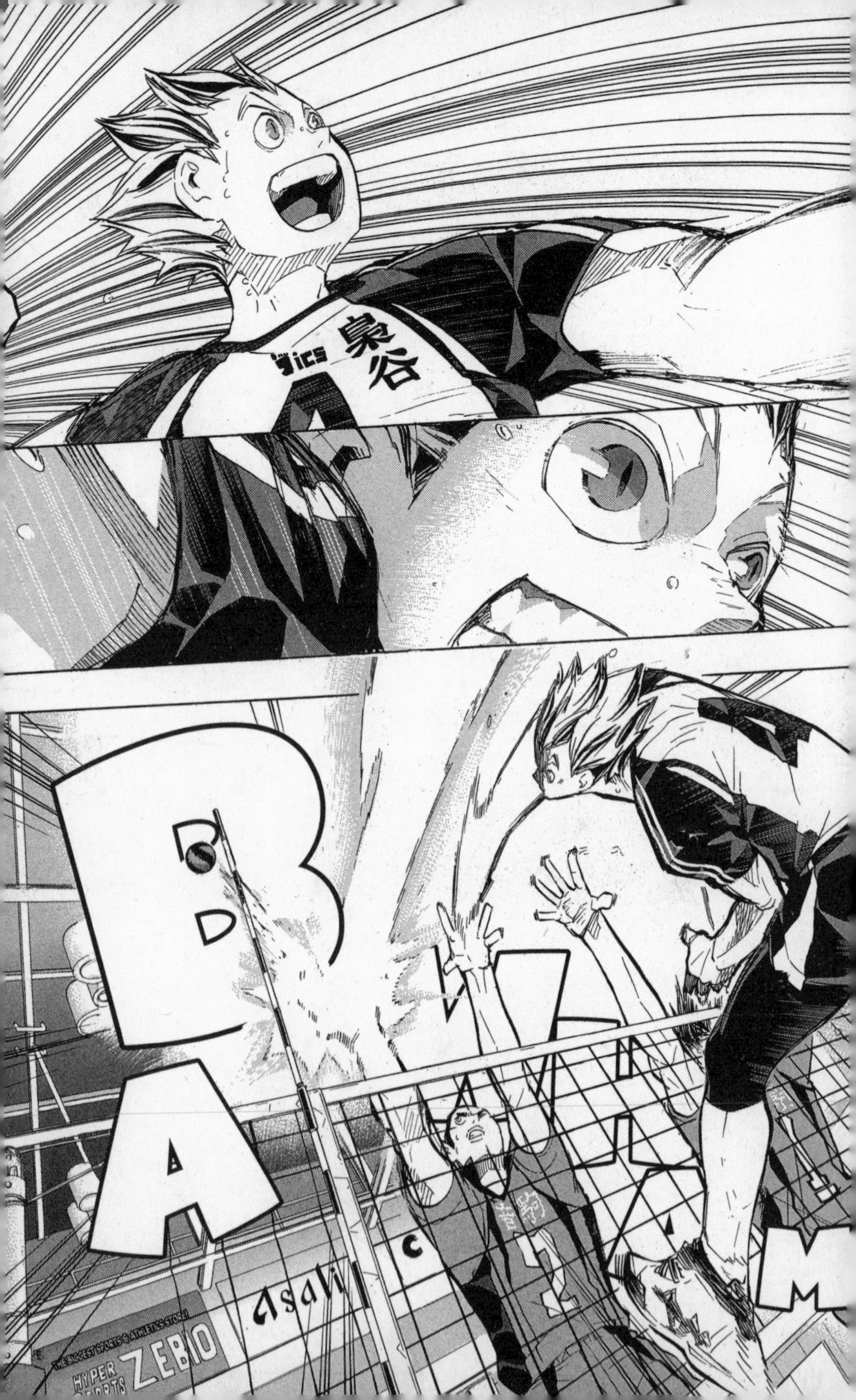
梟谷
BAM
Asahi
THE BIGGEST SPORTS & ATHLETICS STORE!
HYPER SPORTS ZEBIO

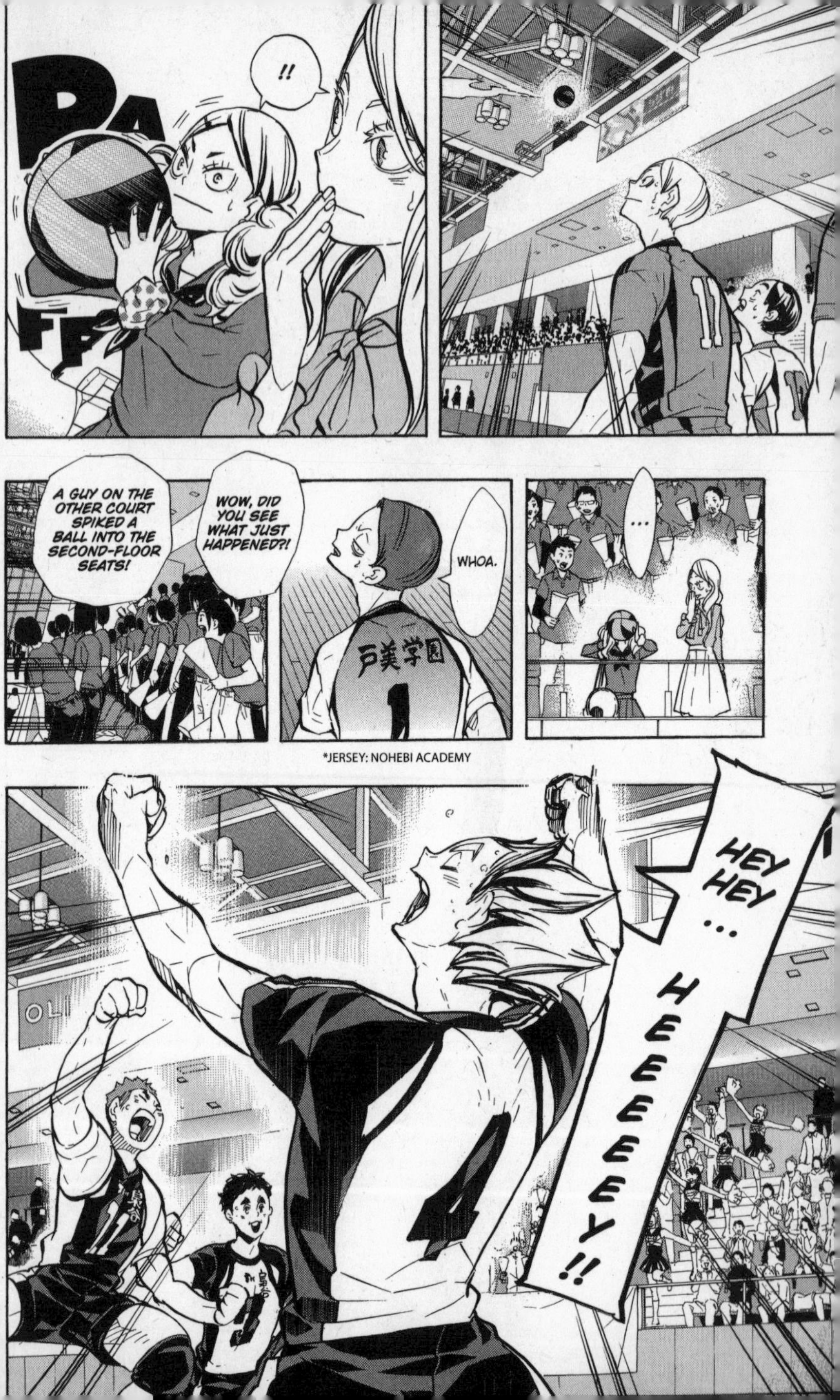
DAFF
!!
...
WHOA.
戸美学園
WOW, DID YOU SEE WHAT JUST HAPPENED?!
A GUY ON THE OTHER COURT SPIKED A BALL INTO THE SECOND-FLOOR SEATS!
HEY HEY ... HEEEEEEY!!

*JERSEY: NOHEBI ACADEMY

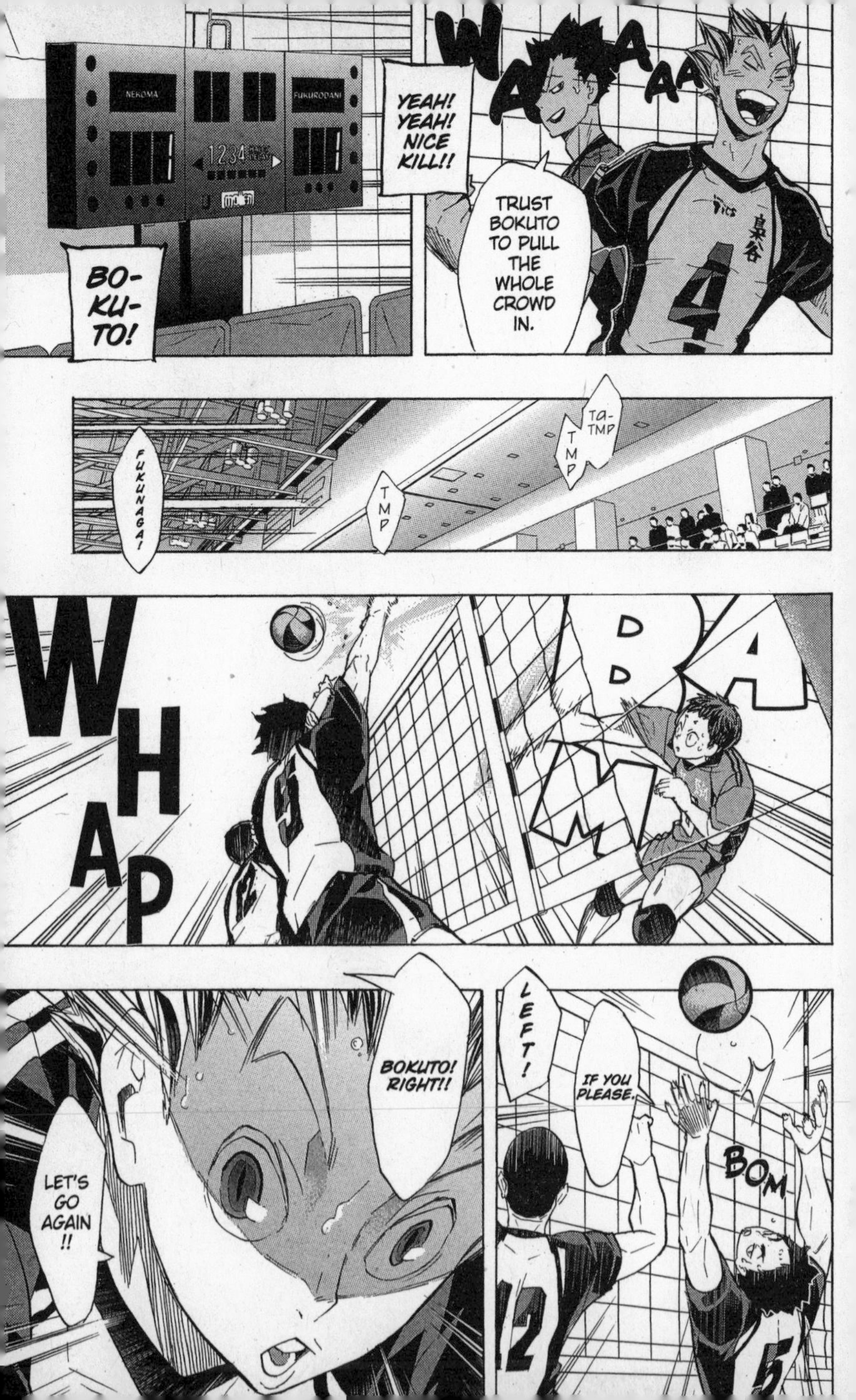
WAAAA
YEAH! YEAH! NICE KILL!!
TRUST BOKUTO TO PULL THE WHOLE CROWD IN.
NEKOMA
FUKURODANI
BO-KU-TO!
TA-TMP
TMP
TMP
FUKUNAGA!
DD
BAM
WHAP
LEFT!
IF YOU PLEASE.
BOM
BOKUTO! RIGHT!!
LET'S GO AGAIN!!

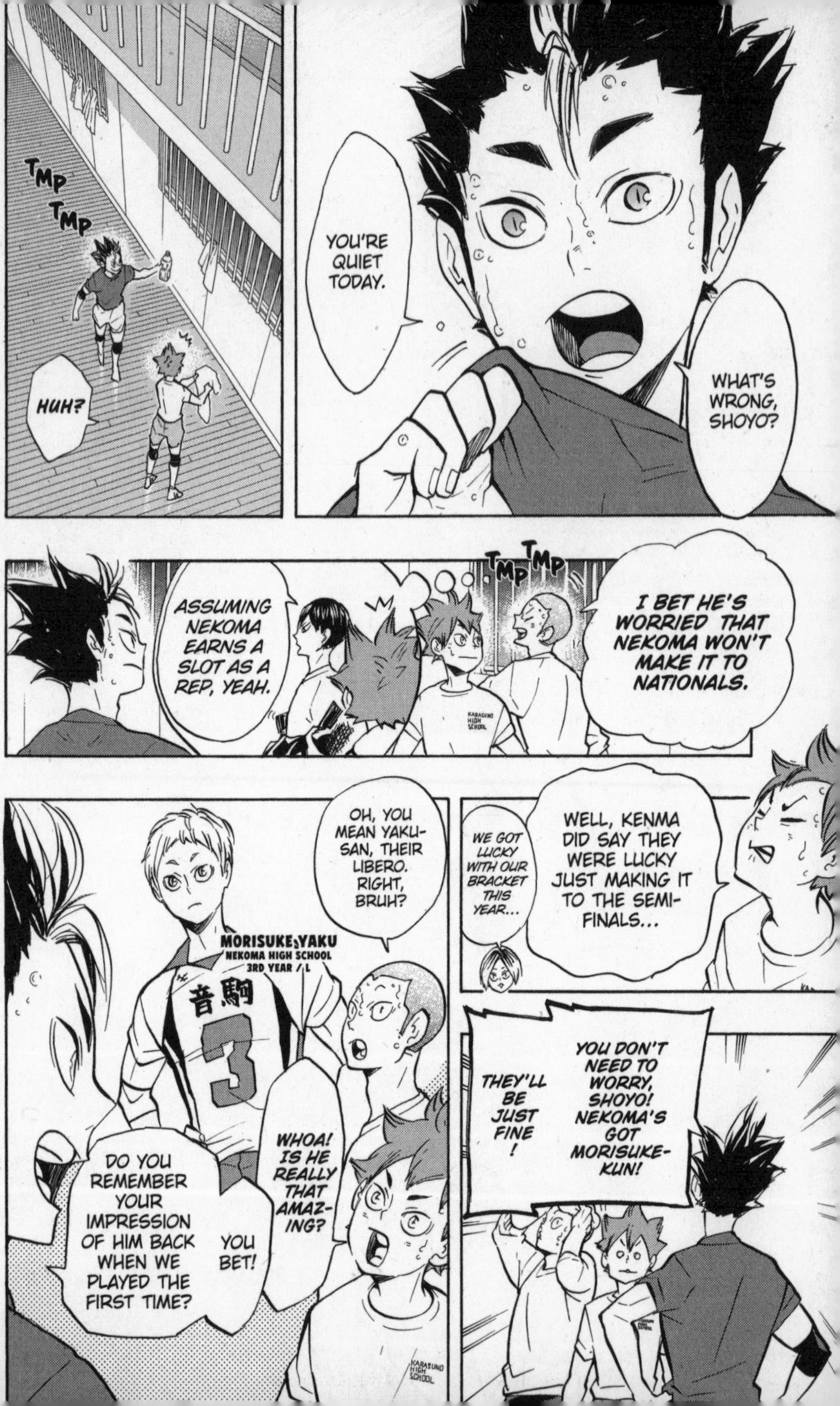
WHAT'S WRONG, SHOYO?
YOU'RE QUIET TODAY.
TMP TMP
HUH?
I BET HE'S WORRIED THAT NEKOMA WON'T MAKE IT TO NATIONALS.
TMP TMP
ASSUMING NEKOMA EARNS A SLOT AS A REP, YEAH.
WELL, KENMA DID SAY THEY WERE LUCKY JUST MAKING IT TO THE SEMI-FINALS...
WE GOT LUCKY WITH OUR BRACKET THIS YEAR...
YOU DON'T NEED TO WORRY, SHOYO! NEKOMA'S GOT MORISUKE-KUN!
THEY'LL BE JUST FINE!
OH, YOU MEAN YAKU-SAN, THEIR LIBERO. RIGHT, BRUH?
MORISUKE YAKU
NEKOMA HIGH SCHOOL
3RD YEAR / L
音駒
3
WHOA! IS HE REALLY THAT AMAZING?
YOU BET!
DO YOU REMEMBER YOUR IMPRESSION OF HIM BACK WHEN WE PLAYED THE FIRST TIME?

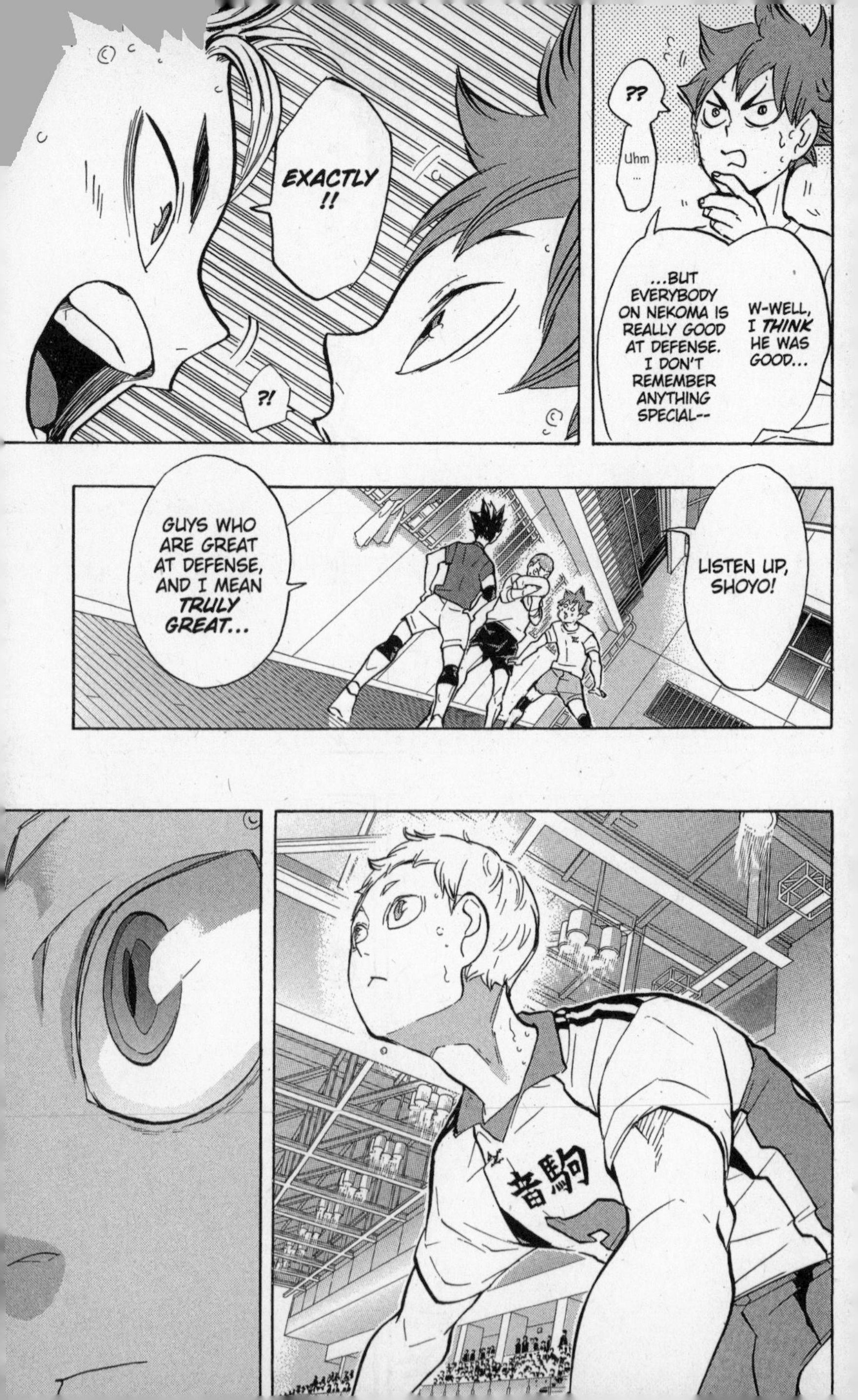
??
Uhm ...
W-WELL, I *THINK* HE WAS GOOD...
...BUT EVERYBODY ON NEKOMA IS REALLY GOOD AT DEFENSE. I DON'T REMEMBER ANYTHING SPECIAL--
EXACTLY !!
?!
LISTEN UP, SHOYO!
GUYS WHO ARE GREAT AT DEFENSE, AND I MEAN *TRULY GREAT...*
音駒

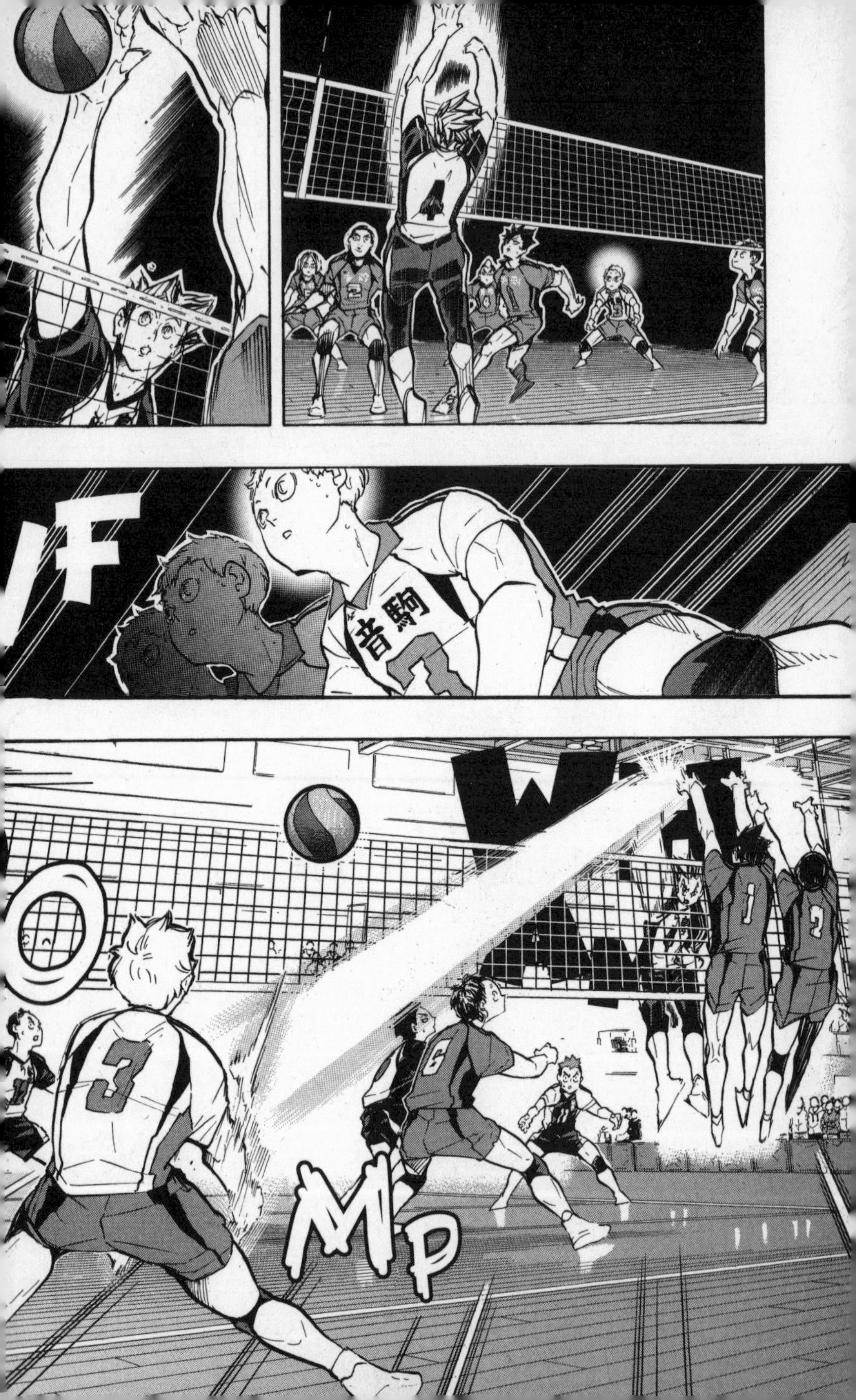
音駒
MP

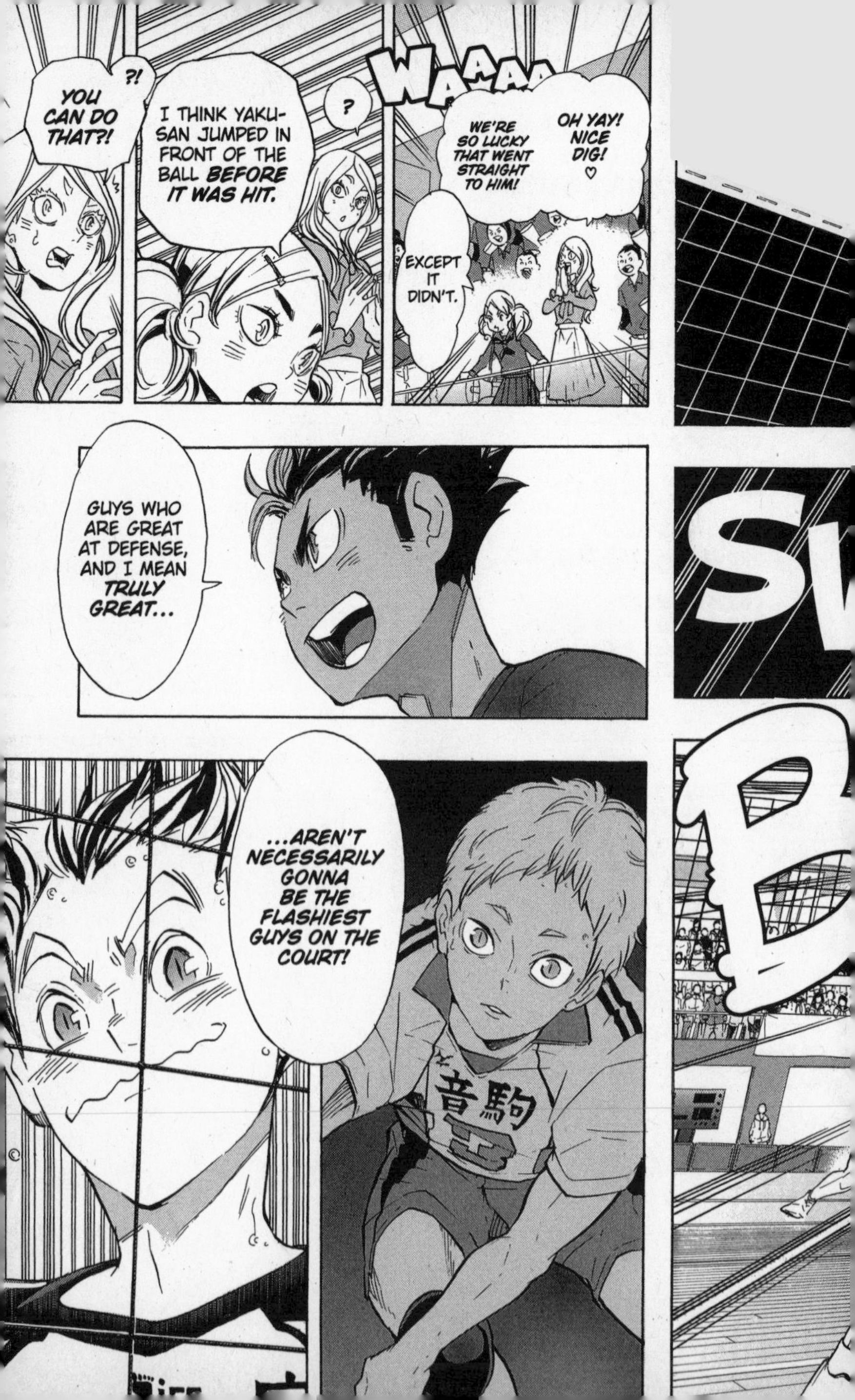
WAAAA
OH YAY! NICE DIG! ♡
WE'RE SO LUCKY THAT WENT STRAIGHT TO HIM!
EXCEPT IT DIDN'T.
?
I THINK YAKU-SAN JUMPED IN FRONT OF THE BALL BEFORE IT WAS HIT.
?!
YOU CAN DO THAT?!
GUYS WHO ARE GREAT AT DEFENSE, AND I MEAN TRULY GREAT...
...AREN'T NECESSARILY GONNA BE THE FLASHIEST GUYS ON THE COURT!
音駒

AKANE YAMAMOTO

**TAKETORA YAMAMOTO'S
YOUNGER SISTER
NEKOMA MIDDLE SCHOOL
CLASS 2-B**

HEIGHT: 4'9"

**WEIGHT: 78 LBS.
(AS OF NOVEMBER, 2ND
YEAR OF MIDDLE SCHOOL)**

BIRTHDAY: MARCH 13

**FAVORITE FOOD:
GROUND CHICKEN OVER RICE**

**CURRENT WORRY:
HER FRIENDS LOOK AT HER
FUNNY WHEN SHE GUSHES
ABOUT VOLLEYBALL.**

**ABILITY PARAMETERS
(5-POINT SCALE)**

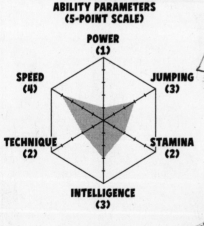

POWER
(1)

JUMPING
(3)

SPEED
(4)

STAMINA
(2)

TECHNIQUE
(2)

INTELLIGENCE
(3)

CHAPTER 192: Engine

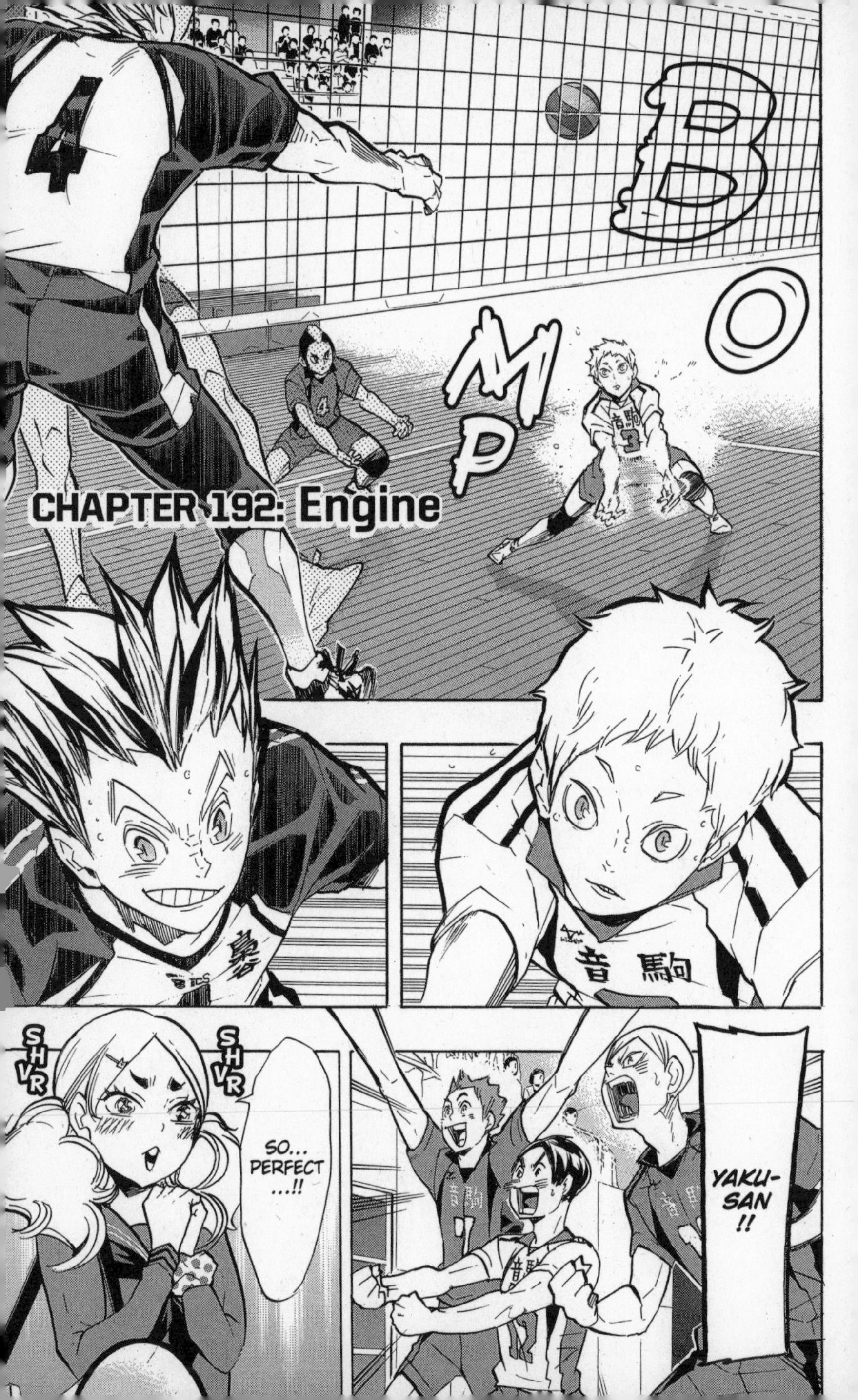
BOMP
YAKU-SAN !!
SHVR SHVR
SO... PERFECT ...!!

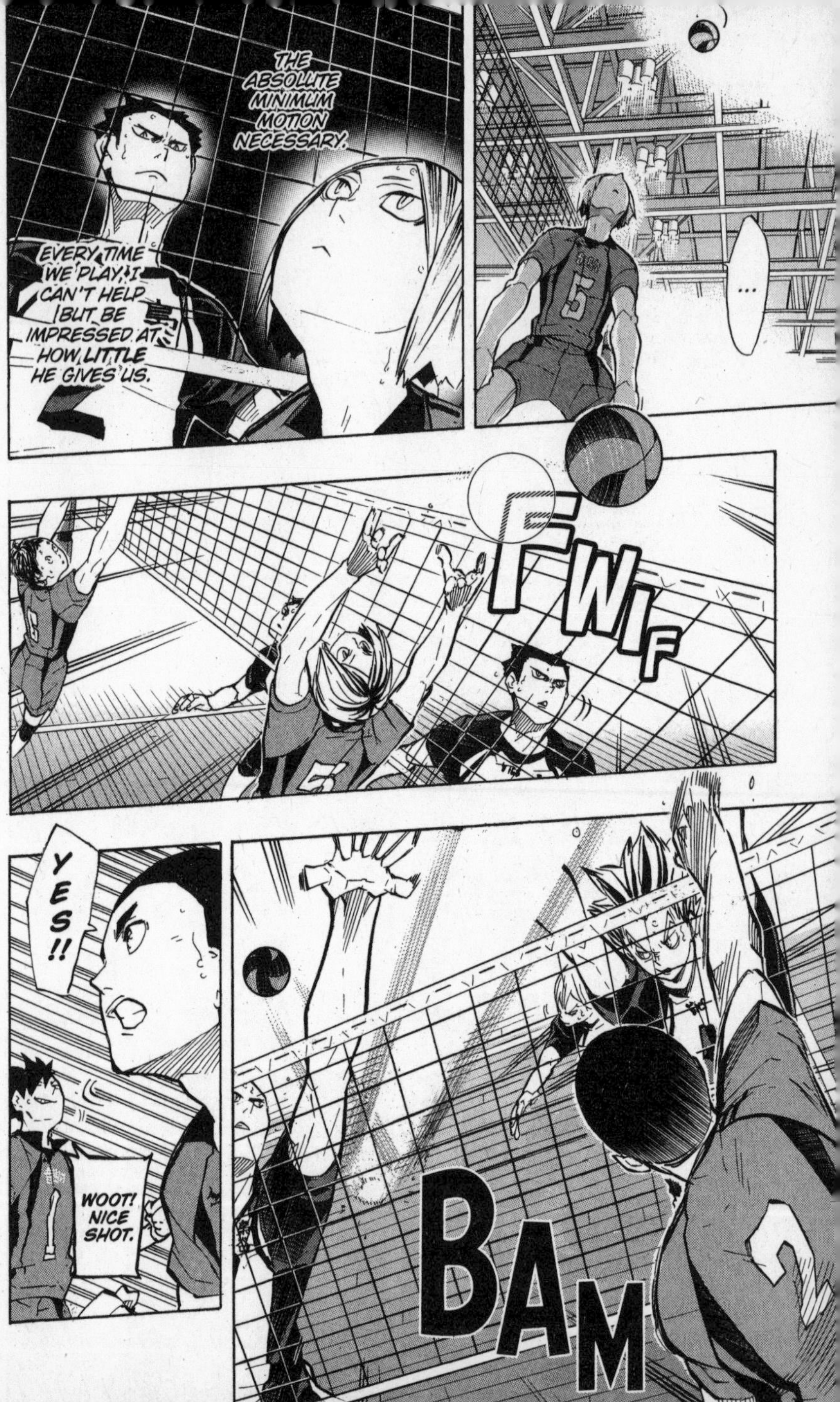
...
THE ABSOLUTE MINIMUM MOTION NECESSARY.
EVERY TIME WE PLAY, I CAN'T HELP BUT BE IMPRESSED AT HOW LITTLE HE GIVES US.
FWIF
BAM
YES!!
WOOT! NICE SHOT.

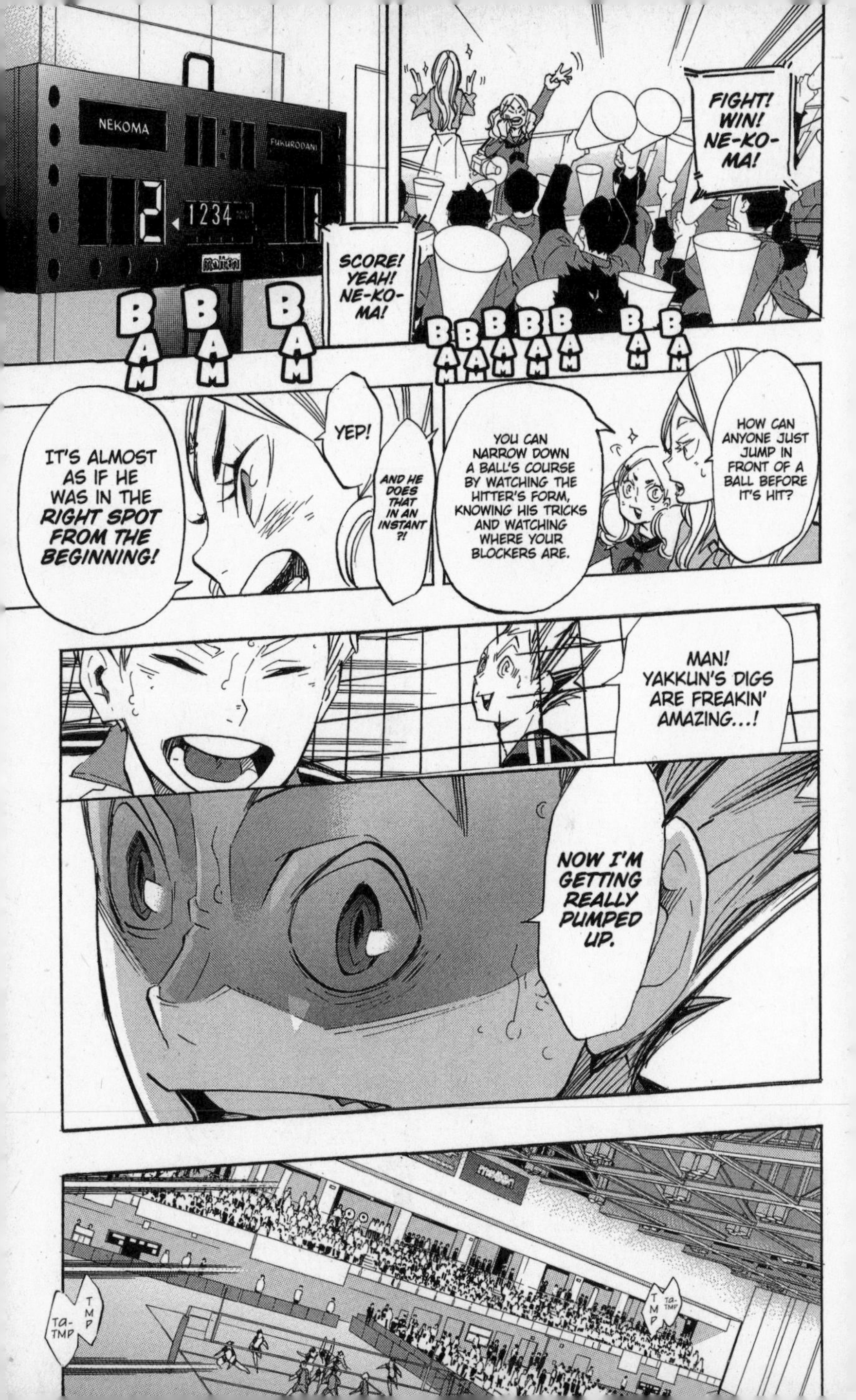
FIGHT! WIN! NE-KO-MA!
SCORE! YEAH! NE-KO-MA!
NEKOMA
FUKURODANI
2
1234
1
BBBBBBB AAAAAAA MMMMMMM
BAM BAM BAM
HOW CAN ANYONE JUST JUMP IN FRONT OF A BALL BEFORE IT'S HIT?
YOU CAN NARROW DOWN A BALL'S COURSE BY WATCHING THE HITTER'S FORM, KNOWING HIS TRICKS AND WATCHING WHERE YOUR BLOCKERS ARE.
AND HE DOES THAT IN AN INSTANT?!
YEP!
IT'S ALMOST AS IF HE WAS IN THE *RIGHT SPOT FROM THE BEGINNING!*
MAN! YAKKUN'S DIGS ARE FREAKIN' AMAZING...!
NOW I'M GETTING REALLY PUMPED UP.
TA-TMP
TMP
TMP
TA-TMP

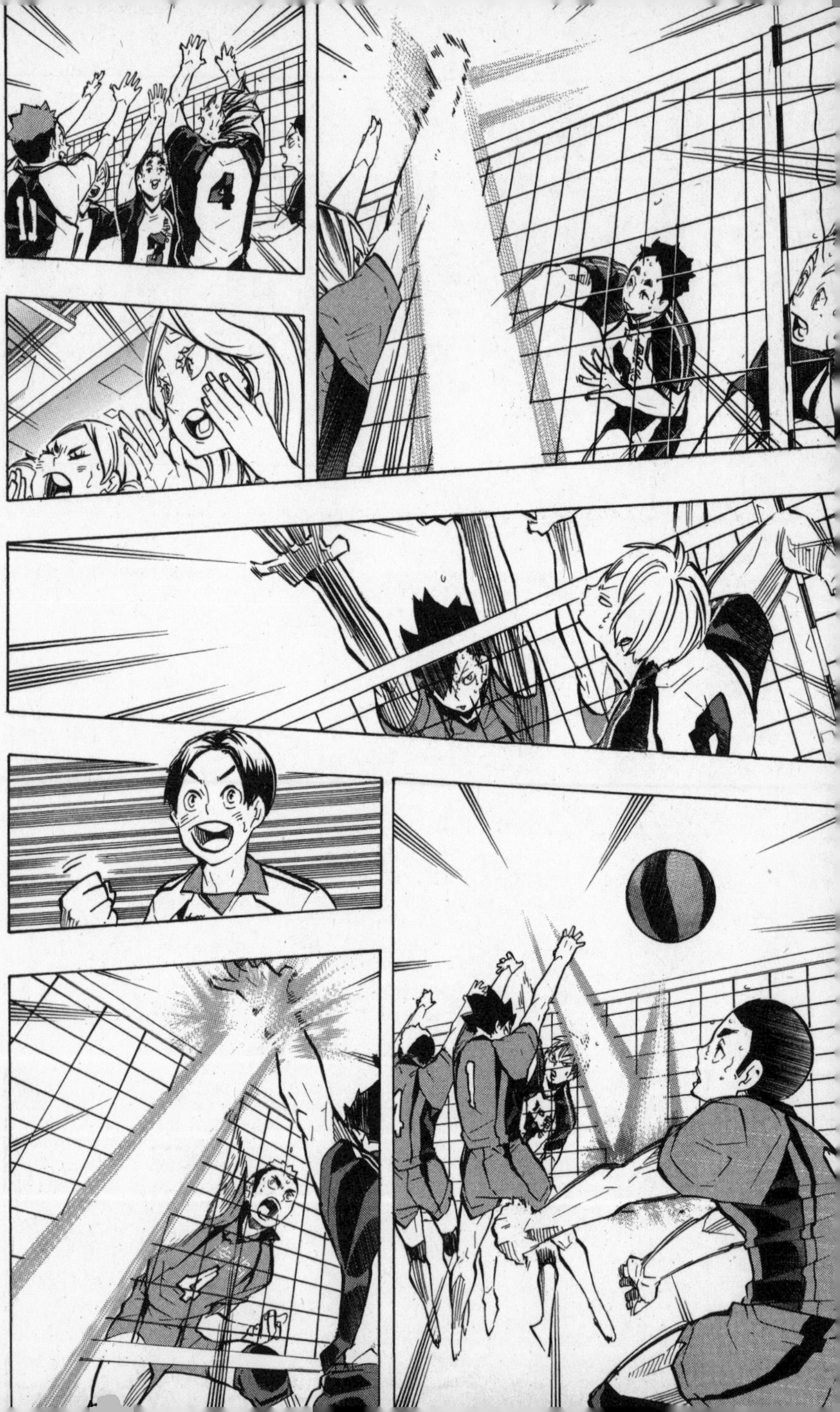

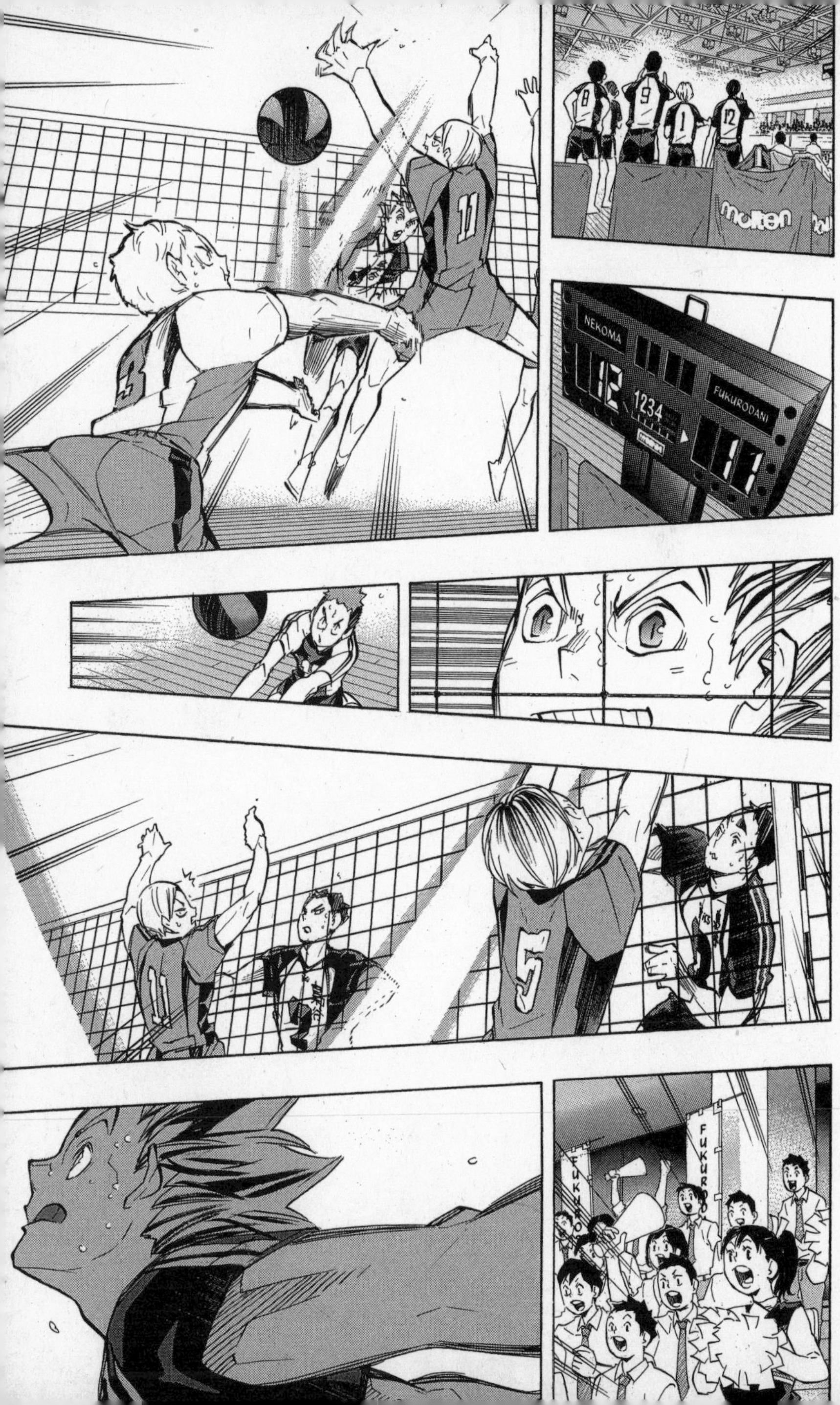
molten
NEKOMA
12
1234
FUKURODANI
11
FUKURO
FUKURO

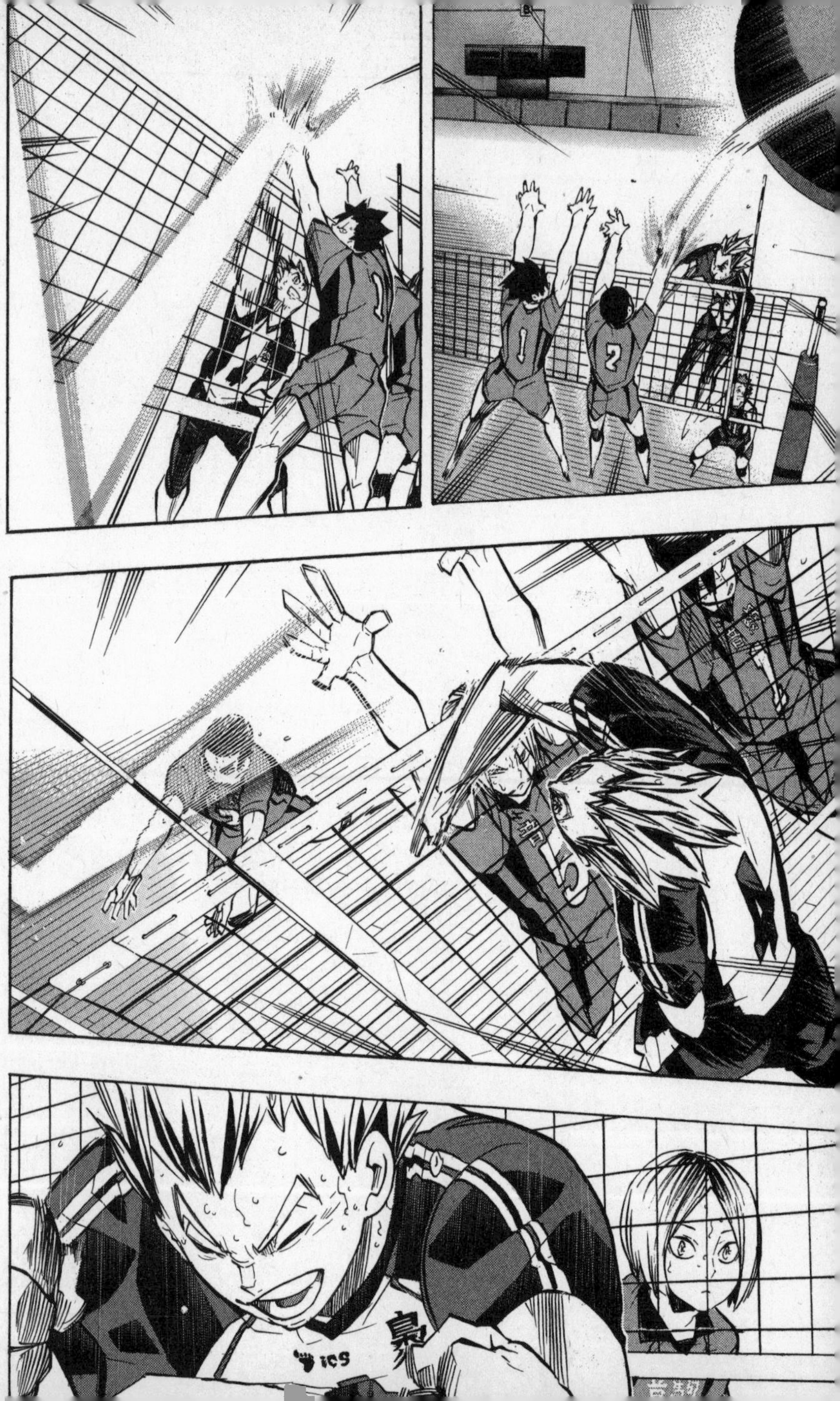

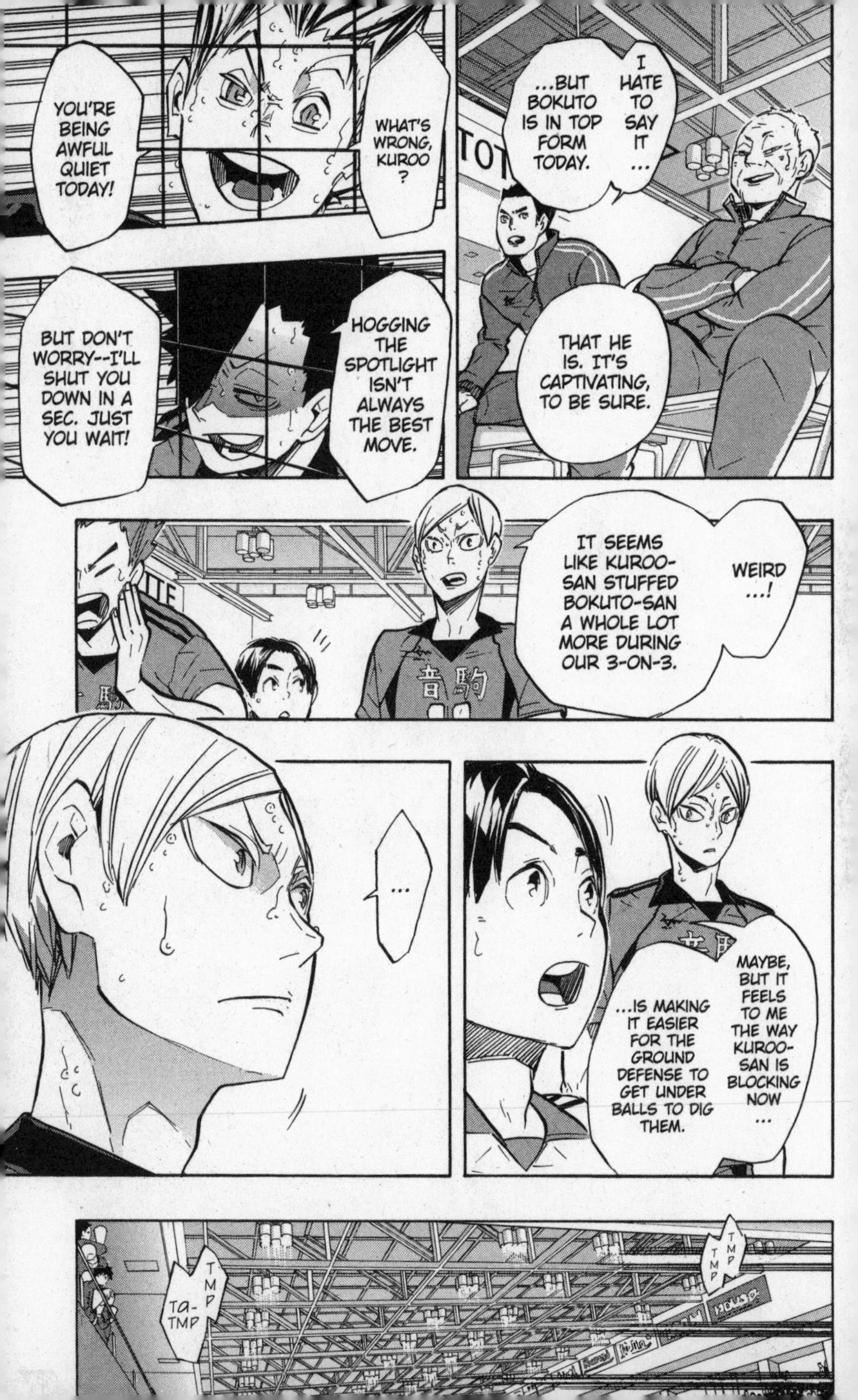

I HATE TO SAY IT...
...BUT BOKUTO IS IN TOP FORM TODAY.
THAT HE IS. IT'S CAPTIVATING, TO BE SURE.
WHAT'S WRONG, KUROO?
YOU'RE BEING AWFUL QUIET TODAY!
HOGGING THE SPOTLIGHT ISN'T ALWAYS THE BEST MOVE.
BUT DON'T WORRY--I'LL SHUT YOU DOWN IN A SEC. JUST YOU WAIT!
WEIRD...!
IT SEEMS LIKE KUROO-SAN STUFFED BOKUTO-SAN A WHOLE LOT MORE DURING OUR 3-ON-3.
MAYBE, BUT IT FEELS TO ME THE WAY KUROO-SAN IS BLOCKING NOW...
...IS MAKING IT EASIER FOR THE GROUND DEFENSE TO GET UNDER BALLS TO DIG THEM.
...
TMP TMP
TMP Ta-TMP

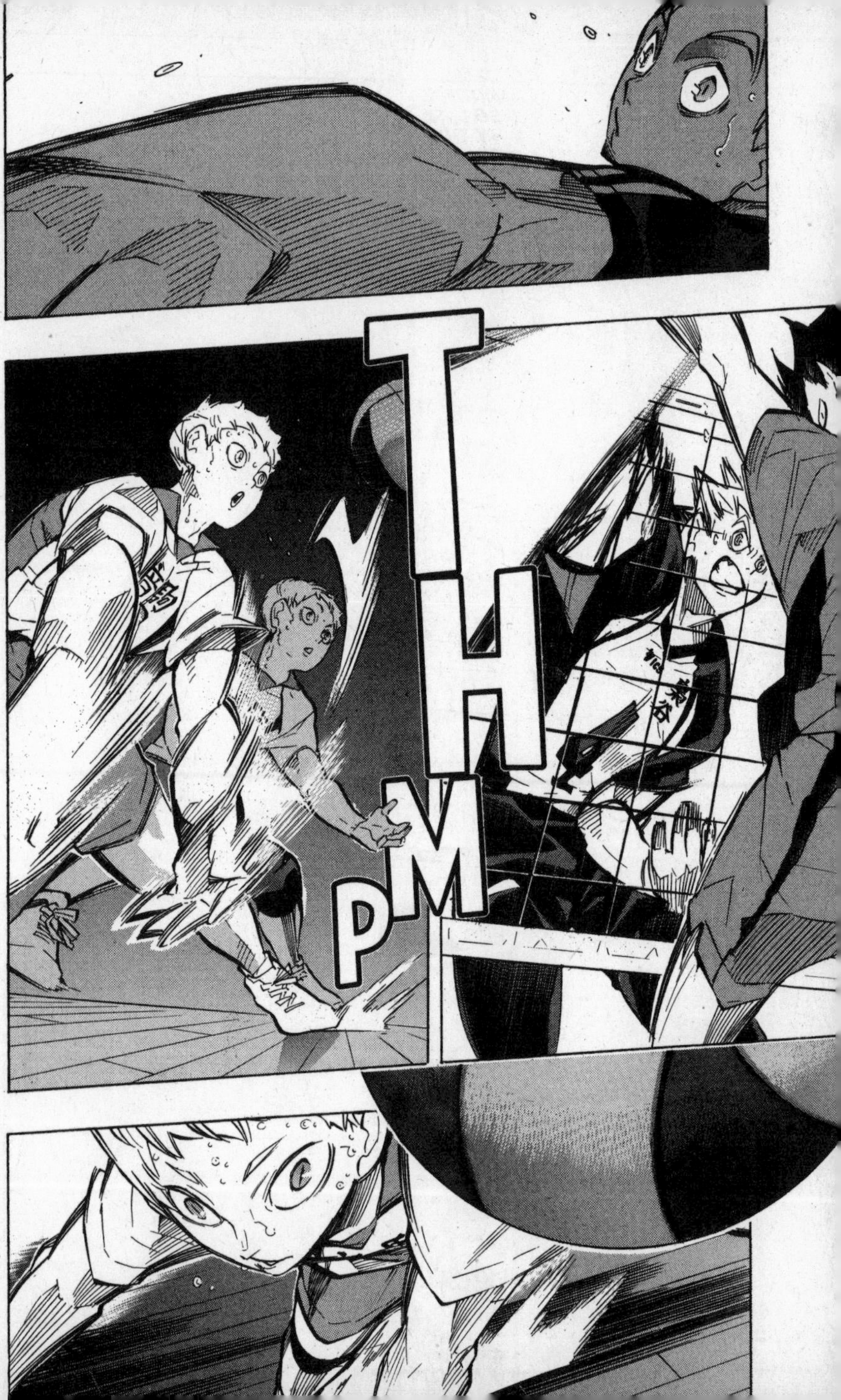
THMP

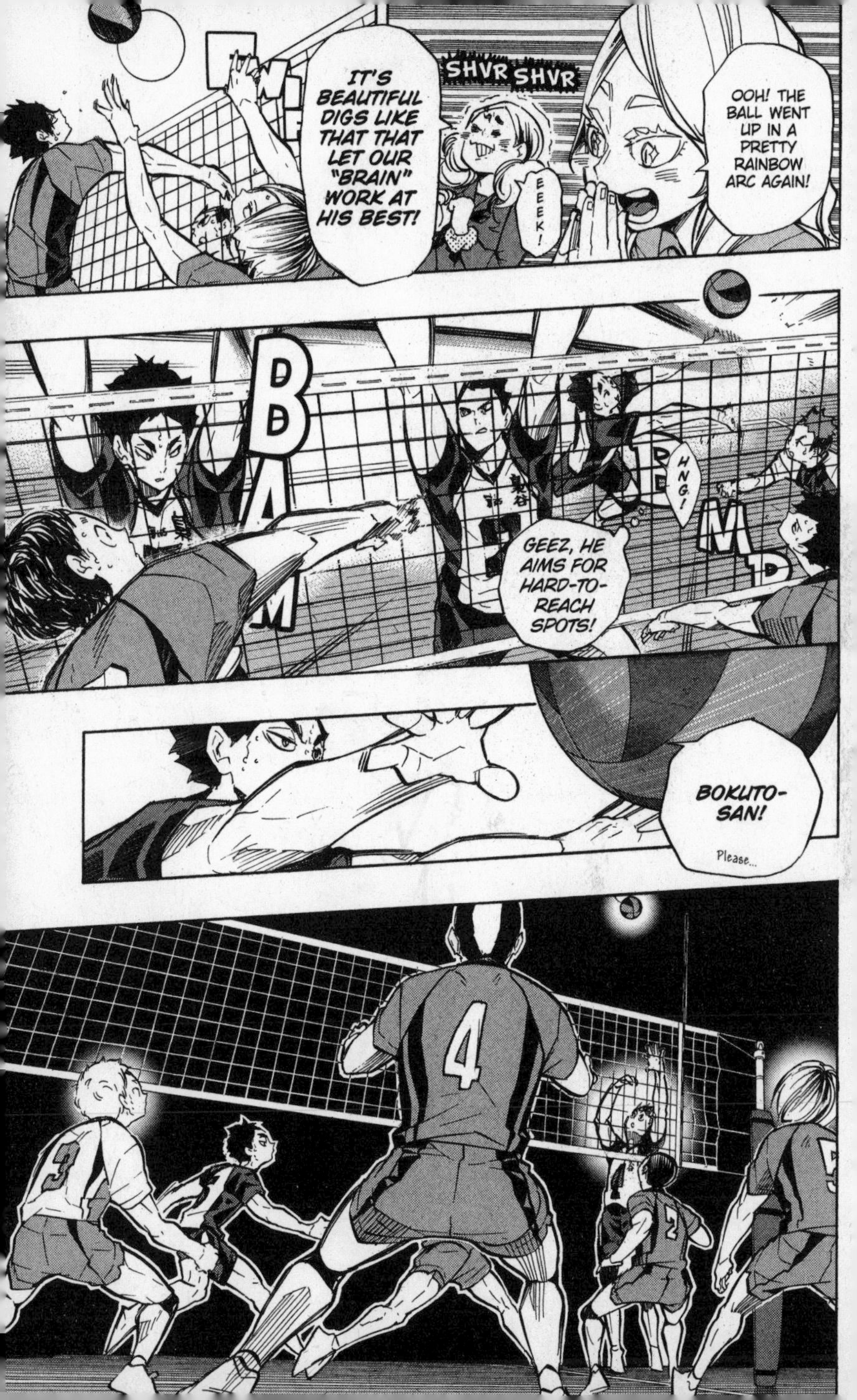
OOH! THE BALL WENT UP IN A PRETTY RAINBOW ARC AGAIN!
EEEK!
SHVR SHVR
IT'S BEAUTIFUL DIGS LIKE THAT THAT LET OUR "BRAIN" WORK AT HIS BEST!
HNG!
GEEZ, HE AIMS FOR HARD-TO-REACH SPOTS!
BAM
BOKUTO-SAN!
Please...

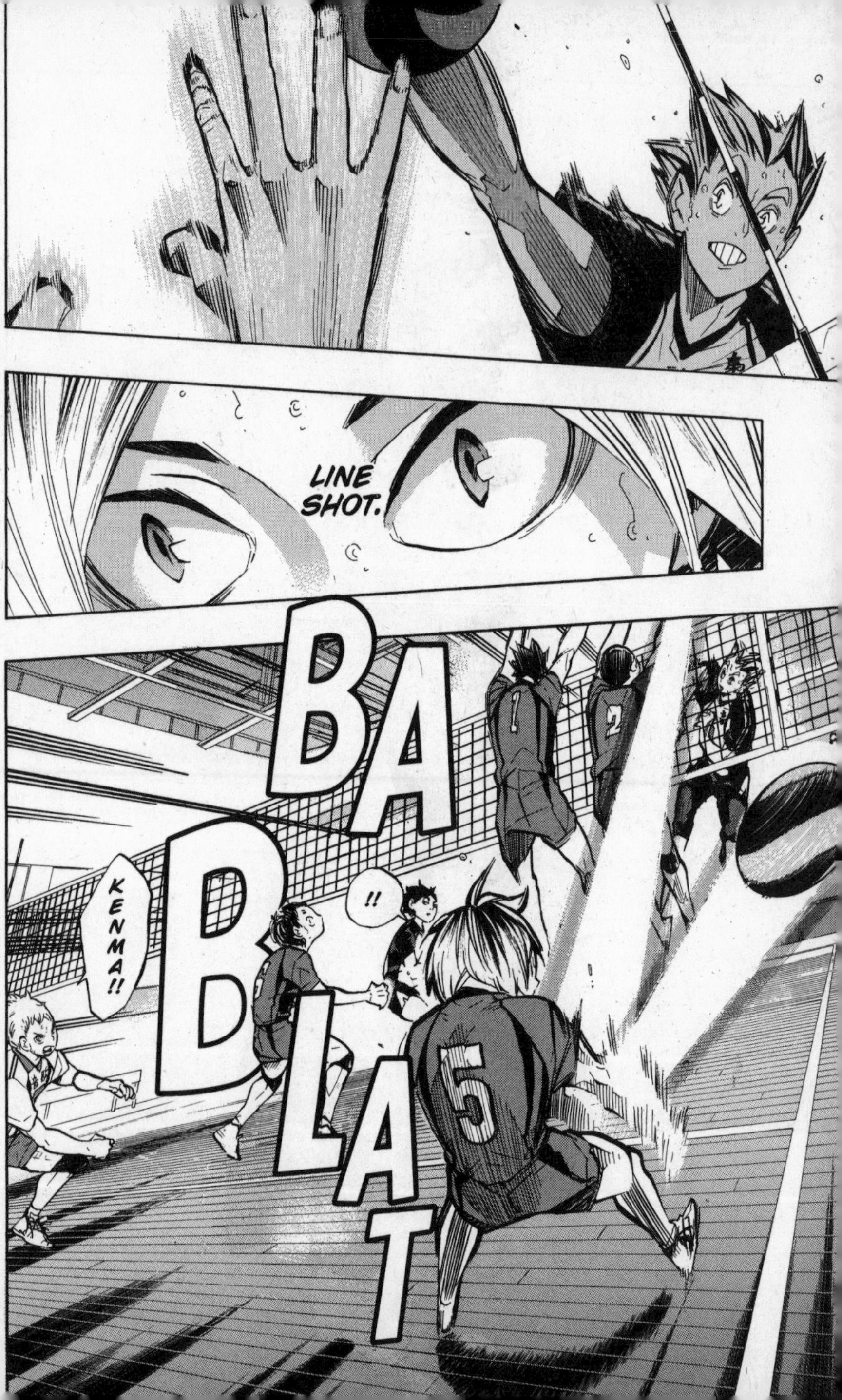
LINE SHOT.
BA
BLAT
!!
KENMA!!

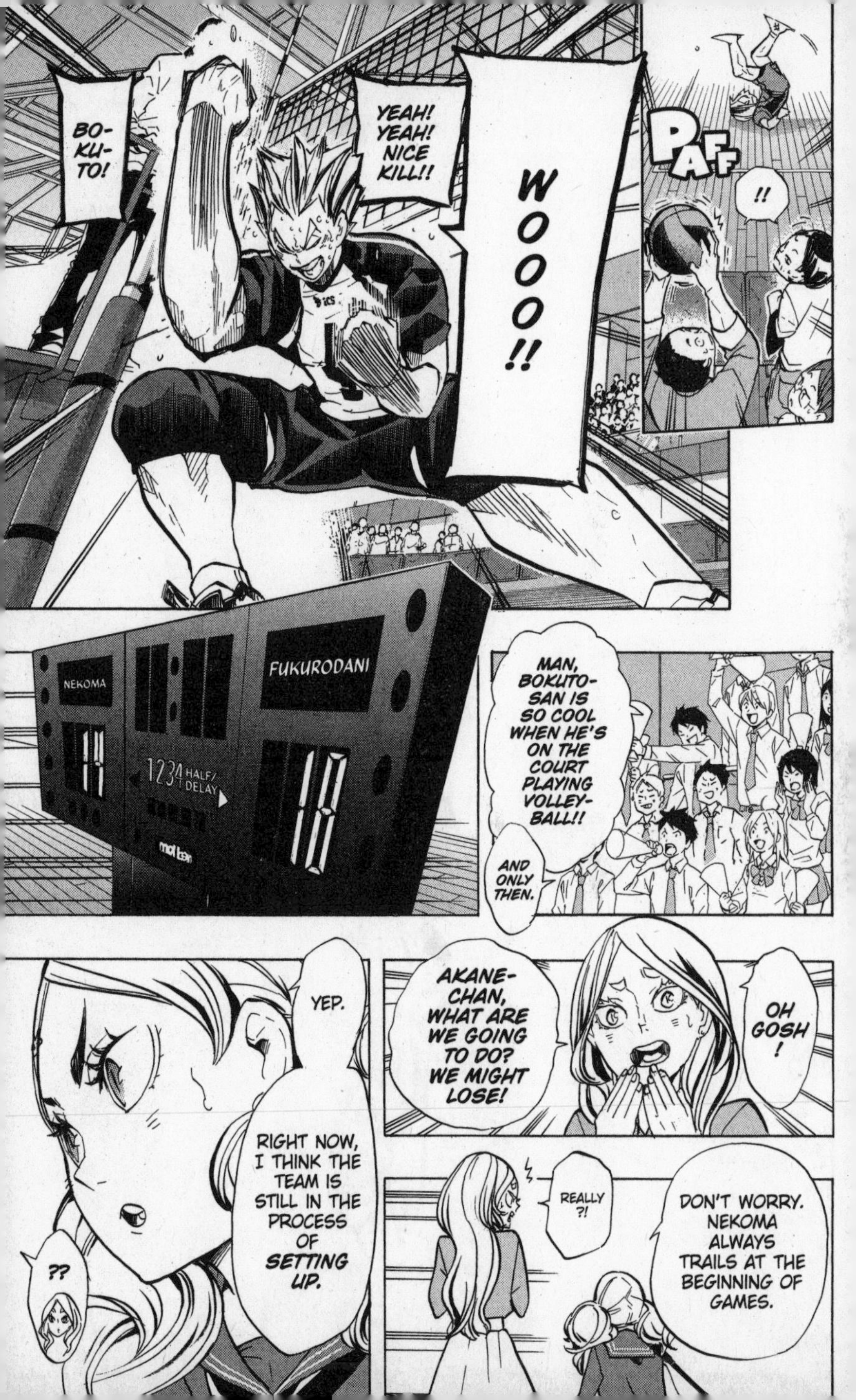
PAFF
!!
WOOOO!!
YEAH! YEAH! NICE KILL!!
BO-KU-TO!
MAN, BOKUTO-SAN IS SO COOL WHEN HE'S ON THE COURT PLAYING VOLLEY-BALL!!
AND ONLY THEN.
FUKURODANI
NEKOMA
1234 HALF/ DELAY
molten
OH GOSH!
AKANE-CHAN, WHAT ARE WE GOING TO DO? WE MIGHT LOSE!
DON'T WORRY. NEKOMA ALWAYS TRAILS AT THE BEGINNING OF GAMES.
REALLY?!
YEP.
RIGHT NOW, I THINK THE TEAM IS STILL IN THE PROCESS OF SETTING UP.
??

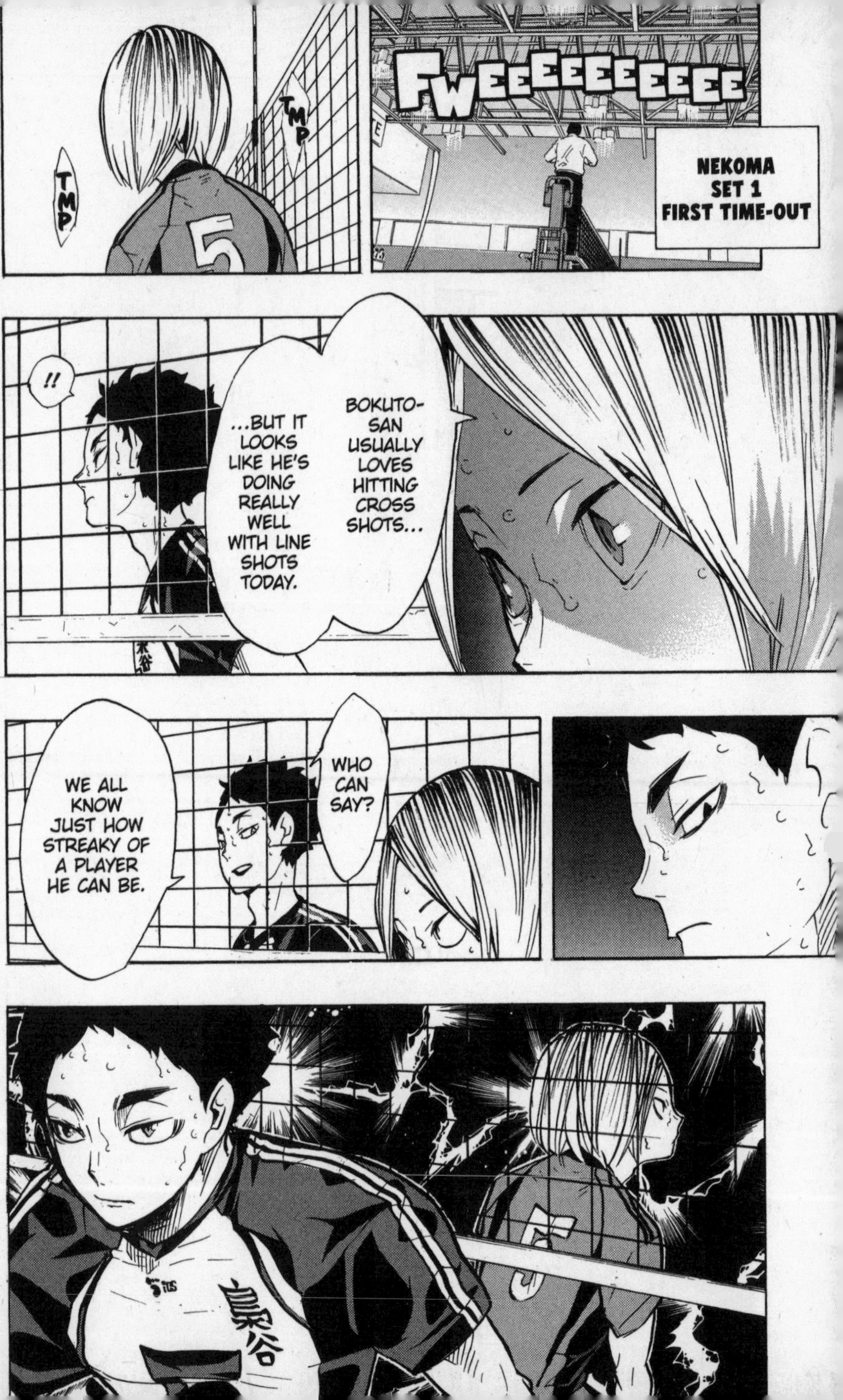
FWEEEEEEEEEE
NEKOMA SET 1 FIRST TIME-OUT
TMP
TMP
BOKUTO-SAN USUALLY LOVES HITTING CROSS SHOTS...
...BUT IT LOOKS LIKE HE'S DOING REALLY WELL WITH LINE SHOTS TODAY.
!!
WHO CAN SAY?
WE ALL KNOW JUST HOW STREAKY OF A PLAYER HE CAN BE.

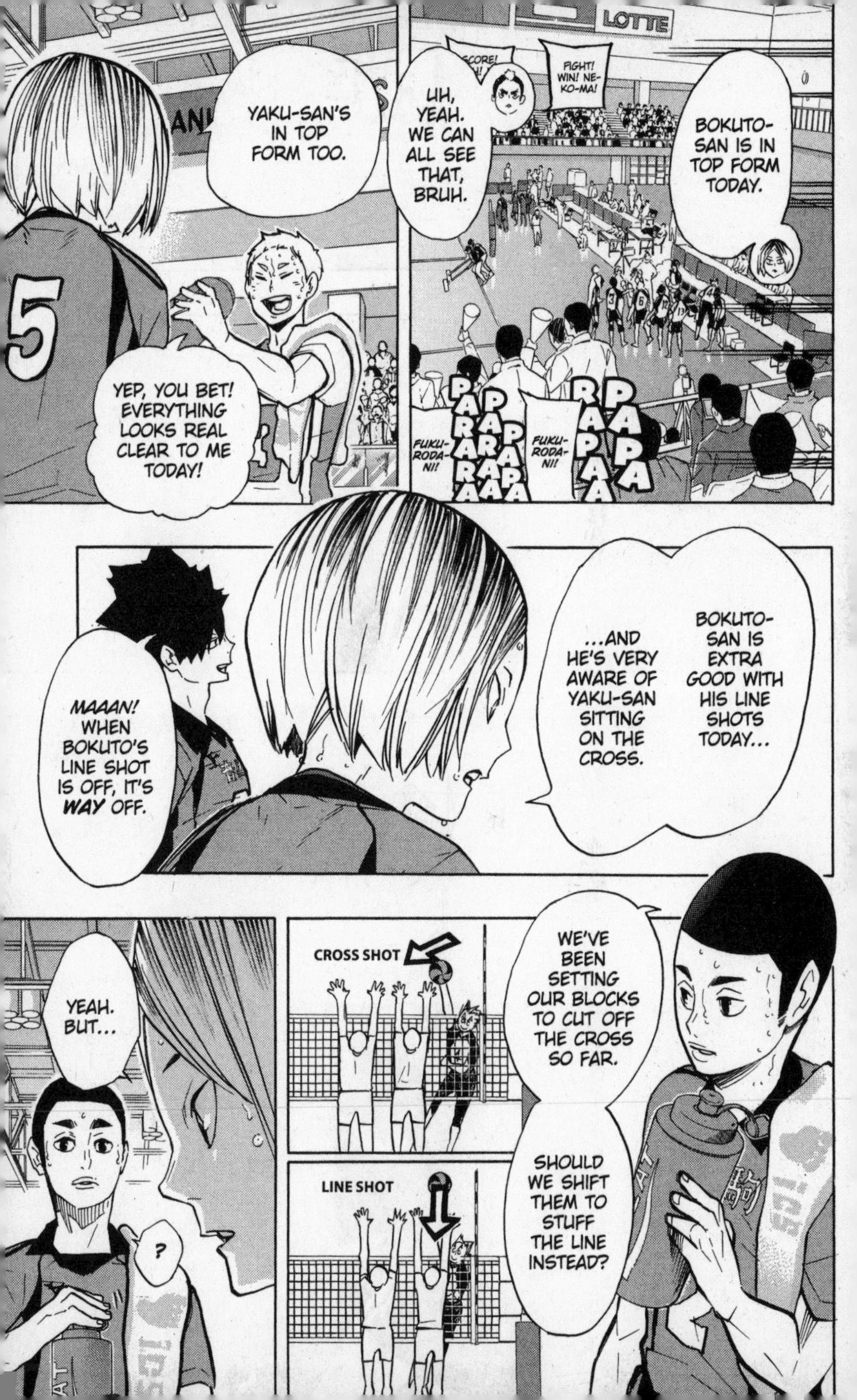
LOTTE
FIGHT! WIN! NE-KO-MA!
BOKUTO-SAN IS IN TOP FORM TODAY.
UH, YEAH. WE CAN ALL SEE THAT, BRUH.
FUKURODANI!
FUKURODANI!
YAKU-SAN'S IN TOP FORM TOO.
YEP, YOU BET! EVERYTHING LOOKS REAL CLEAR TO ME TODAY!
BOKUTO-SAN IS EXTRA GOOD WITH HIS LINE SHOTS TODAY...
...AND HE'S VERY AWARE OF YAKU-SAN SITTING ON THE CROSS.
MAAAN! WHEN BOKUTO'S LINE SHOT IS OFF, IT'S ***WAY*** OFF.
WE'VE BEEN SETTING OUR BLOCKS TO CUT OFF THE CROSS SO FAR.
SHOULD WE SHIFT THEM TO STUFF THE LINE INSTEAD?
CROSS SHOT
LINE SHOT
YEAH. BUT...
?

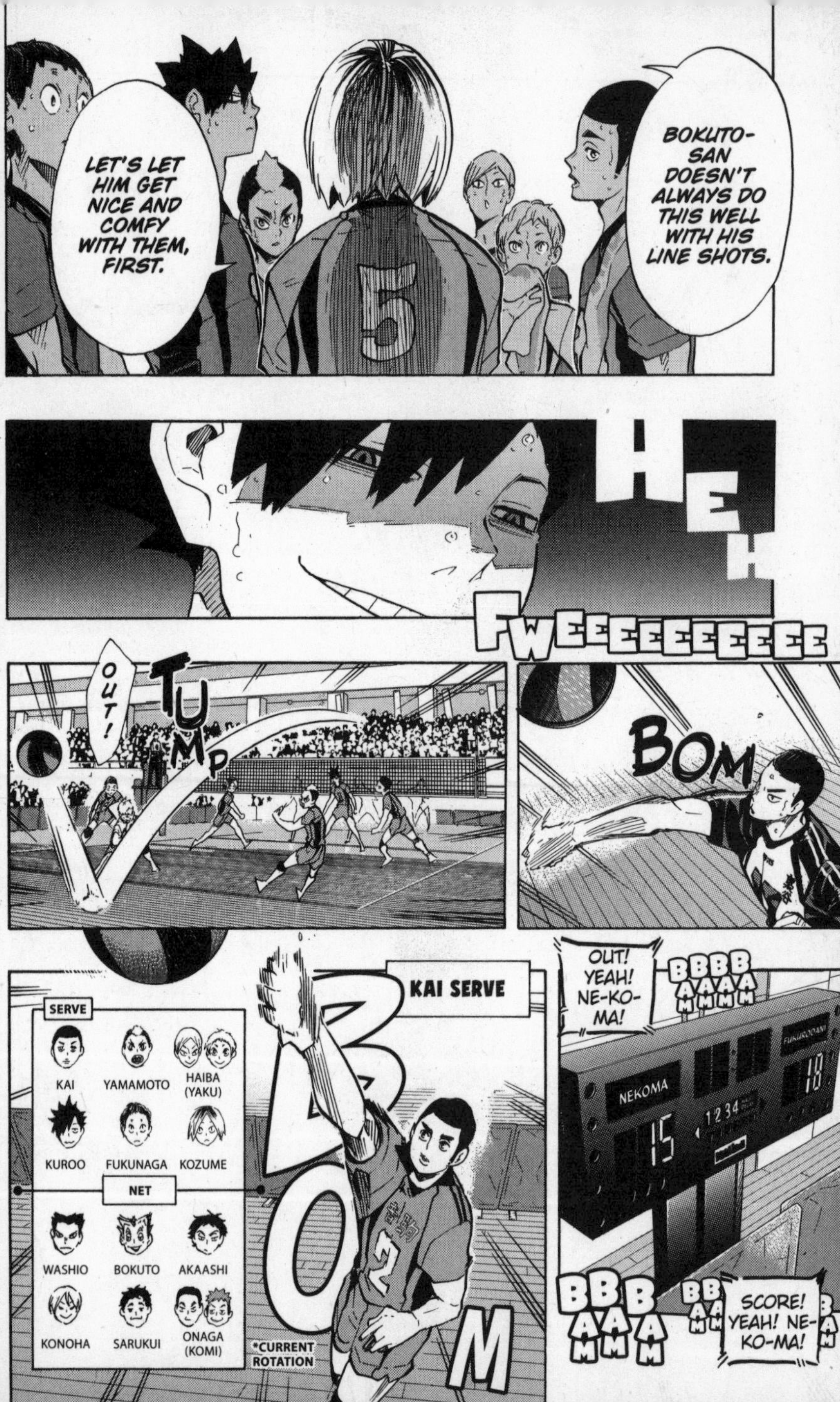
BOKUTO-SAN DOESN'T ALWAYS DO THIS WELL WITH HIS LINE SHOTS.
LET'S LET HIM GET NICE AND COMFY WITH THEM, FIRST.
HEH
FWEEEEEEEEEE
BOM
OUT!
TUMP
OUT! YEAH! NE-KO-MA!
BBBB AAAA MMMM
FUKURODANI
NEKOMA
18
15
1234
BBB AAA MMM
BB AA MM
SCORE! YEAH! NE-KO-MA!
B A M
KAI SERVE
BOOM
SERVE
KAI
YAMAMOTO
HAIBA (YAKU)
KUROO
FUKUNAGA
KOZUME
NET
WASHIO
BOKUTO
AKAASHI
KONOHA
SARUKUI
ONAGA (KOMI)
*CURRENT ROTATION

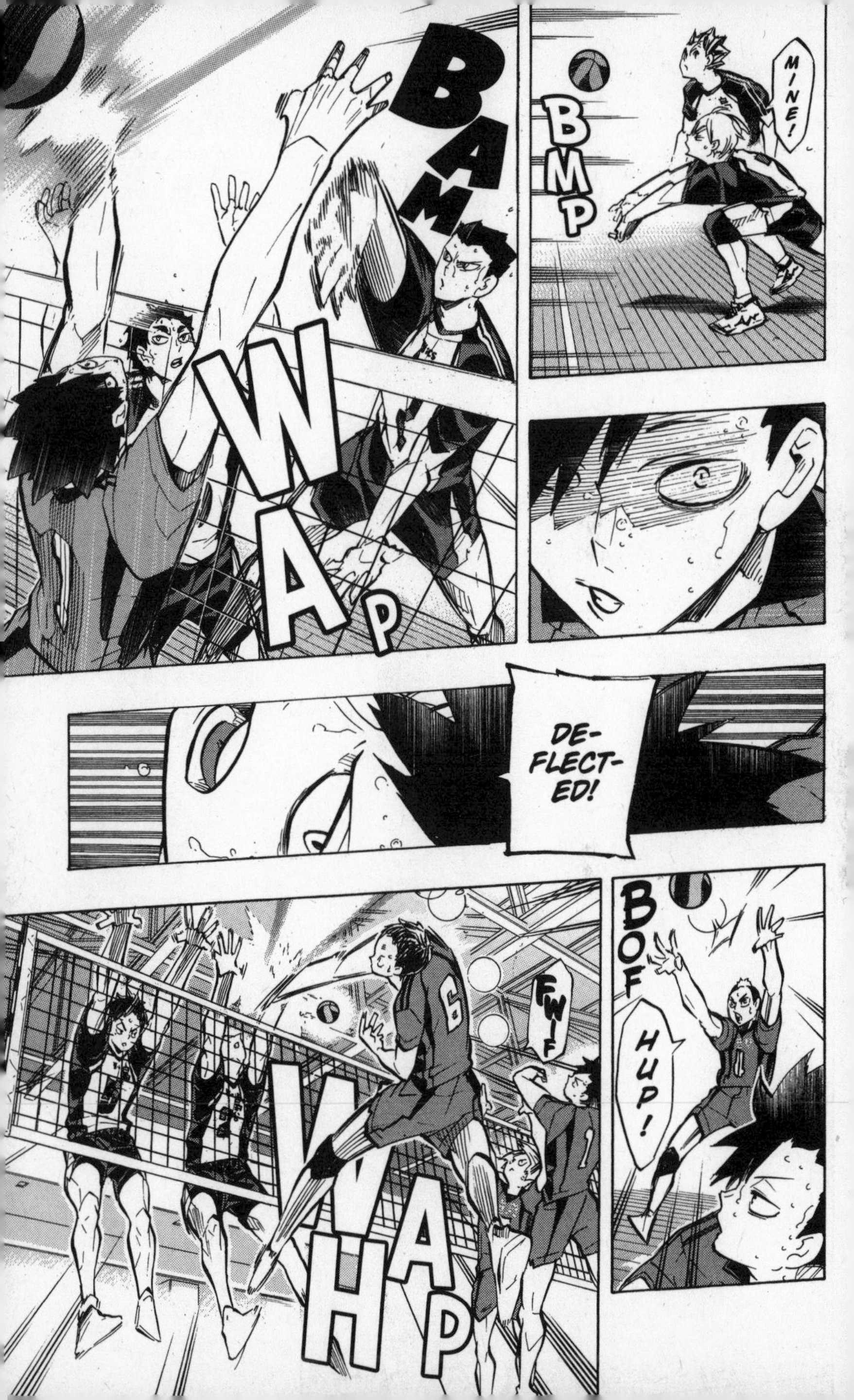
MINE!
BUMP
BAM
WAP
DE-FLECT-ED!
BOF
HUP!
FWIF
WHAP

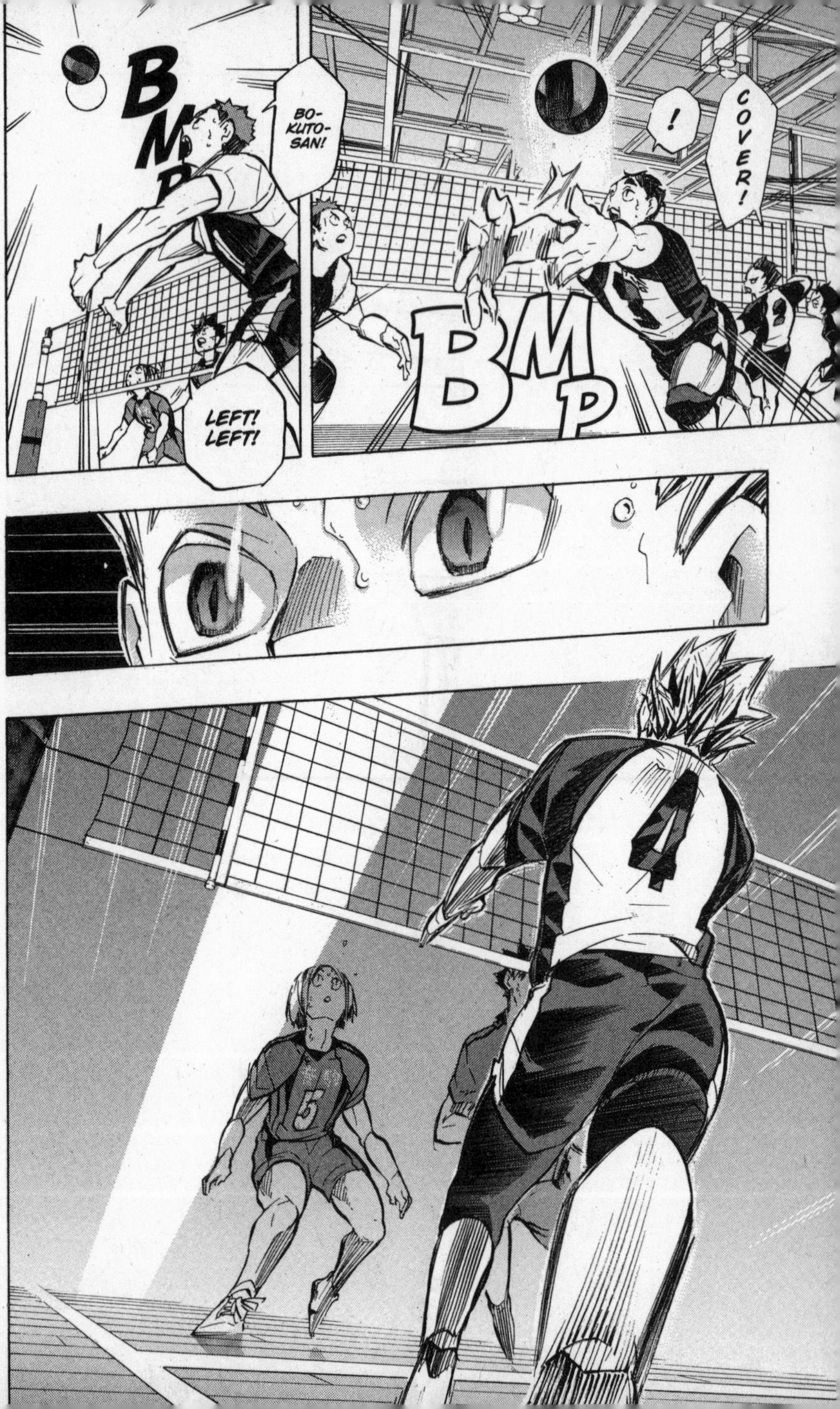
COVER!
!
BMP
BO-KUTO-SAN!
BMP
LEFT! LEFT!

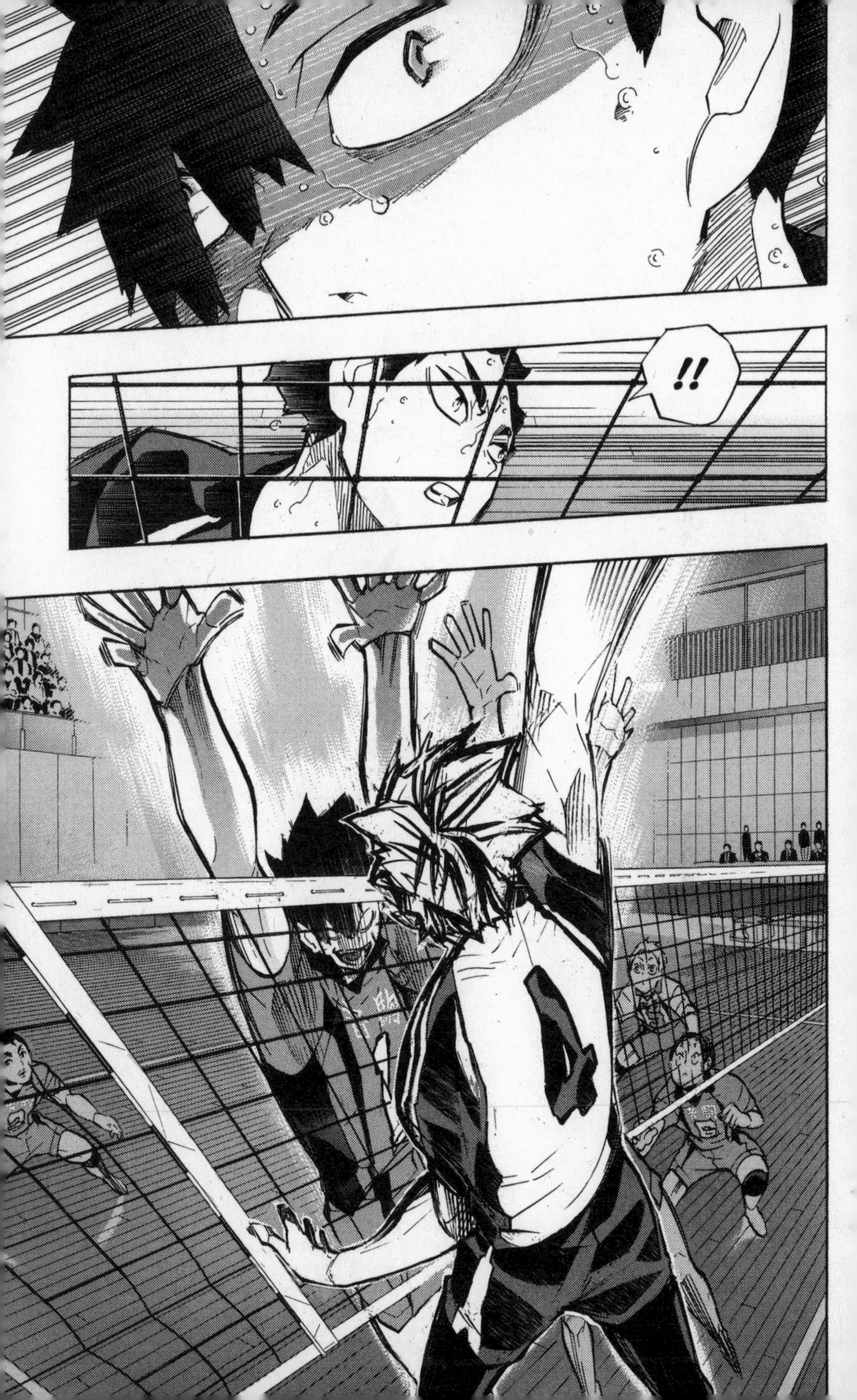
!!

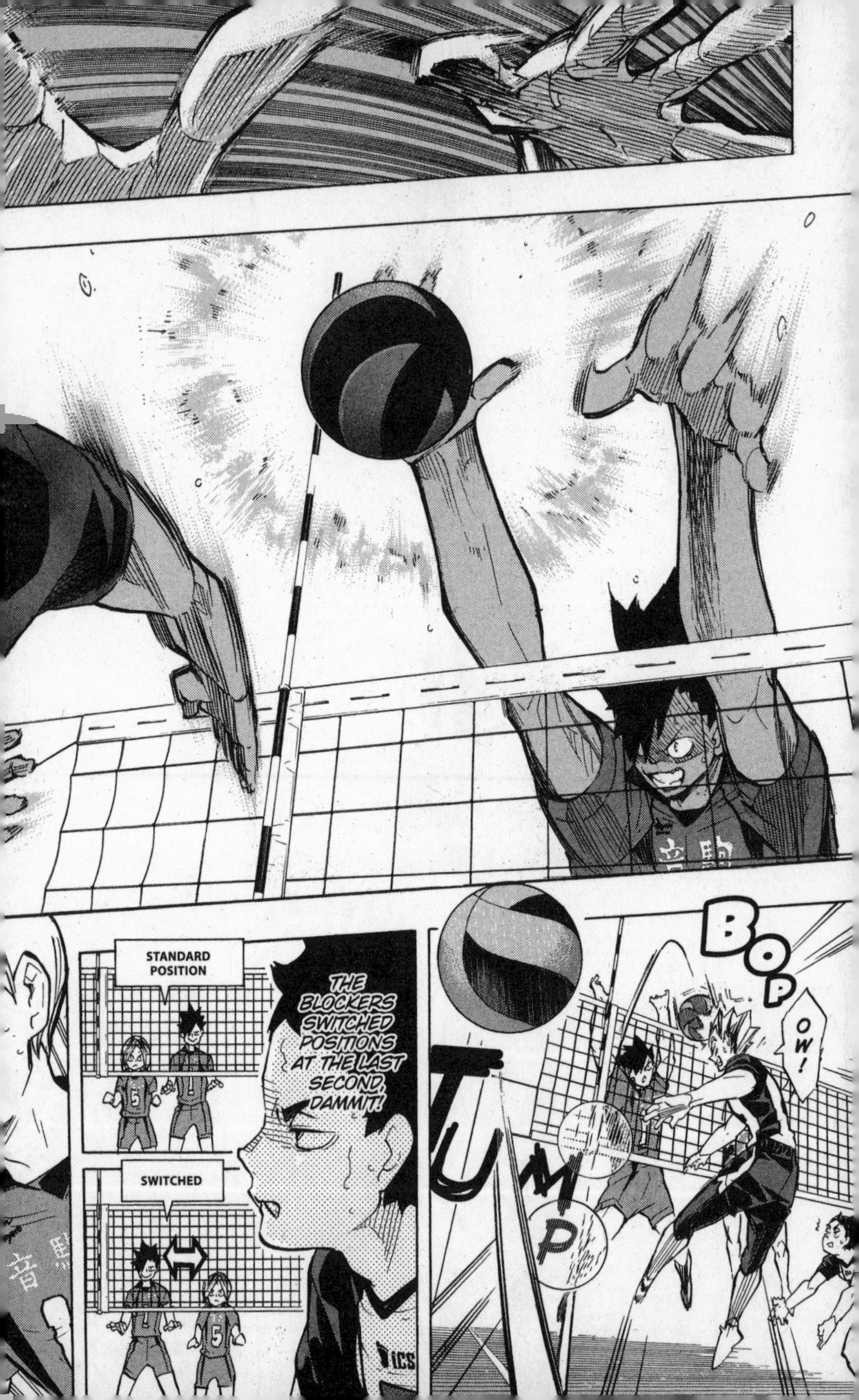
BOP
OW!
TUMP
THE BLOCKERS SWITCHED POSITIONS AT THE LAST SECOND, DAMMIT!
STANDARD POSITION
SWITCHED

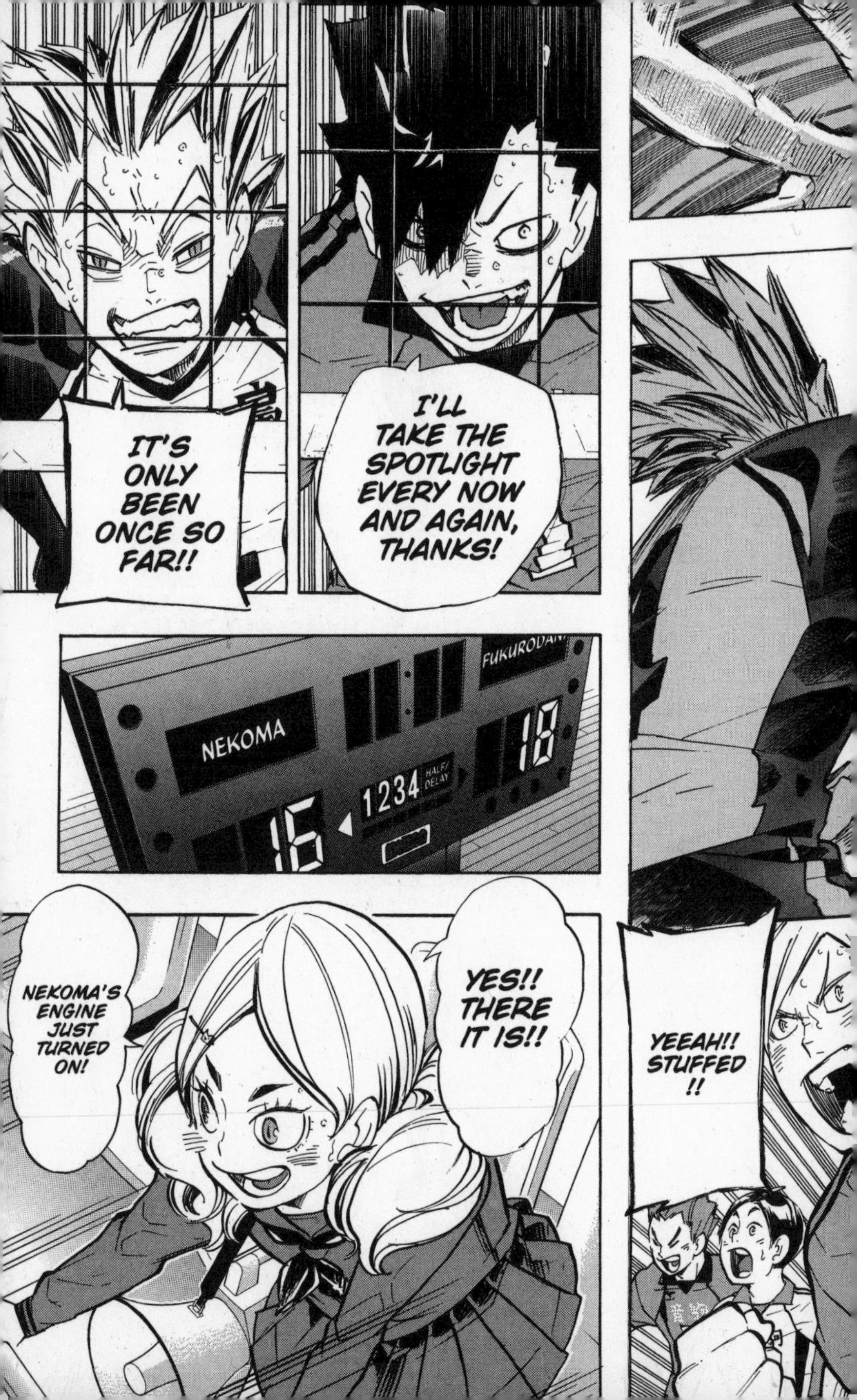
I'LL TAKE THE SPOTLIGHT EVERY NOW AND AGAIN, THANKS!
IT'S ONLY BEEN ONCE SO FAR!!
FUKURODANI
NEKOMA
18
1234 HALF/DELAY
16
YEEAH!! STUFFED !!
YES!! THERE IT IS!!
NEKOMA'S ENGINE JUST TURNED ON!

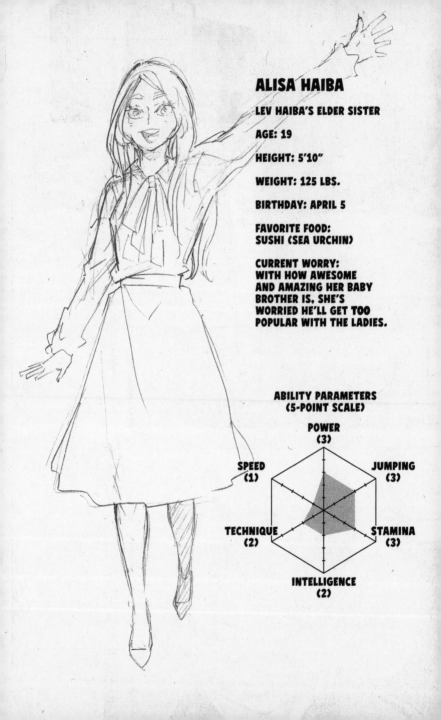

ALISA HAIBA

LEV HAIBA'S ELDER SISTER

AGE: 19

HEIGHT: 5'10"

WEIGHT: 125 LBS.

BIRTHDAY: APRIL 5

FAVORITE FOOD:
SUSHI (SEA URCHIN)

CURRENT WORRY:
WITH HOW AWESOME
AND AMAZING HER BABY
BROTHER IS, SHE'S
WORRIED HE'LL GET TOO
POPULAR WITH THE LADIES.

ABILITY PARAMETERS
(5-POINT SCALE)

POWER
(3)

SPEED
(1)

JUMPING
(3)

TECHNIQUE
(2)

STAMINA
(3)

INTELLIGENCE
(2)

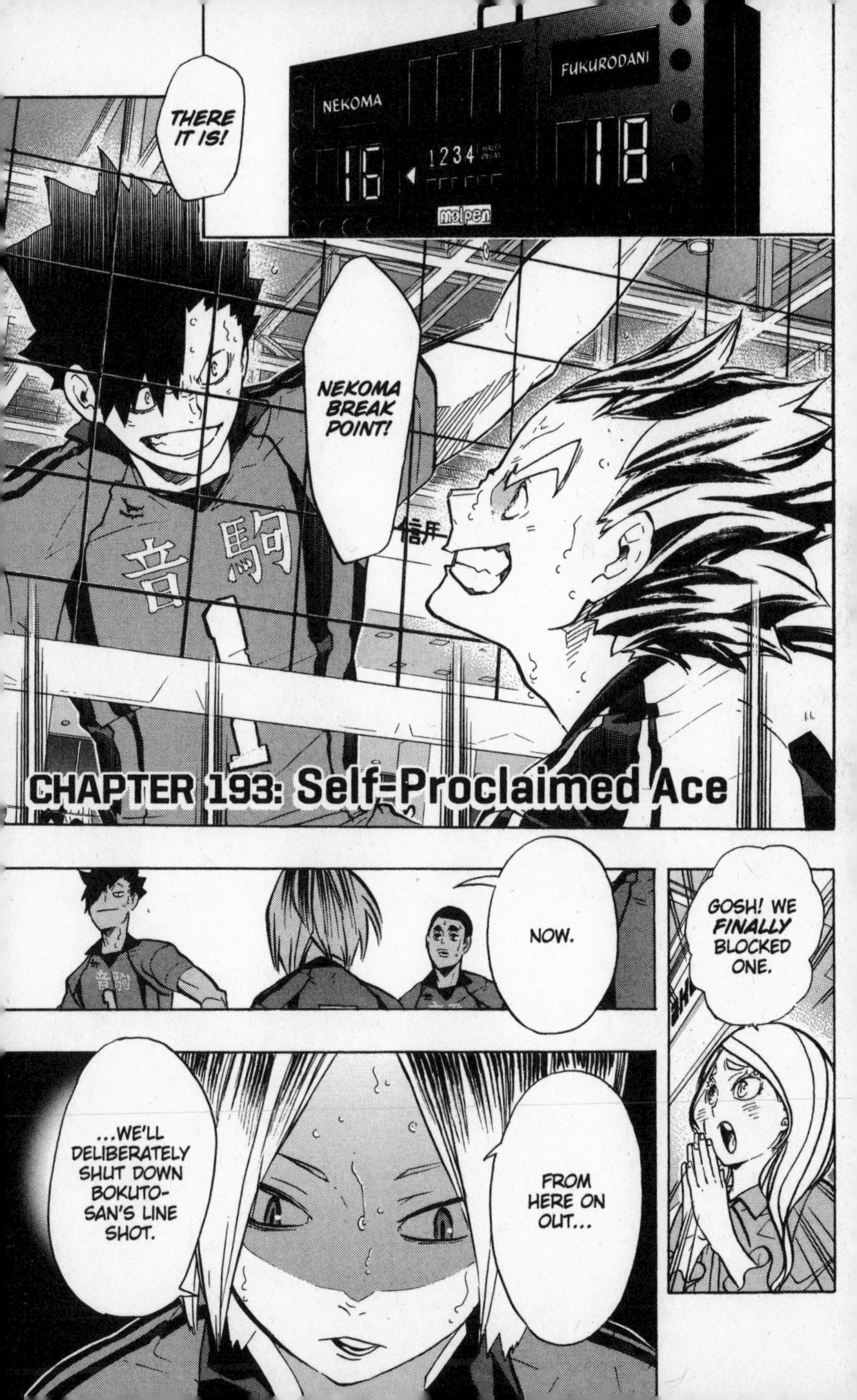
FUKURODANI
NEKOMA
16
18
THERE IT IS!
NEKOMA BREAK POINT!
CHAPTER 193: Self-Proclaimed Ace
GOSH! WE FINALLY BLOCKED ONE.
NOW.
FROM HERE ON OUT...
...WE'LL DELIBERATELY SHUT DOWN BOKUTO-SAN'S LINE SHOT.

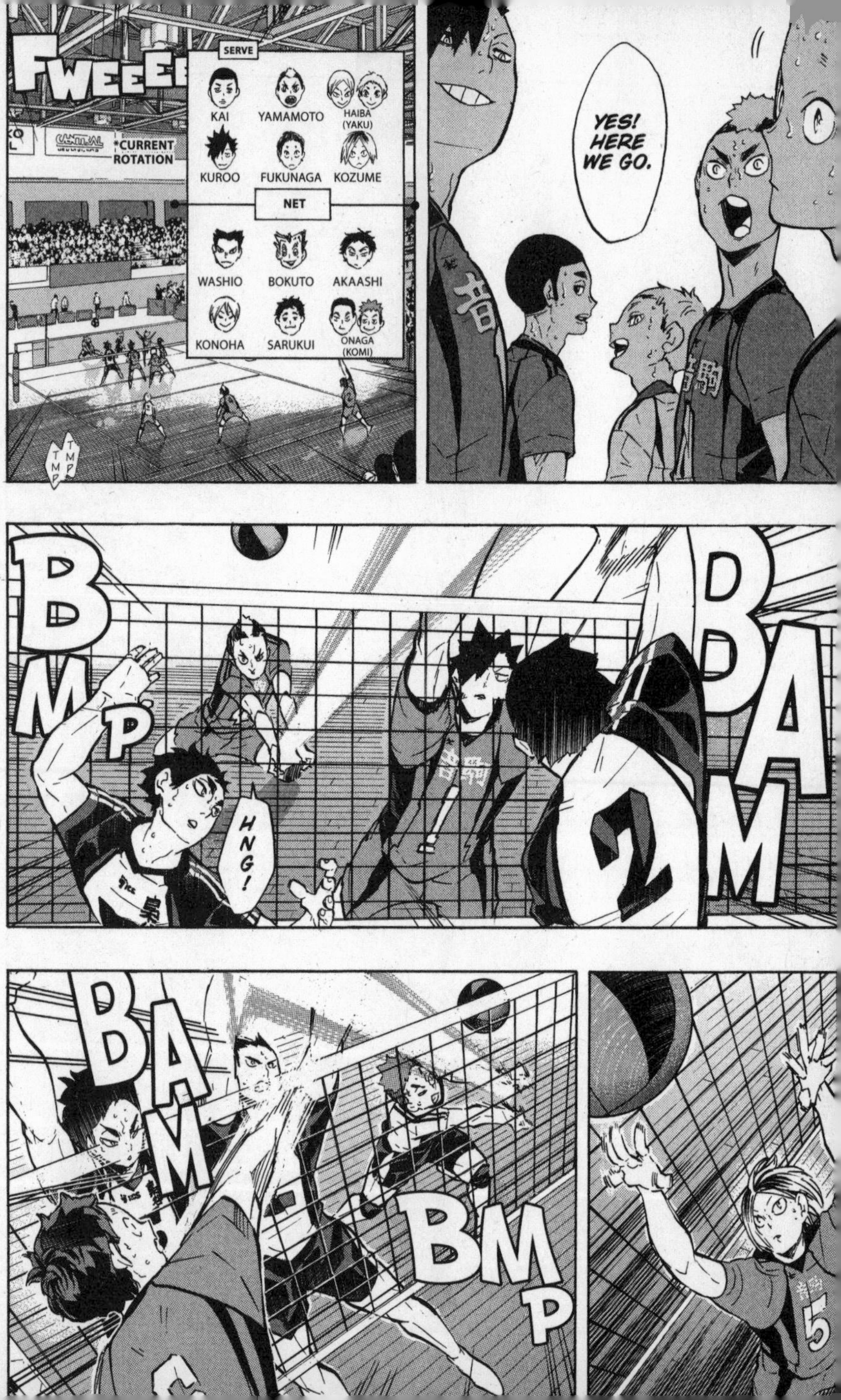
YES! HERE WE GO.
FWEEEE
CURRENT ROTATION
SERVE
KAI
YAMAMOTO
HAIBA (YAKU)
KUROO
FUKUNAGA
KOZUME
NET
WASHIO
BOKUTO
AKAASHI
KONOHA
SARUKUI
ONAGA (KOMI)
TMP TMP
BAMM
HNG!
BMP
BAM
BMP

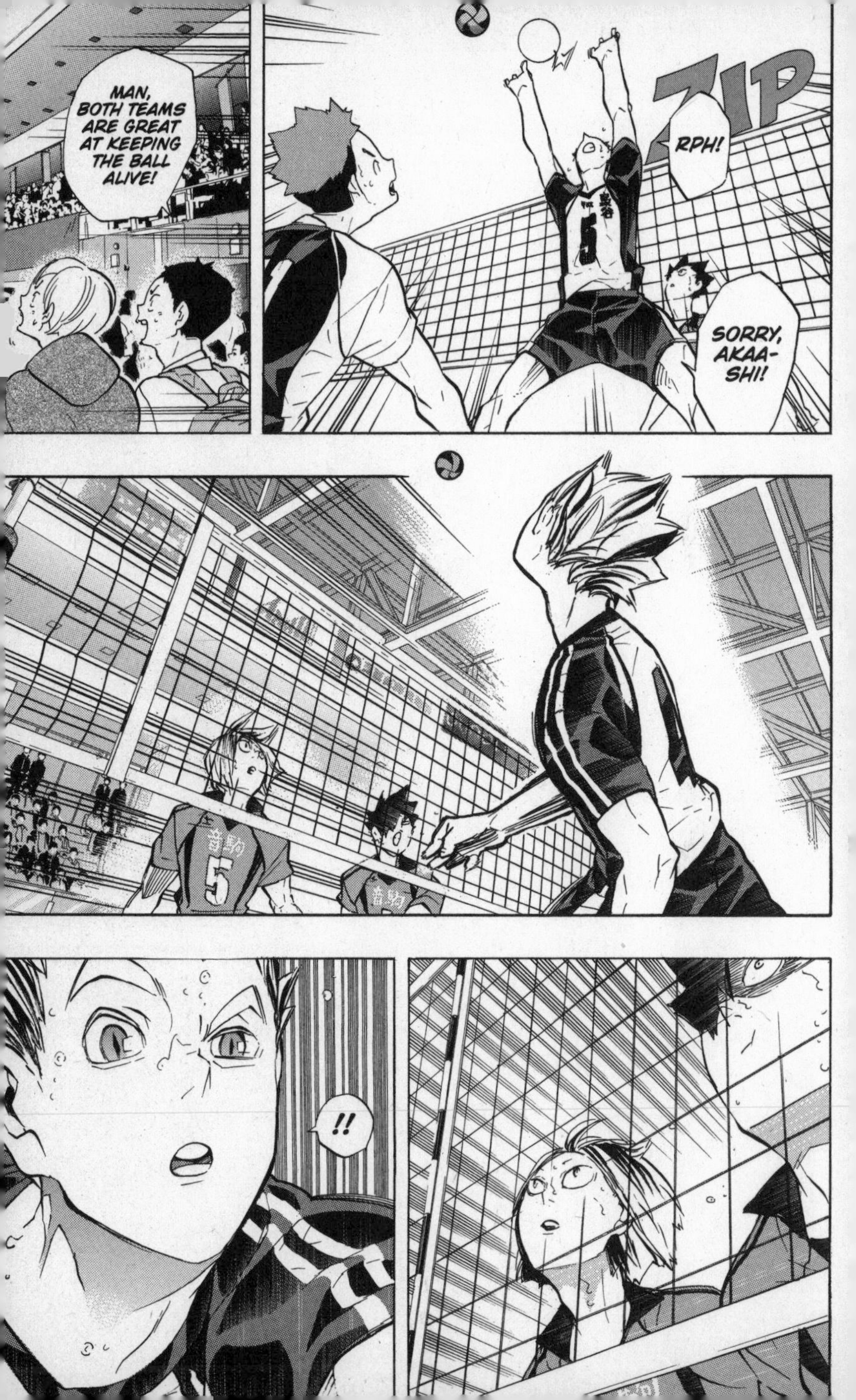
ZIP
RPH!
SORRY, AKAA-SHI!
MAN, BOTH TEAMS ARE GREAT AT KEEPING THE BALL ALIVE!
!!

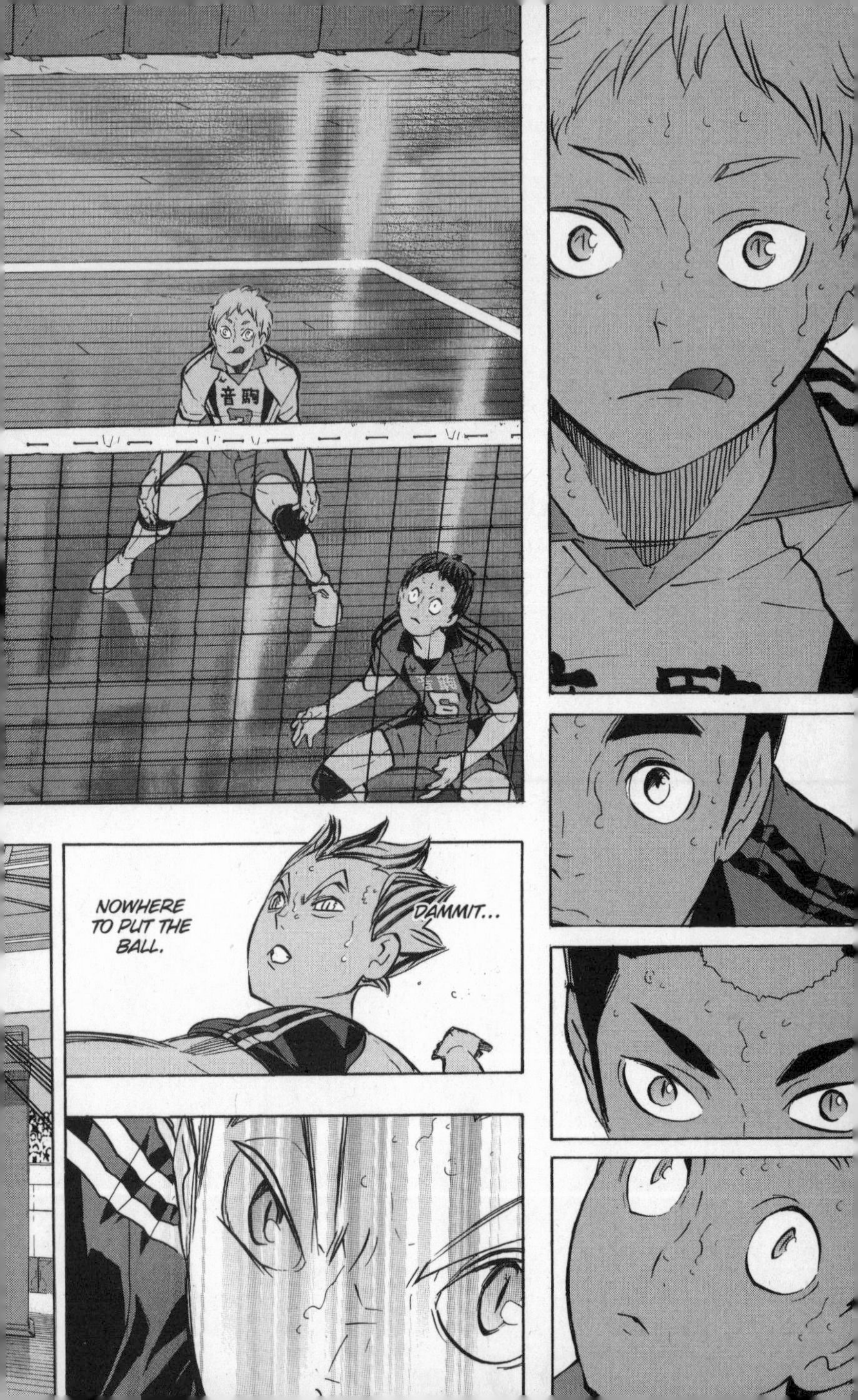
音駒
DAMMIT...
NOWHERE TO PUT THE BALL.

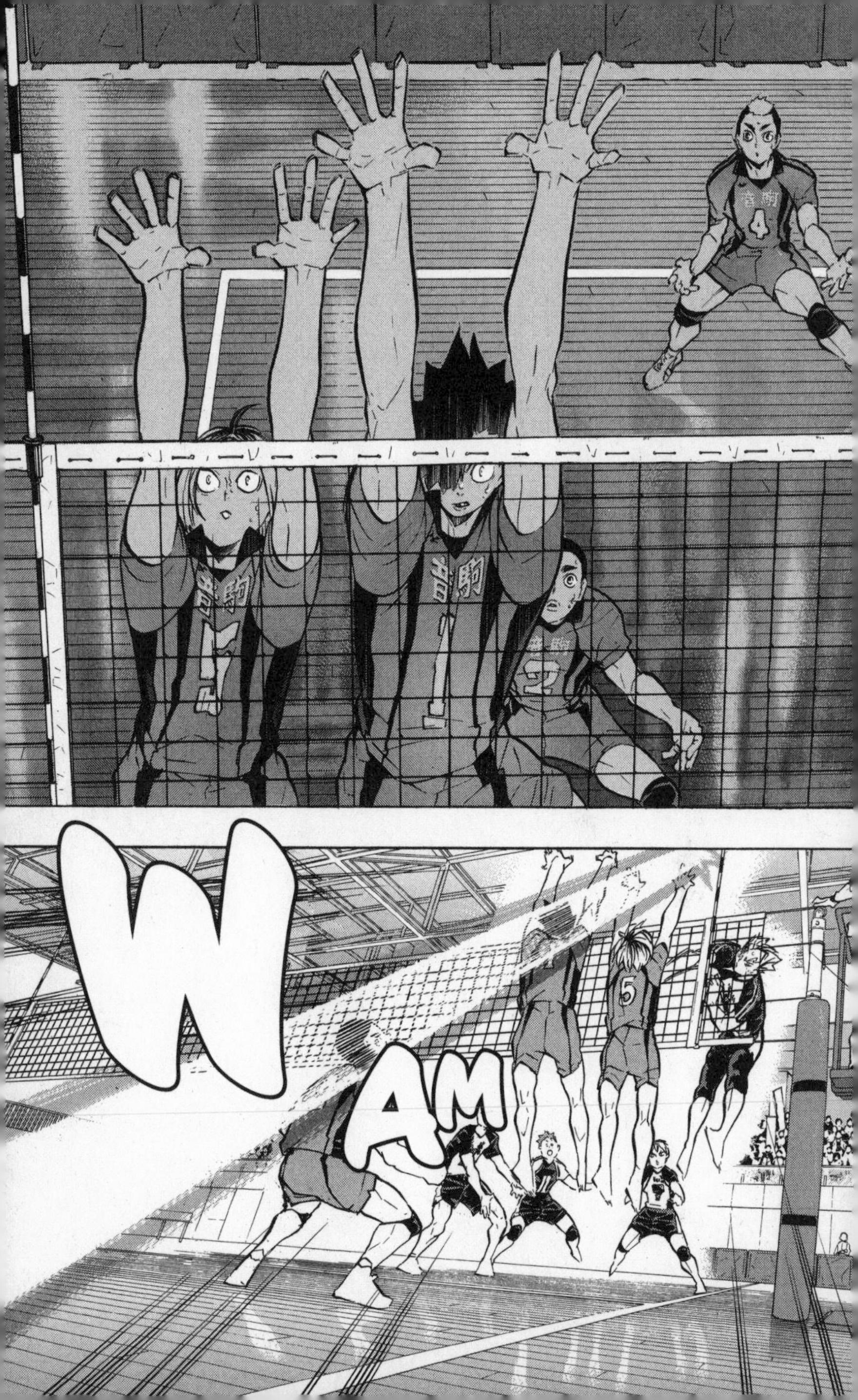
WAM

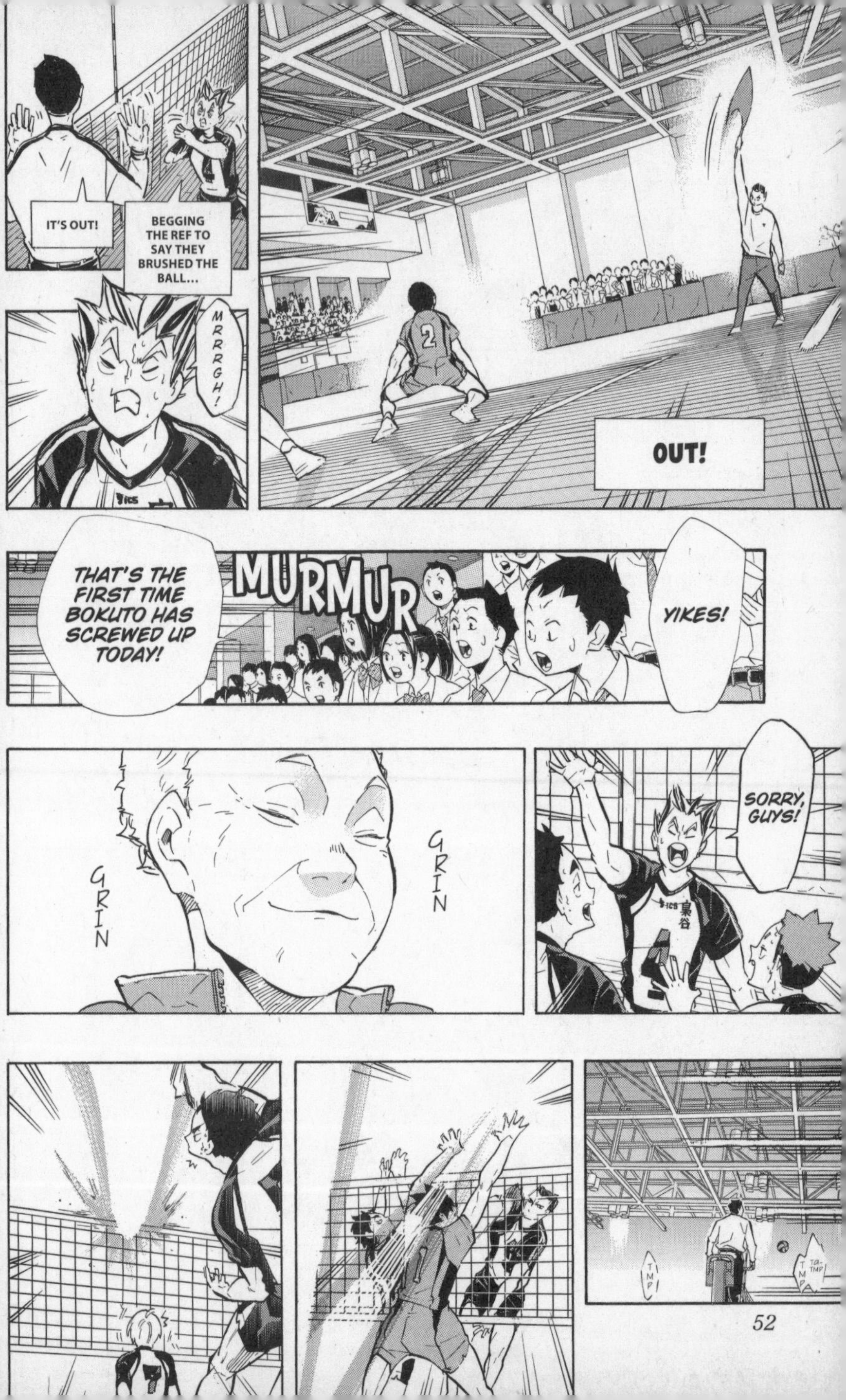
OUT!
BEGGING THE REF TO SAY THEY BRUSHED THE BALL...
IT'S OUT!
MRRRGH!
YIKES!
MURMUR
THAT'S THE FIRST TIME BOKUTO HAS SCREWED UP TODAY!
SORRY, GUYS!
GRIN
GRIN
TA-TMP
TMP
TMP

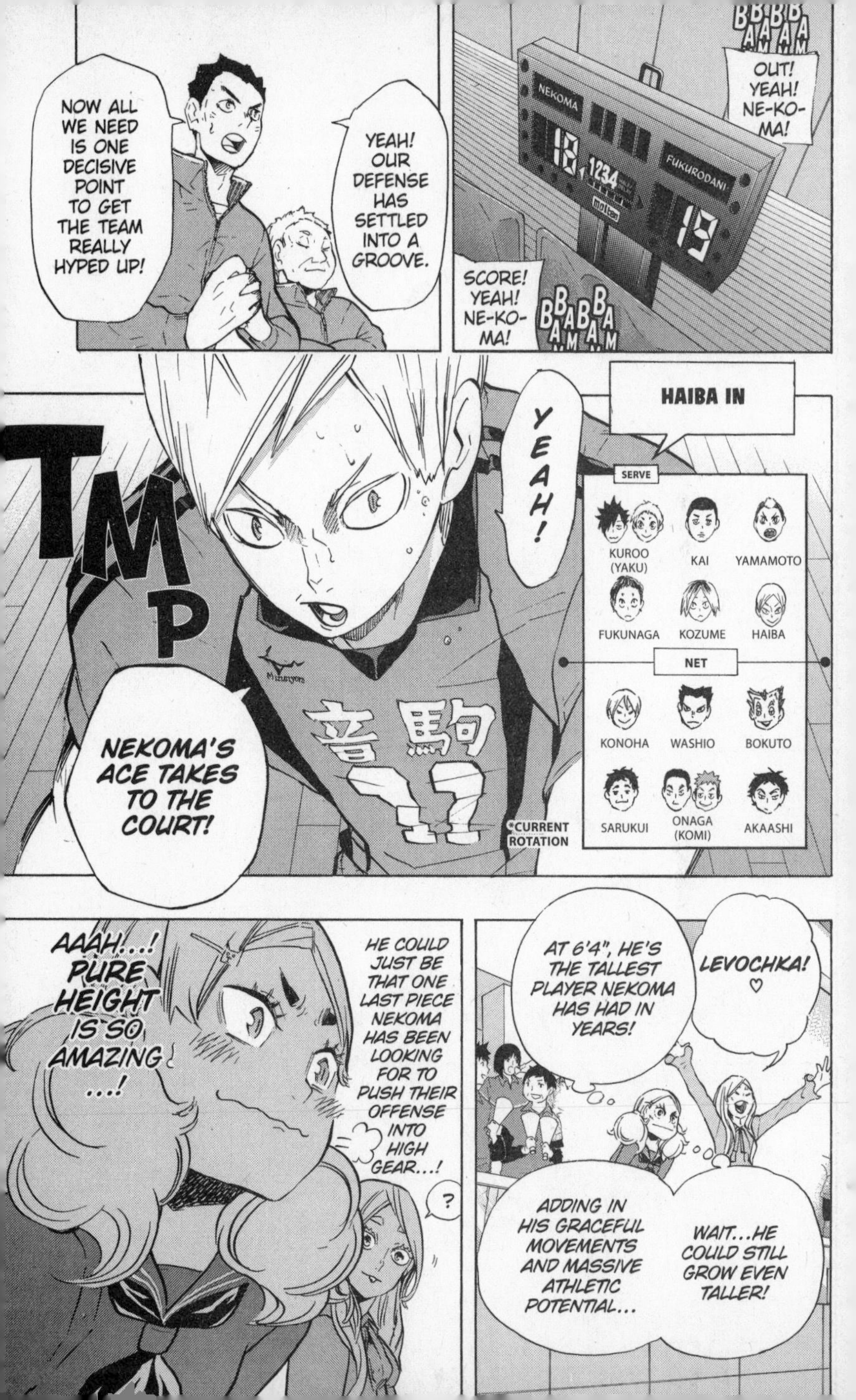
BBBB AAAA MMM
OUT! YEAH! NE-KO-MA!
NEKOMA
18
1234
FUKURODANI
19
SCORE! YEAH! NE-KO-MA!
BBBB AAAA MMMM
YEAH! OUR DEFENSE HAS SETTLED INTO A GROOVE.
NOW ALL WE NEED IS ONE DECISIVE POINT TO GET THE TEAM REALLY HYPED UP!
HAIBA IN
SERVE
KUROO (YAKU)
KAI
YAMAMOTO
FUKUNAGA
KOZUME
HAIBA
NET
KONOHA
WASHIO
BOKUTO
SARUKUI
ONAGA (KOMI)
AKAASHI
*CURRENT ROTATION
YEAH!
TMP
NEKOMA'S ACE TAKES TO THE COURT!
LEVOCHKA! ♡
AT 6'4", HE'S THE TALLEST PLAYER NEKOMA HAS HAD IN YEARS!
ADDING IN HIS GRACEFUL MOVEMENTS AND MASSIVE ATHLETIC POTENTIAL...
WAIT...HE COULD STILL GROW EVEN TALLER!
HE COULD JUST BE THAT ONE LAST PIECE NEKOMA HAS BEEN LOOKING FOR TO PUSH THEIR OFFENSE INTO HIGH GEAR...!
AAAH...! PURE HEIGHT IS SO AMAZING...!
?

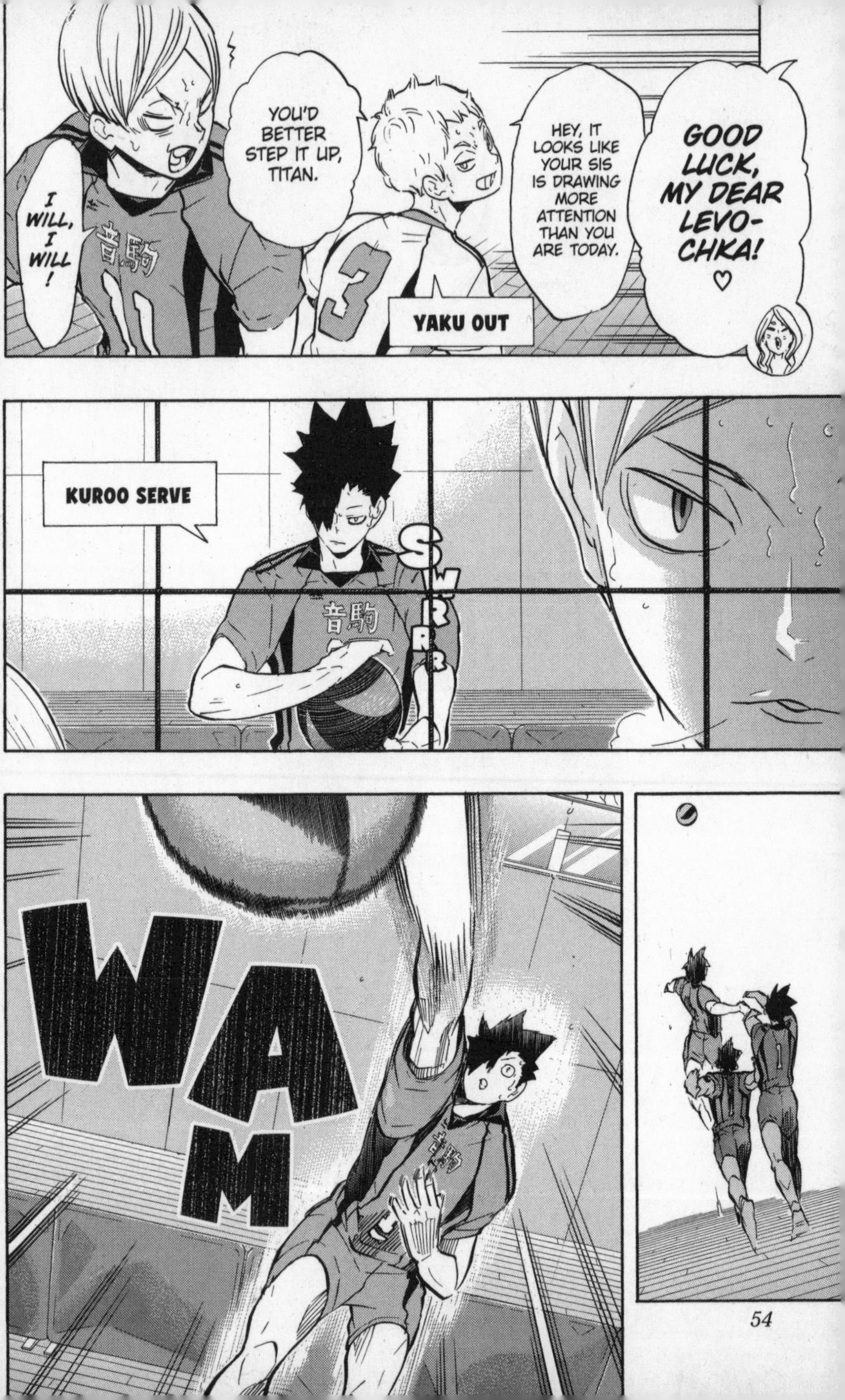
GOOD LUCK, MY DEAR LEVOCHKA! ♡
HEY, IT LOOKS LIKE YOUR SIS IS DRAWING MORE ATTENTION THAN YOU ARE TODAY.
YAKU OUT
YOU'D BETTER STEP IT UP, TITAN.
I WILL, I WILL!
SWRRR
KUROO SERVE
WAM

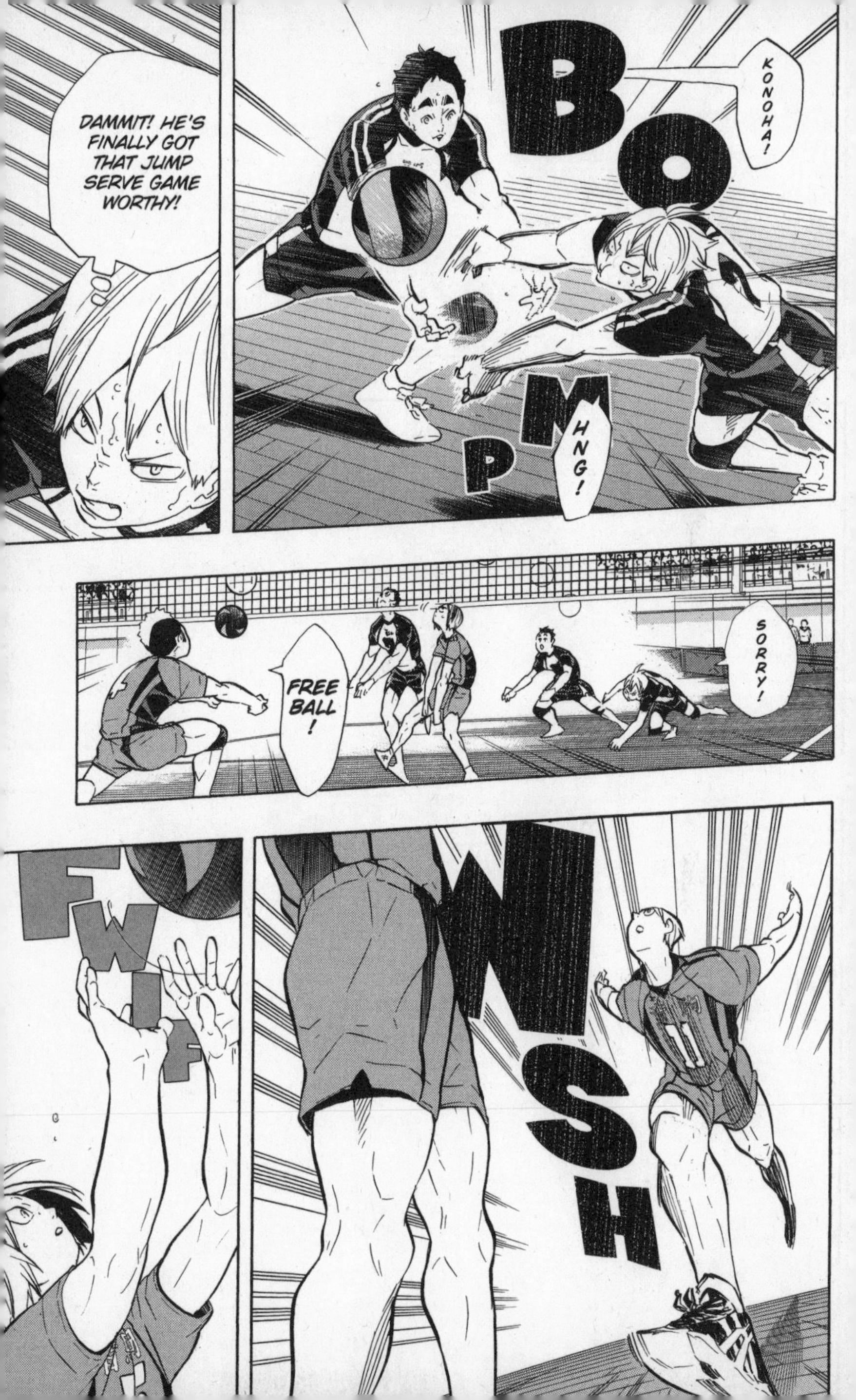
KONOHA!
BOMP
HNG!
DAMMIT! HE'S FINALLY GOT THAT JUMP SERVE GAME WORTHY!
SORRY!
FREE BALL!
WNSH
FWIF

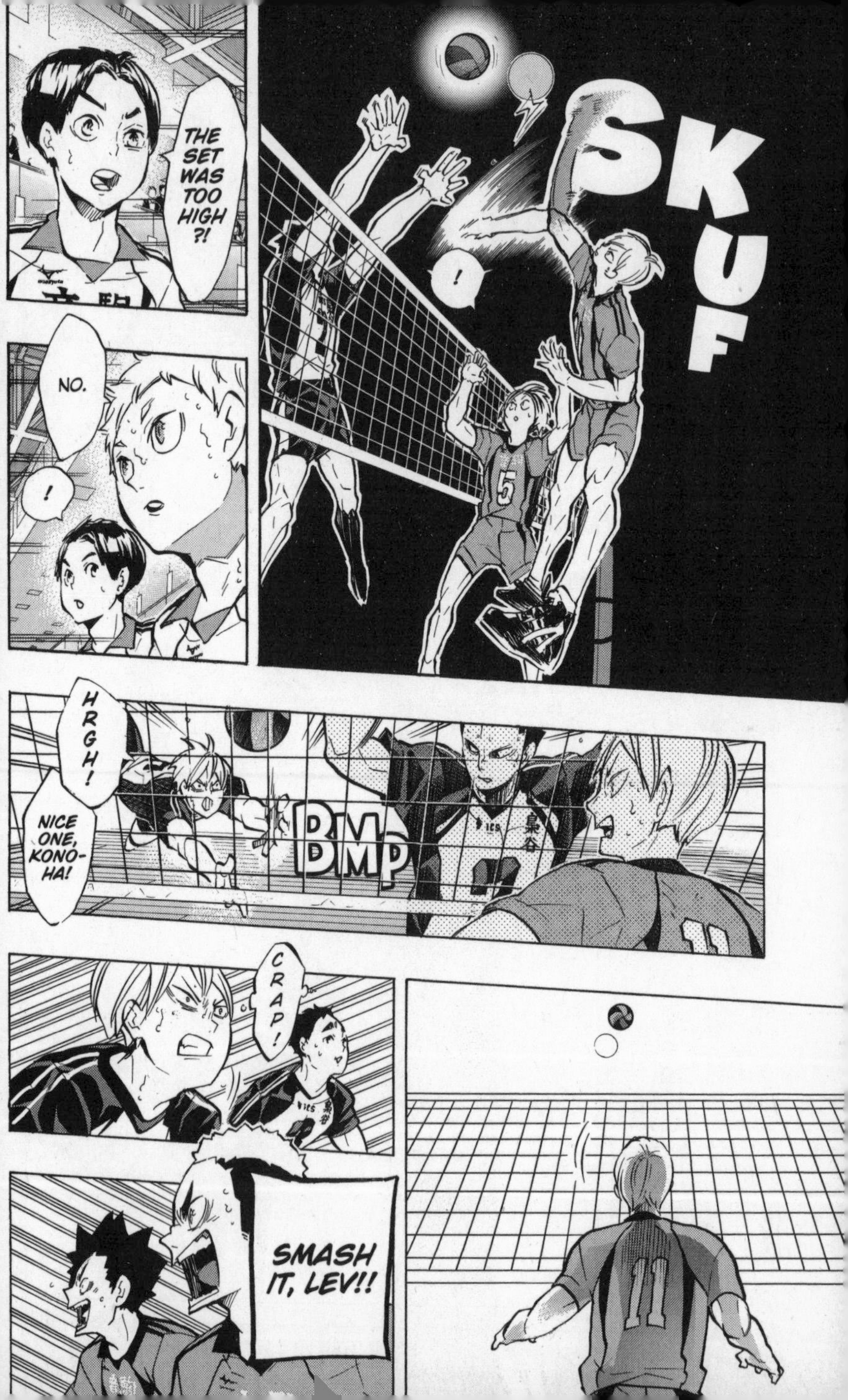
SKUF
!
THE SET WAS TOO HIGH?!
NO.
!
HRGH!
NICE ONE, KONOHA!
BMP
CRAP!
SMASH IT, LEV!!

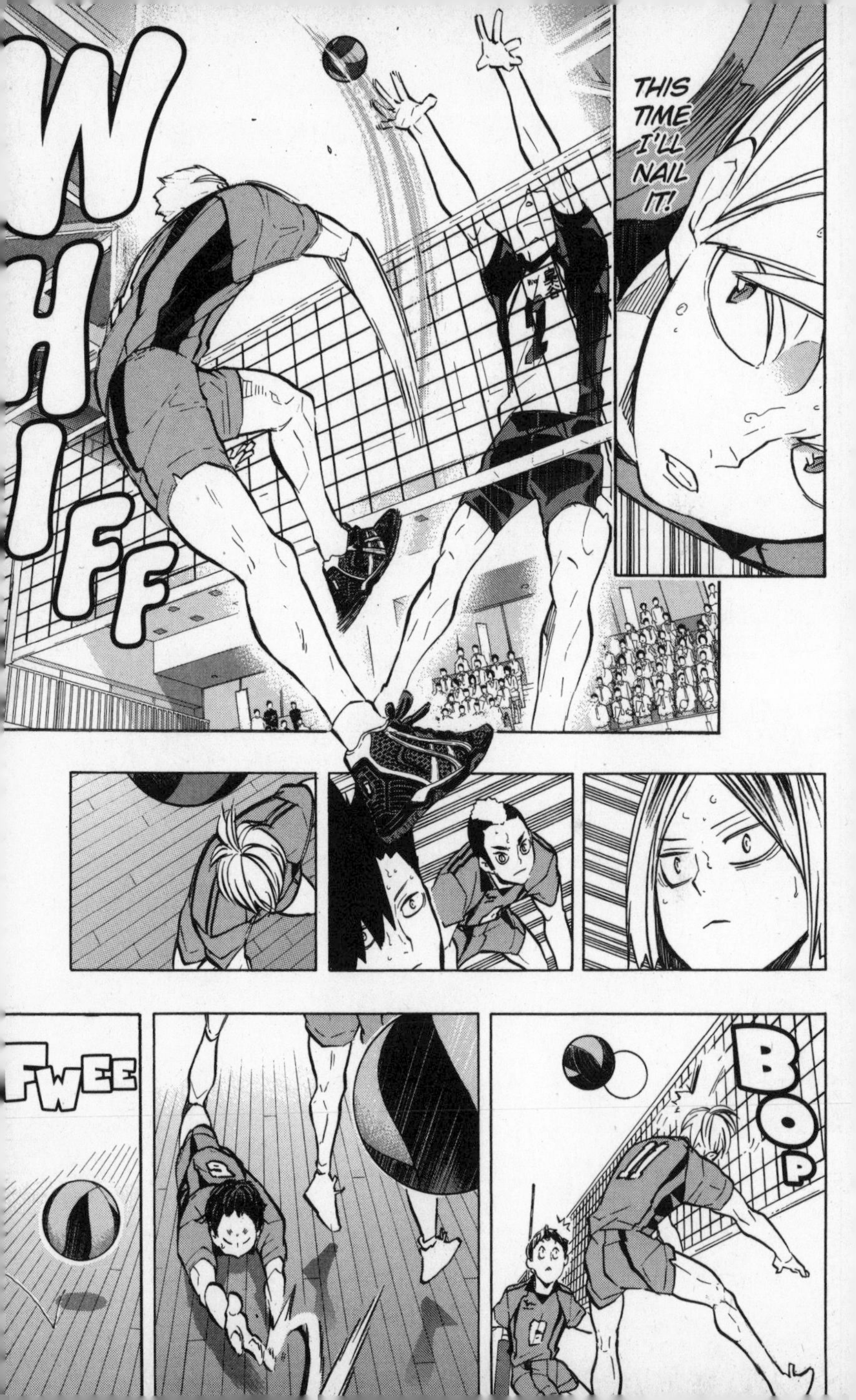
THIS TIME I'LL NAIL IT!
WHIFF
BOOP
FWEE

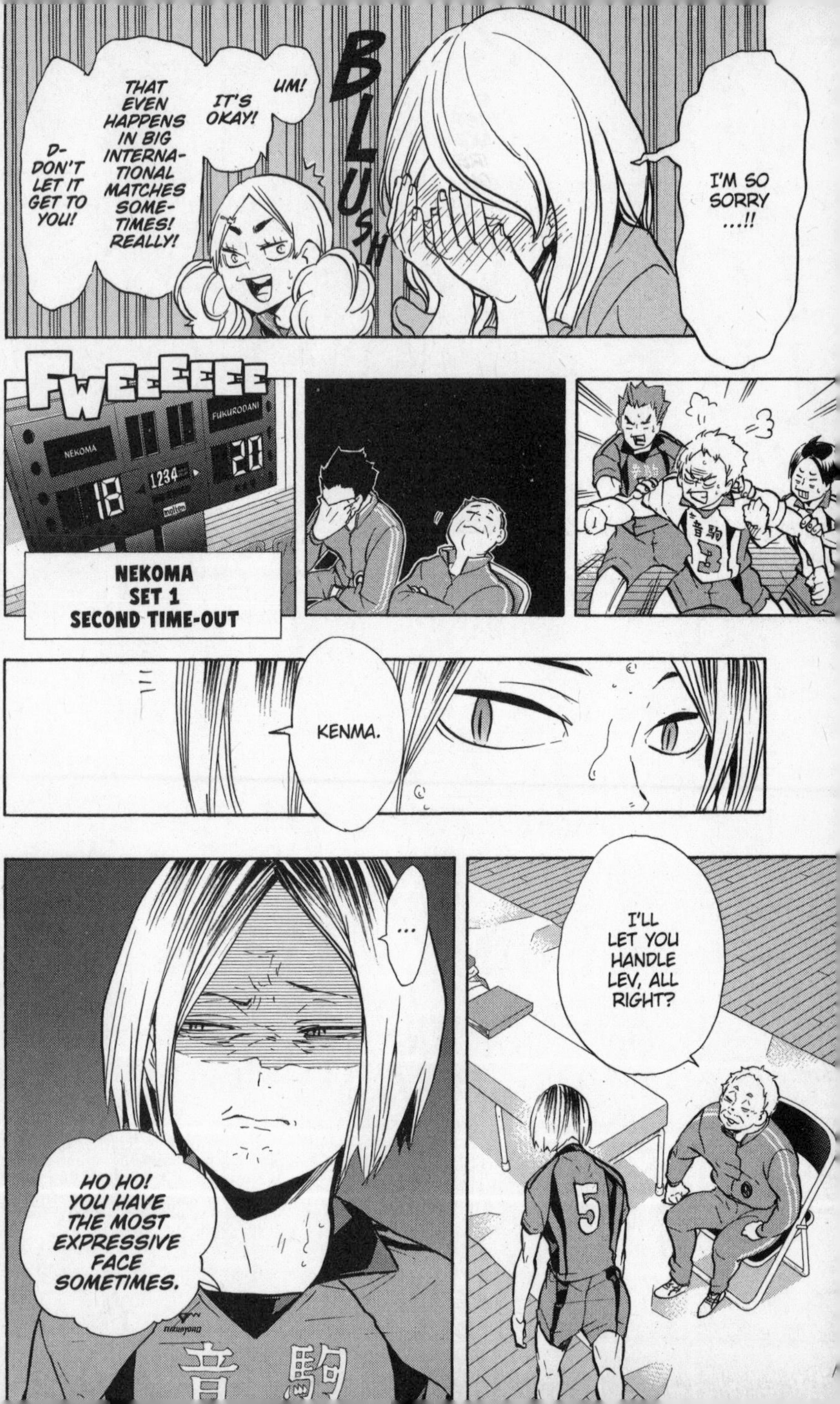
I'M SO SORRY ...!!
BLUSH
UM!
IT'S OKAY!
THAT EVEN HAPPENS IN BIG INTERNATIONAL MATCHES SOMETIMES! REALLY!
D-DON'T LET IT GET TO YOU!
FWEEEEEE
FUKURODANI
NEKOMA
18
20
NEKOMA SET 1 SECOND TIME-OUT
KENMA.
I'LL LET YOU HANDLE LEV, ALL RIGHT?
...
HO HO! YOU HAVE THE MOST EXPRESSIVE FACE SOMETIMES.

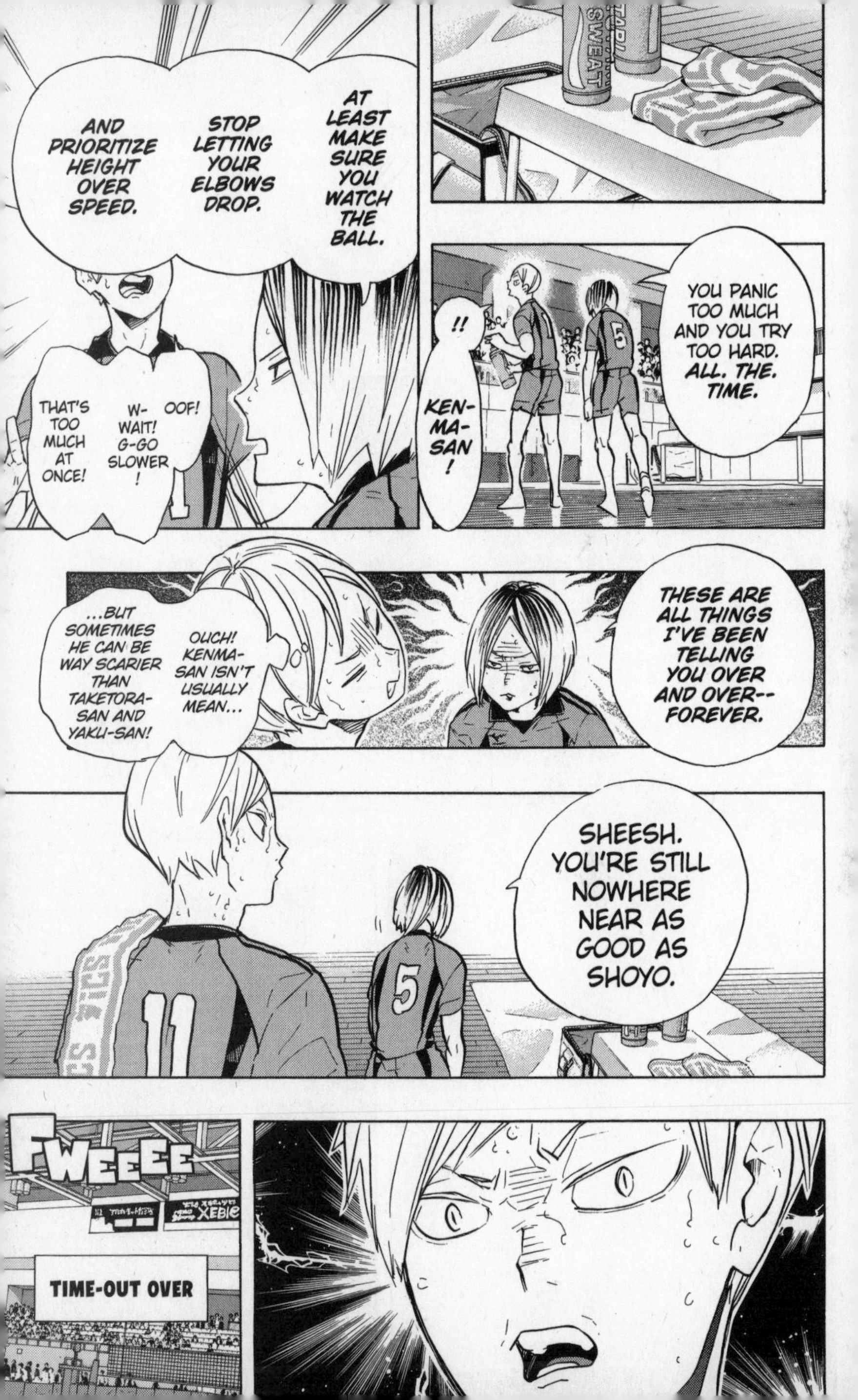
SWEAT
YOU PANIC TOO MUCH AND YOU TRY TOO HARD. ALL. THE. TIME.
!!
KEN-MA-SAN!
AT LEAST MAKE SURE YOU WATCH THE BALL.
STOP LETTING YOUR ELBOWS DROP.
AND PRIORITIZE HEIGHT OVER SPEED.
OOF!
W-WAIT! G-GO SLOWER!
THAT'S TOO MUCH AT ONCE!
THESE ARE ALL THINGS I'VE BEEN TELLING YOU OVER AND OVER--FOREVER.
OUCH! KENMA-SAN ISN'T USUALLY MEAN...
...BUT SOMETIMES HE CAN BE WAY SCARIER THAN TAKETORA-SAN AND YAKU-SAN!
SHEESH. YOU'RE STILL NOWHERE NEAR AS GOOD AS SHOYO.
FWEEEE
TIME-OUT OVER

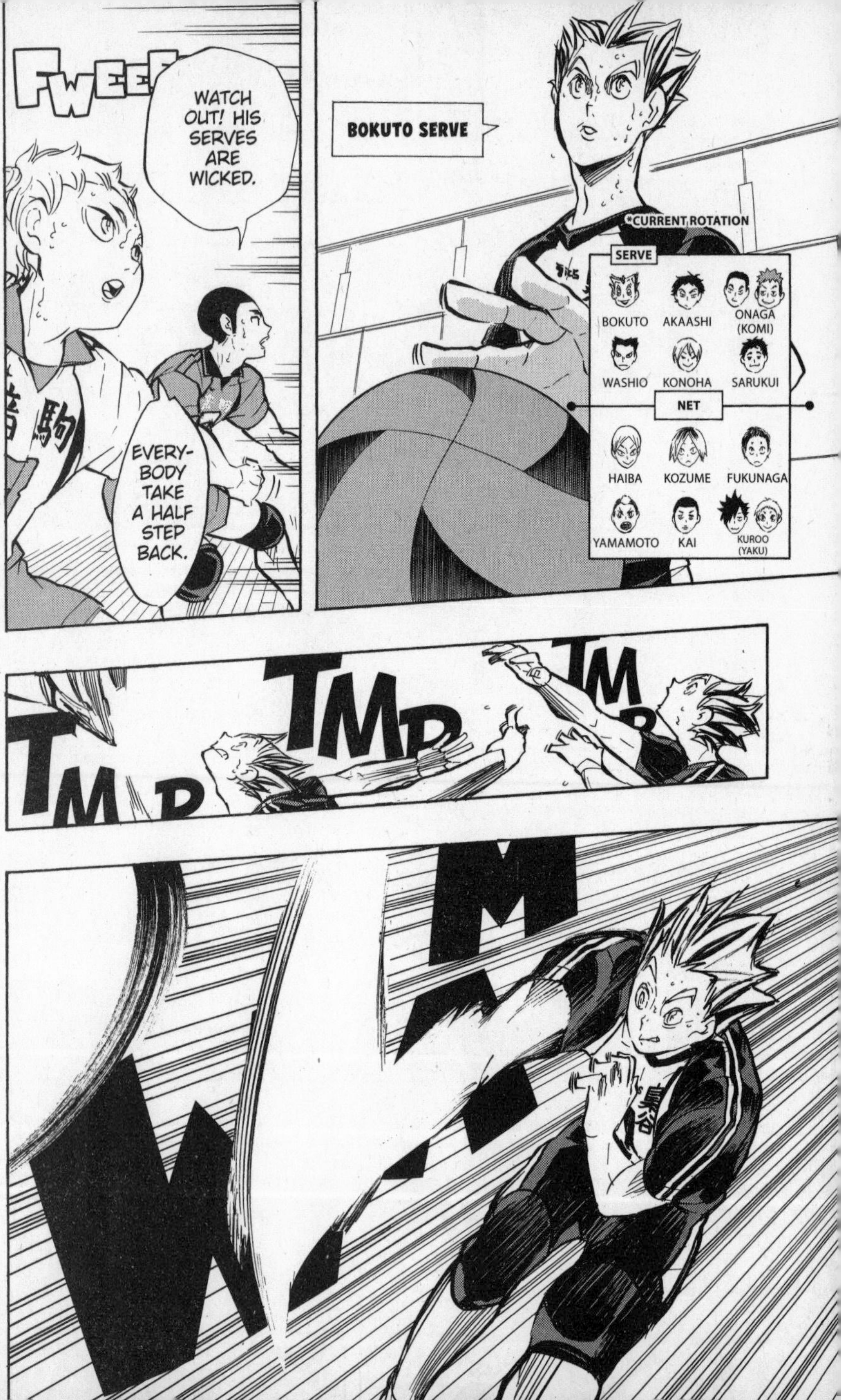
BOKUTO SERVE
*CURRENT ROTATION
SERVE
BOKUTO
AKAASHI
ONAGA (KOMI)
WASHIO
KONOHA
SARUKUI
NET
HAIBA
KOZUME
FUKUNAGA
YAMAMOTO
KAI
KUROO (YAKU)
FWEE
WATCH OUT! HIS SERVES ARE WICKED.
EVERY-BODY TAKE A HALF STEP BACK.
TMP
TMP
TMP

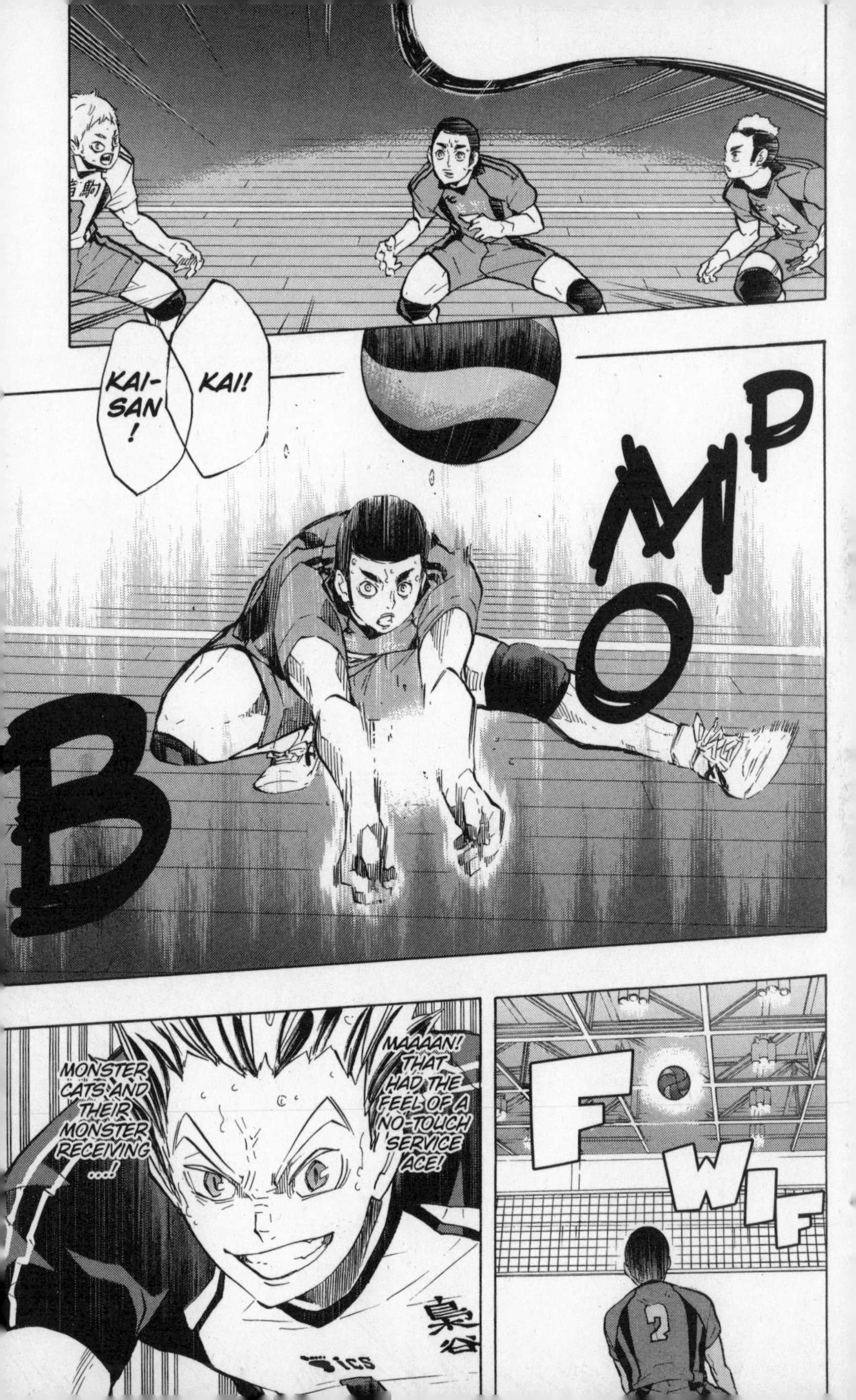
KAI!
KAI-SAN!
BOMP
FWIF
MAAAAN! THAT HAD THE FEEL OF A NO-TOUCH SERVICE ACE!
MONSTER CATS AND THEIR MONSTER RECEIVING ...!

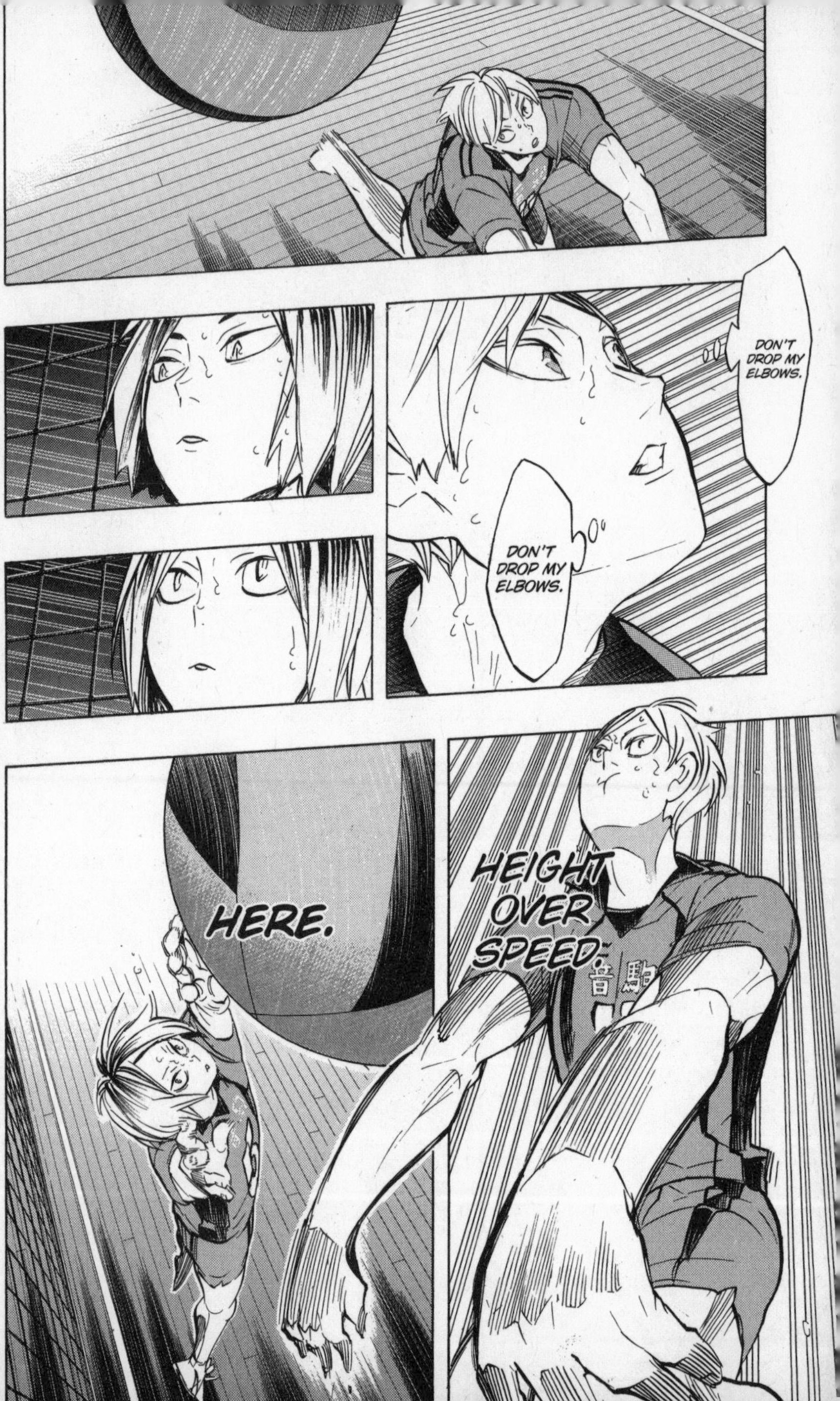
DON'T DROP MY ELBOWS.
DON'T DROP MY ELBOWS.
HEIGHT OVER SPEED.
HERE.

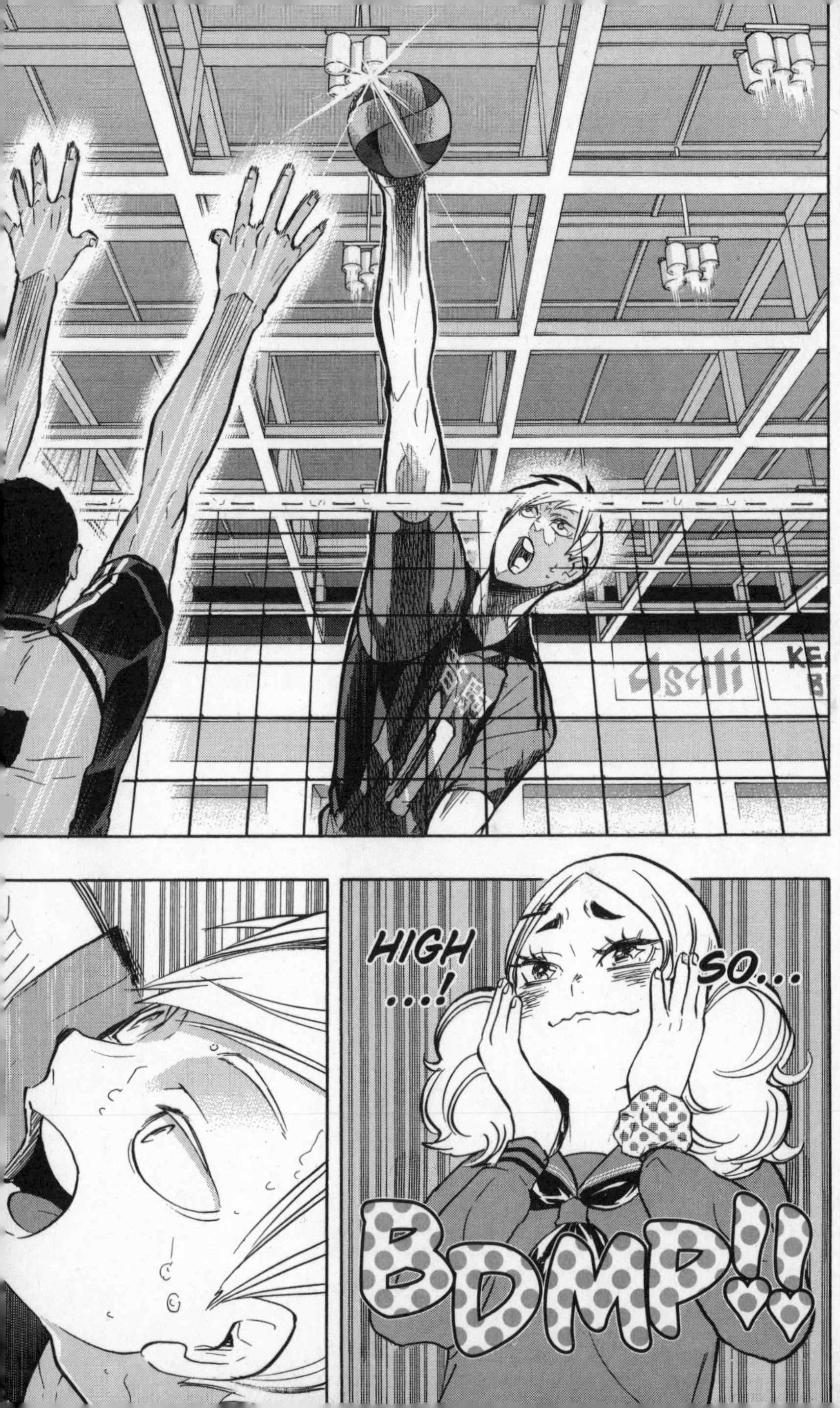
SO...
HIGH ...!
BDMP!!

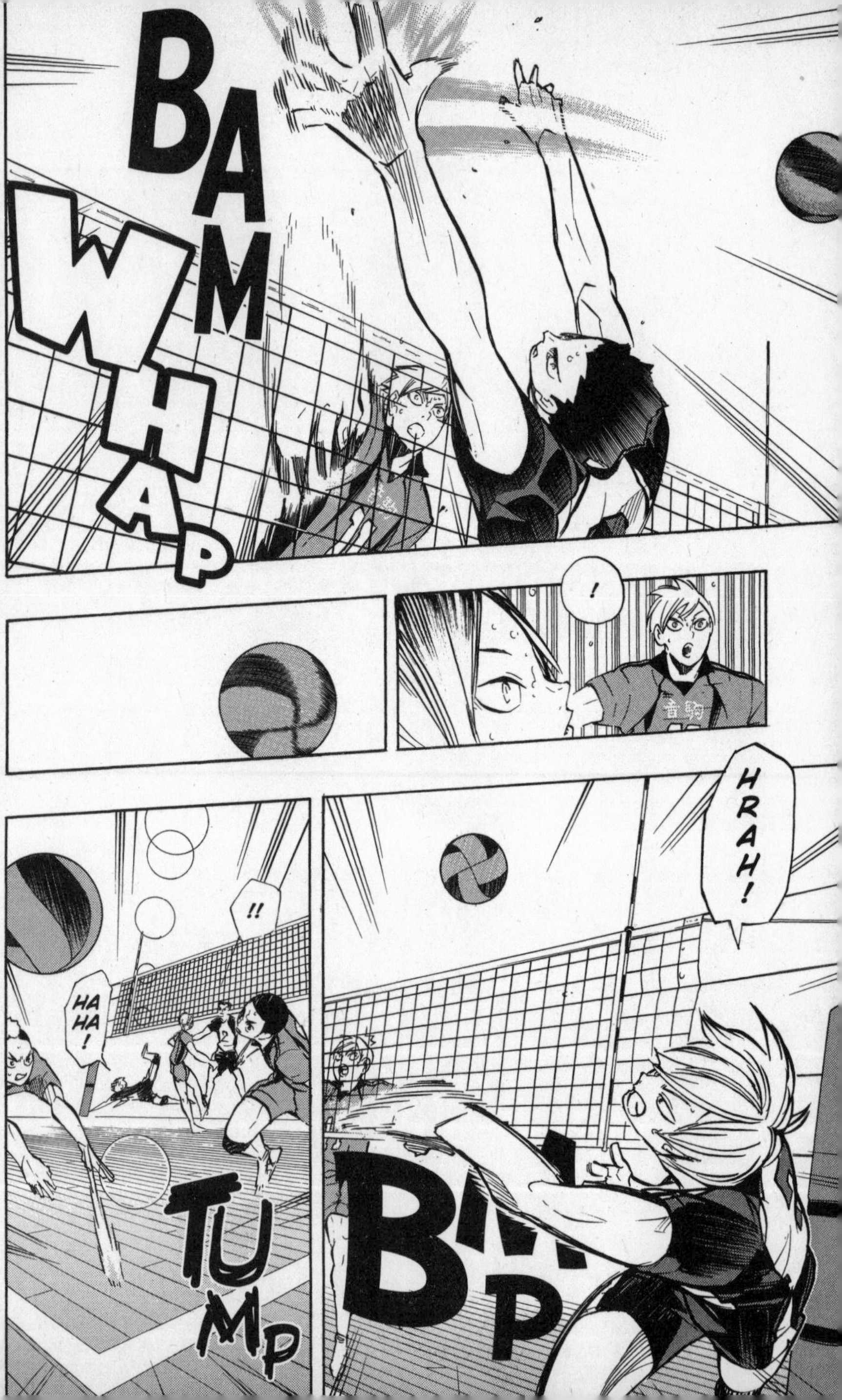
BAMM
WHHAP
!
HRAH!
!!
HA HA!
TUMP

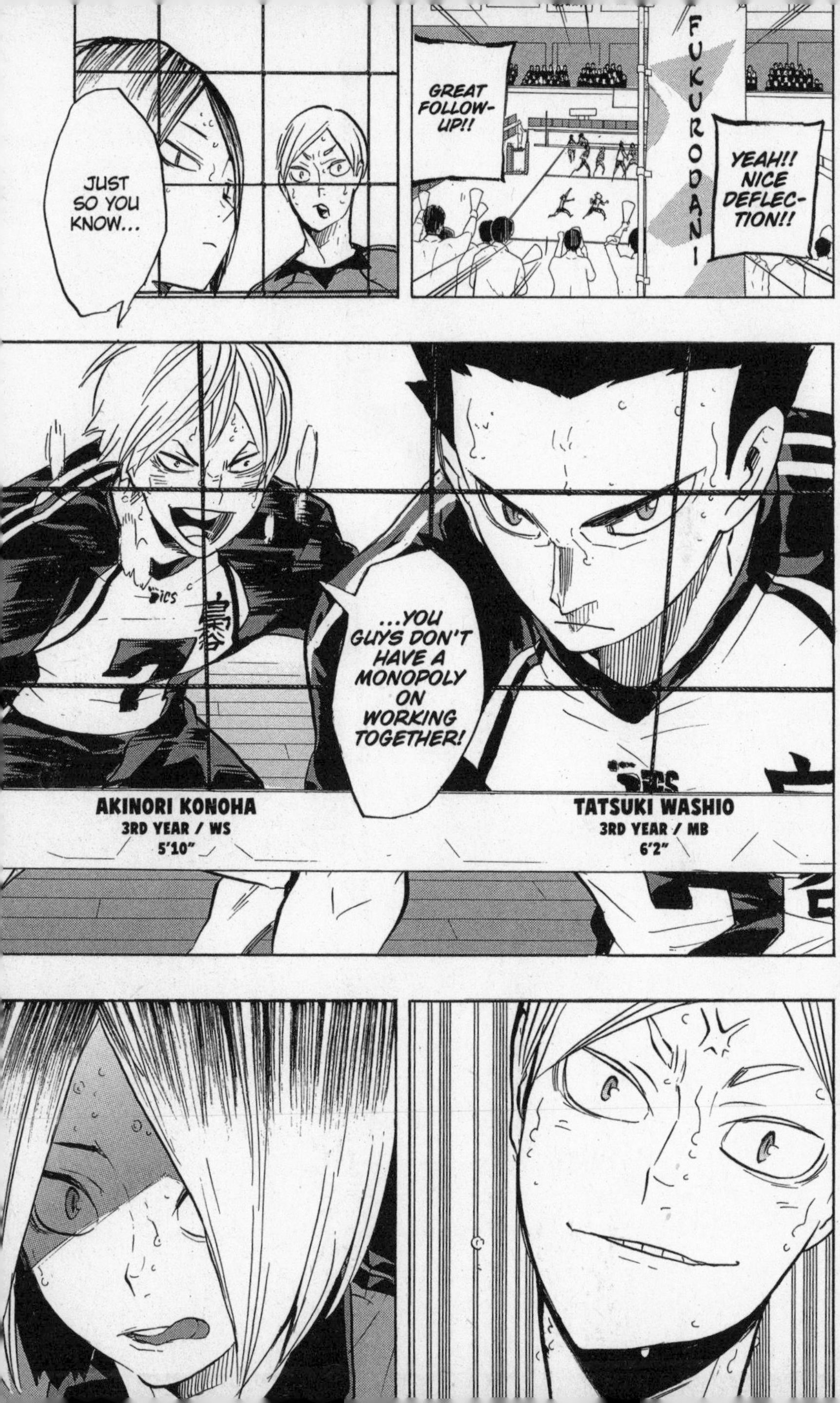
FUKURODANI
YEAH!! NICE DEFLECTION!!
GREAT FOLLOW-UP!!
JUST SO YOU KNOW...
...YOU GUYS DON'T HAVE A MONOPOLY ON WORKING TOGETHER!
TATSUKI WASHIO
3RD YEAR / MB
6'2"
AKINORI KONOHA
3RD YEAR / WS
5'10"

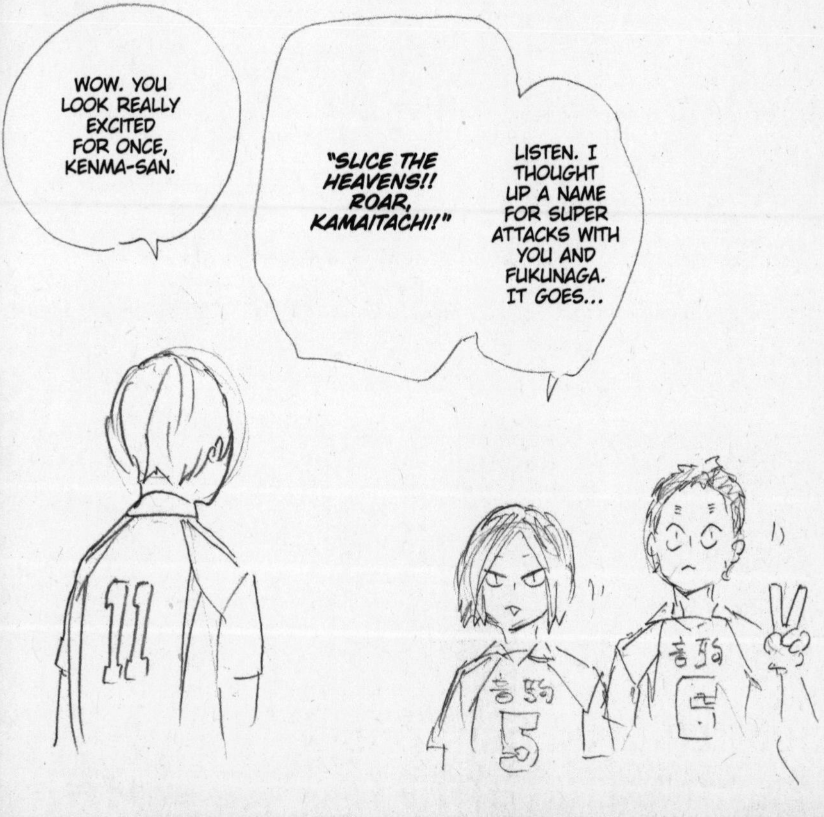
LISTEN. I THOUGHT UP A NAME FOR SUPER ATTACKS WITH YOU AND FUKUNAGA. IT GOES...
"SLICE THE HEAVENS!! ROAR, KAMAITACHI!"
WOW. YOU LOOK REALLY EXCITED FOR ONCE, KENMA-SAN.

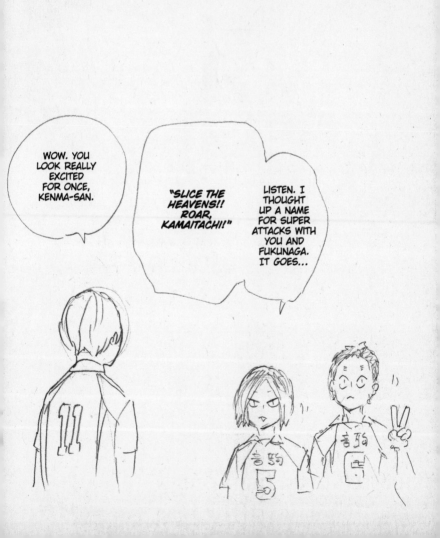

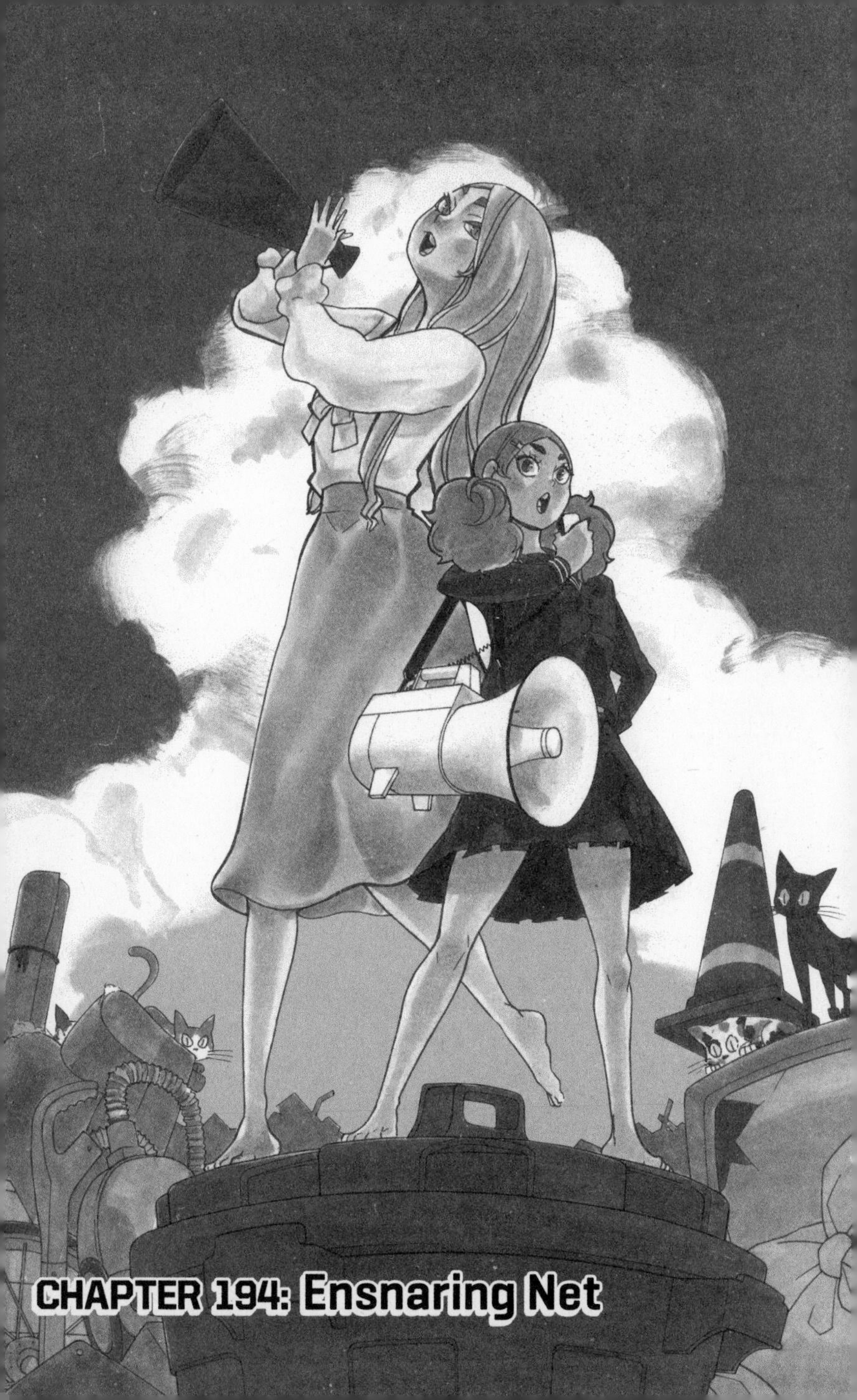
CHAPTER 194: Ensnaring Net

HAIKYU!!

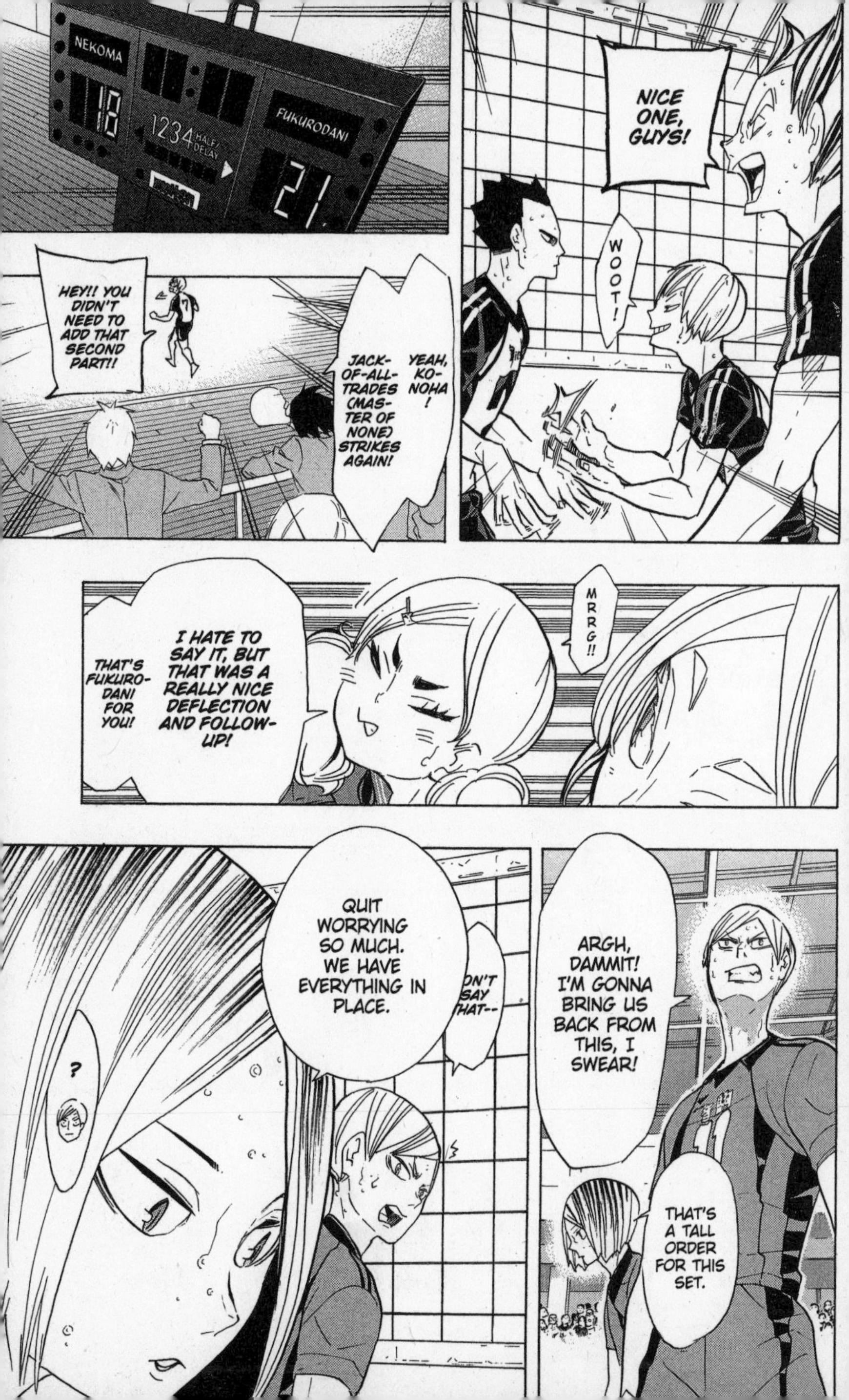
NICE ONE, GUYS!
WOOT!
NEKOMA
18
1234 HALF/DELAY
FUKURODANI
21
YEAH, KONOHA!
JACK-OF-ALL-TRADES (MASTER OF NONE) STRIKES AGAIN!
HEY!! YOU DIDN'T NEED TO ADD THAT SECOND PART!!
MRRG!!
I HATE TO SAY IT, BUT THAT WAS A REALLY NICE DEFLECTION AND FOLLOW-UP!
THAT'S FUKURODANI FOR YOU!
ARGH, DAMMIT! I'M GONNA BRING US BACK FROM THIS, I SWEAR!
THAT'S A TALL ORDER FOR THIS SET.
ON'T SAY THAT--
QUIT WORRYING SO MUCH. WE HAVE EVERYTHING IN PLACE.
?

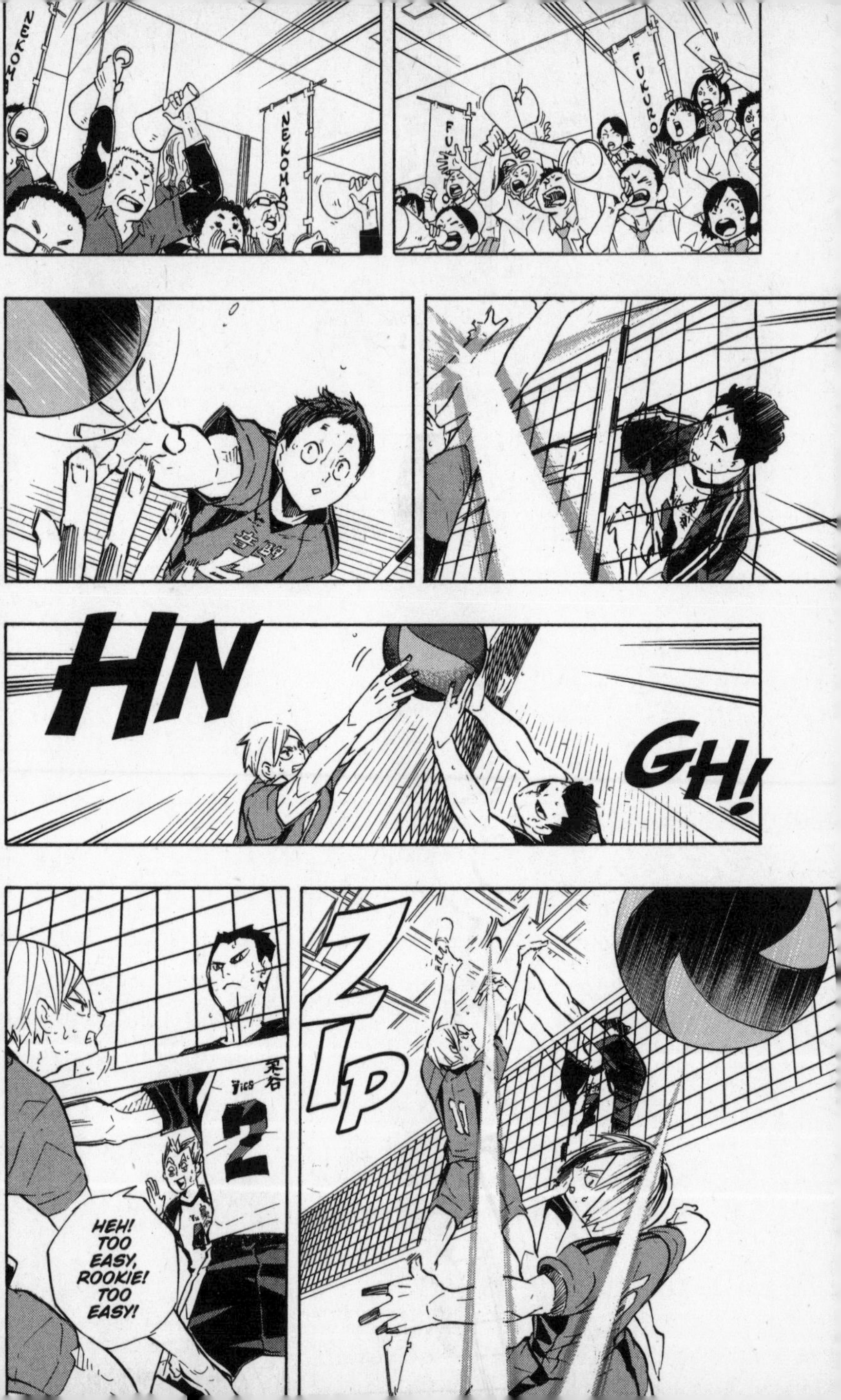
FUKURO
FU
NEKOMA
NEKOM
HN
GH!
ZIP
HEH! TOO EASY, ROOKIE! TOO EASY!

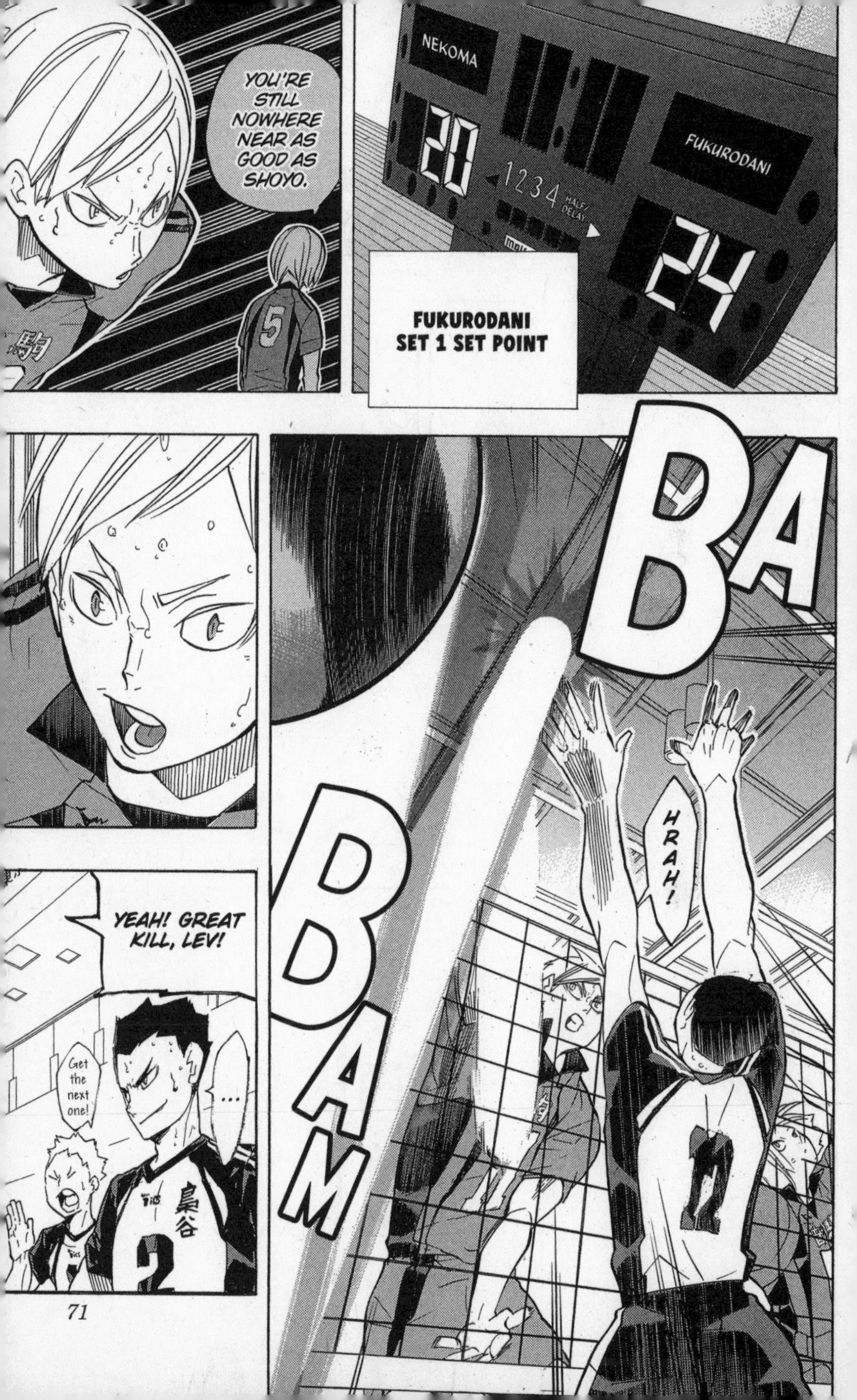
NEKOMA
20
FUKURODANI
24
FUKURODANI SET 1 SET POINT
YOU'RE STILL NOWHERE NEAR AS GOOD AS SHOYO.
BA
BAM
HRAH!
YEAH! GREAT KILL, LEV!
...
Get the next one!

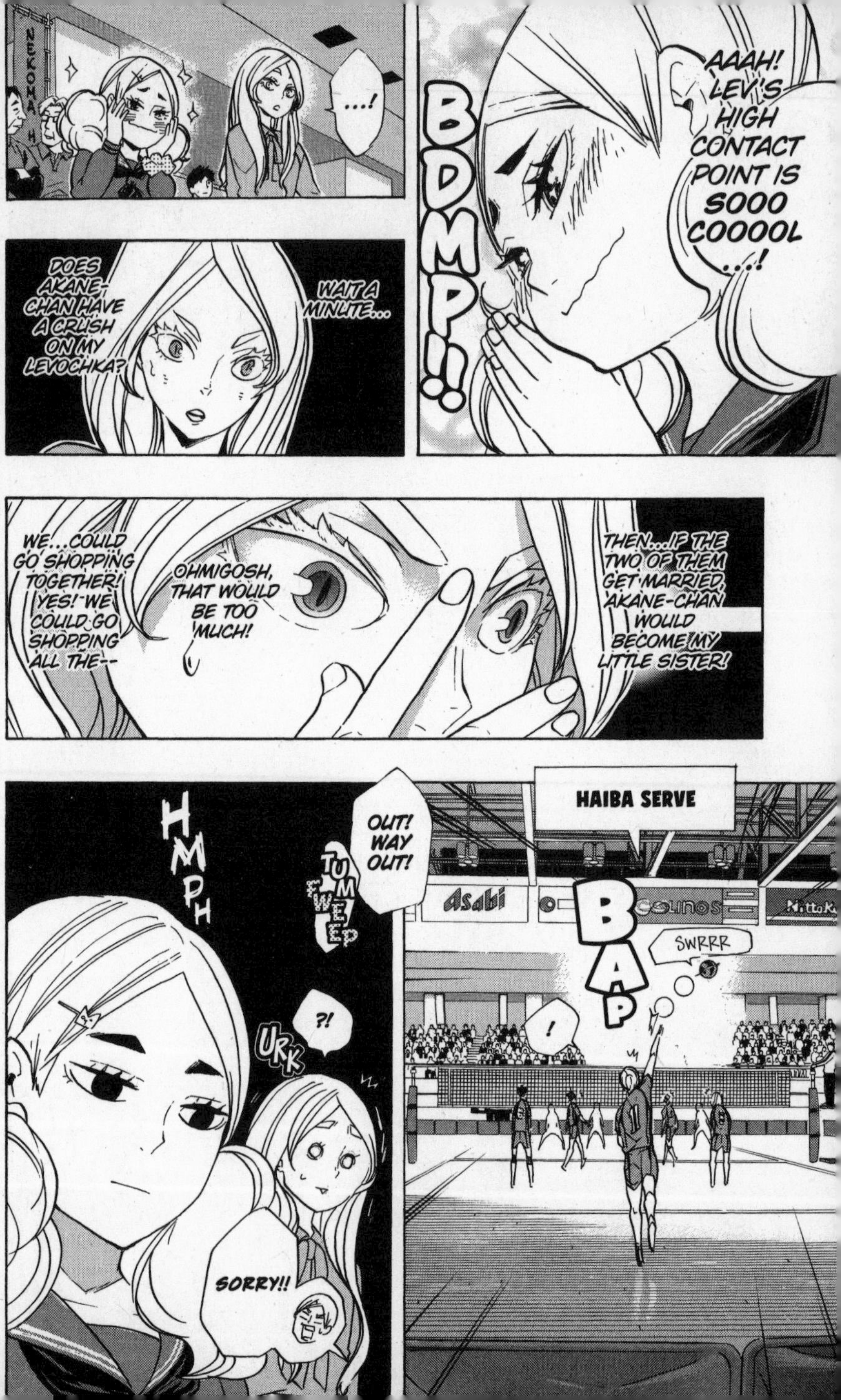

BDMP!!
AAAH! LEV'S HIGH CONTACT POINT IS SOOO COOOOL...!
....!
WAIT A MINUTE...
DOES AKANE-CHAN HAVE A CRUSH ON MY LEVOCHKA?
THEN...IF THE TWO OF THEM GET MARRIED, AKANE-CHAN WOULD BECOME MY LITTLE SISTER!
OHMIGOSH, THAT WOULD BE TOO MUCH!
WE...COULD GO SHOPPING TOGETHER! YES! WE COULD GO SHOPPING ALL THE--
HAIBA SERVE
BAP
SWRRR
!
OUT! WAY OUT!
TWEEP
HMPH
?!
URK
SORRY!!

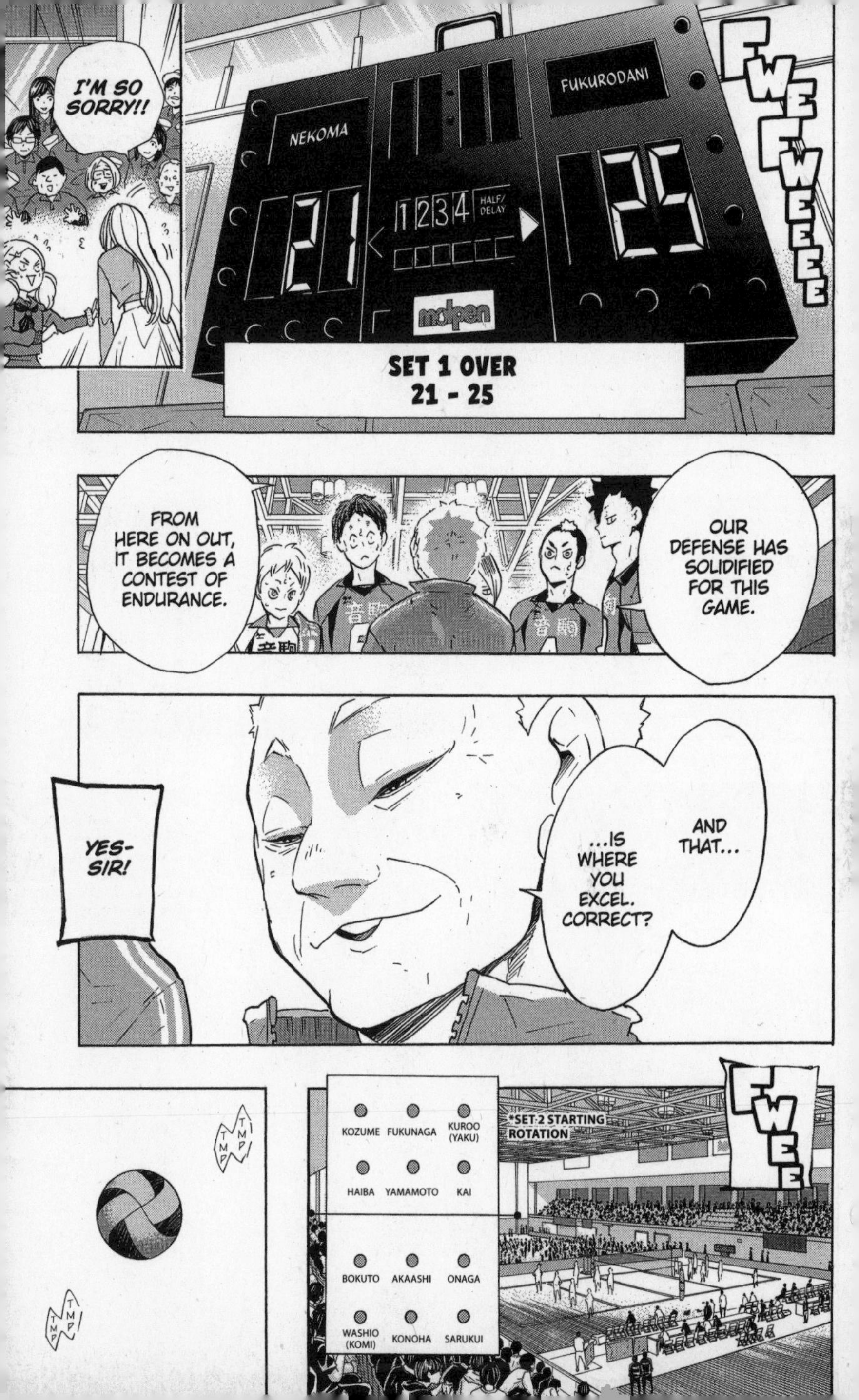
FWEEWEEE
FUKURODANI
NEKOMA
21
1234
HALF/ DELAY
25
SET 1 OVER
21 - 25
I'M SO SORRY!!
OUR DEFENSE HAS SOLIDIFIED FOR THIS GAME.
FROM HERE ON OUT, IT BECOMES A CONTEST OF ENDURANCE.
AND THAT...
...IS WHERE YOU EXCEL. CORRECT?
YES-SIR!
FWEE
*SET 2 STARTING ROTATION
KOZUME FUKUNAGA KUROO (YAKU)
HAIBA YAMAMOTO KAI
BOKUTO AKAASHI ONAGA
WASHIO (KOMI) KONOHA SARUKUI
TMP TMP
TMP TMP

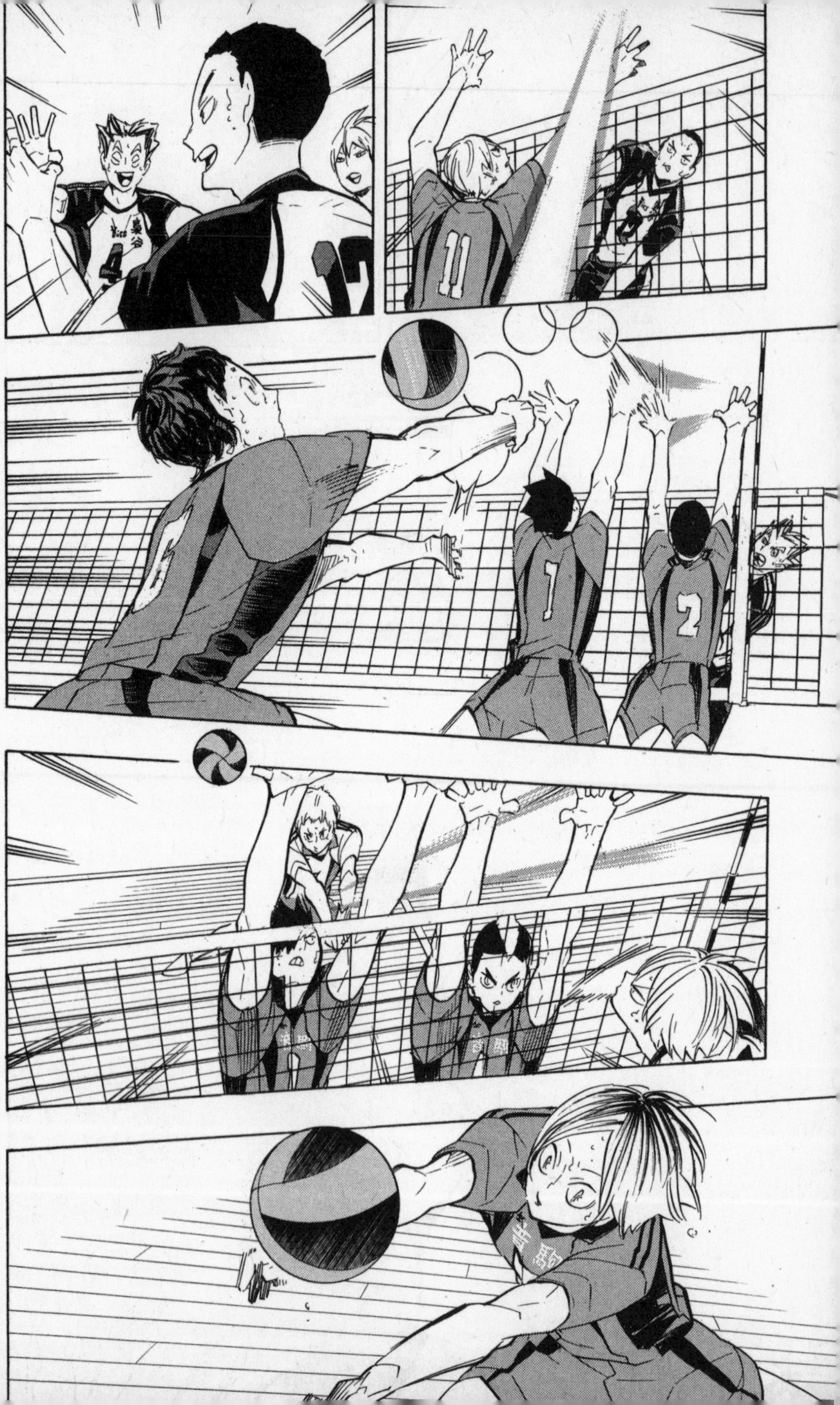

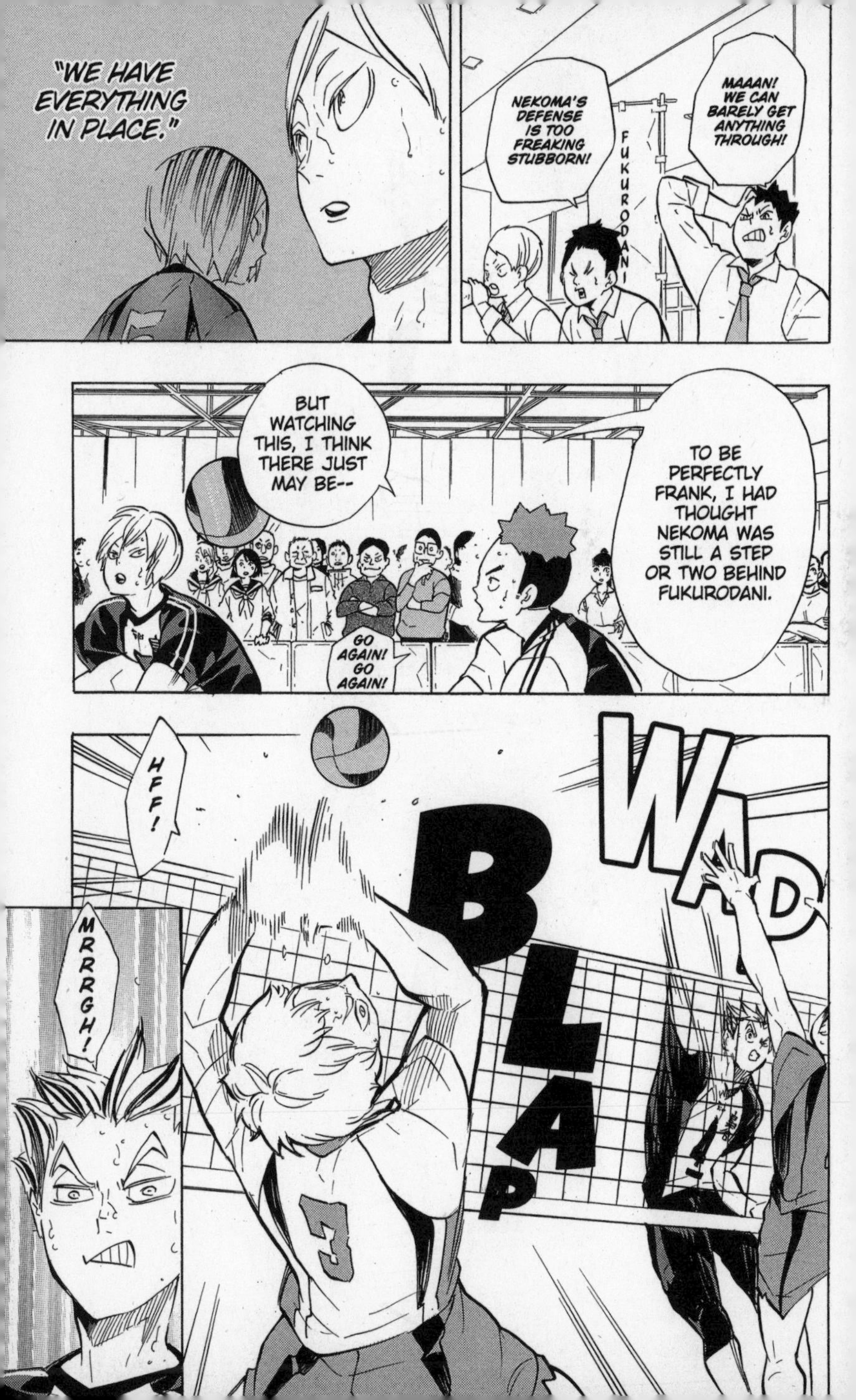

MAAAN! WE CAN BARELY GET ANYTHING THROUGH!
NEKOMA'S DEFENSE IS TOO FREAKING STUBBORN!
FUKURODANI
"WE HAVE EVERYTHING IN PLACE."
TO BE PERFECTLY FRANK, I HAD THOUGHT NEKOMA WAS STILL A STEP OR TWO BEHIND FUKURODANI.
BUT WATCHING THIS, I THINK THERE JUST MAY BE--
GO AGAIN! GO AGAIN!
WAD
HFF!
BLAP
MRRRGH!

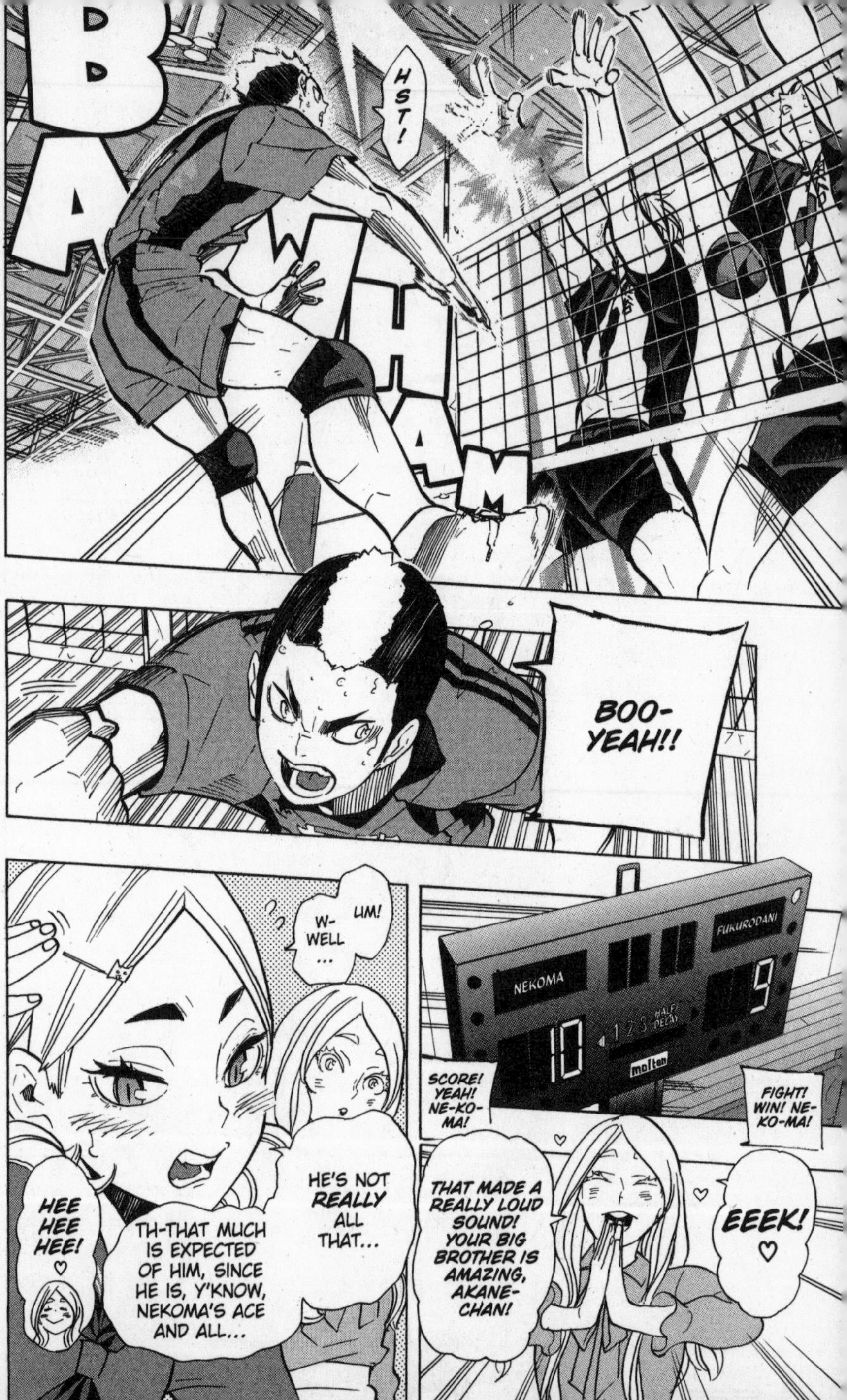
HST!
BAWHAM
BOO-YEAH!!
FIGHT! WIN! NE-KO-MA!
FUKURODANI
NEKOMA
9
10
HALF DELAY
molten
SCORE! YEAH! NE-KO-MA!
EEEK!
THAT MADE A REALLY LOUD SOUND! YOUR BIG BROTHER IS AMAZING, AKANE-CHAN!
UM!
W-WELL...
HE'S NOT REALLY ALL THAT...
TH-THAT MUCH IS EXPECTED OF HIM, SINCE HE IS, Y'KNOW, NEKOMA'S ACE AND ALL...
HEE HEE HEE!

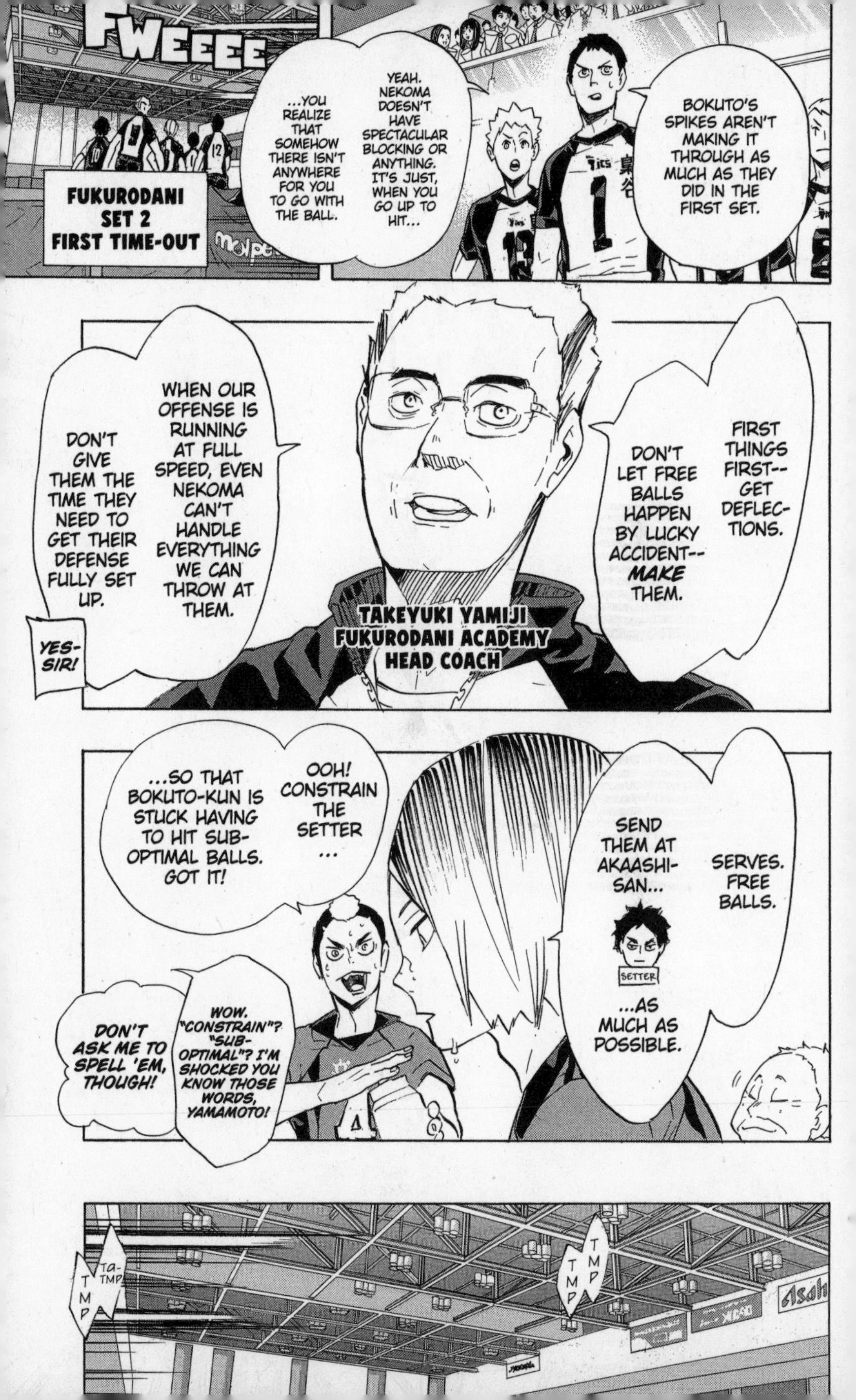

BOKUTO'S SPIKES AREN'T MAKING IT THROUGH AS MUCH AS THEY DID IN THE FIRST SET.
YEAH. NEKOMA DOESN'T HAVE SPECTACULAR BLOCKING OR ANYTHING. IT'S JUST, WHEN YOU GO UP TO HIT...
...YOU REALIZE THAT SOMEHOW THERE ISN'T ANYWHERE FOR YOU TO GO WITH THE BALL.
FWEEEE
FUKURODANI SET 2 FIRST TIME-OUT
FIRST THINGS FIRST--GET DEFLEC-TIONS.
DON'T LET FREE BALLS HAPPEN BY LUCKY ACCIDENT--MAKE THEM.
TAKEYUKI YAMIJI FUKURODANI ACADEMY HEAD COACH
WHEN OUR OFFENSE IS RUNNING AT FULL SPEED, EVEN NEKOMA CAN'T HANDLE EVERYTHING WE CAN THROW AT THEM.
DON'T GIVE THEM THE TIME THEY NEED TO GET THEIR DEFENSE FULLY SET UP.
YES-SIR!
SERVES. FREE BALLS.
SEND THEM AT AKAASHI-SAN...
SETTER
...AS MUCH AS POSSIBLE.
OOH! CONSTRAIN THE SETTER ...
...SO THAT BOKUTO-KUN IS STUCK HAVING TO HIT SUB-OPTIMAL BALLS. GOT IT!
WOW. "CONSTRAIN"? "SUB-OPTIMAL"? I'M SHOCKED YOU KNOW THOSE WORDS, YAMAMOTO!
DON'T ASK ME TO SPELL 'EM, THOUGH!
TMP TMP
TMP
TA-TMP
TMP

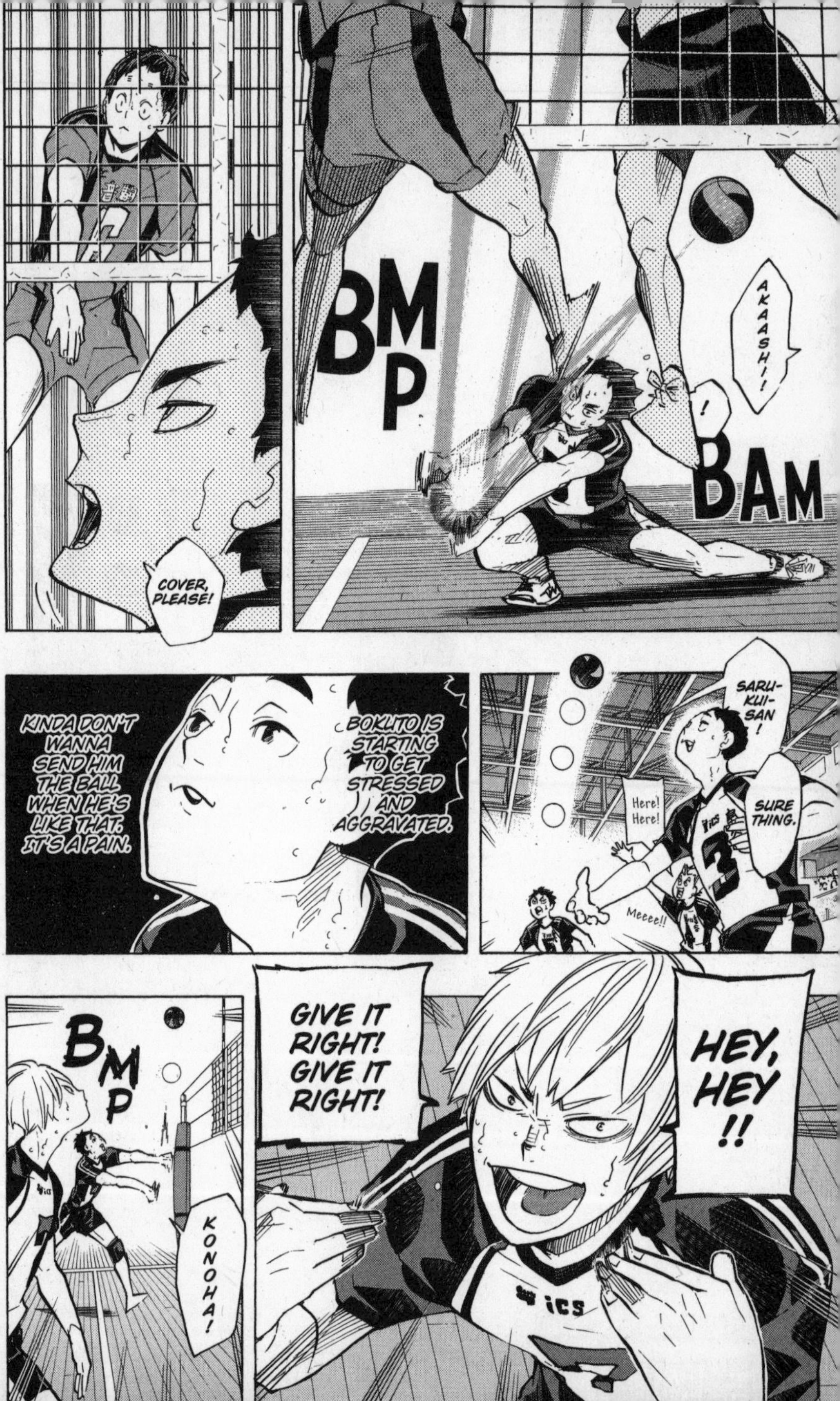
AKAASHI!!
BMP
!
BAM
COVER, PLEASE!
SARUKUI-SAN!
SURE THING.
Here! Here!
Meeee!!
BOKUTO IS STARTING TO GET STRESSED AND AGGRAVATED.
KINDA DON'T WANNA SEND HIM THE BALL WHEN HE'S LIKE THAT. IT'S A PAIN.
HEY, HEY!!
GIVE IT RIGHT! GIVE IT RIGHT!
BMP
KONOHA!

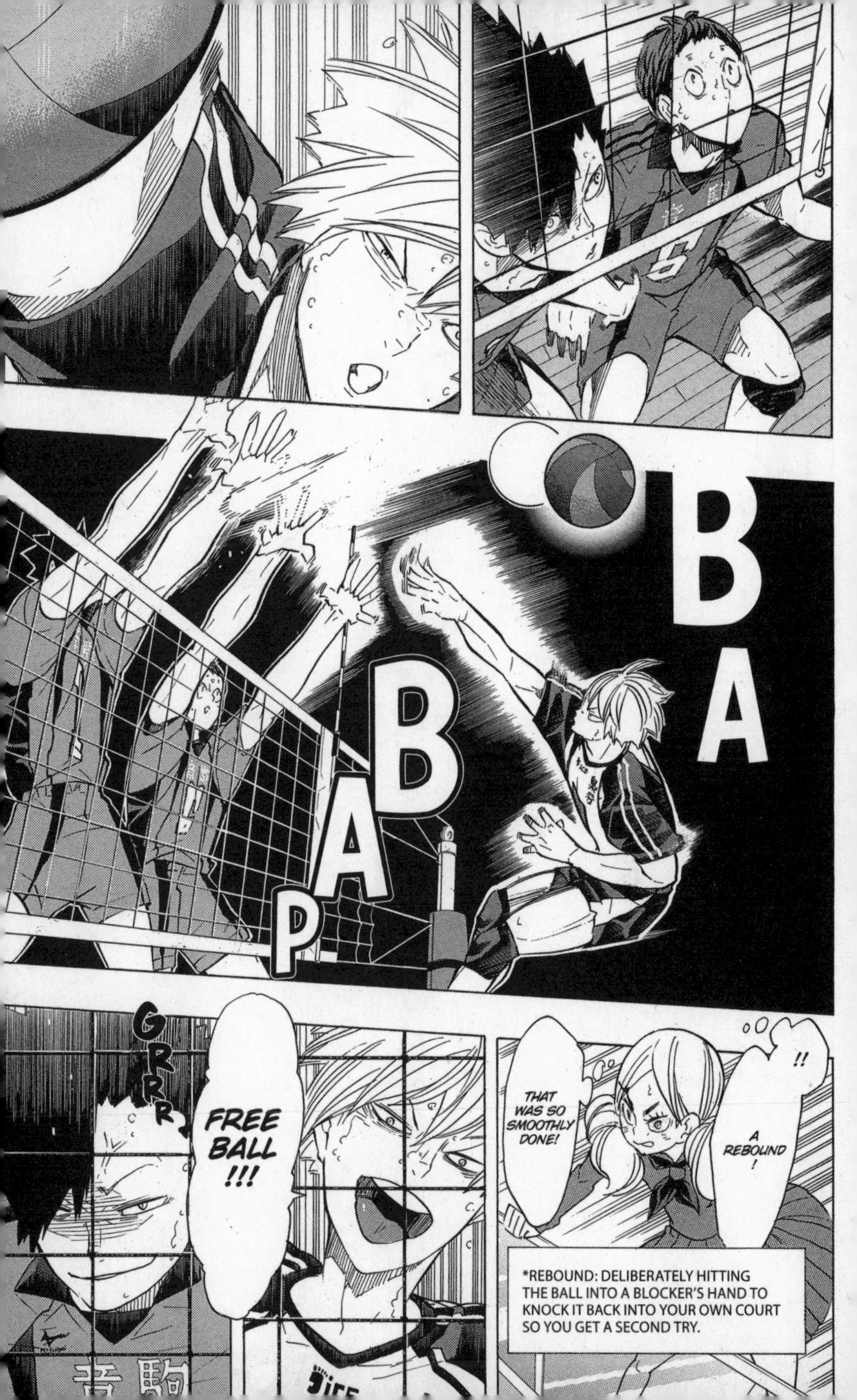
BA
PAB
!!
A REBOUND!
THAT WAS SO SMOOTHLY DONE!
*REBOUND: DELIBERATELY HITTING THE BALL INTO A BLOCKER'S HAND TO KNOCK IT BACK INTO YOUR OWN COURT SO YOU GET A SECOND TRY.
FREE BALL!!!
GRRR

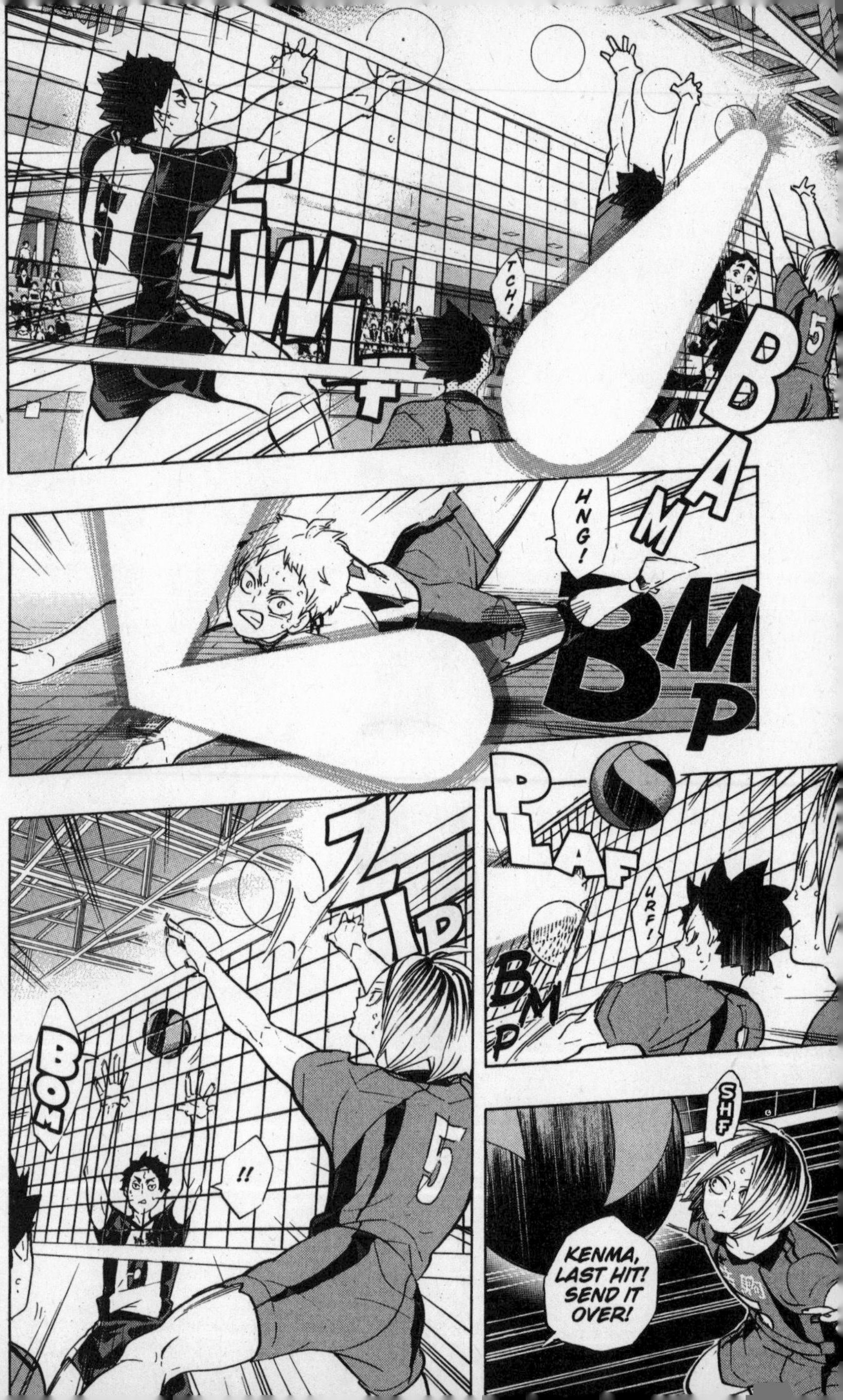
BAM
TCH!
HNG!
BMP
PLAF
URF!
BMP
SHF
KENMA, LAST HIT! SEND IT OVER!
ZID
BOM
!!

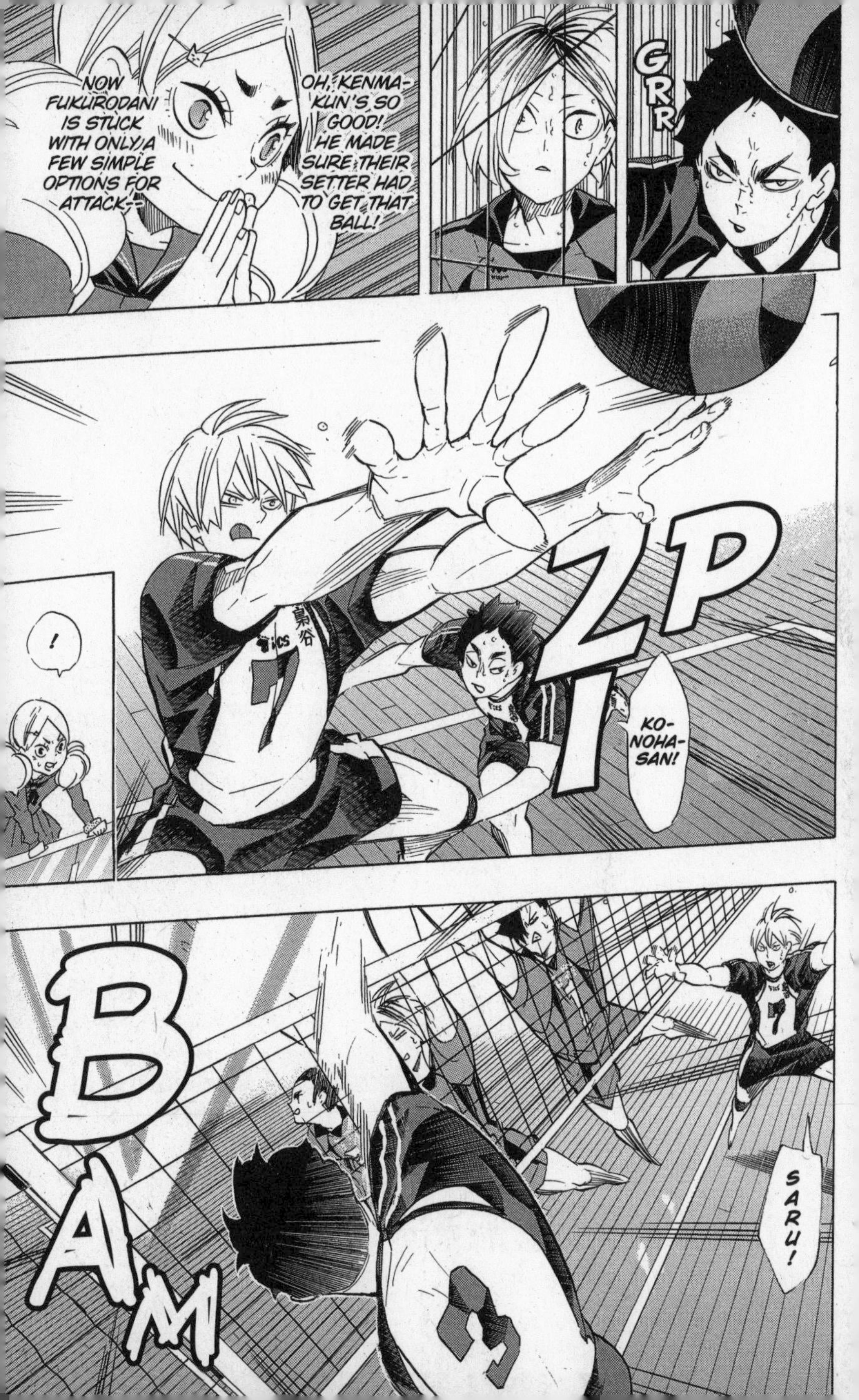
GRR
OH, KENMA-KUN'S SO GOOD! HE MADE SURE THEIR SETTER HAD TO GET THAT BALL!
NOW FUKURODANI IS STUCK WITH ONLY A FEW SIMPLE OPTIONS FOR ATTACK--
ZP
KO-NOHA-SAN!
!
SARU!
BAM

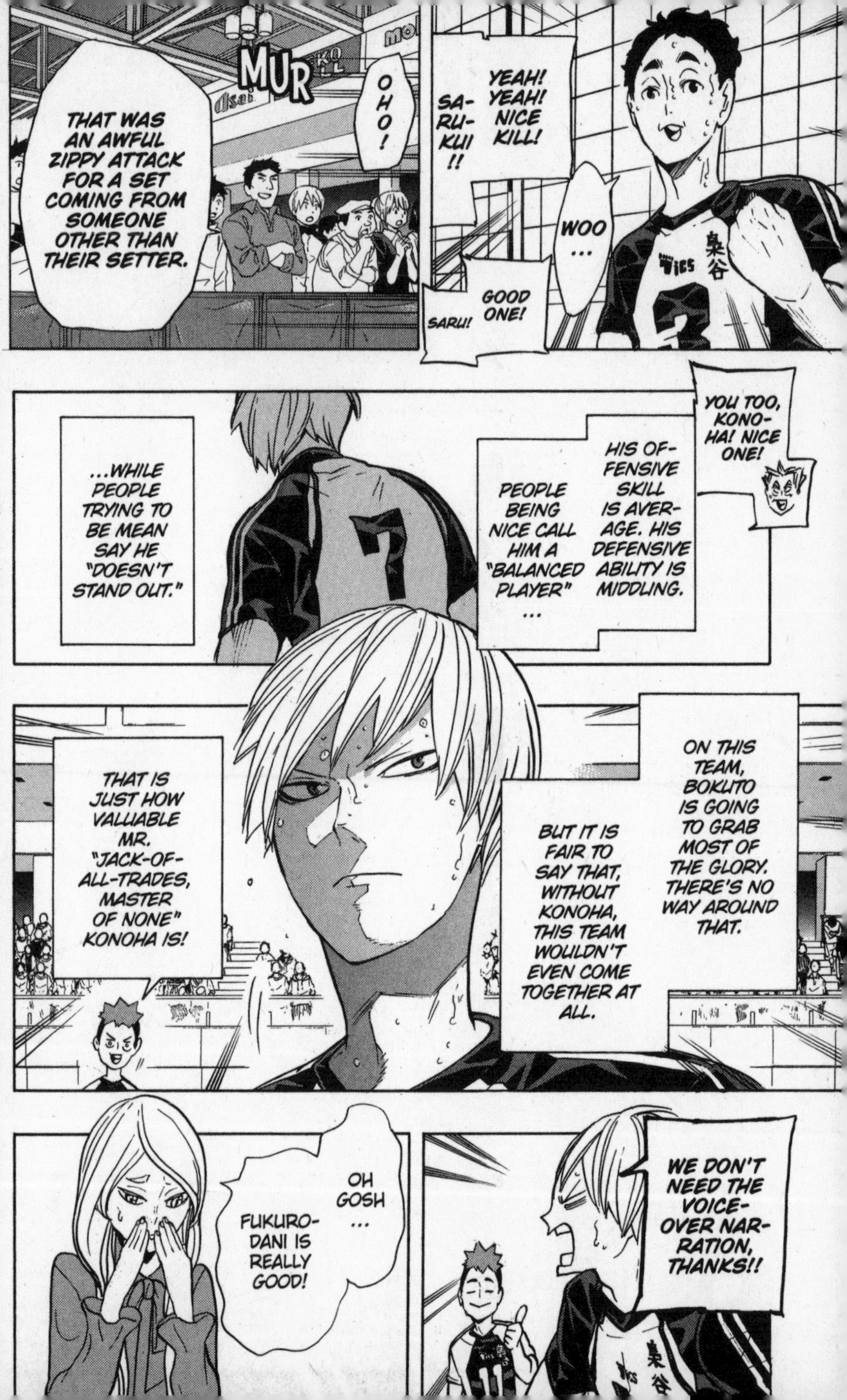
YEAH! YEAH! NICE KILL!
SA-RU-KUI!!
WOO...
GOOD ONE!
SARU!
MUR
OHO!
THAT WAS AN AWFUL ZIPPY ATTACK FOR A SET COMING FROM SOMEONE OTHER THAN THEIR SETTER.
YOU TOO, KONO-HA! NICE ONE!
HIS OF-FENSIVE SKILL IS AVER-AGE. HIS DEFENSIVE ABILITY IS MIDDLING.
PEOPLE BEING NICE CALL HIM A "BALANCED PLAYER"...
...WHILE PEOPLE TRYING TO BE MEAN SAY HE "DOESN'T STAND OUT."
ON THIS TEAM, BOKUTO IS GOING TO GRAB MOST OF THE GLORY. THERE'S NO WAY AROUND THAT.
BUT IT IS FAIR TO SAY THAT, WITHOUT KONOHA, THIS TEAM WOULDN'T EVEN COME TOGETHER AT ALL.
THAT IS JUST HOW VALUABLE MR. "JACK-OF-ALL-TRADES, MASTER OF NONE" KONOHA IS!
WE DON'T NEED THE VOICE-OVER NAR-RATION, THANKS!!
OH GOSH...
FUKURO-DANI IS REALLY GOOD!

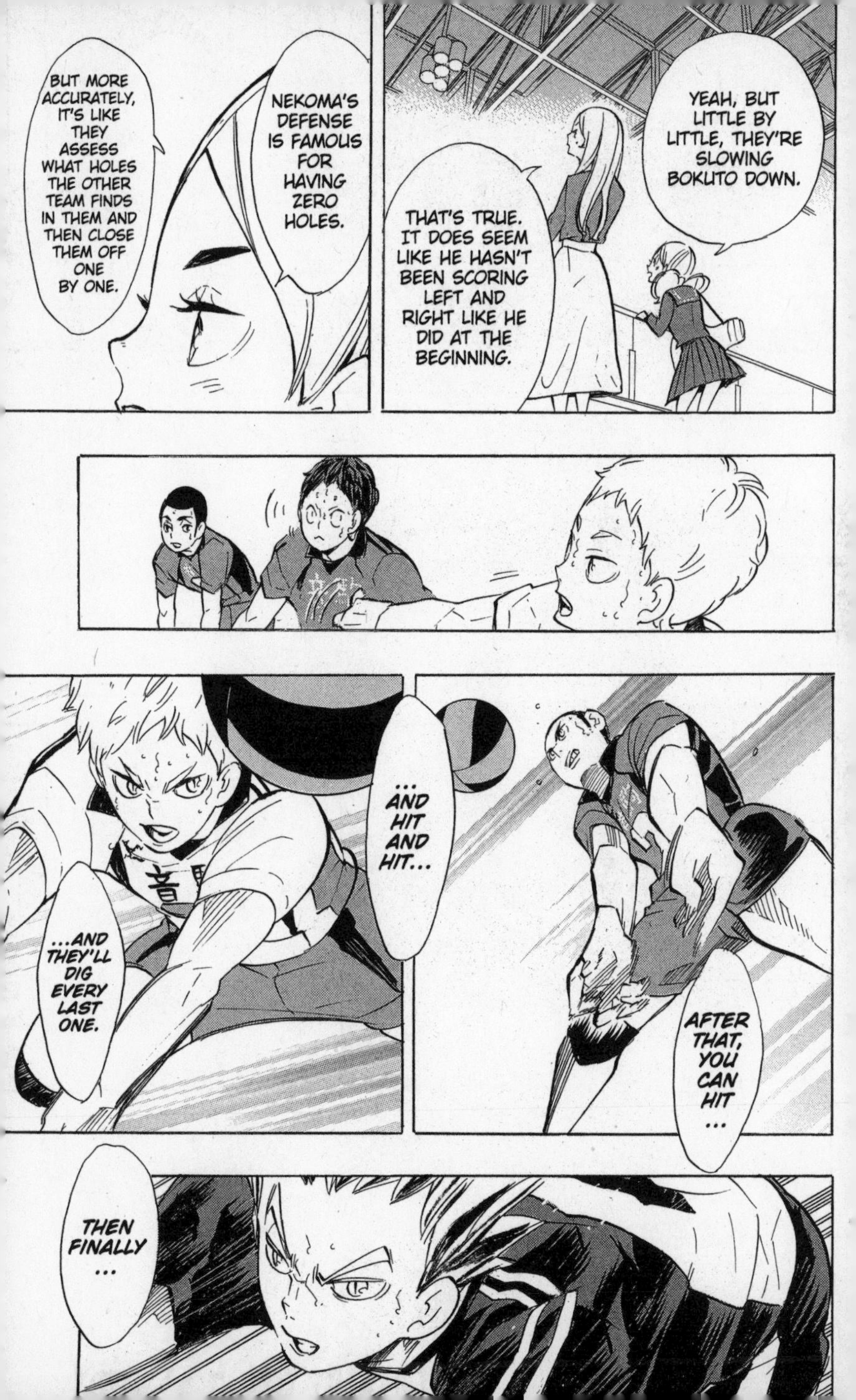
YEAH, BUT LITTLE BY LITTLE, THEY'RE SLOWING BOKUTO DOWN.
THAT'S TRUE. IT DOES SEEM LIKE HE HASN'T BEEN SCORING LEFT AND RIGHT LIKE HE DID AT THE BEGINNING.
NEKOMA'S DEFENSE IS FAMOUS FOR HAVING ZERO HOLES.
BUT MORE ACCURATELY, IT'S LIKE THEY ASSESS WHAT HOLES THE OTHER TEAM FINDS IN THEM AND THEN CLOSE THEM OFF ONE BY ONE.
AFTER THAT, YOU CAN HIT...
...AND HIT AND HIT...
...AND THEY'LL DIG EVERY LAST ONE.
THEN FINALLY...

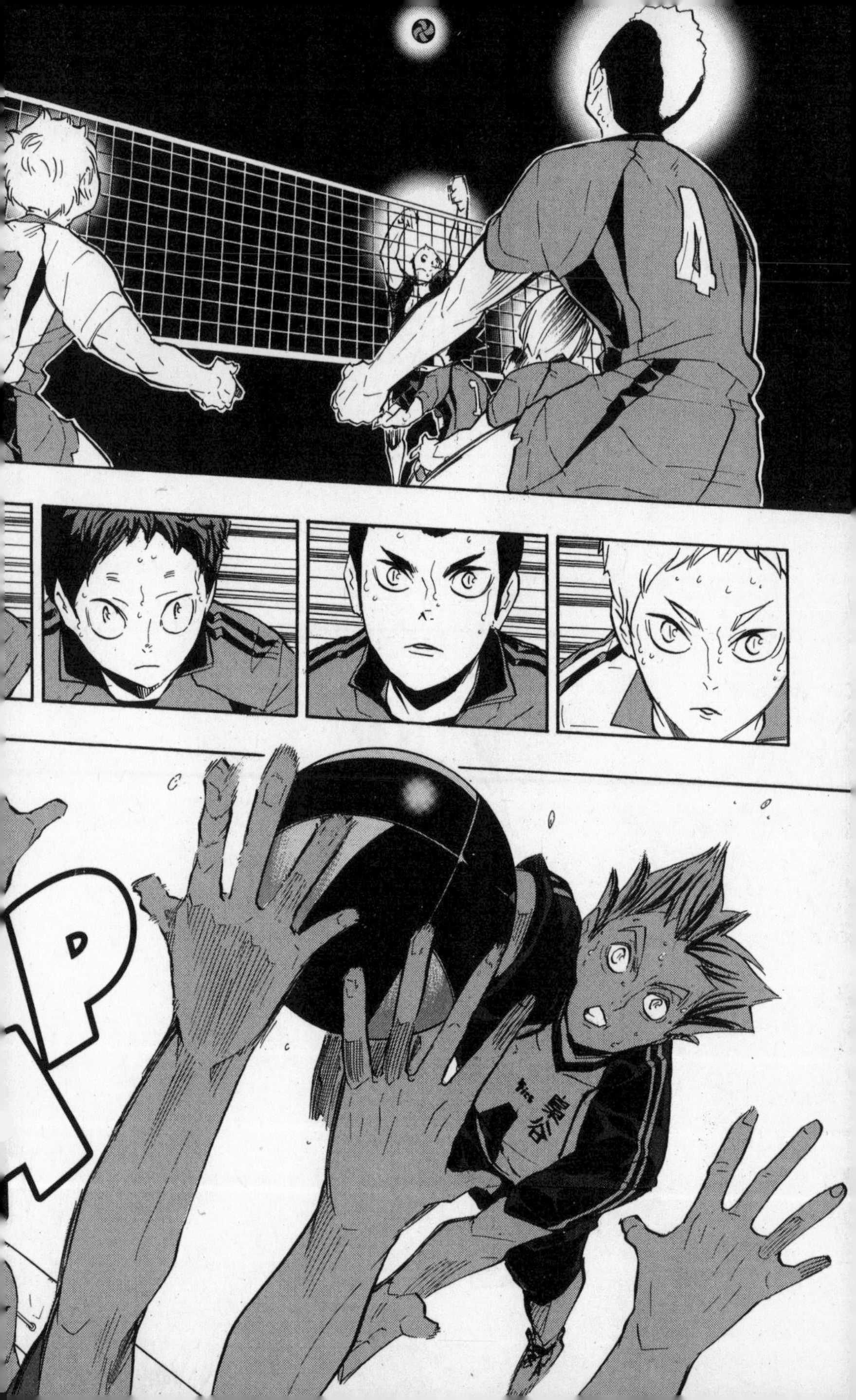

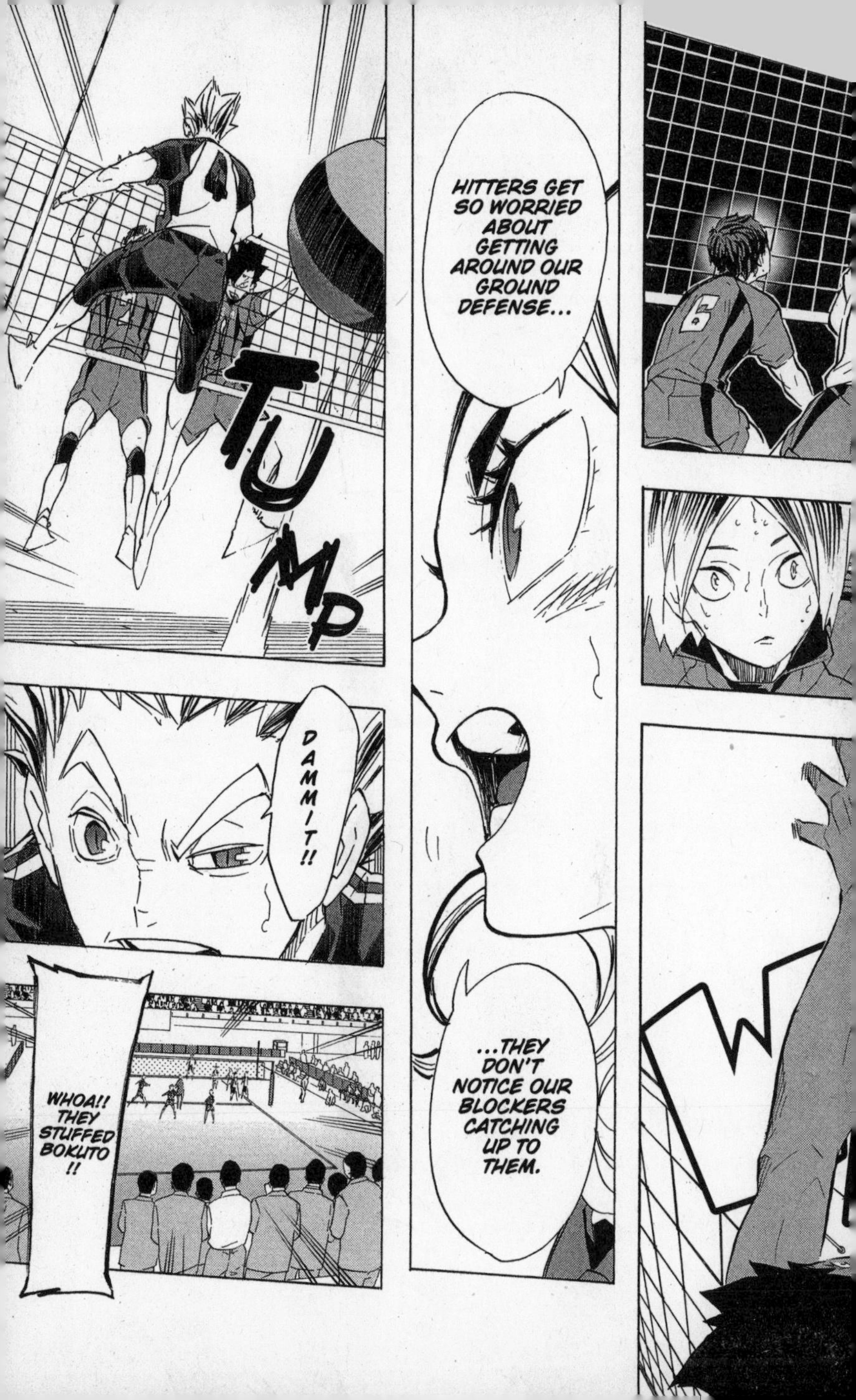
HITTERS GET SO WORRIED ABOUT GETTING AROUND OUR GROUND DEFENSE...
...THEY DON'T NOTICE OUR BLOCKERS CATCHING UP TO THEM.
TUMP
DAMMIT!!
WHOA!! THEY STUFFED BOKUTO!!

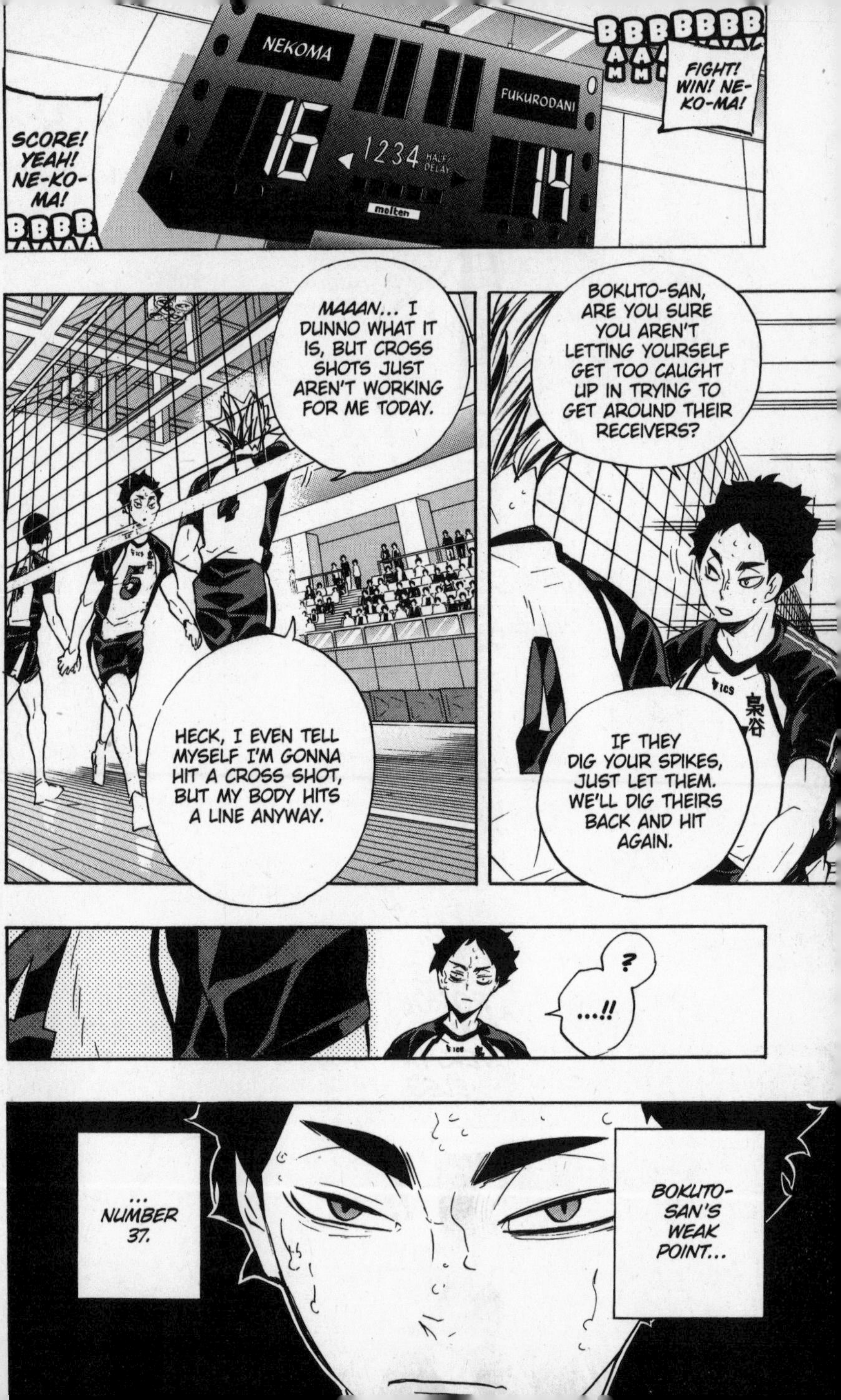
BBBBBBB
AAA
MMM
FIGHT! WIN! NE-KO-MA!
NEKOMA
FUKURODANI
16
1234
14
molten
SCORE! YEAH! NE-KO-MA!
BBBB
AAAA
BOKUTO-SAN, ARE YOU SURE YOU AREN'T LETTING YOURSELF GET TOO CAUGHT UP IN TRYING TO GET AROUND THEIR RECEIVERS?
IF THEY DIG YOUR SPIKES, JUST LET THEM. WE'LL DIG THEIRS BACK AND HIT AGAIN.
MAAAN... I DUNNO WHAT IT IS, BUT CROSS SHOTS JUST AREN'T WORKING FOR ME TODAY.
HECK, I EVEN TELL MYSELF I'M GONNA HIT A CROSS SHOT, BUT MY BODY HITS A LINE ANYWAY.
?
...!!
BOKUTO-SAN'S WEAK POINT...
...NUMBER 37.

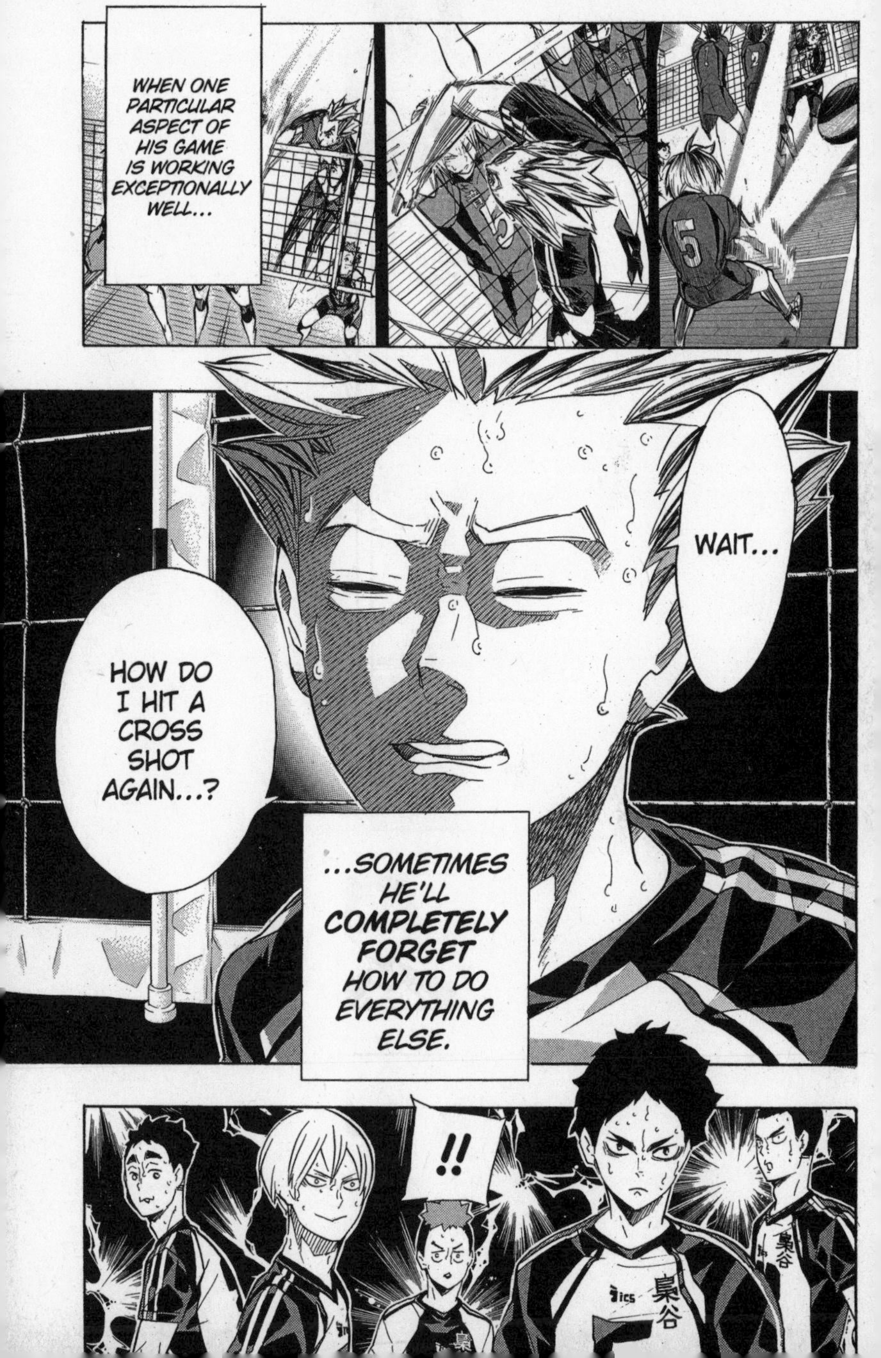
WHEN ONE PARTICULAR ASPECT OF HIS GAME IS WORKING EXCEPTIONALLY WELL...
WAIT...
HOW DO I HIT A CROSS SHOT AGAIN...?
...SOMETIMES HE'LL COMPLETELY FORGET HOW TO DO EVERYTHING ELSE.
!!

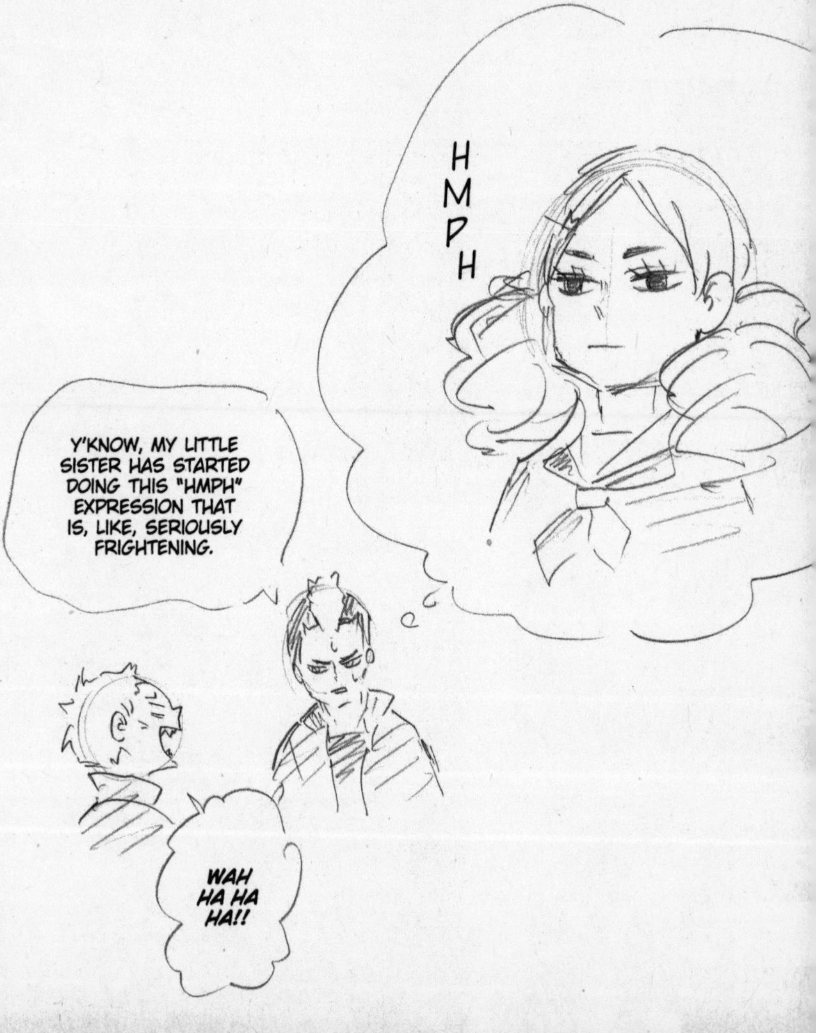
HMPH
Y'KNOW, MY LITTLE SISTER HAS STARTED DOING THIS "HMPH" EXPRESSION THAT IS, LIKE, SERIOUSLY FRIGHTENING.
WAH HA HA HA!!

CHAPTER 195: Land vs. Air

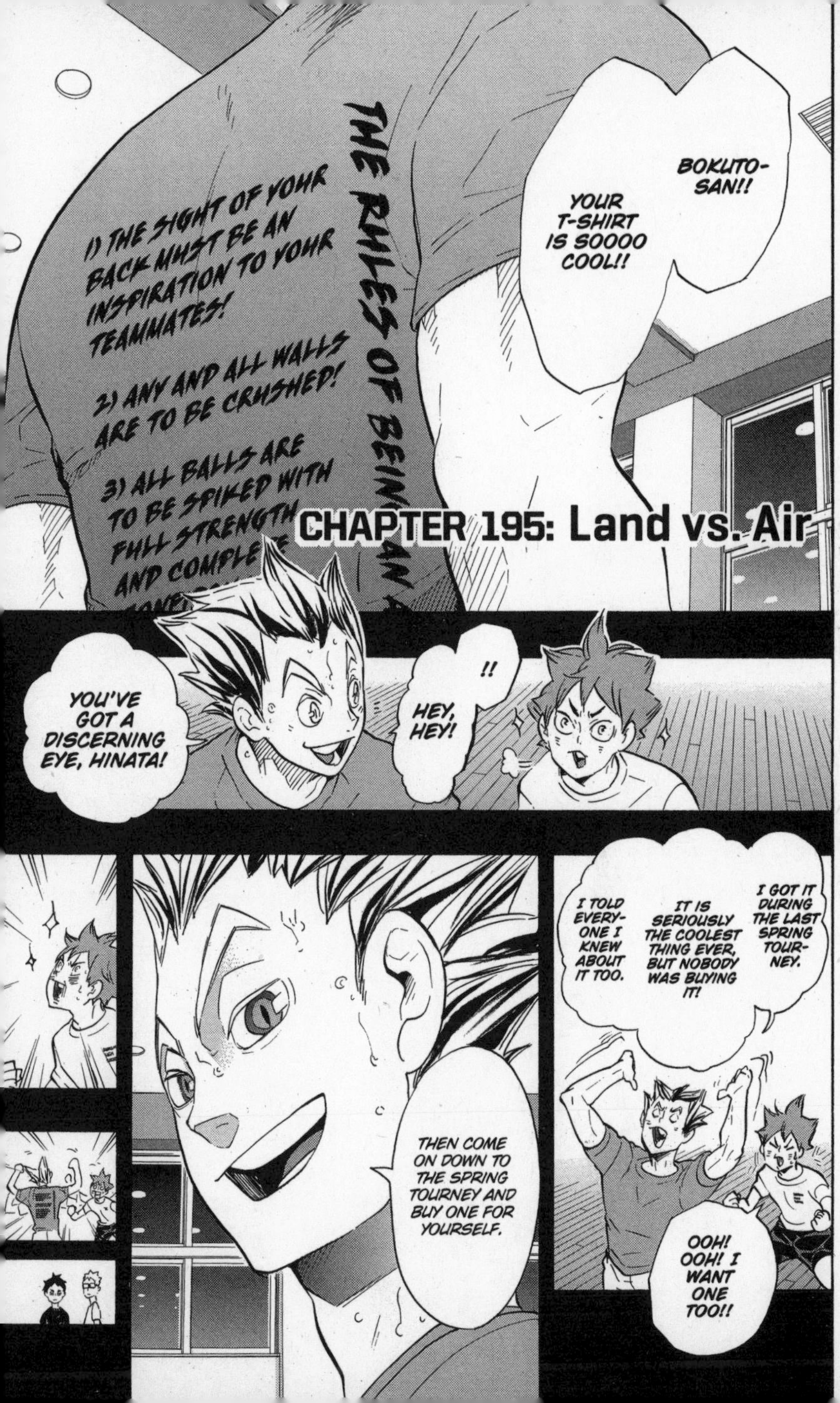
BOKUTO-SAN!!
YOUR T-SHIRT IS SOOOO COOL!!
THE RULES OF BEING AN A
1) THE SIGHT OF YOUR BACK MUST BE AN INSPIRATION TO YOUR TEAMMATES!
2) ANY AND ALL WALLS ARE TO BE CRUSHED!
3) ALL BALLS ARE TO BE SPIKED WITH FULL STRENGTH AND COMPLE
!!
HEY, HEY!
YOU'VE GOT A DISCERNING EYE, HINATA!
I GOT IT DURING THE LAST SPRING TOURNEY.
IT IS SERIOUSLY THE COOLEST THING EVER, BUT NOBODY WAS BUYING IT!
I TOLD EVERYONE I KNEW ABOUT IT TOO.
OOH! OOH! I WANT ONE TOO!!
THEN COME ON DOWN TO THE SPRING TOURNEY AND BUY ONE FOR YOURSELF.

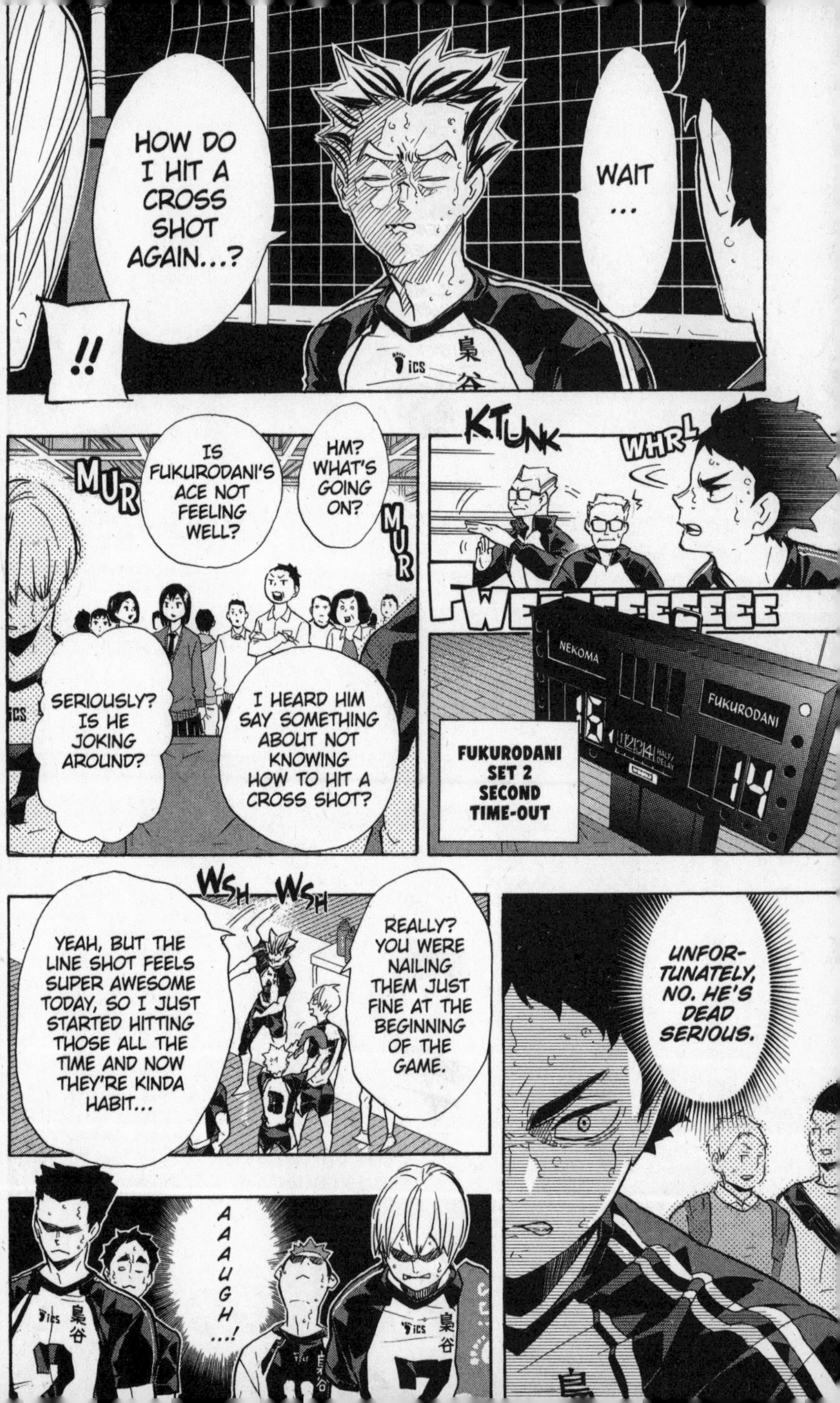
WAIT ...
HOW DO I HIT A CROSS SHOT AGAIN...?
!!
KTUNK
WHRL
FWEEEEEEEE
NEKOMA
16
FUKURODANI
14
FUKURODANI SET 2 SECOND TIME-OUT
HM? WHAT'S GOING ON?
MUR
IS FUKURODANI'S ACE NOT FEELING WELL?
MUR
I HEARD HIM SAY SOMETHING ABOUT NOT KNOWING HOW TO HIT A CROSS SHOT?
SERIOUSLY? IS HE JOKING AROUND?
UNFORTUNATELY, NO. HE'S DEAD SERIOUS.
WSH WSH
REALLY? YOU WERE NAILING THEM JUST FINE AT THE BEGINNING OF THE GAME.
YEAH, BUT THE LINE SHOT FEELS SUPER AWESOME TODAY, SO I JUST STARTED HITTING THOSE ALL THE TIME AND NOW THEY'RE KINDA HABIT...
AAAAUGH...!

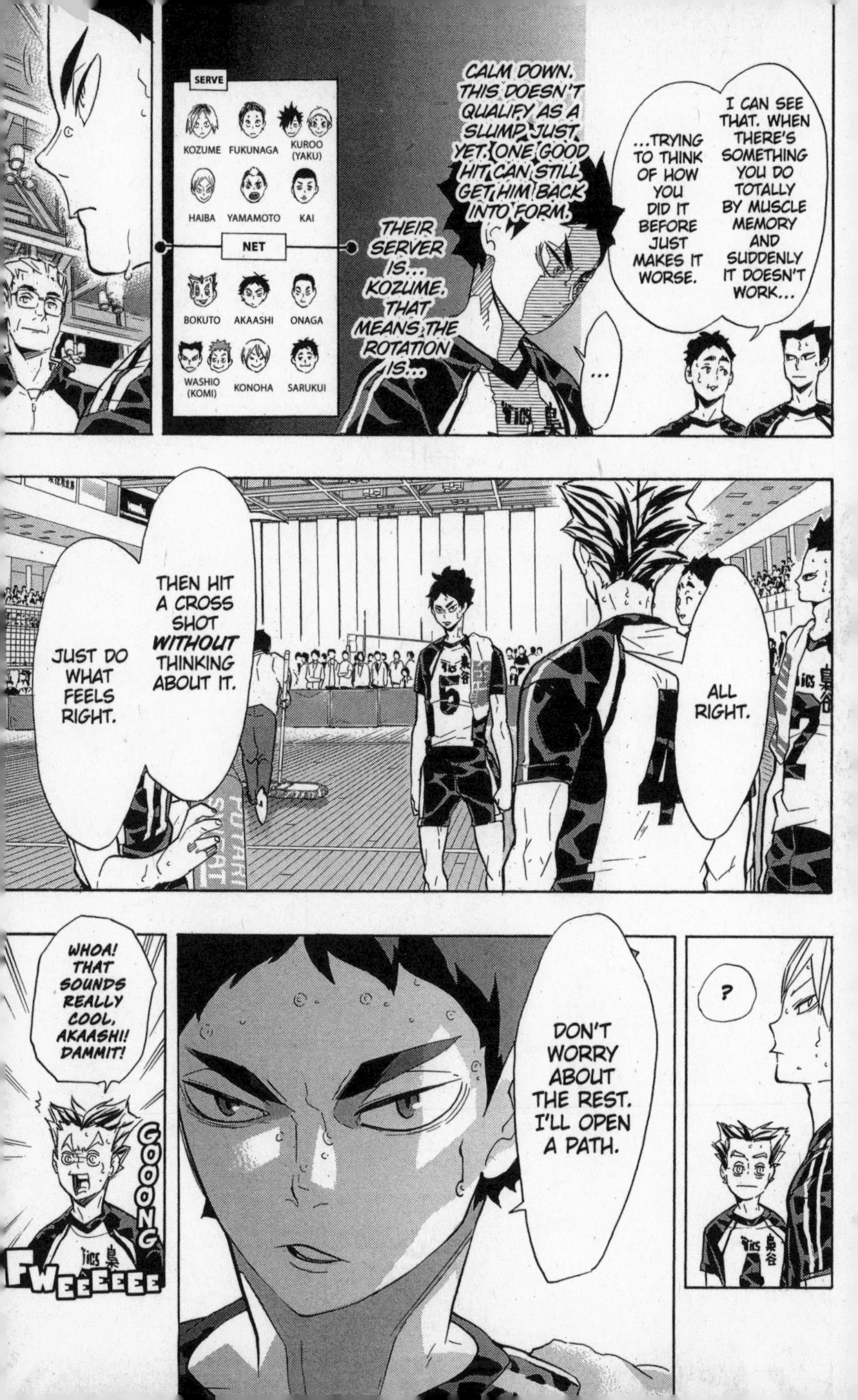
I CAN SEE THAT. WHEN THERE'S SOMETHING YOU DO TOTALLY BY MUSCLE MEMORY AND SUDDENLY IT DOESN'T WORK...
...TRYING TO THINK OF HOW YOU DID IT BEFORE JUST MAKES IT WORSE.
...
CALM DOWN. THIS DOESN'T QUALIFY AS A SLUMP JUST YET. ONE GOOD HIT CAN STILL GET HIM BACK INTO FORM.
THEIR SERVER IS... KOZUME. THAT MEANS THE ROTATION IS...
SERVE
KOZUME
FUKUNAGA
KUROO (YAKU)
HAIBA
YAMAMOTO
KAI
NET
BOKUTO
AKAASHI
ONAGA
WASHIO (KOMI)
KONOHA
SARUKUI
ALL RIGHT.
THEN HIT A CROSS SHOT *WITHOUT* THINKING ABOUT IT.
JUST DO WHAT FEELS RIGHT.
?
DON'T WORRY ABOUT THE REST. I'LL OPEN A PATH.
WHOA! THAT SOUNDS REALLY COOL, AKAASHI! DAMMIT!
GOOOONG
FWEEEEEE

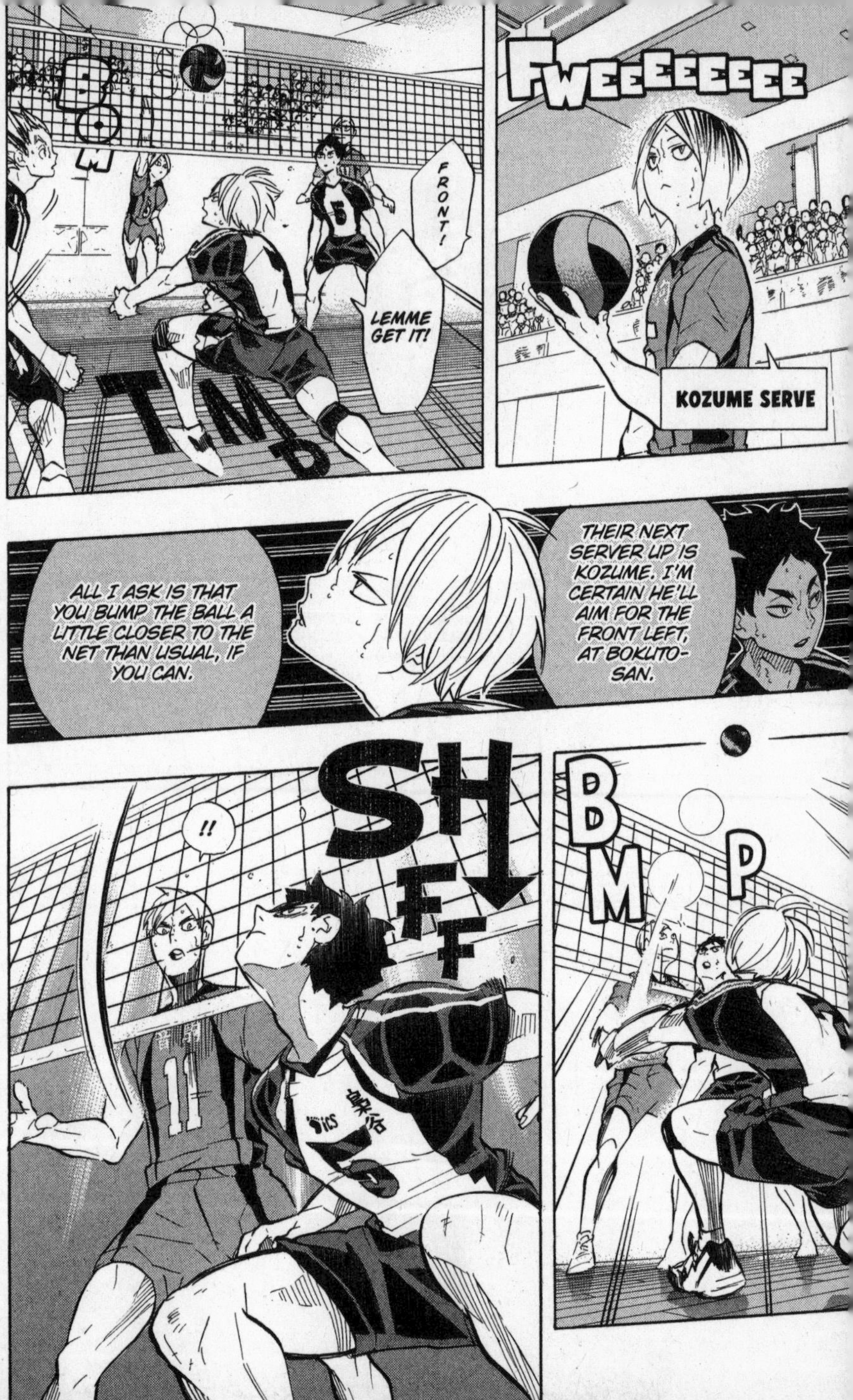
FWEEEEEEEE
KOZUME SERVE
FRONT!
LEMME GET IT!
TMP
THEIR NEXT SERVER UP IS KOZUME. I'M CERTAIN HE'LL AIM FOR THE FRONT LEFT, AT BOKUTO-SAN.
ALL I ASK IS THAT YOU BUMP THE BALL A LITTLE CLOSER TO THE NET THAN USUAL, IF YOU CAN.
BMP
!!
SHFF

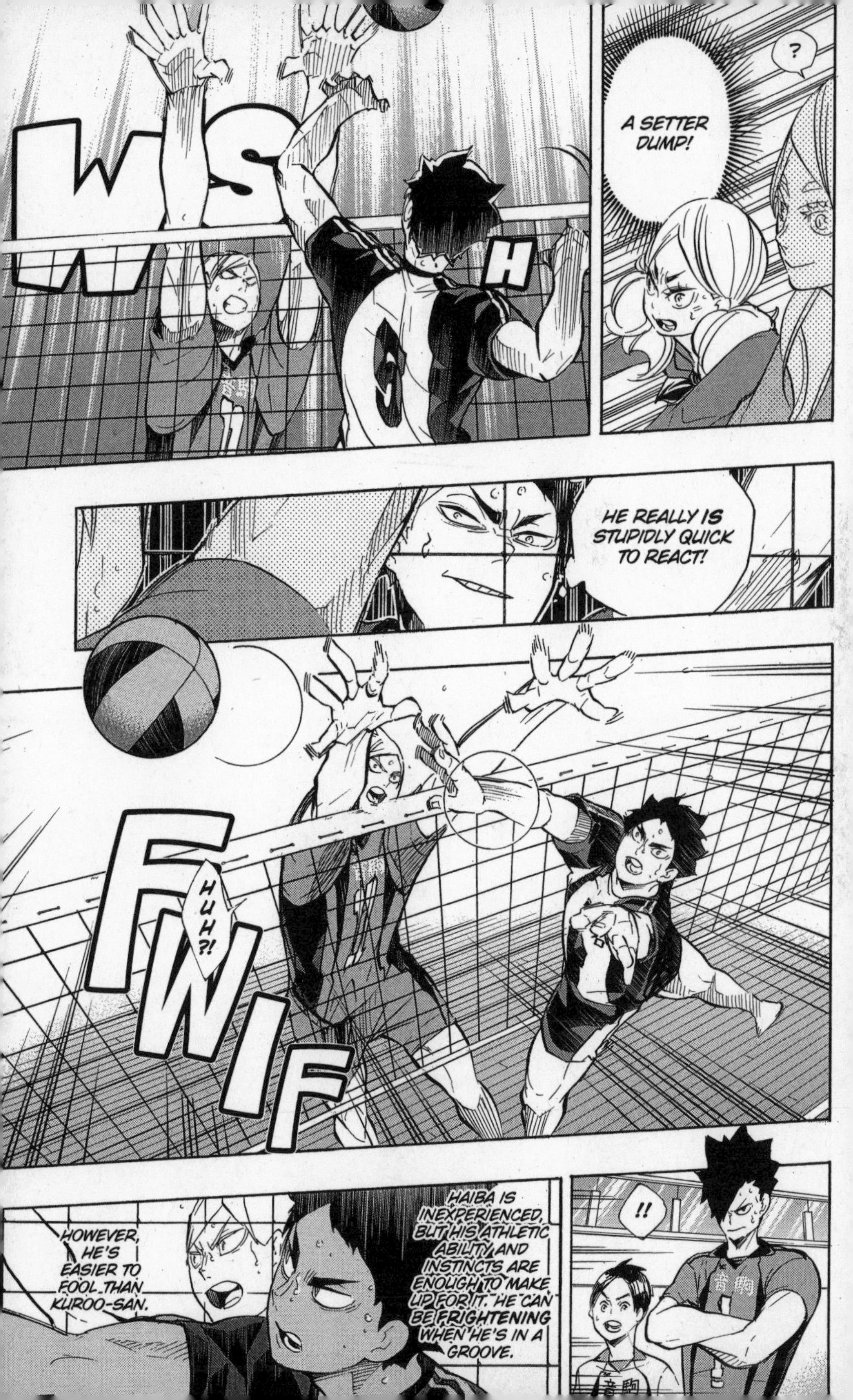
?
A SETTER DUMP!
WSH
HE REALLY IS STUPIDLY QUICK TO REACT!
HUH?!
FWIF
!!
HAIBA IS INEXPERIENCED, BUT HIS ATHLETIC ABILITY AND INSTINCTS ARE ENOUGH TO MAKE UP FOR IT. HE CAN BE FRIGHTENING WHEN HE'S IN A GROOVE.
HOWEVER, HE'S EASIER TO FOOL THAN KUROO-SAN.

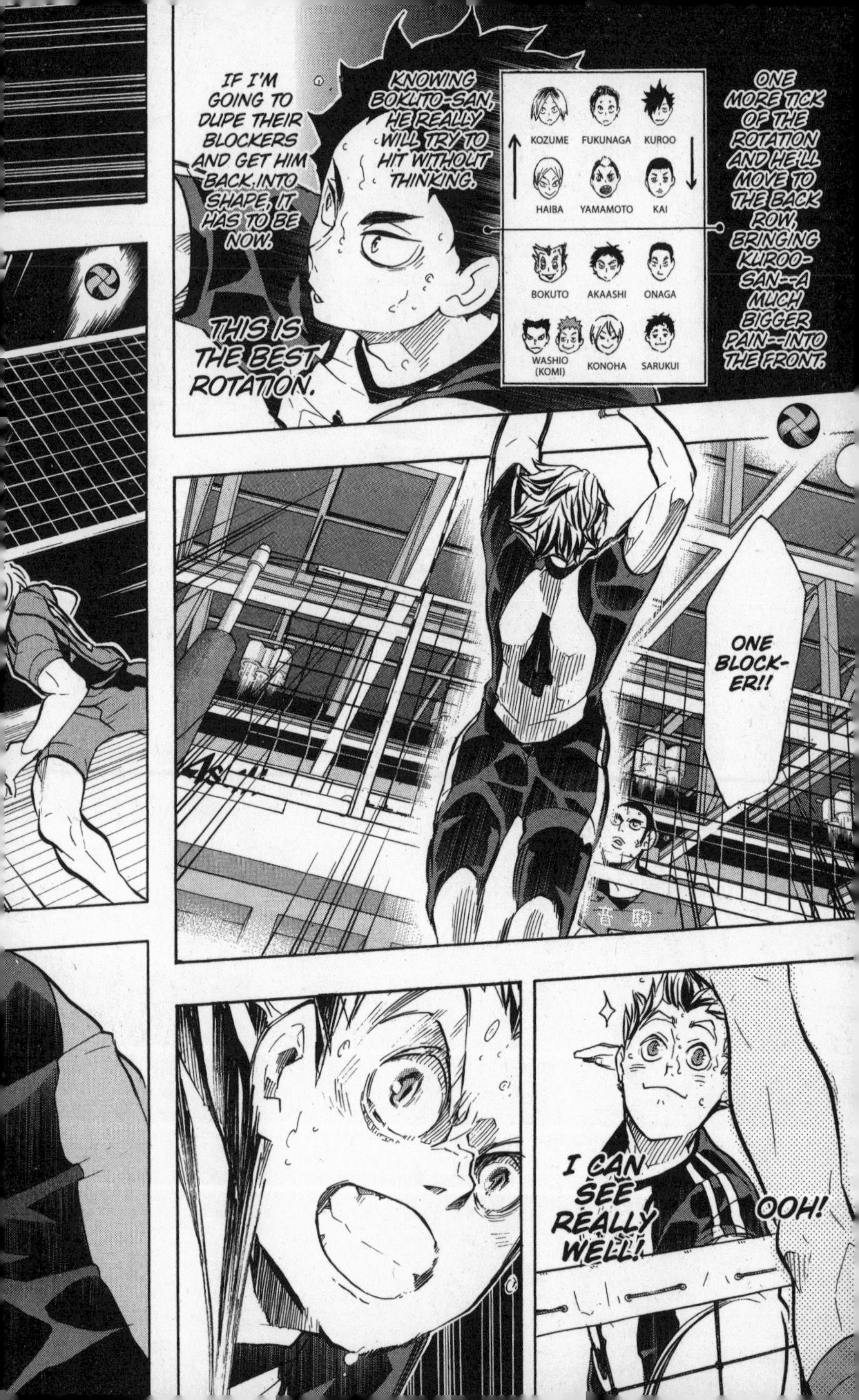
ONE MORE TICK OF THE ROTATION AND HE'LL MOVE TO THE BACK ROW, BRINGING KUROO-SAN--A MUCH BIGGER PAIN--INTO THE FRONT.
KOZUME
FUKUNAGA
KUROO
HAIBA
YAMAMOTO
KAI
BOKUTO
AKAASHI
ONAGA
WASHIO (KOMI)
KONOHA
SARUKUI
KNOWING BOKUTO-SAN, HE REALLY WILL TRY TO HIT WITHOUT THINKING.
IF I'M GOING TO DUPE THEIR BLOCKERS AND GET HIM BACK INTO SHAPE, IT HAS TO BE NOW.
THIS IS THE BEST ROTATION.
ONE BLOCKER!!
OOH!
I CAN SEE REALLY WELL!

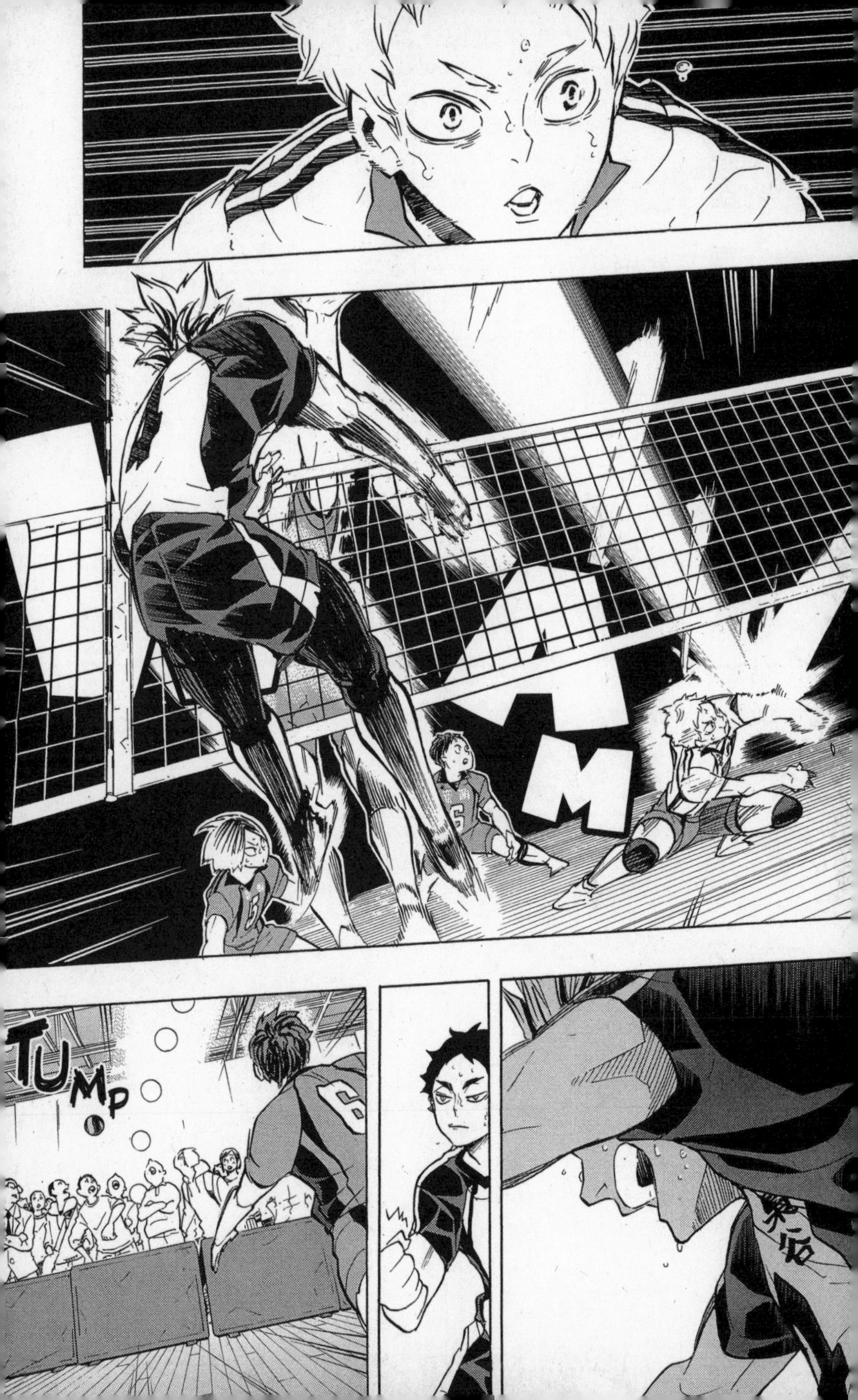
TUMP

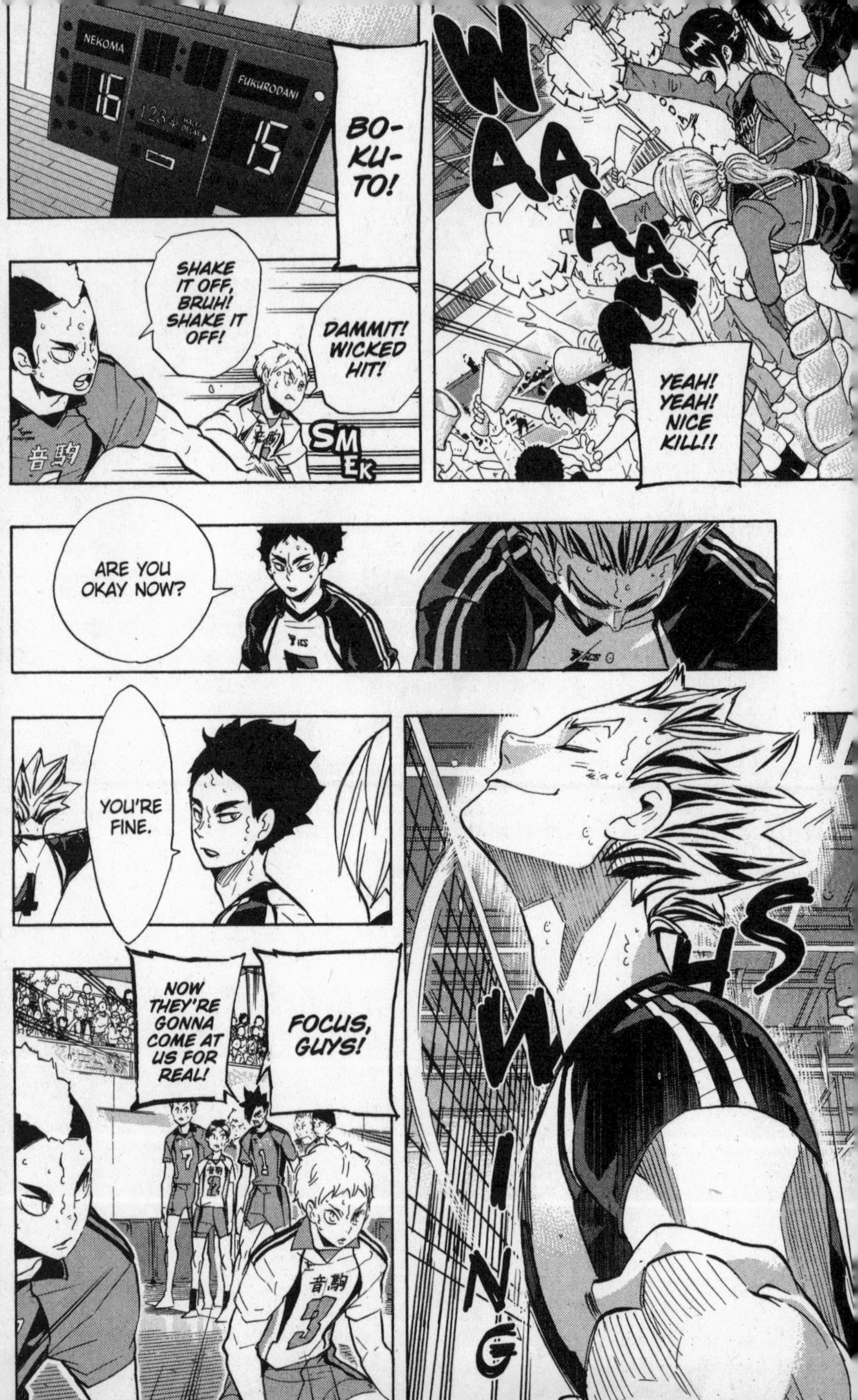
WAAAAA
YEAH! YEAH! NICE KILL!!
NEKOMA
16
FUKURODANI
15
BO-KU-TO!
DAMMIT! WICKED HIT!
SHAKE IT OFF, BRUH! SHAKE IT OFF!
SMEK
ARE YOU OKAY NOW?
SHWING
YOU'RE FINE.
FOCUS, GUYS!
NOW THEY'RE GONNA COME AT US FOR REAL!

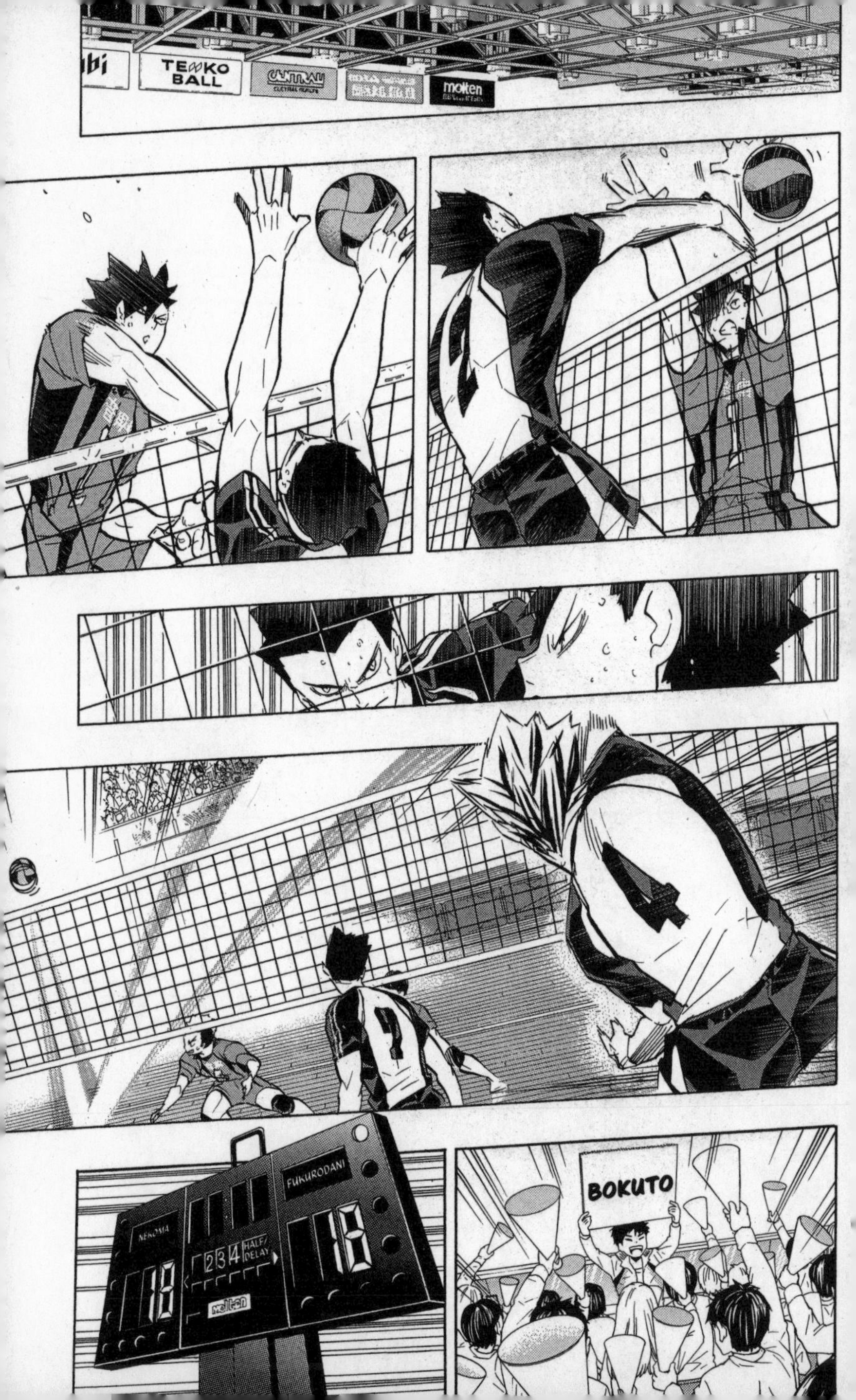

molten
TENKO BALL
BOKUTO
FUKURODANI
NEKOMA
18
2 3 4
HALF/ DELAY
18
molten

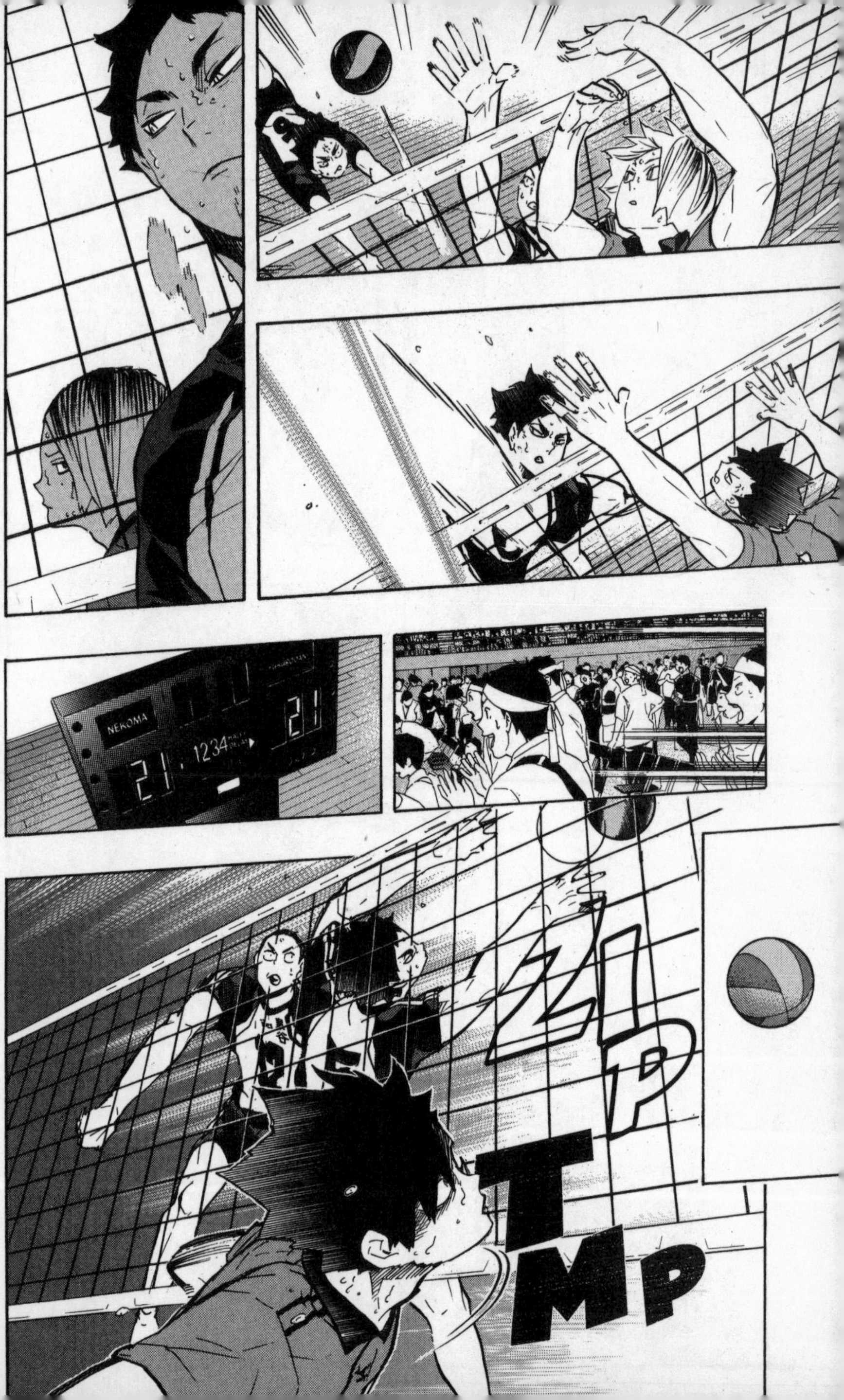
NEKOMA
21
1234
21
ZIP
TMP

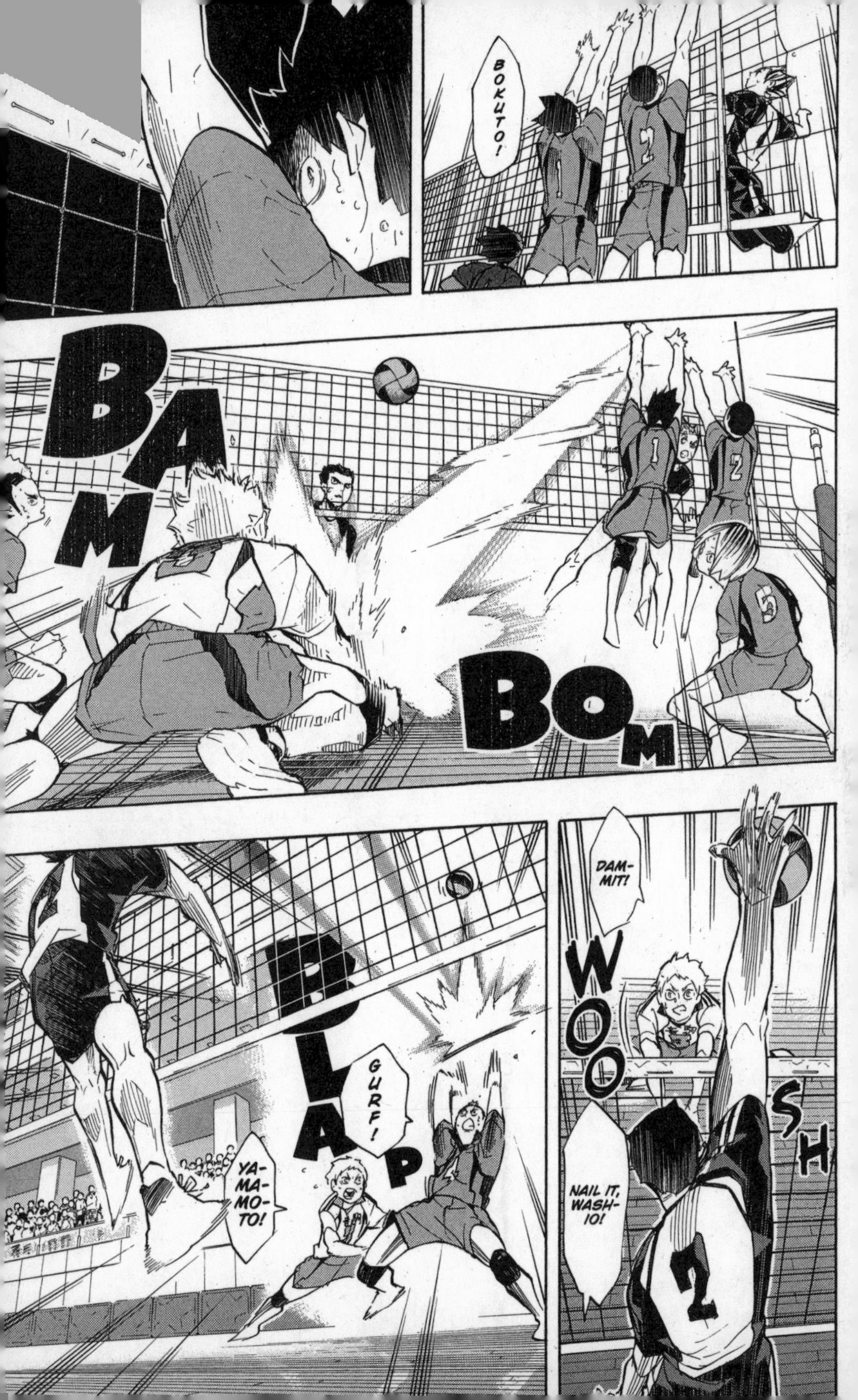
BOKUTO!
BAM
BOOM
DAM-
MIT!
WOOSH
NAIL IT,
WASH-
IO!
BLAP
GURF!
YA-
MA-
MO-
TO!

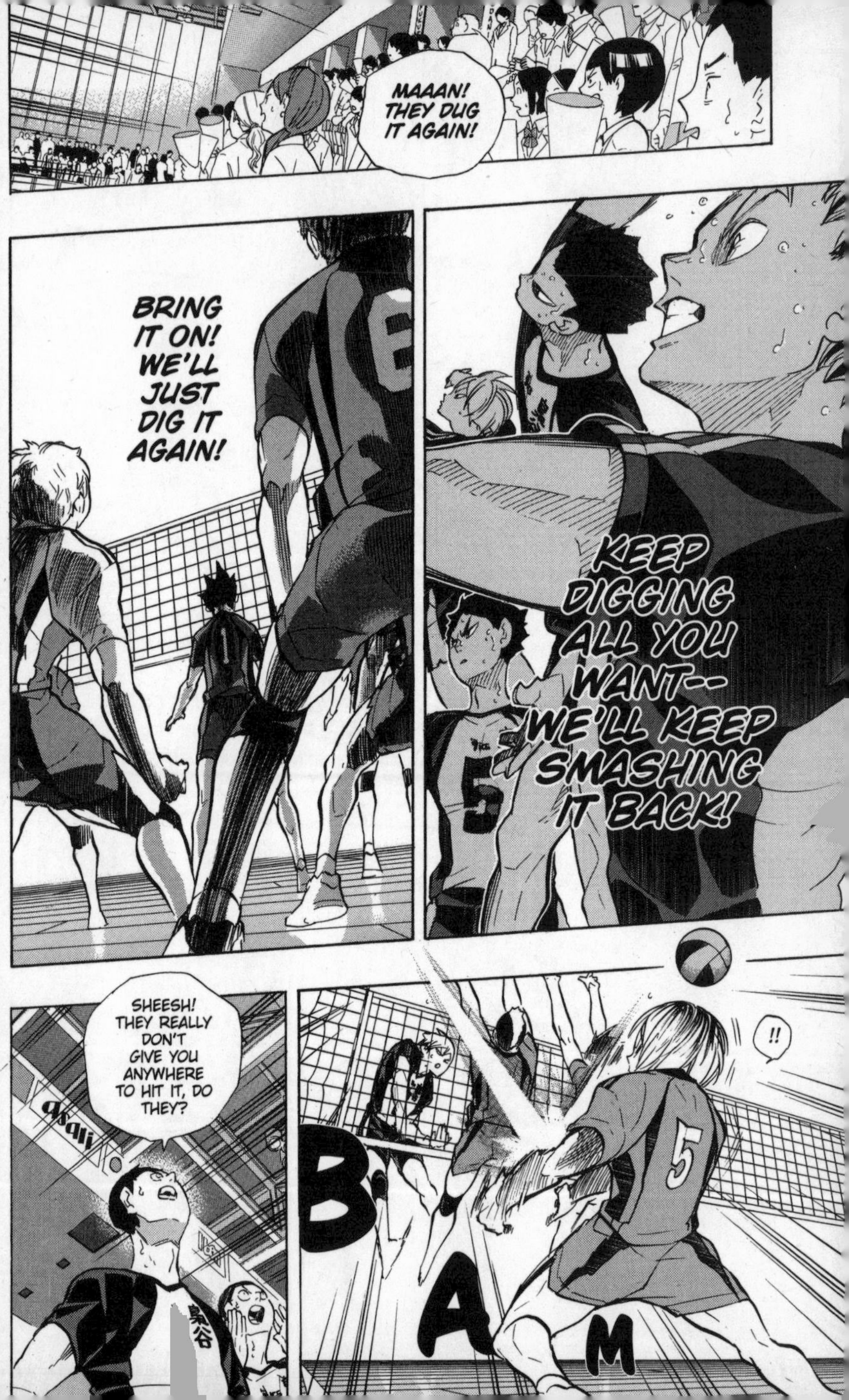
MAAAN! THEY DUG IT AGAIN!
KEEP DIGGING ALL YOU WANT-- WE'LL KEEP SMASHING IT BACK!
BRING IT ON! WE'LL JUST DIG IT AGAIN!
!!
BAM
SHEESH! THEY REALLY DON'T GIVE YOU ANYWHERE TO HIT IT, DO THEY?

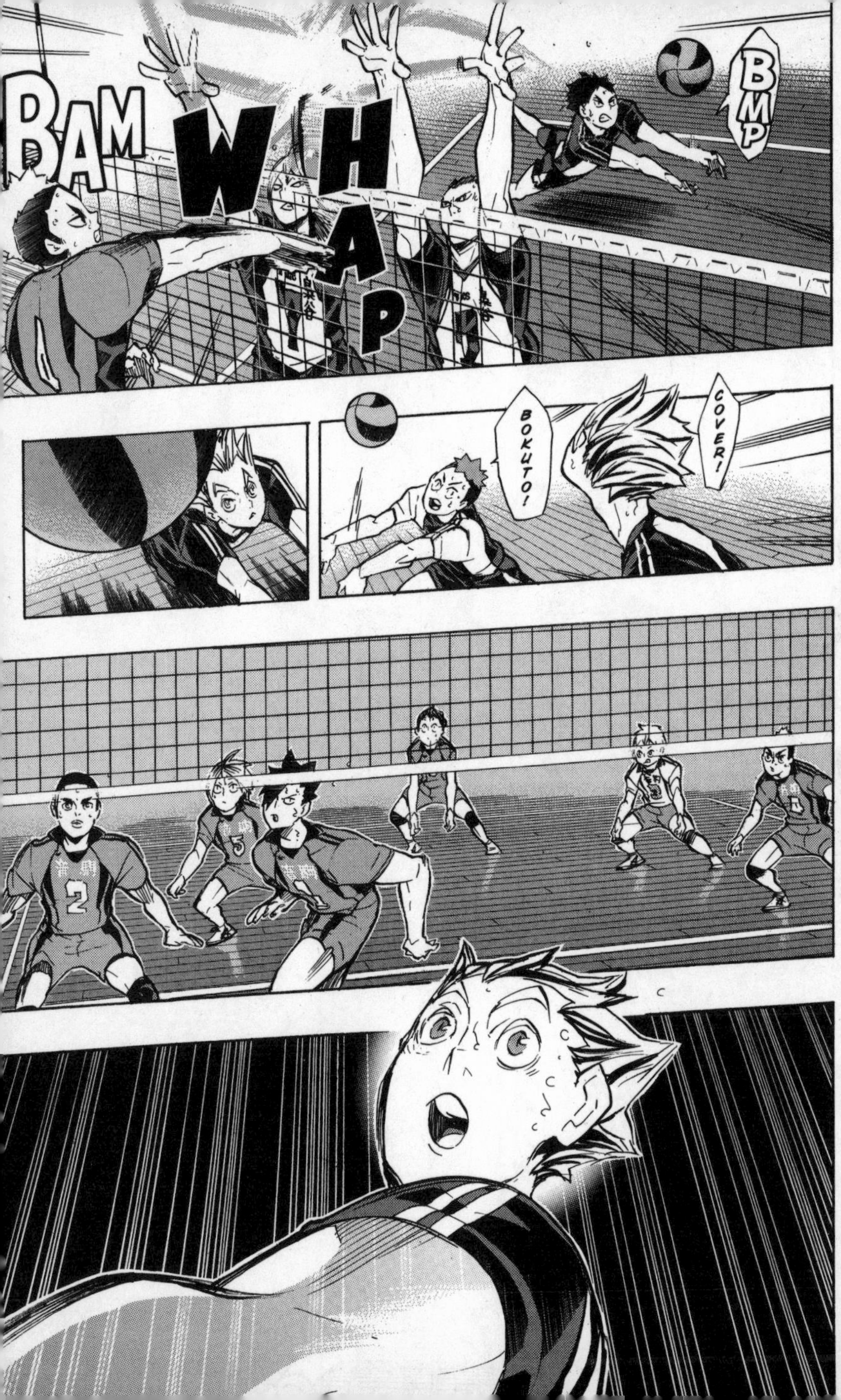
BMP
WHAP
BAM
COVER!
BOKUTO!

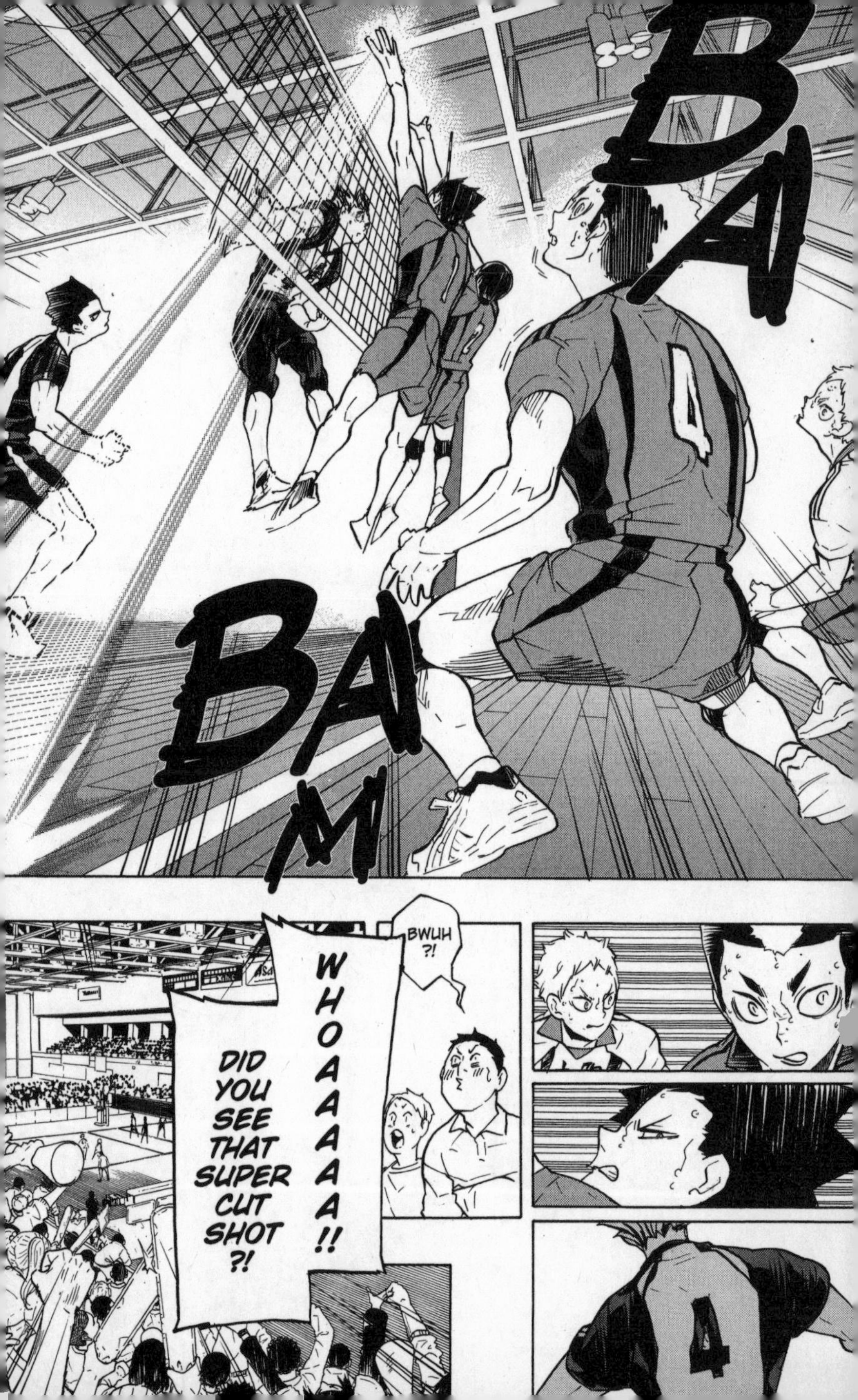
BA
BAM
BWUH ?!
WHOAAAAAAA!!
DID YOU SEE THAT SUPER CUT SHOT?!

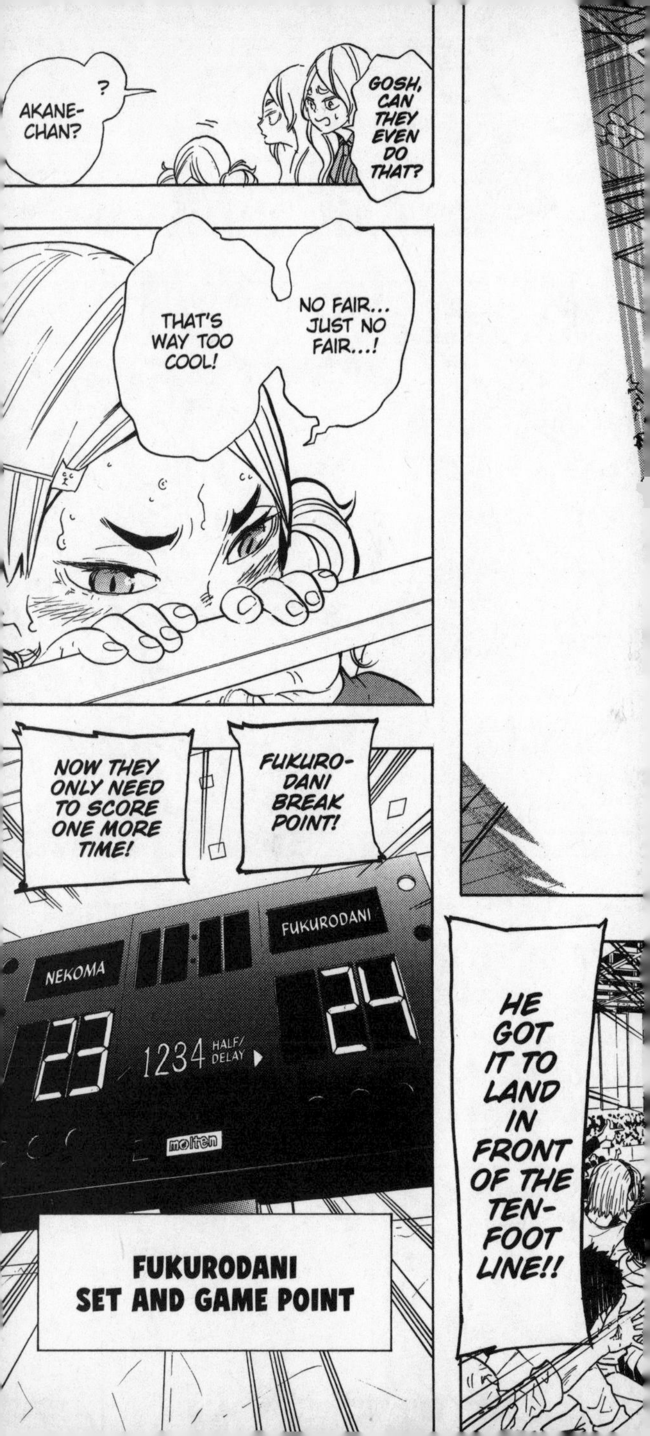
HE GOT IT TO LAND IN FRONT OF THE TEN-FOOT LINE!!
GOSH, CAN THEY EVEN DO THAT?
?
AKANE-CHAN?
NO FAIR... JUST NO FAIR...!
THAT'S WAY TOO COOL!
FUKURO-DANI BREAK POINT!
NOW THEY ONLY NEED TO SCORE ONE MORE TIME!
FUKURODANI
NEKOMA
24
23
1234 HALF/ DELAY
molten
FUKURODANI SET AND GAME POINT

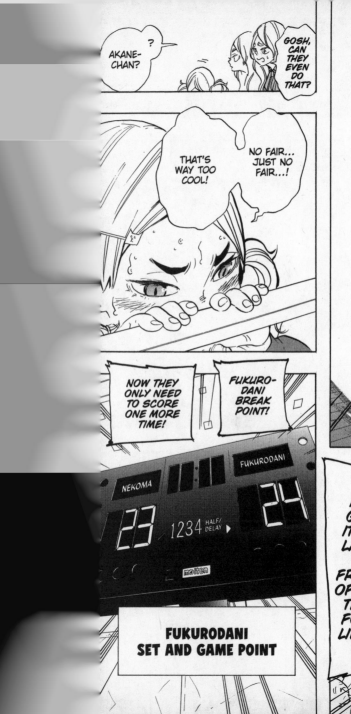

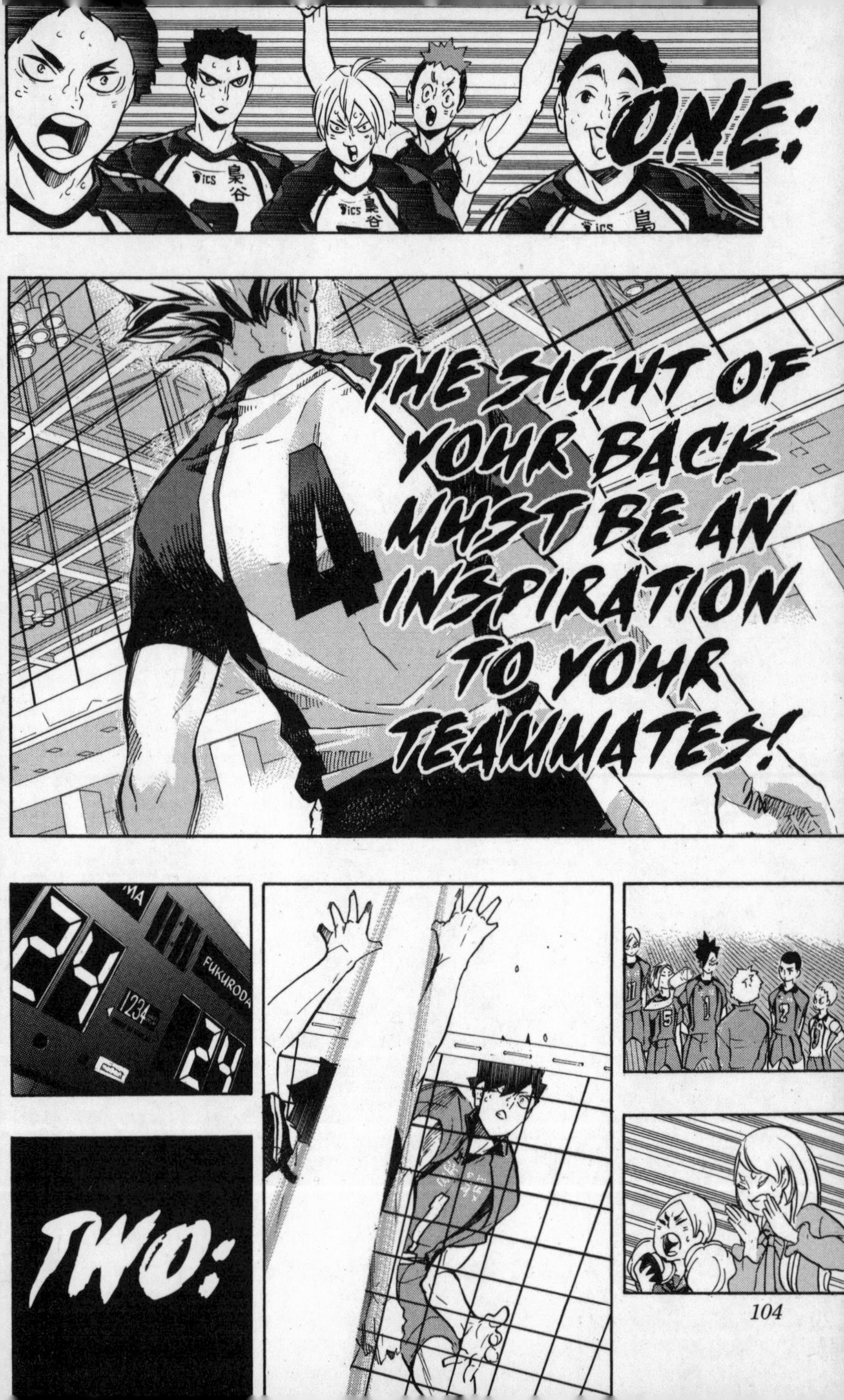
ONE:
THE SIGHT OF YOUR BACK MUST BE AN INSPIRATION TO YOUR TEAMMATES!
24
FUKURODA
24
TWO:

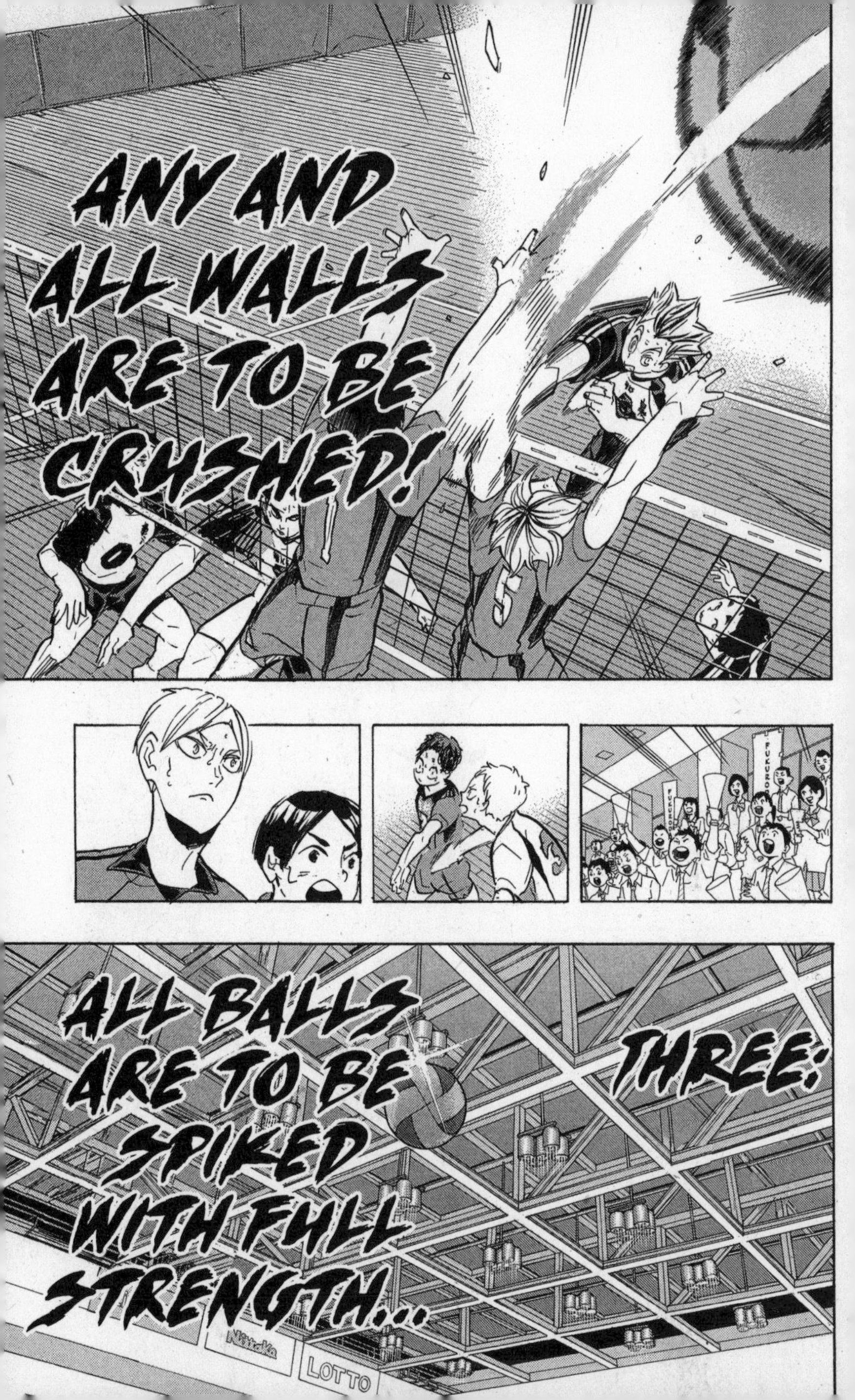
ANY AND ALL WALLS ARE TO BE CRUSHED!
THREE:
ALL BALLS ARE TO BE SPIKED WITH FULL STRENGTH...
LOTTO

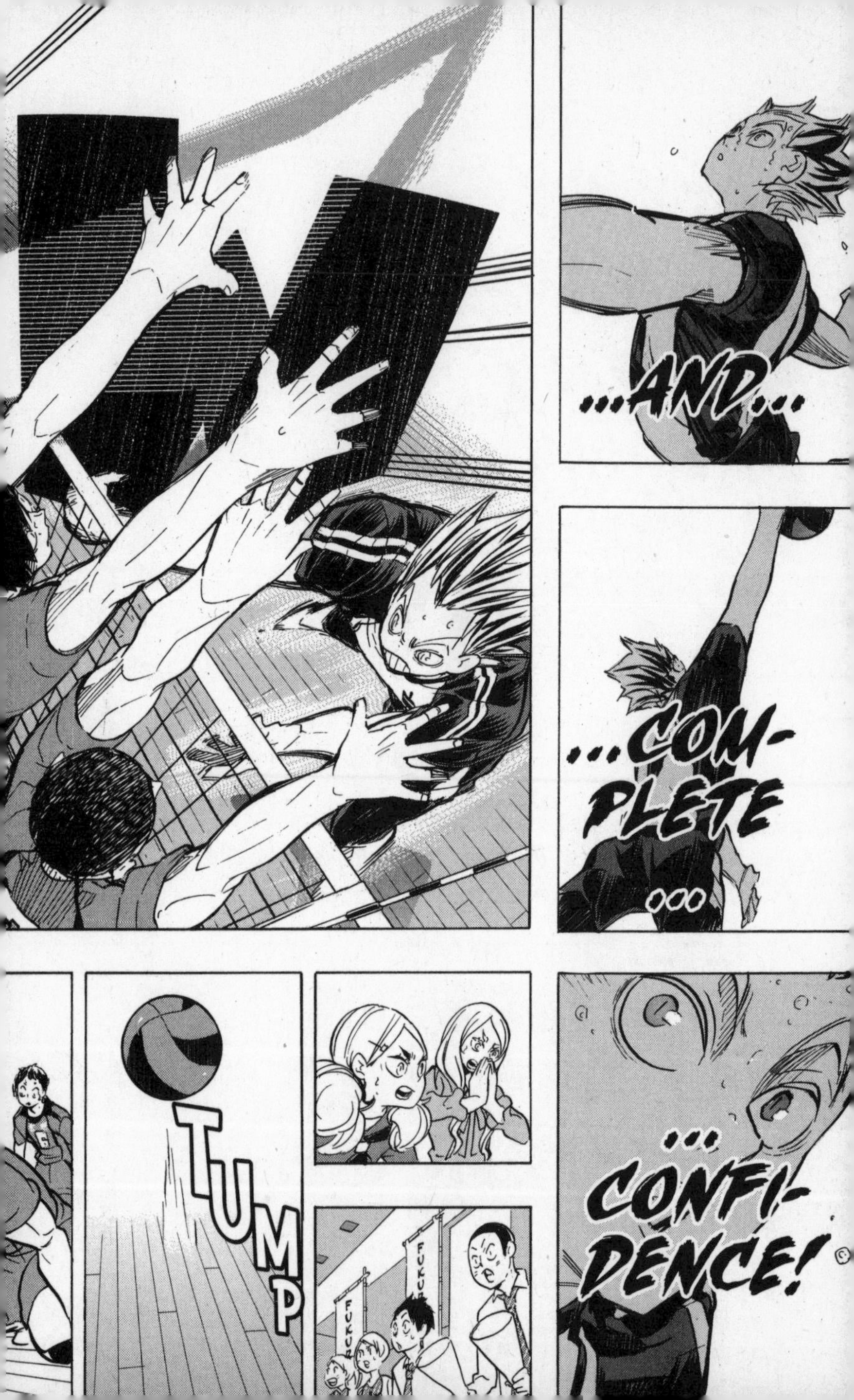
...AND...
...COM-PLETE...
...CONFI-DENCE!
TUMP

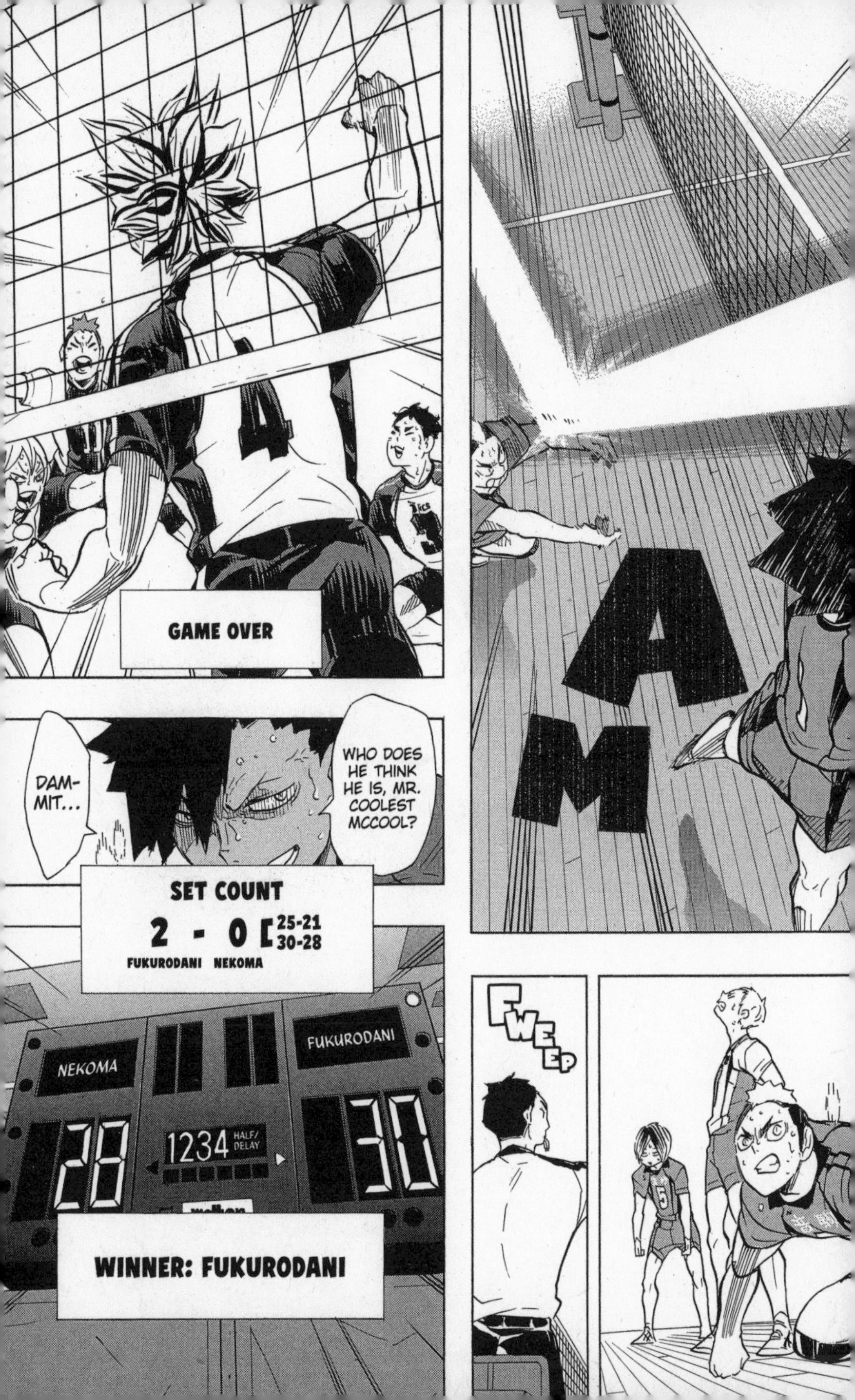
BAM
GAME OVER
WHO DOES HE THINK HE IS, MR. COOLEST MCCOOL?
DAM-MIT...
SET COUNT
2 - 0 [25-21 30-28
FUKURODANI NEKOMA
FWEEP
FUKURODANI
NEKOMA
28
1234 HALF/DELAY
30
WINNER: FUKURODANI

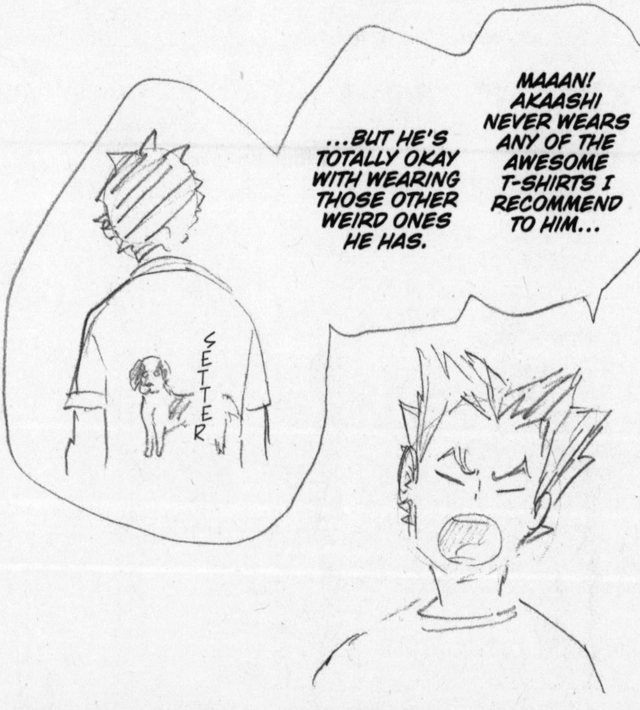
MAAAN! AKAASHI NEVER WEARS ANY OF THE AWESOME T-SHIRTS I RECOMMEND TO HIM...
...BUT HE'S TOTALLY OKAY WITH WEARING THOSE OTHER WEIRD ONES HE HAS.
SETTER

CHAPTER 196: Backs to the Wall

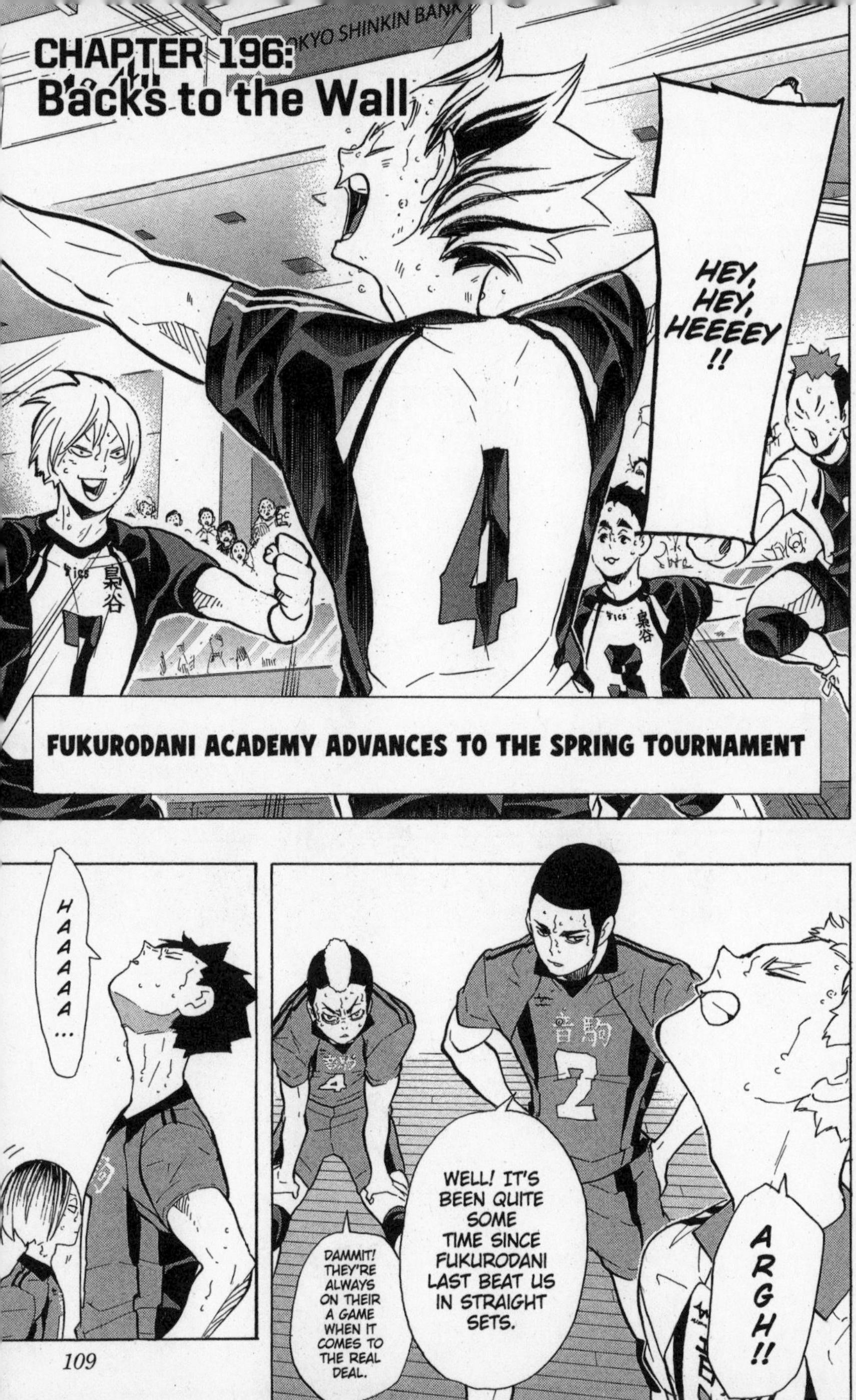
OKYO SHINKIN BANK
HEY, HEY, HEEEEY!!
FUKURODANI ACADEMY ADVANCES TO THE SPRING TOURNAMENT
ARGH!!
WELL! IT'S BEEN QUITE SOME TIME SINCE FUKURODANI LAST BEAT US IN STRAIGHT SETS.
DAMMIT! THEY'RE ALWAYS ON THEIR A GAME WHEN IT COMES TO THE REAL DEAL.
HAAAAA...

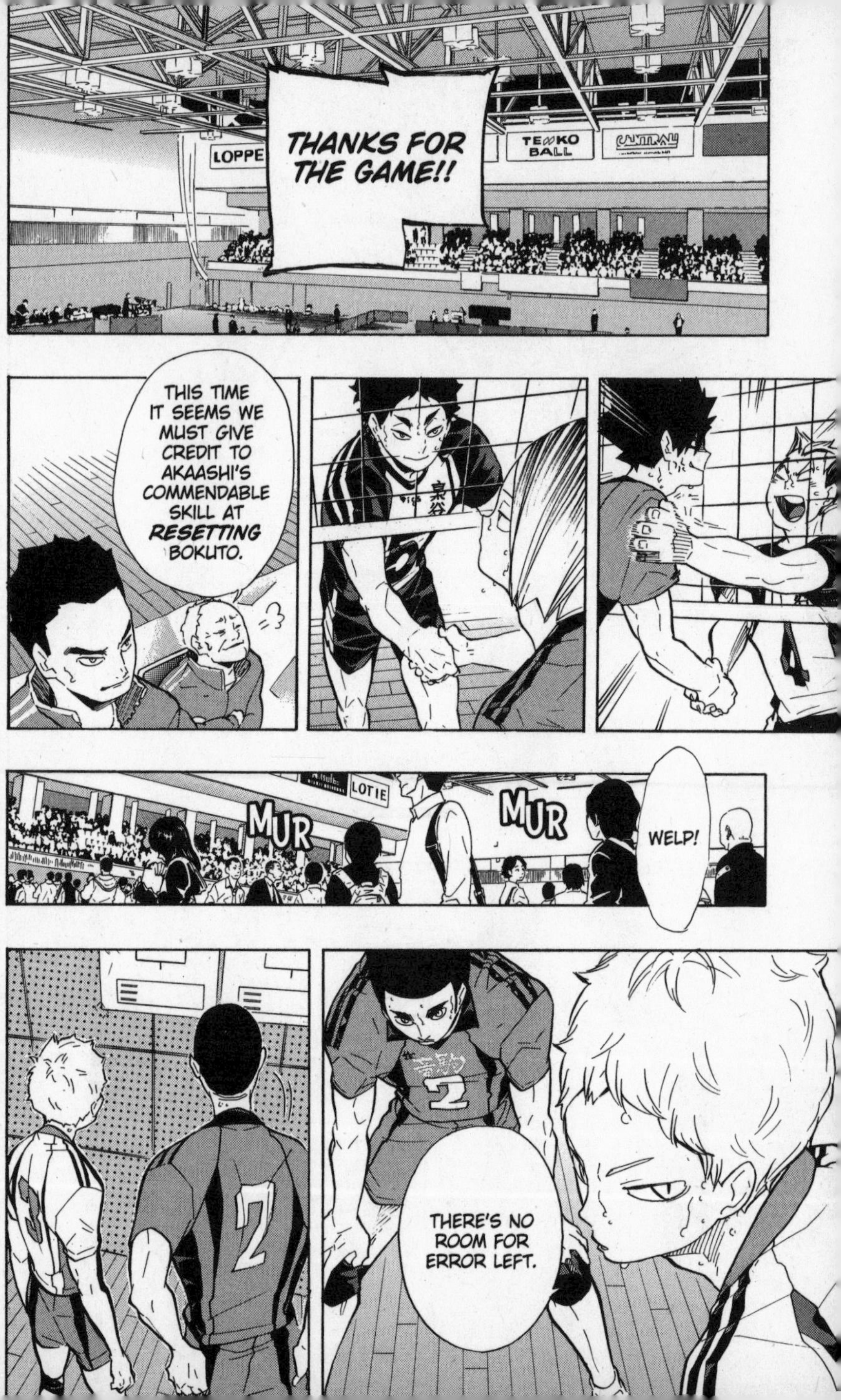
THANKS FOR THE GAME!!
TE KO BALL
LOPPE
THIS TIME IT SEEMS WE MUST GIVE CREDIT TO AKAASHI'S COMMENDABLE SKILL AT *RESETTING* BOKUTO.
WELP!
MUR
MUR
LOTIE
THERE'S NO ROOM FOR ERROR LEFT.

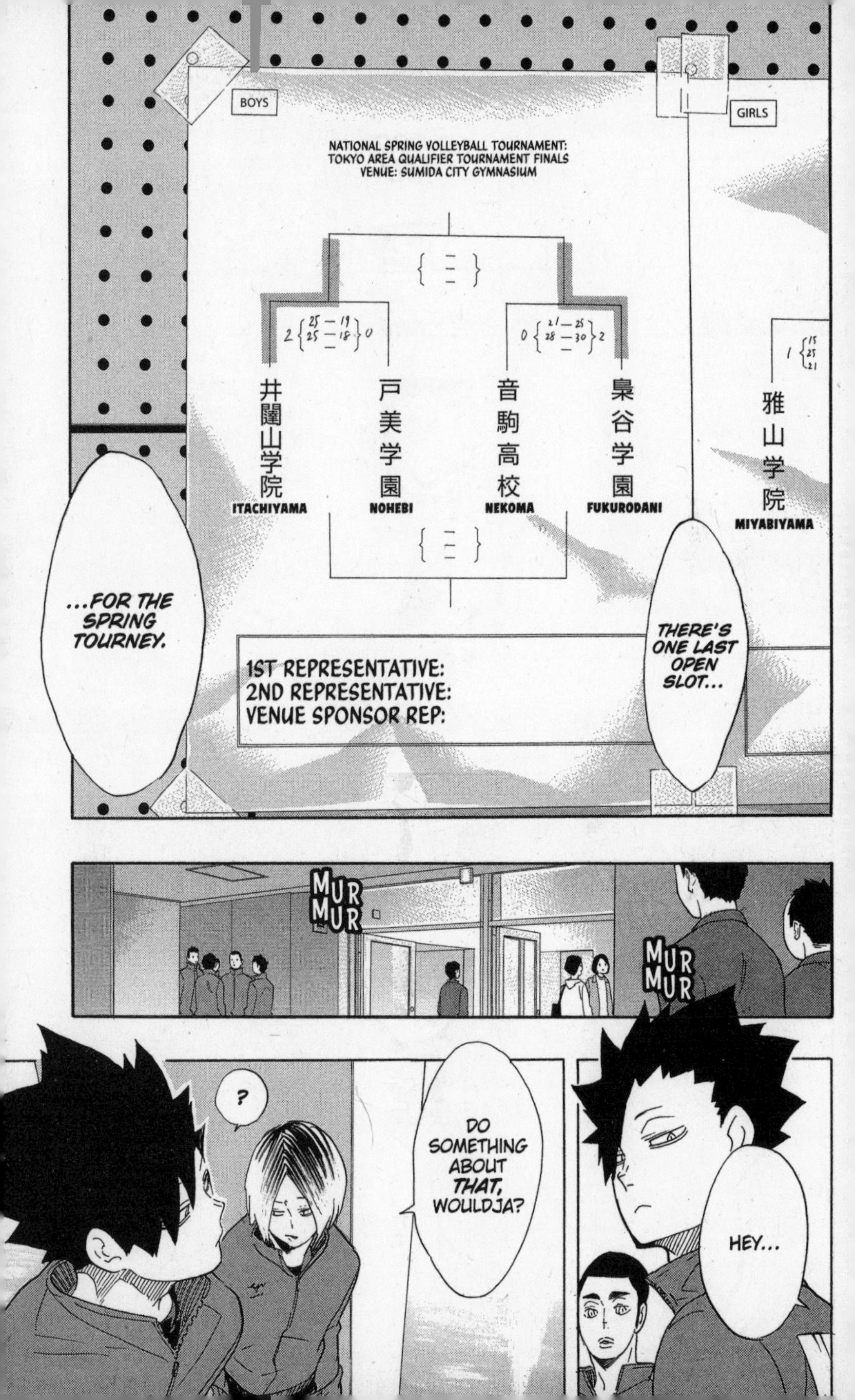

GIRLS
BOYS
NATIONAL SPRING VOLLEYBALL TOURNAMENT:
TOKYO AREA QUALIFIER TOURNAMENT FINALS
VENUE: SUMIDA CITY GYMNASIUM
THERE'S ONE LAST OPEN SLOT...
雅山学院
MIYABIYAMA
梟谷学園
FUKURODANI
音駒高校
NEKOMA
戸美学園
NOHEBI
井闥山学院
ITACHIYAMA
1ST REPRESENTATIVE:
2ND REPRESENTATIVE:
VENUE SPONSOR REP:
...FOR THE SPRING TOURNEY.
MUR MUR
MUR MUR
HEY...
DO SOMETHING ABOUT THAT, WOULDJA?
?

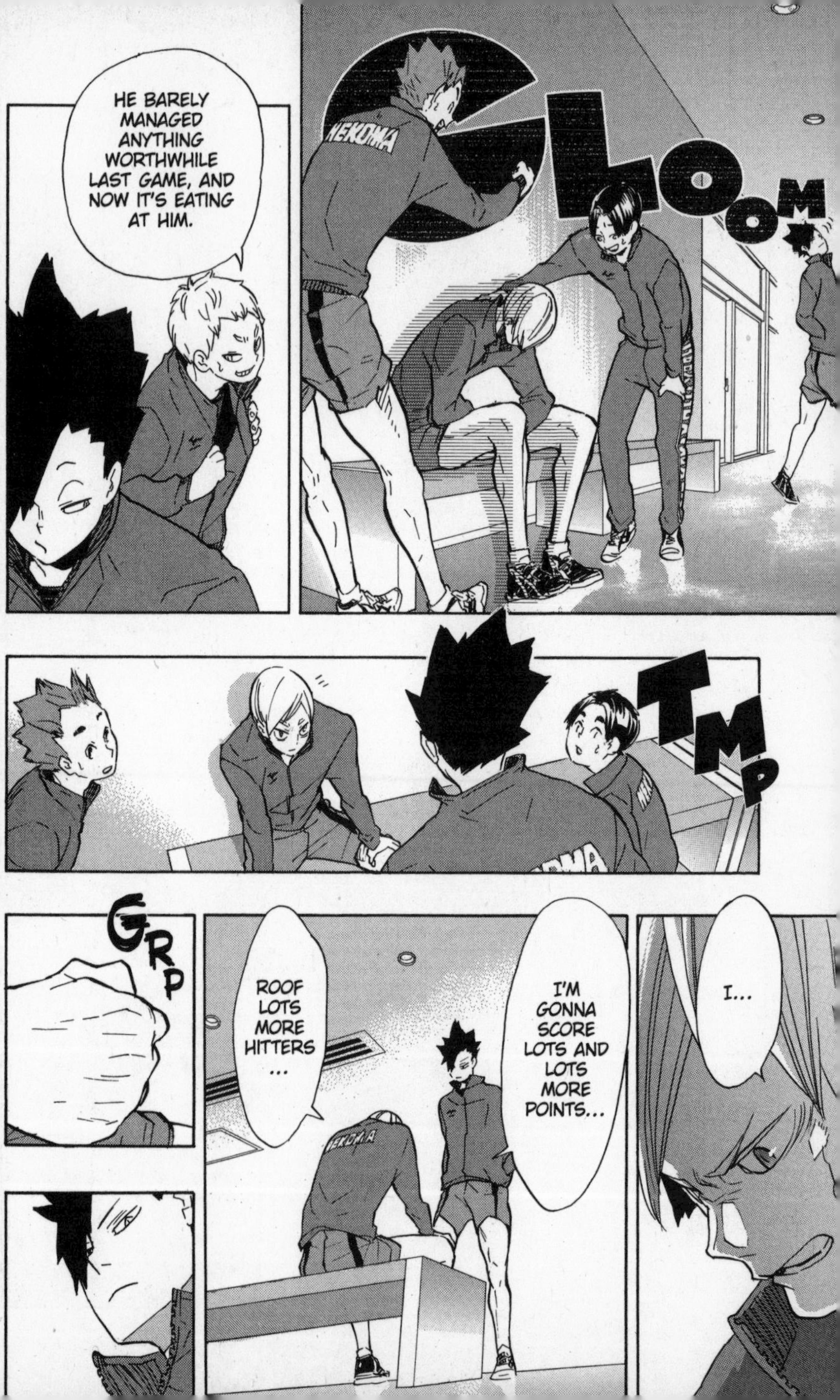

GLOOM
HE BARELY MANAGED ANYTHING WORTHWHILE LAST GAME, AND NOW IT'S EATING AT HIM.
TMP
I...
I'M GONNA SCORE LOTS AND LOTS MORE POINTS...
ROOF LOTS MORE HITTERS ...
GRP

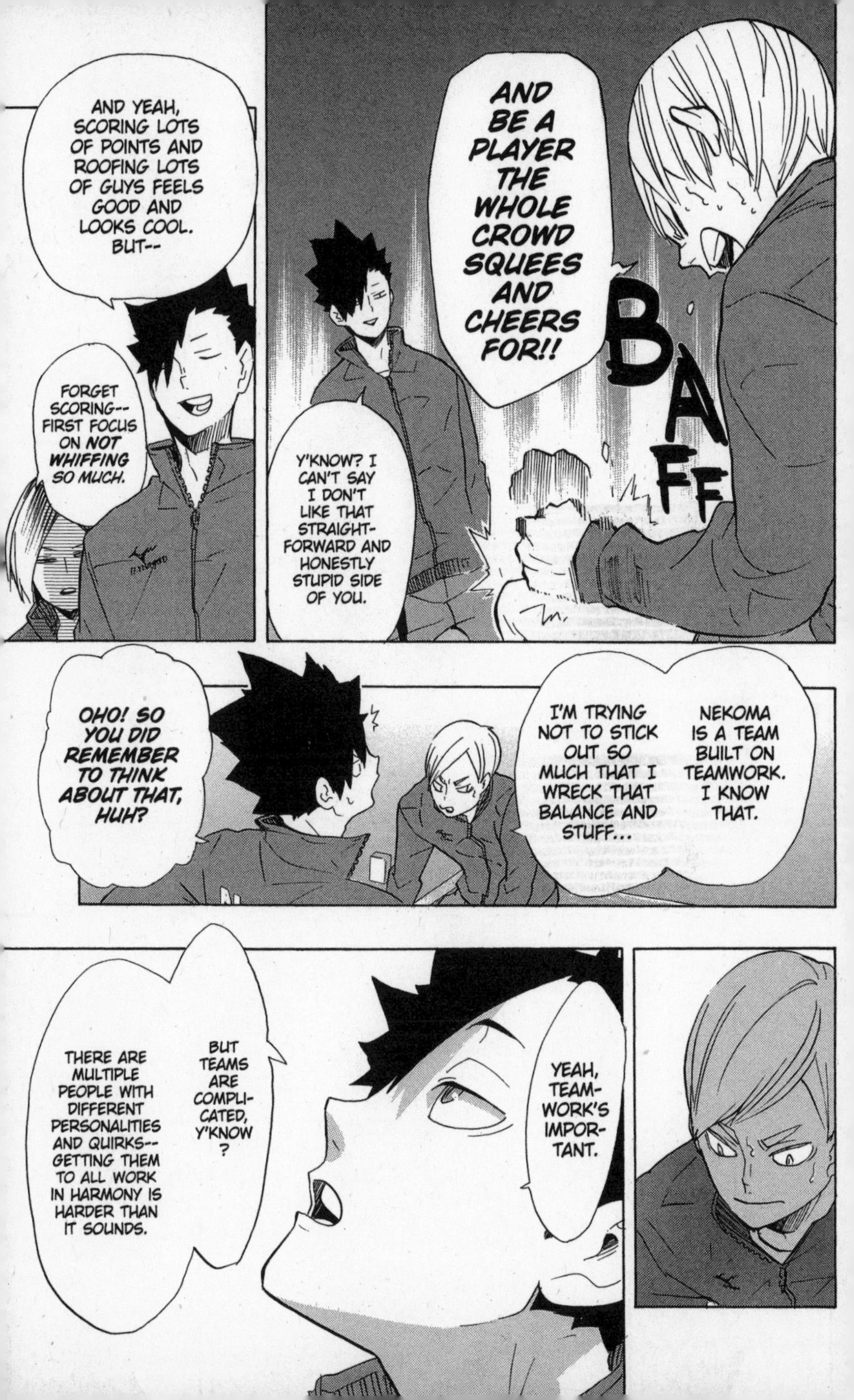
AND BE A PLAYER THE WHOLE CROWD SQUEES AND CHEERS FOR!!
BAFF
Y'KNOW? I CAN'T SAY I DON'T LIKE THAT STRAIGHT-FORWARD AND HONESTLY STUPID SIDE OF YOU.
AND YEAH, SCORING LOTS OF POINTS AND ROOFING LOTS OF GUYS FEELS GOOD AND LOOKS COOL. BUT--
FORGET SCORING-- FIRST FOCUS ON *NOT WHIFFING* SO MUCH.
NEKOMA IS A TEAM BUILT ON TEAMWORK. I KNOW THAT.
I'M TRYING NOT TO STICK OUT SO MUCH THAT I WRECK THAT BALANCE AND STUFF...
OHO! SO YOU DID REMEMBER TO THINK ABOUT THAT, HUH?
YEAH, TEAM-WORK'S IMPOR-TANT.
BUT TEAMS ARE COMPLI-CATED, Y'KNOW?
THERE ARE MULTIPLE PEOPLE WITH DIFFERENT PERSONALITIES AND QUIRKS-- GETTING THEM TO ALL WORK IN HARMONY IS HARDER THAN IT SOUNDS.

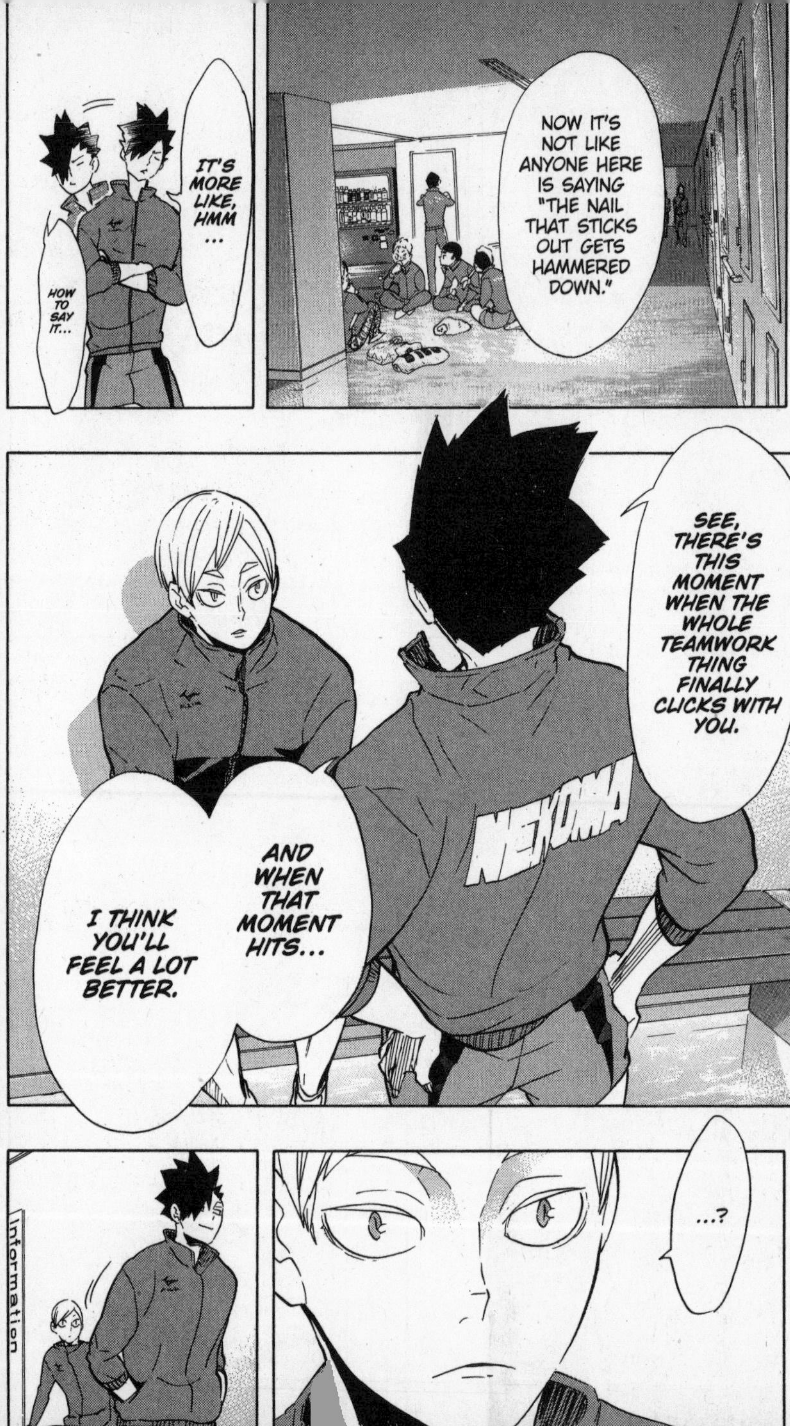
NOW IT'S NOT LIKE ANYONE HERE IS SAYING "THE NAIL THAT STICKS OUT GETS HAMMERED DOWN."
IT'S MORE LIKE, HMM...
HOW TO SAY IT...
SEE, THERE'S THIS MOMENT WHEN THE WHOLE TEAMWORK THING FINALLY CLICKS WITH YOU.
NEKOMA
AND WHEN THAT MOMENT HITS...
I THINK YOU'LL FEEL A LOT BETTER.
...?
Information

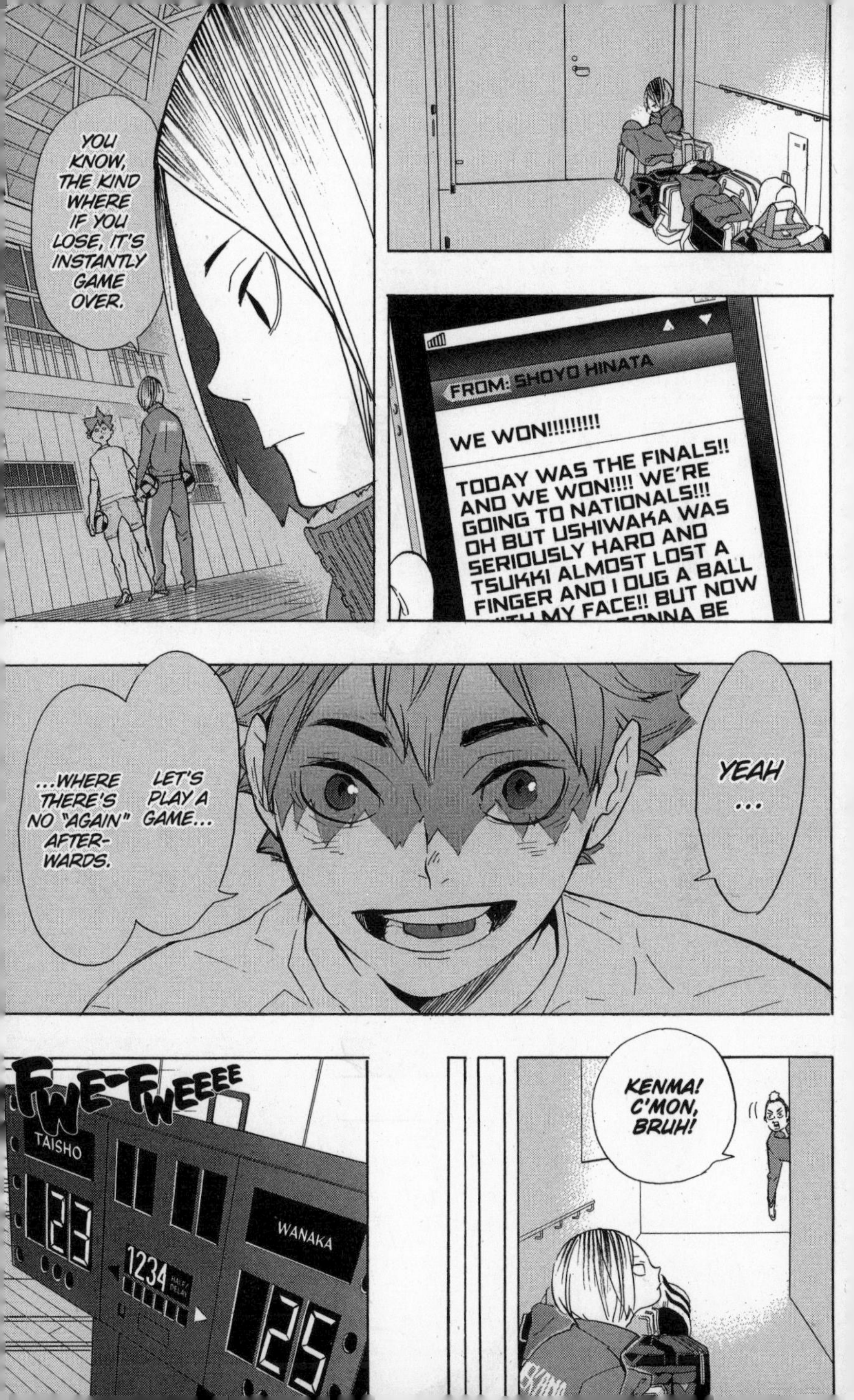
FROM: SHOYO HINATA
WE WON!!!!!!!!!
TODAY WAS THE FINALS!! AND WE WON!!!! WE'RE GOING TO NATIONALS!!! OH BUT USHIWAKA WAS SERIOUSLY HARD AND TSUKKI ALMOST LOST A FINGER AND I DUG A BALL
YOU KNOW, THE KIND WHERE IF YOU LOSE, IT'S INSTANTLY GAME OVER.
YEAH...
LET'S PLAY A GAME...
...WHERE THERE'S NO "AGAIN" AFTER-WARDS.
KENMA! C'MON, BRUH!
FWE-FWEEEE
TAISHO
23
1234
WANAKA
25

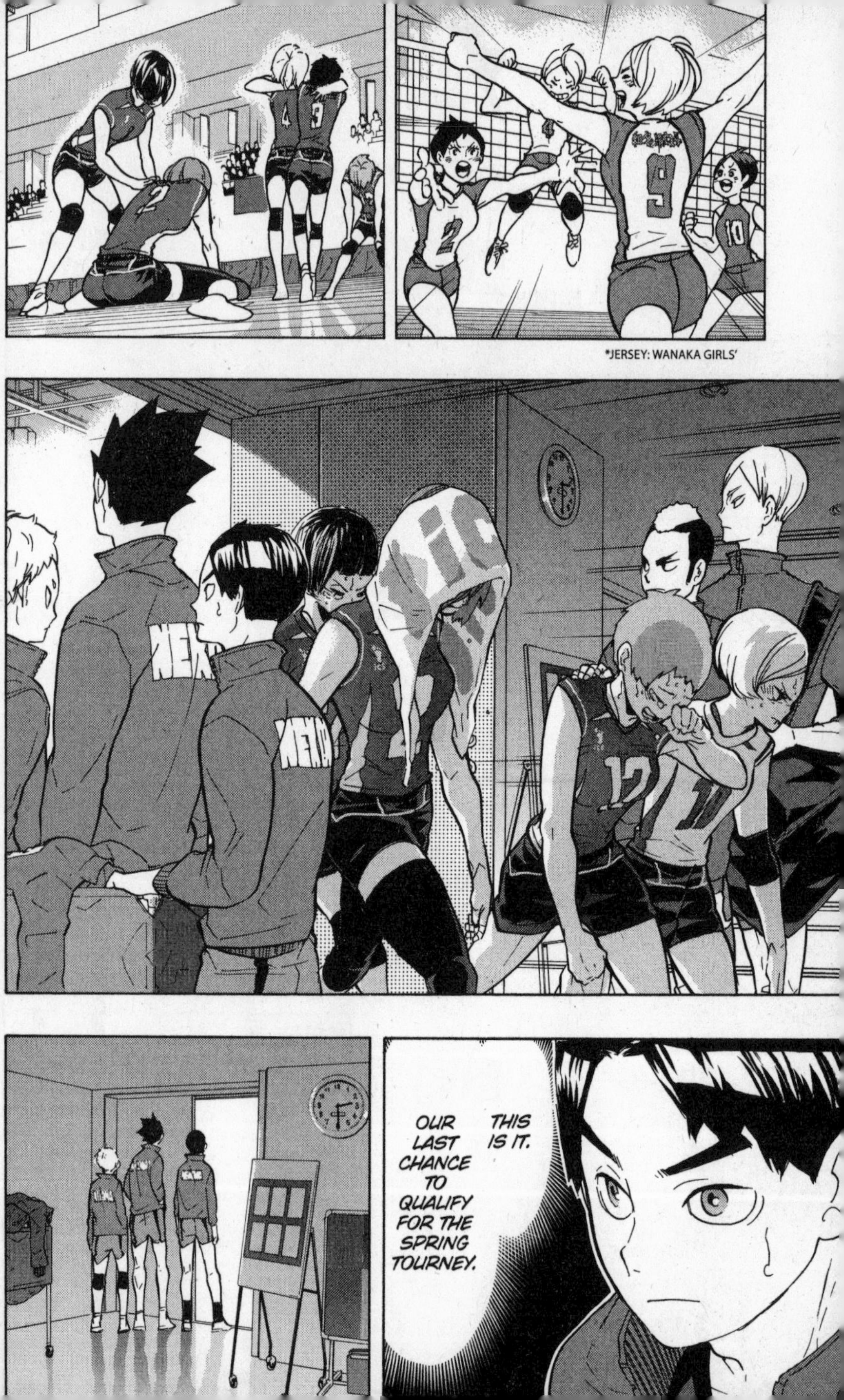
*JERSEY: WANAKA GIRLS'
THIS IS IT.
OUR LAST CHANCE TO QUALIFY FOR THE SPRING TOURNEY.

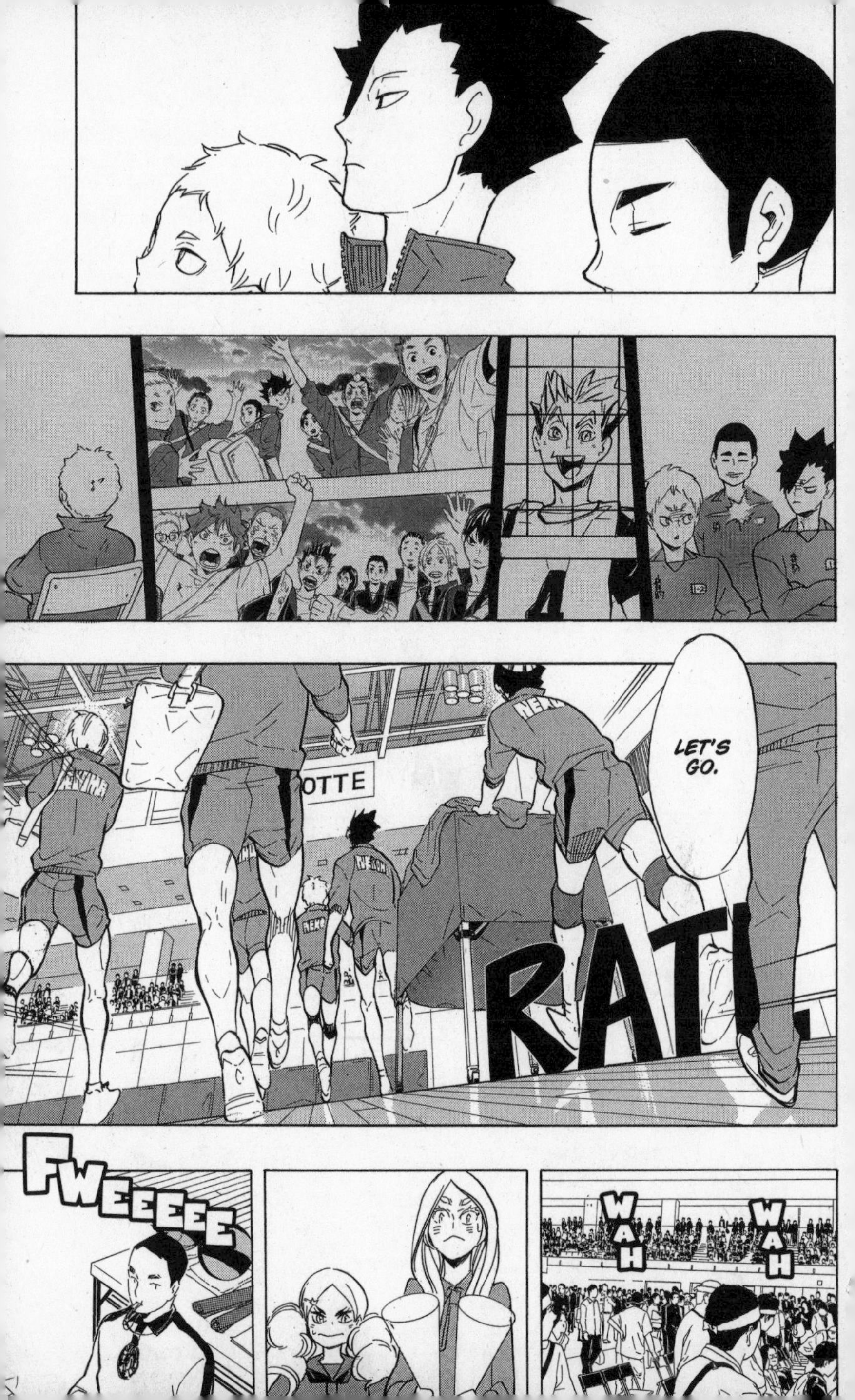
OTTE
LET'S GO.
RATL
FWEEEEEE
WAH
WAH

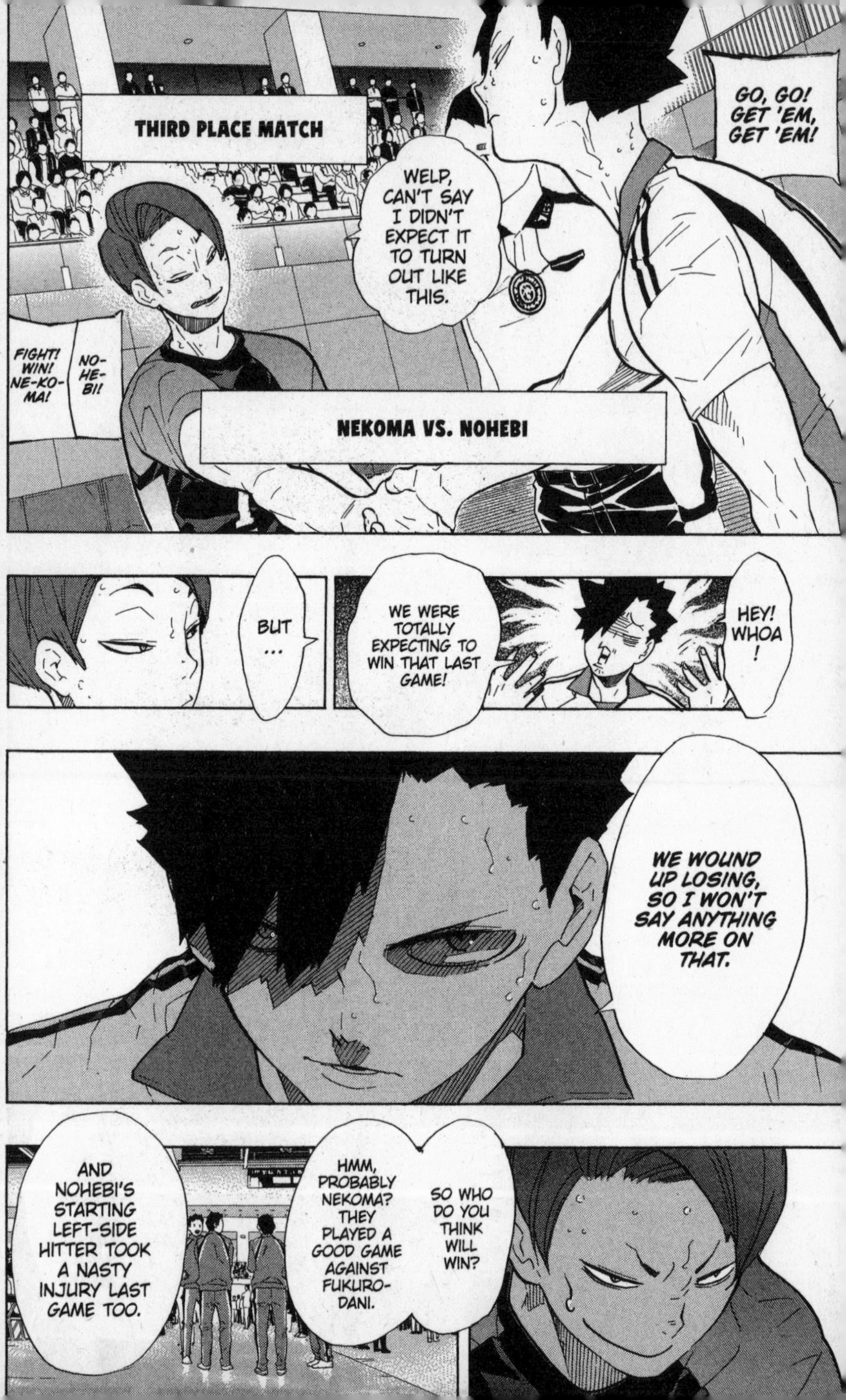
GO, GO! GET 'EM, GET 'EM!
THIRD PLACE MATCH
WELP, CAN'T SAY I DIDN'T EXPECT IT TO TURN OUT LIKE THIS.
NO-HE-BI!
FIGHT! WIN! NE-KO-MA!
NEKOMA VS. NOHEBI
HEY! WHOA!
WE WERE TOTALLY EXPECTING TO WIN THAT LAST GAME!
BUT...
WE WOUND UP LOSING, SO I WON'T SAY ANYTHING MORE ON THAT.
SO WHO DO YOU THINK WILL WIN?
HMM, PROBABLY NEKOMA? THEY PLAYED A GOOD GAME AGAINST FUKURO-DANI.
AND NOHEBI'S STARTING LEFT-SIDE HITTER TOOK A NASTY INJURY LAST GAME TOO.

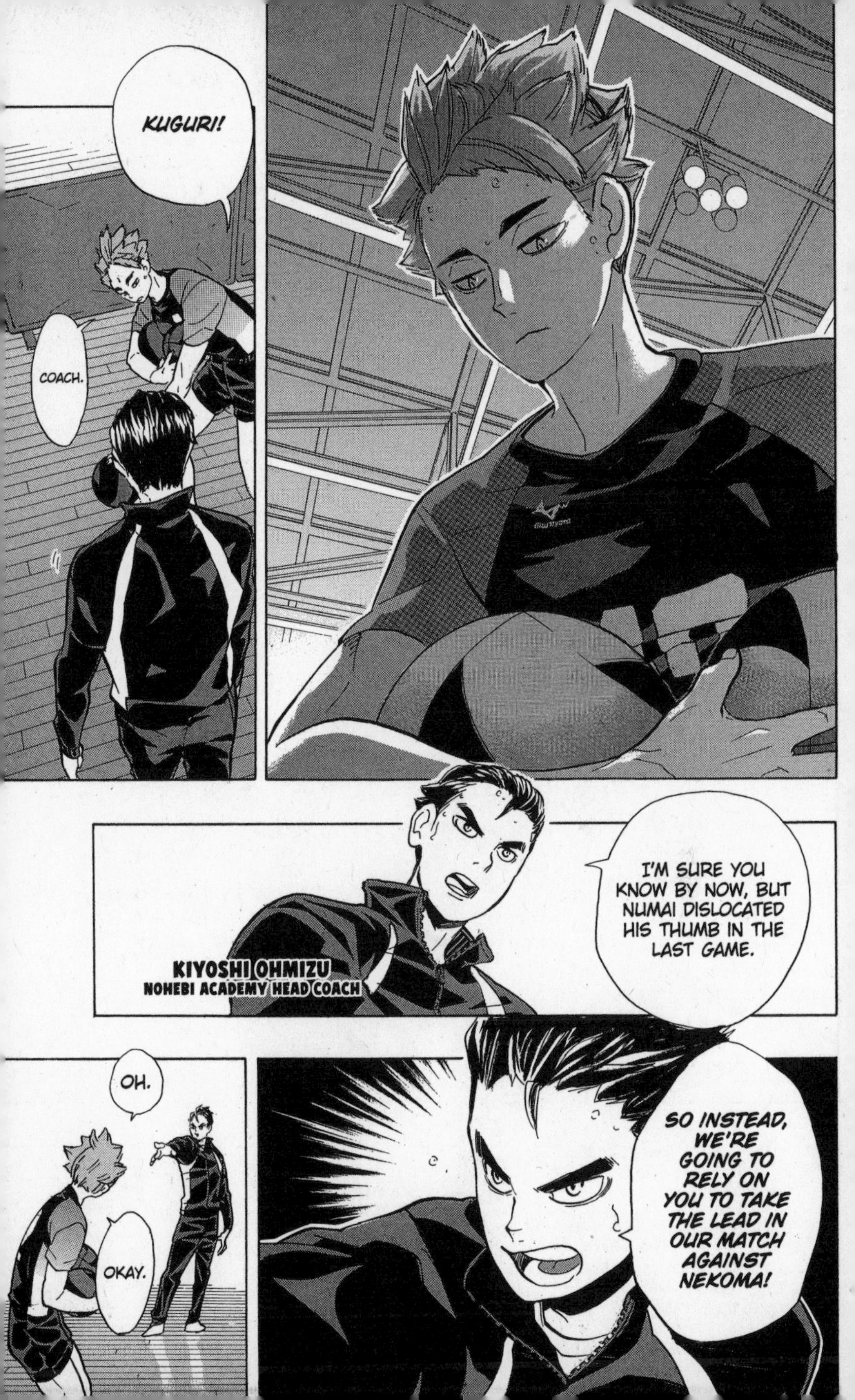
KUGURI!
COACH.
I'M SURE YOU KNOW BY NOW, BUT NUMAI DISLOCATED HIS THUMB IN THE LAST GAME.
KIYOSHI OHMIZU
NOHEBI ACADEMY HEAD COACH
SO INSTEAD, WE'RE GOING TO RELY ON YOU TO TAKE THE LEAD IN OUR MATCH AGAINST NEKOMA!
OH.
OKAY.

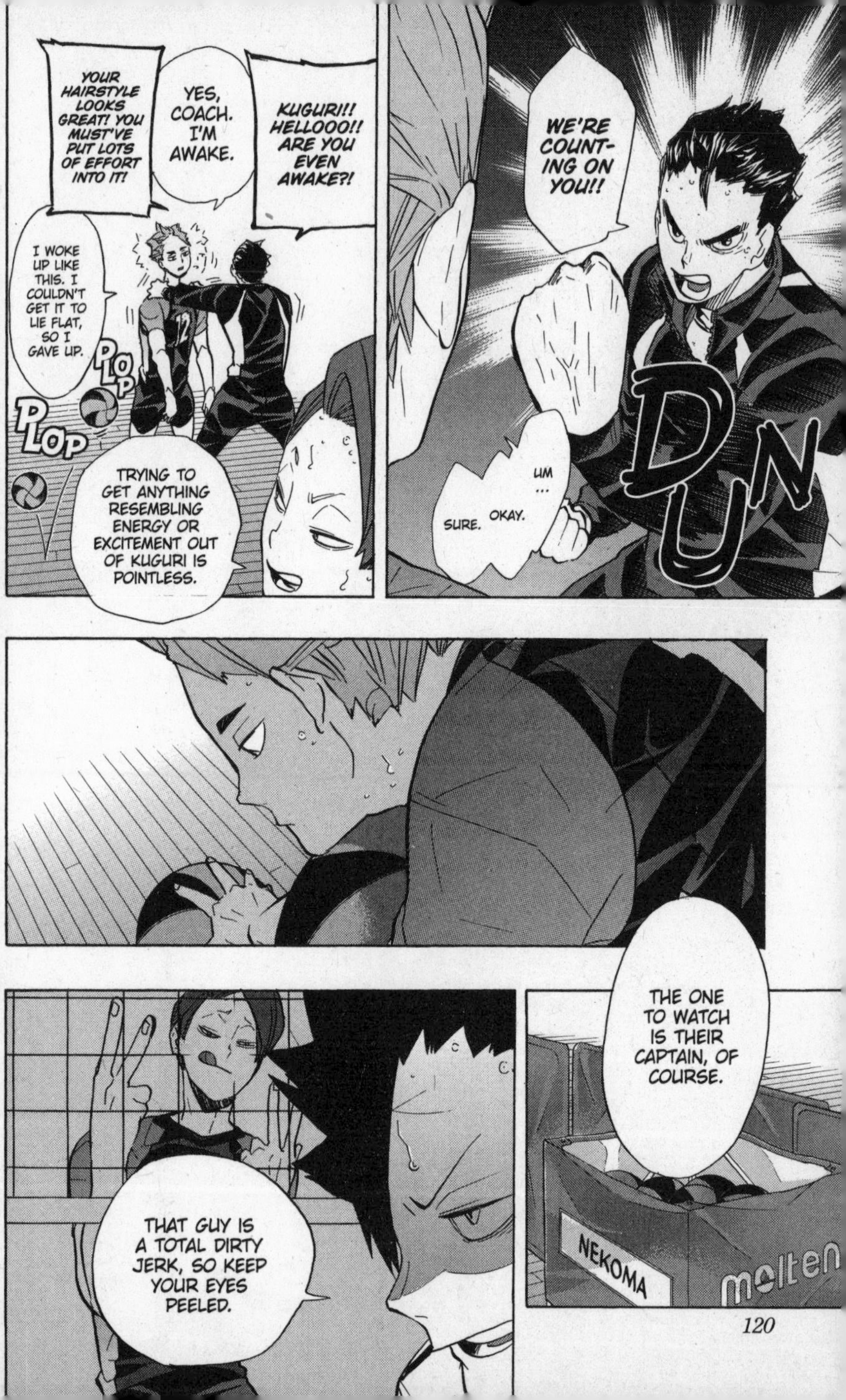
WE'RE COUNTING ON YOU!!
DUN
UM... SURE. OKAY.
KUGURI!! HELLOOO!! ARE YOU EVEN AWAKE?!
YES, COACH. I'M AWAKE.
YOUR HAIRSTYLE LOOKS GREAT! YOU MUST'VE PUT LOTS OF EFFORT INTO IT!
I WOKE UP LIKE THIS. I COULDN'T GET IT TO LIE FLAT, SO I GAVE UP.
PLOP
PLOP
TRYING TO GET ANYTHING RESEMBLING ENERGY OR EXCITEMENT OUT OF KUGURI IS POINTLESS.
THE ONE TO WATCH IS THEIR CAPTAIN, OF COURSE.
NEKOMA
molten
THAT GUY IS A TOTAL DIRTY JERK, SO KEEP YOUR EYES PEELED.

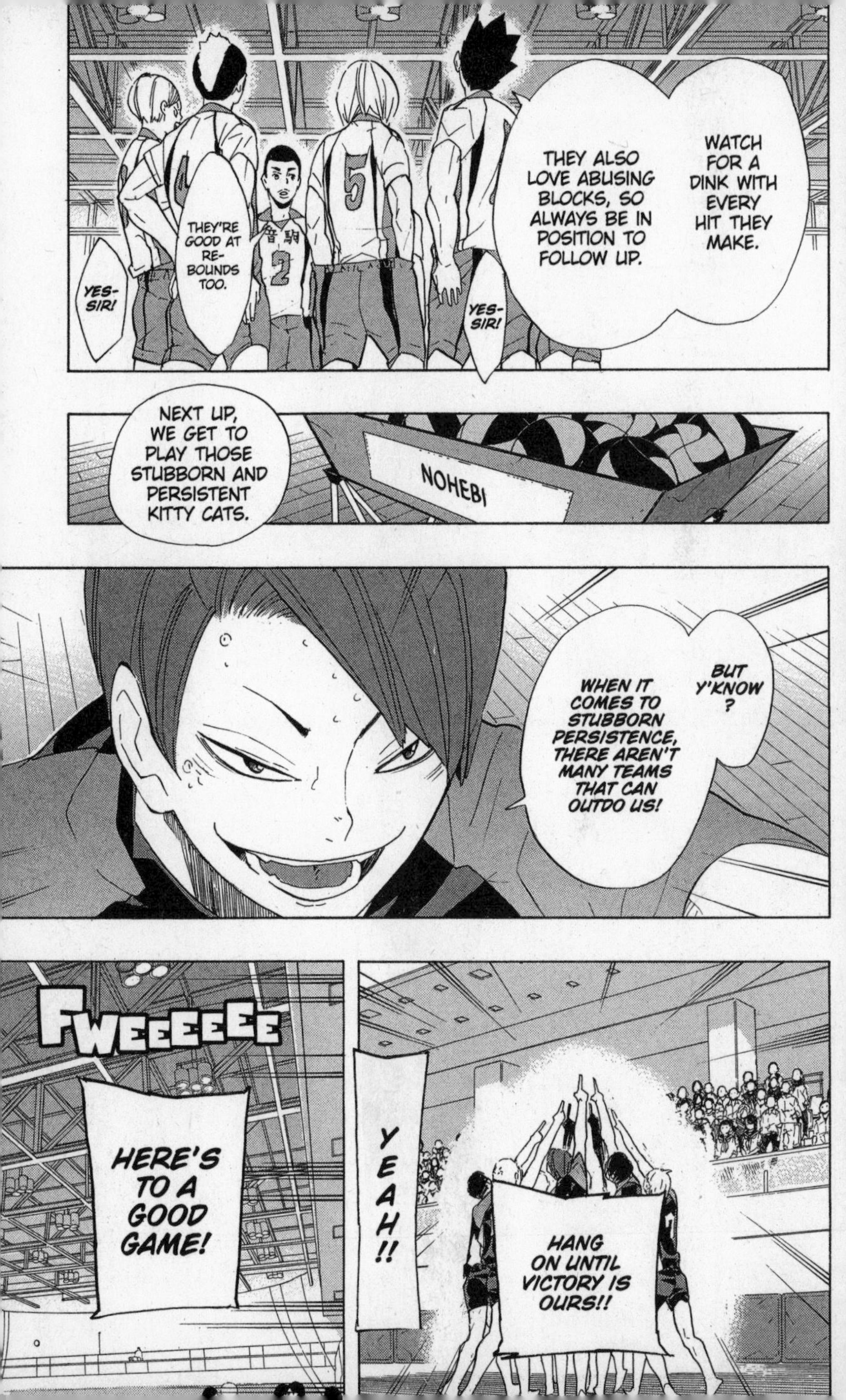
WATCH FOR A DINK WITH EVERY HIT THEY MAKE.
THEY ALSO LOVE ABUSING BLOCKS, SO ALWAYS BE IN POSITION TO FOLLOW UP.
YES-SIR!
THEY'RE GOOD AT RE-BOUNDS TOO.
YES-SIR!
NOHEBI
NEXT UP, WE GET TO PLAY THOSE STUBBORN AND PERSISTENT KITTY CATS.
BUT Y'KNOW?
WHEN IT COMES TO STUBBORN PERSISTENCE, THERE AREN'T MANY TEAMS THAT CAN OUTDO US!
HANG ON UNTIL VICTORY IS OURS!!
YEAH!!
FWEEEEEE
HERE'S TO A GOOD GAME!

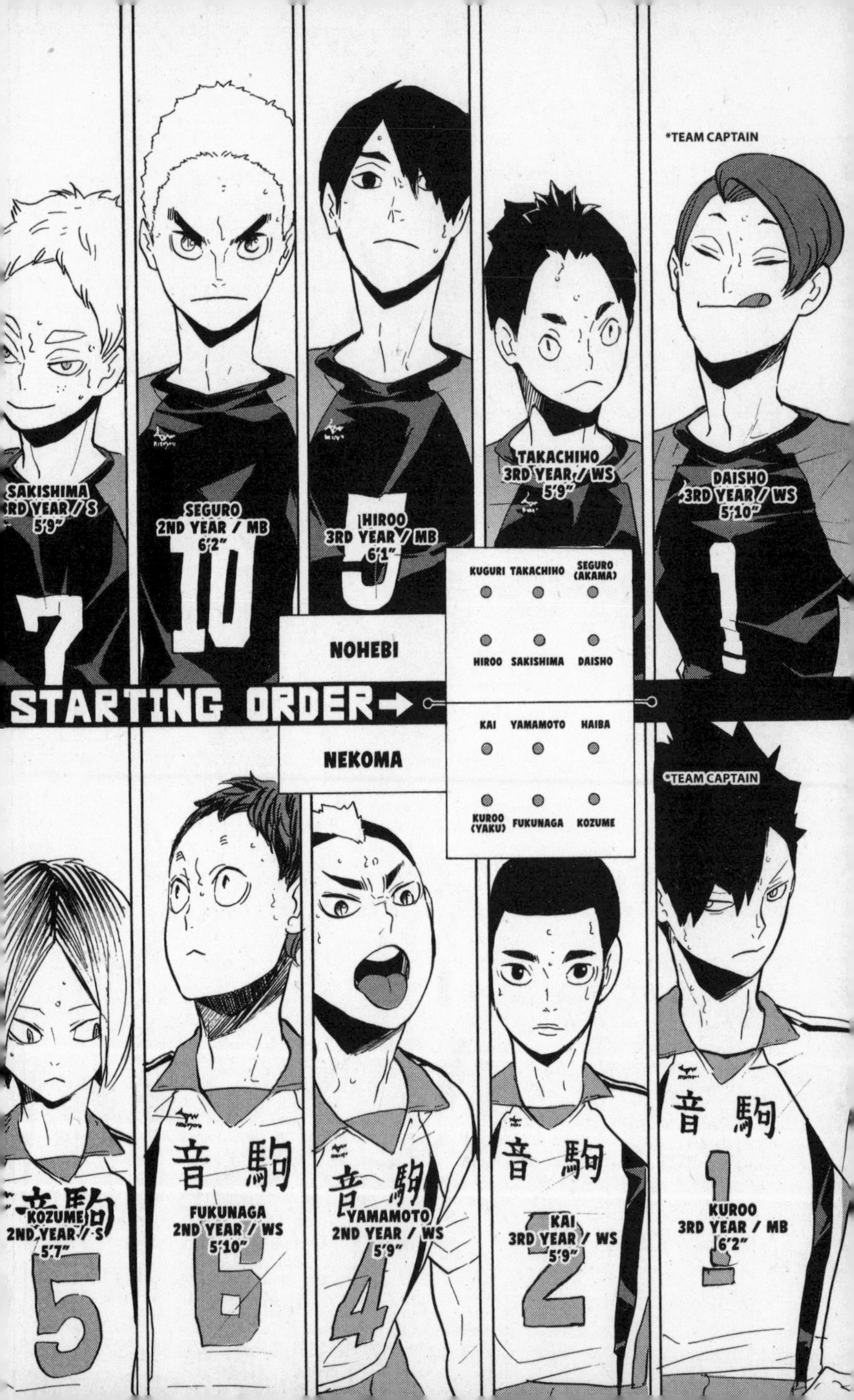
*TEAM CAPTAIN
DAISHO
3RD YEAR / WS
5'10"
TAKACHIHO
3RD YEAR / WS
5'9"
HIROO
3RD YEAR / MB
6'1"
SEGURO
2ND YEAR / MB
6'2"
SAKISHIMA
3RD YEAR / S
5'9"
STARTING ORDER→
NOHEBI
KUGURI TAKACHIHO SEGURO (AKAMA)
HIROO SAKISHIMA DAISHO
NEKOMA
KAI YAMAMOTO HAIBA
KUROO (YAKU) FUKUNAGA KOZUME
*TEAM CAPTAIN
音駒
KUROO
3RD YEAR / MB
6'2"
音駒
KAI
3RD YEAR / WS
5'9"
音駒
YAMAMOTO
2ND YEAR / WS
5'9"
音駒
FUKUNAGA
2ND YEAR / WS
5'10"
音駒
KOZUME
2ND YEAR / S
5'7"

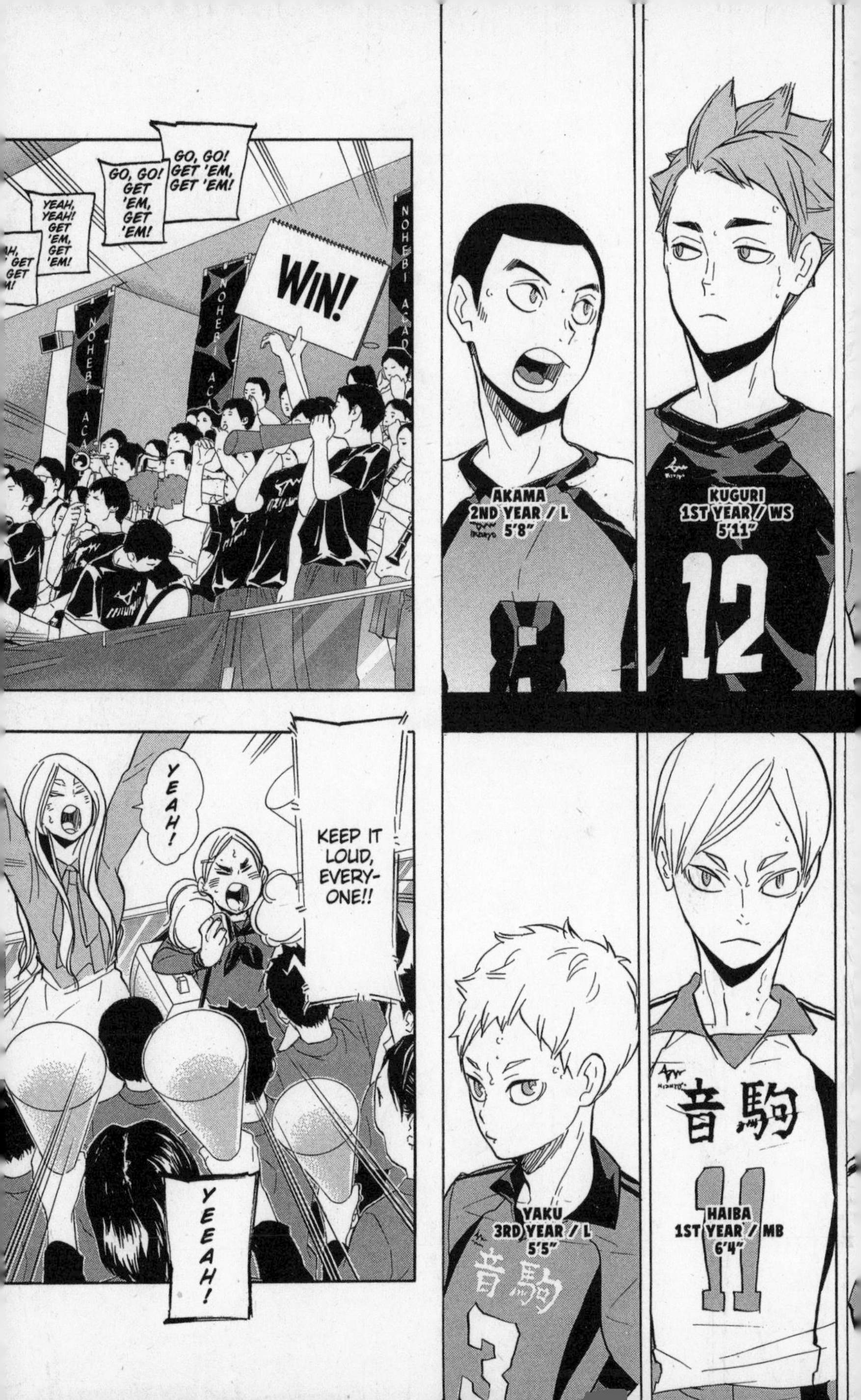
KUGURI
1ST YEAR / WS
5'11"
12
AKAMA
2ND YEAR / L
5'8"
GO, GO! GET 'EM, GET 'EM!
GO, GO! GET 'EM, GET 'EM!
WIN!
YEAH, YEAH! GET 'EM, GET 'EM!
NOHEBI ACAD
HAIBA
1ST YEAR / MB
6'4"
音駒
11
YAKU
3RD YEAR / L
5'5"
音駒
3
KEEP IT LOUD, EVERY-ONE!!
YEAH!
YEEEAH!

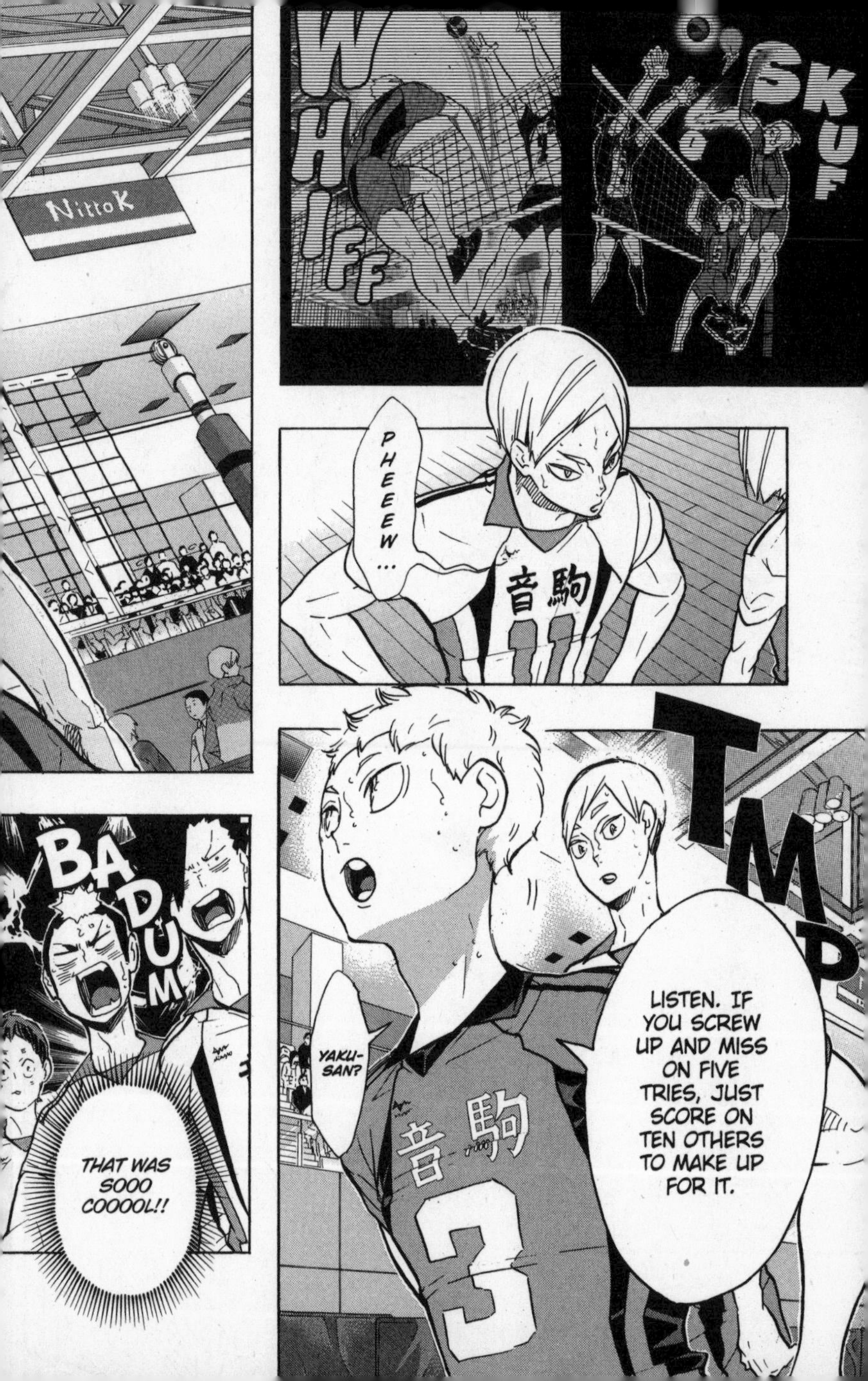
SKUF
WHIFF
PHEEEW...
NittoK
TMP
LISTEN. IF YOU SCREW UP AND MISS ON FIVE TRIES, JUST SCORE ON TEN OTHERS TO MAKE UP FOR IT.
YAKU-SAN?
BADUM
THAT WAS SOOO COOOOL!!

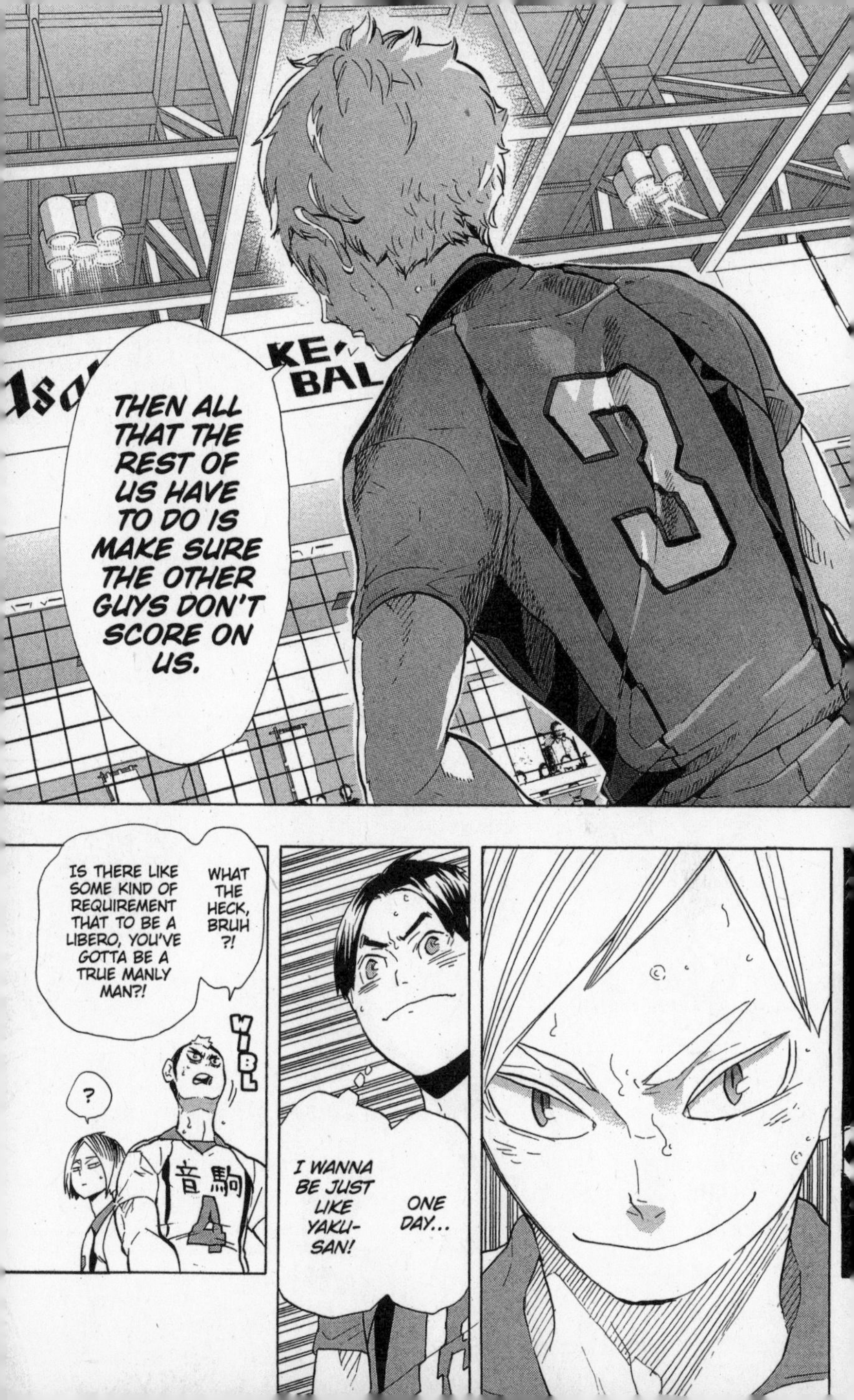
THEN ALL THAT THE REST OF US HAVE TO DO IS MAKE SURE THE OTHER GUYS DON'T SCORE ON US.
ONE DAY...
I WANNA BE JUST LIKE YAKU-SAN!
WHAT THE HECK, BRUH?!
IS THERE LIKE SOME KIND OF REQUIREMENT THAT TO BE A LIBERO, YOU'VE GOTTA BE A TRUE MANLY MAN?!
WIBL
?
音駒
4

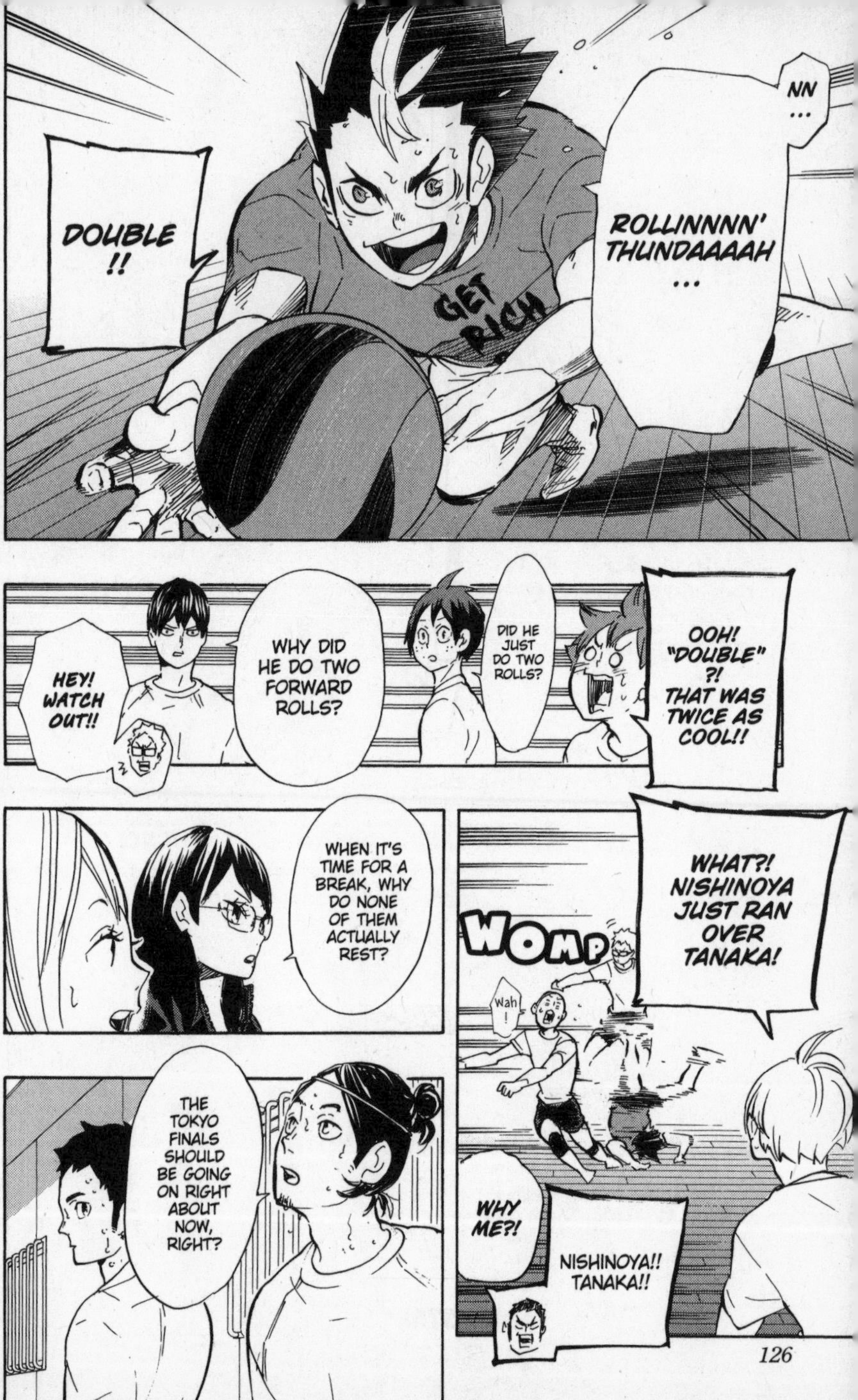
NN ...
ROLLINNNN' THUNDAAAAH ...
DOUBLE !!
OOH! "DOUBLE" ?! THAT WAS TWICE AS COOL!!
DID HE JUST DO TWO ROLLS?
WHY DID HE DO TWO FORWARD ROLLS?
HEY! WATCH OUT!!
WHAT?! NISHINOYA JUST RAN OVER TANAKA!
WOMP
Wah !
WHY ME?!
NISHINOYA!! TANAKA!!
WHEN IT'S TIME FOR A BREAK, WHY DO NONE OF THEM ACTUALLY REST?
THE TOKYO FINALS SHOULD BE GOING ON RIGHT ABOUT NOW, RIGHT?

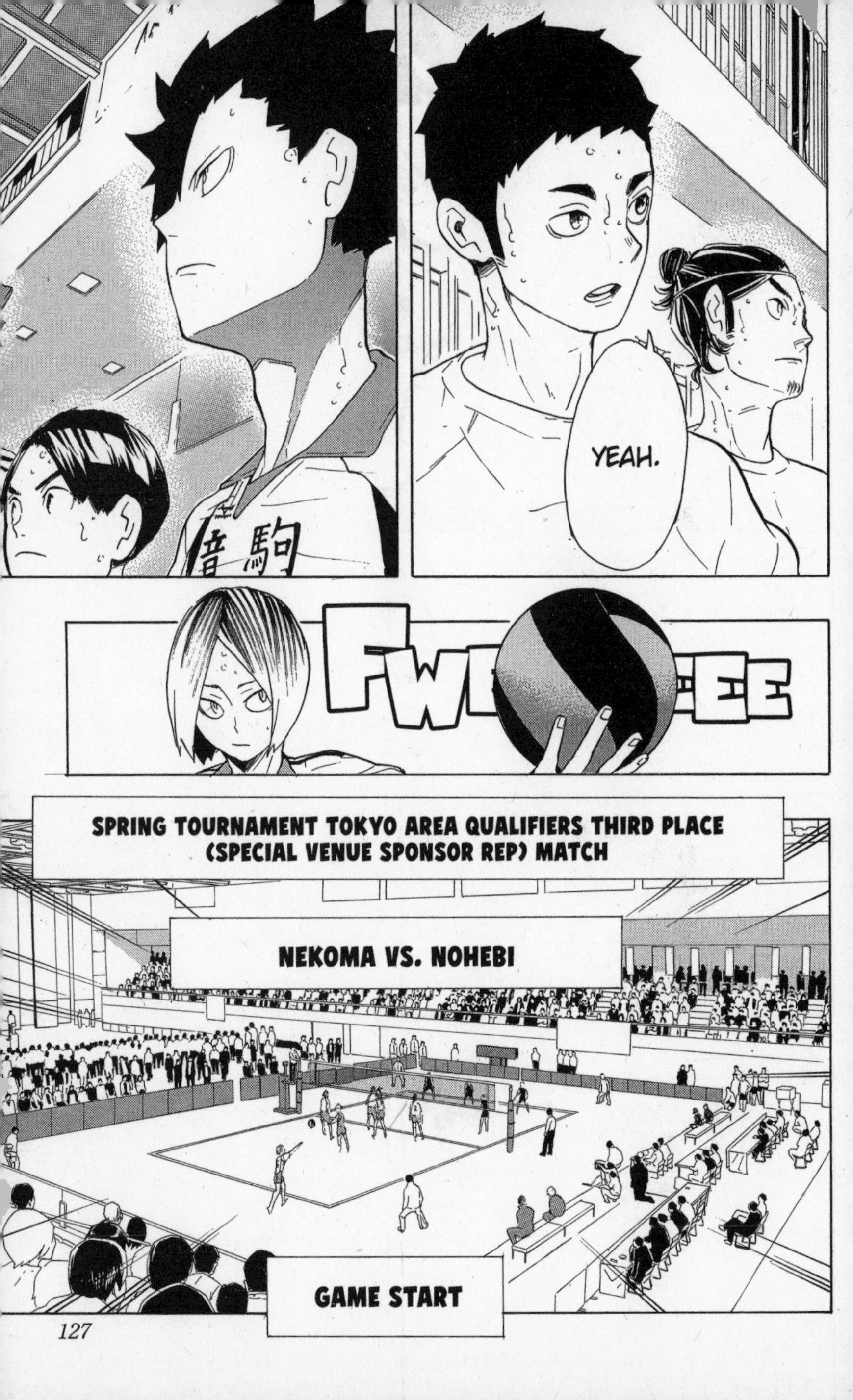
YEAH.
FW EEE
SPRING TOURNAMENT TOKYO AREA QUALIFIERS THIRD PLACE (SPECIAL VENUE SPONSOR REP) MATCH
NEKOMA VS. NOHEBI
GAME START

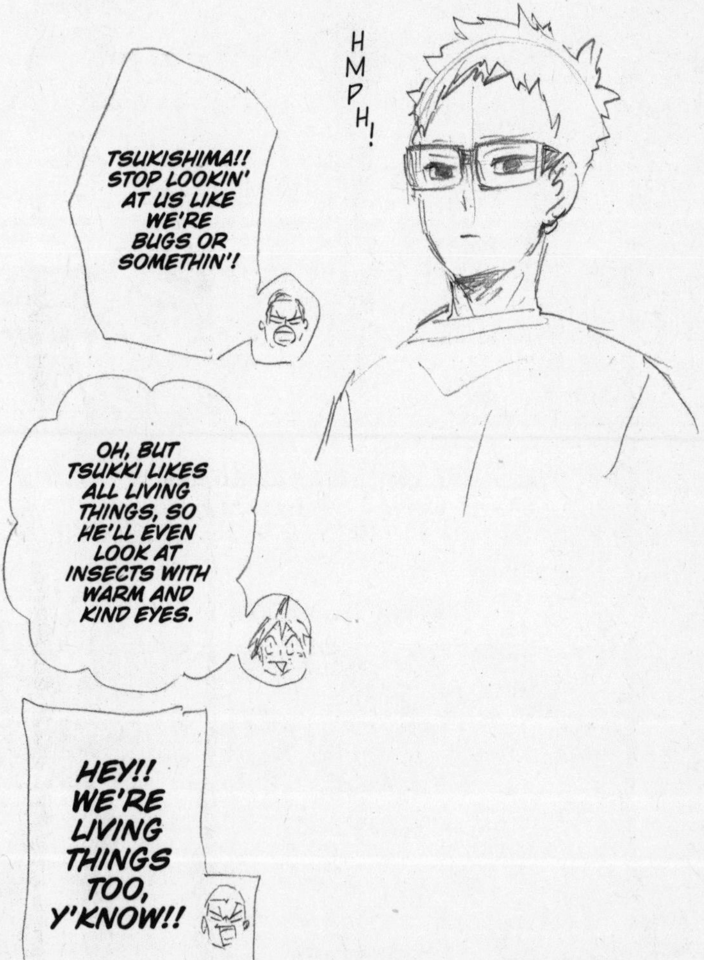
HMPH!
TSUKISHIMA!! STOP LOOKIN' AT US LIKE WE'RE BUGS OR SOMETHIN'!
OH, BUT TSUKKI LIKES ALL LIVING THINGS, SO HE'LL EVEN LOOK AT INSECTS WITH WARM AND KIND EYES.
HEY!! WE'RE LIVING THINGS TOO, Y'KNOW!!

CHAPTER 197: Snakes vs. Cats

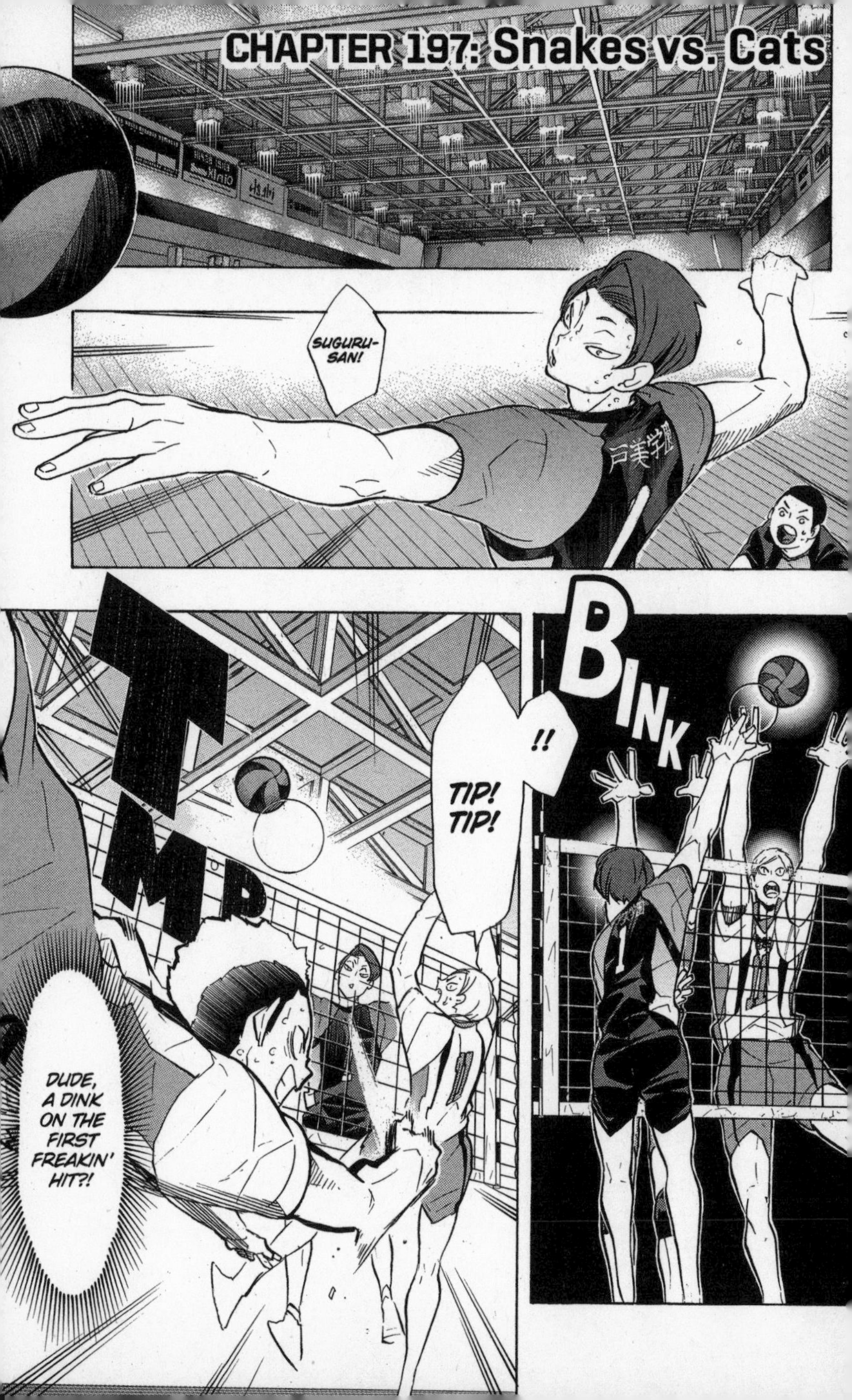
SUGURU-SAN!
BINK
!!
TIP! TIP!
TMP
DUDE, A DINK ON THE FIRST FREAKIN' HIT?!

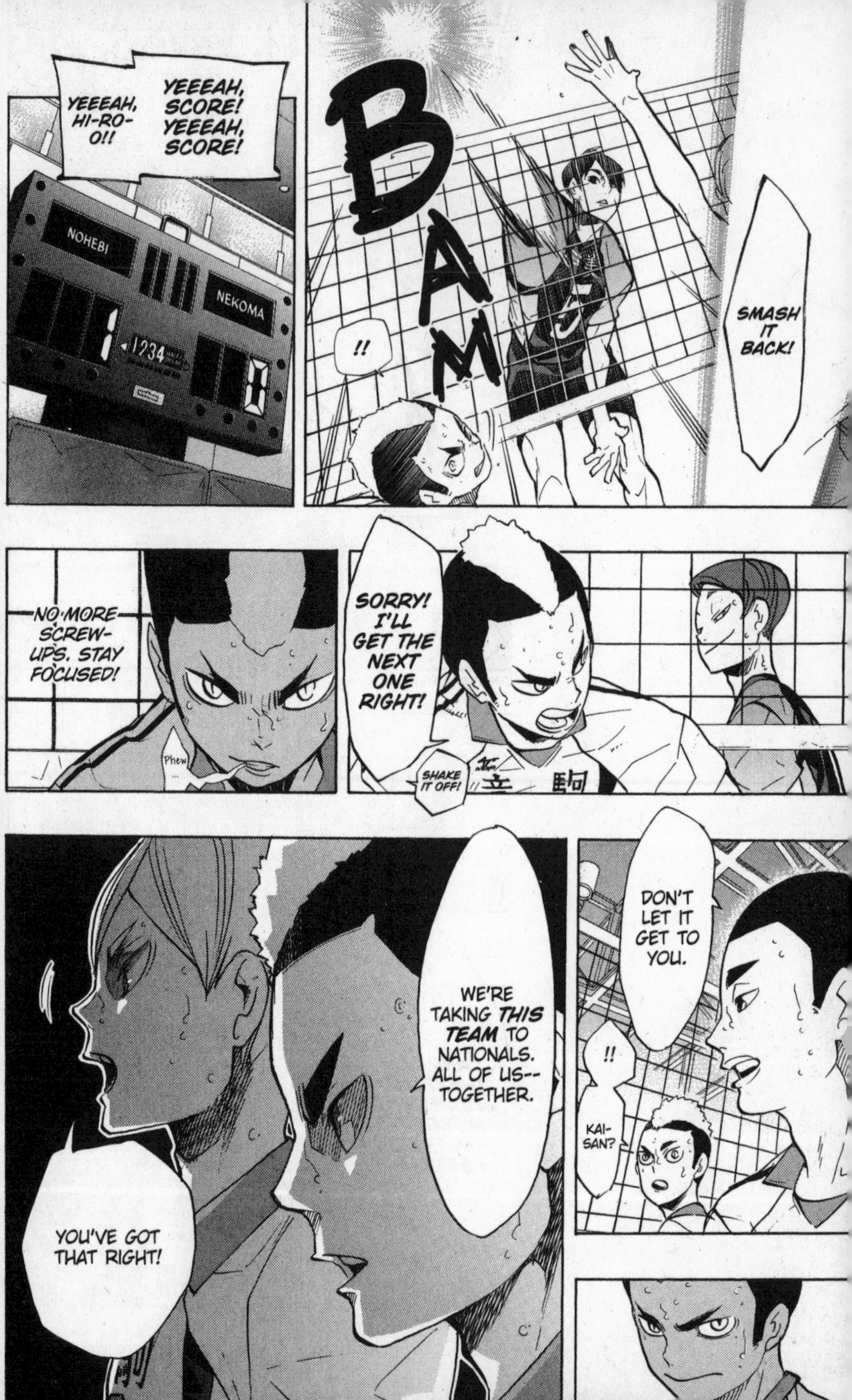
SMASH IT BACK!
BAM
!!
YEEEAH, SCORE! YEEEAH, SCORE!
YEEEAH, HI-RO-O!!
NOHEBI
NEKOMA
1234
SORRY! I'LL GET THE NEXT ONE RIGHT!
SHAKE IT OFF!
NO MORE SCREW-UPS. STAY FOCUSED!
Phew...
DON'T LET IT GET TO YOU.
!!
KAI-SAN?
WE'RE TAKING *THIS TEAM* TO NATIONALS. ALL OF US-- TOGETHER.
YOU'VE GOT THAT RIGHT!

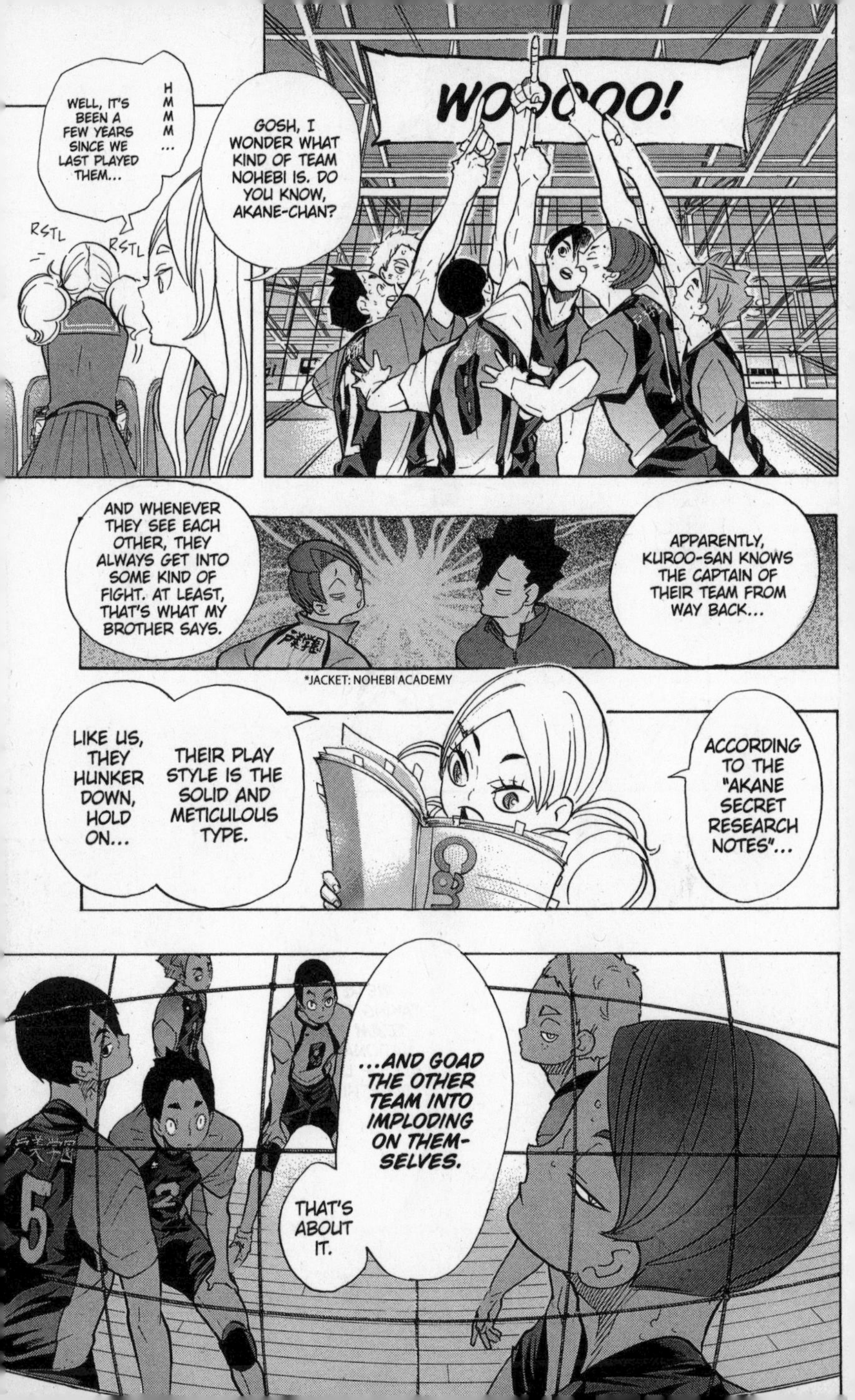
WOOOOO!
GOSH, I WONDER WHAT KIND OF TEAM NOHEBI IS. DO YOU KNOW, AKANE-CHAN?
HMMM...
WELL, IT'S BEEN A FEW YEARS SINCE WE LAST PLAYED THEM...
RSTL
RSTL
APPARENTLY, KUROO-SAN KNOWS THE CAPTAIN OF THEIR TEAM FROM WAY BACK...
AND WHENEVER THEY SEE EACH OTHER, THEY ALWAYS GET INTO SOME KIND OF FIGHT. AT LEAST, THAT'S WHAT MY BROTHER SAYS.
*JACKET: NOHEBI ACADEMY
ACCORDING TO THE "AKANE SECRET RESEARCH NOTES"...
THEIR PLAY STYLE IS THE SOLID AND METICULOUS TYPE.
LIKE US, THEY HUNKER DOWN, HOLD ON...
...AND GOAD THE OTHER TEAM INTO IMPLODING ON THEM-SELVES.
THAT'S ABOUT IT.

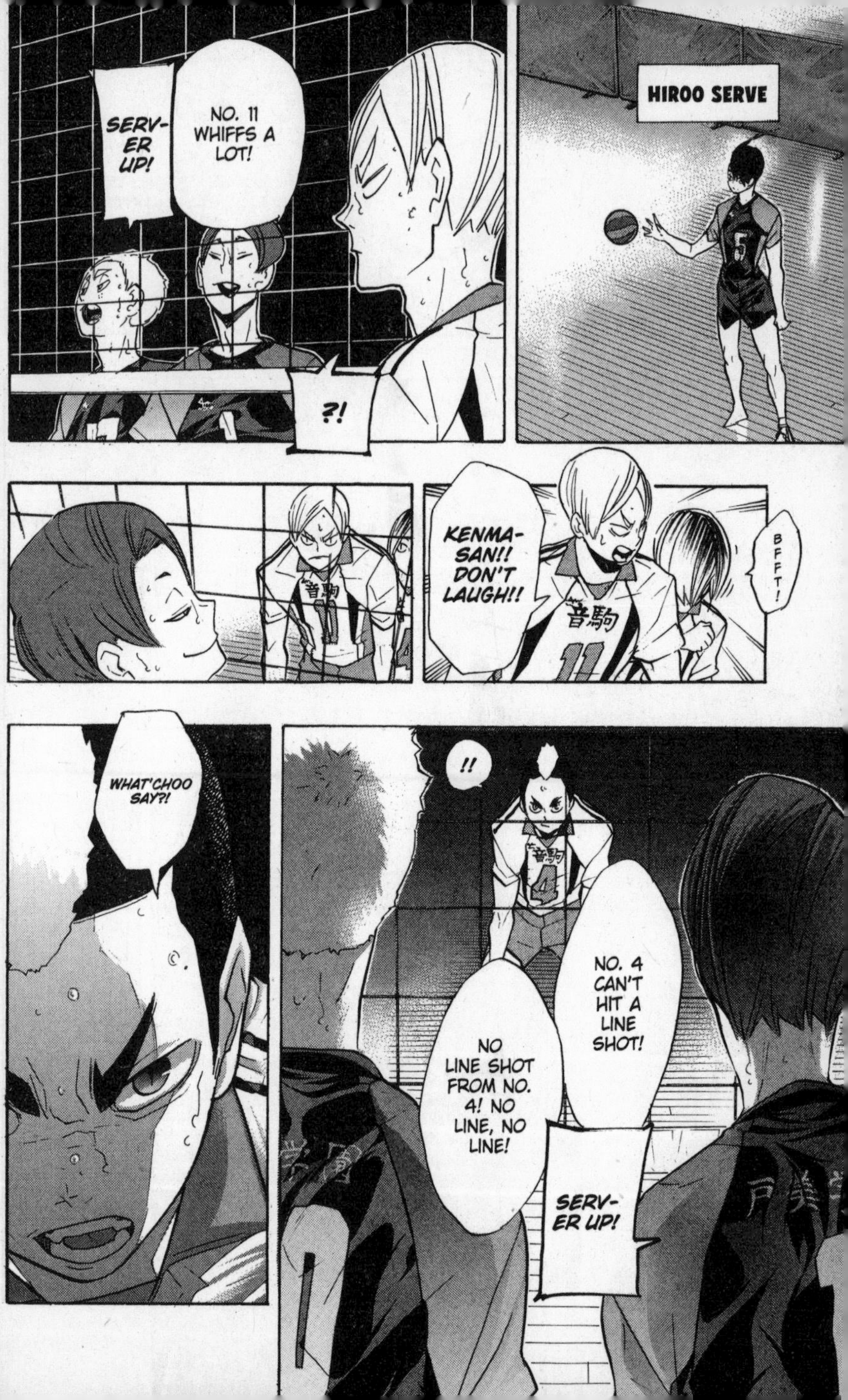
HIROO SERVE
NO. 11 WHIFFS A LOT!
SERV-ER UP!
?!
BFFT!
KENMA-SAN!! DON'T LAUGH!!
NO. 4 CAN'T HIT A LINE SHOT!
!!
NO LINE SHOT FROM NO. 4! NO LINE, NO LINE!
SERV-ER UP!
WHAT'CHOO SAY?!

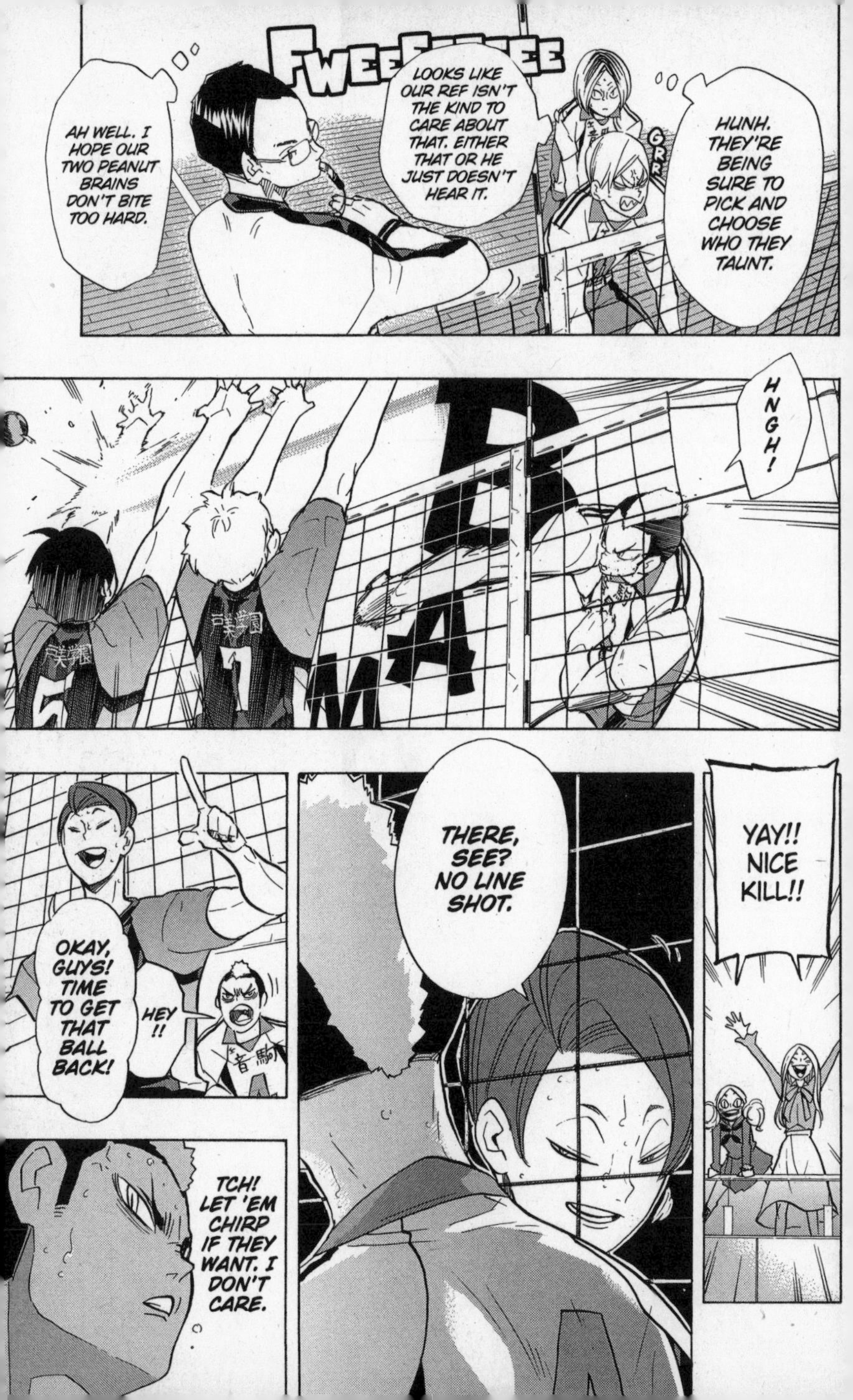

HUNH. THEY'RE BEING SURE TO PICK AND CHOOSE WHO THEY TAUNT.
GRR
FWEE
LOOKS LIKE OUR REF ISN'T THE KIND TO CARE ABOUT THAT. EITHER THAT OR HE JUST DOESN'T HEAR IT.
AH WELL. I HOPE OUR TWO PEANUT BRAINS DON'T BITE TOO HARD.
HNGH!
YAY!! NICE KILL!!
THERE, SEE? NO LINE SHOT.
OKAY, GUYS! TIME TO GET THAT BALL BACK!
HEY!!
TCH! LET 'EM CHIRP IF THEY WANT. I DON'T CARE.

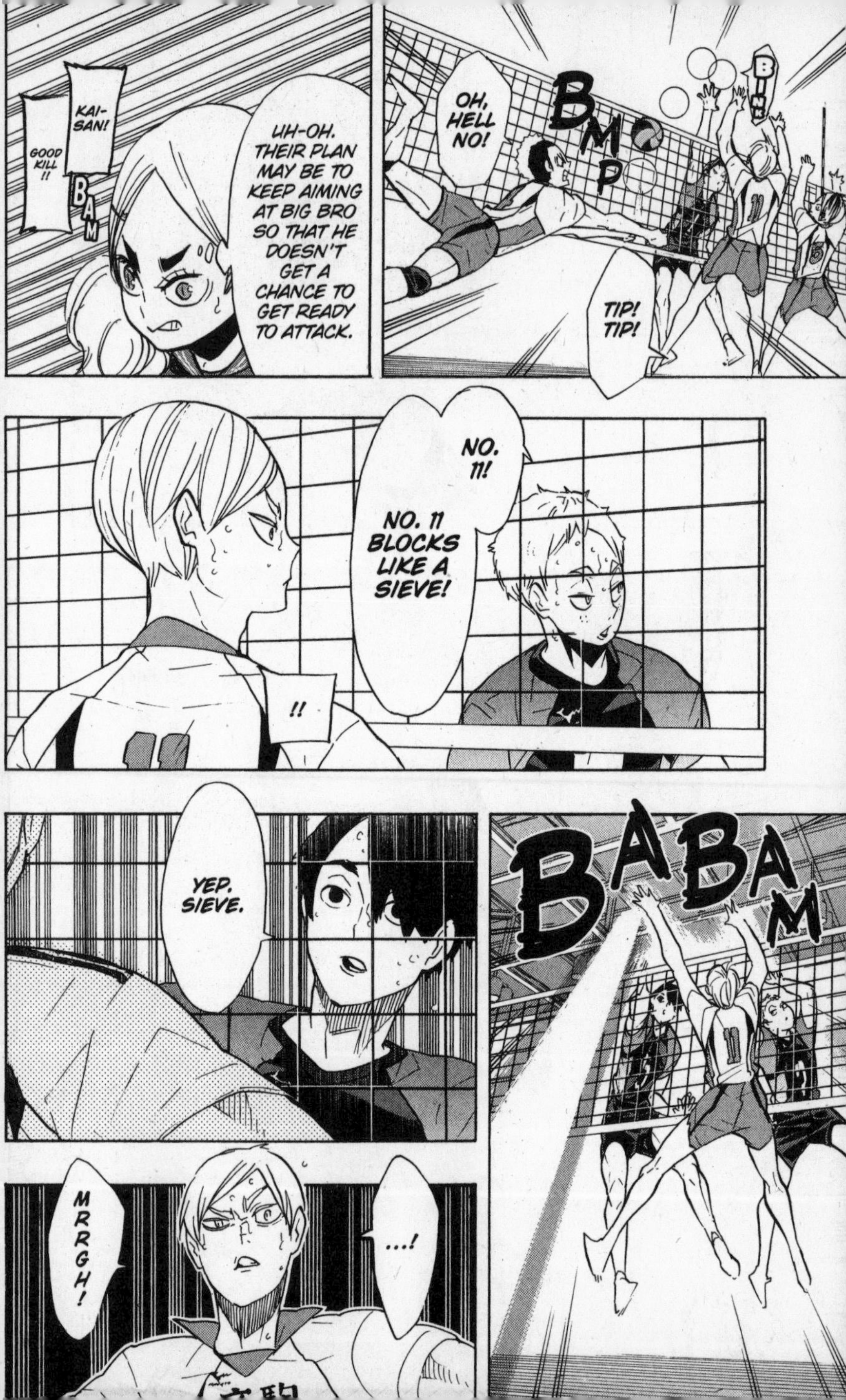
OH, HELL NO!
BMP
BINK
TIP! TIP!
UH-OH. THEIR PLAN MAY BE TO KEEP AIMING AT BIG BRO SO THAT HE DOESN'T GET A CHANCE TO GET READY TO ATTACK.
KAI-SAN!
GOOD KILL !!
BAM
NO. 11!
NO. 11 BLOCKS LIKE A SIEVE!
!!
BABAM
YEP. SIEVE.
...!
MRRGH!

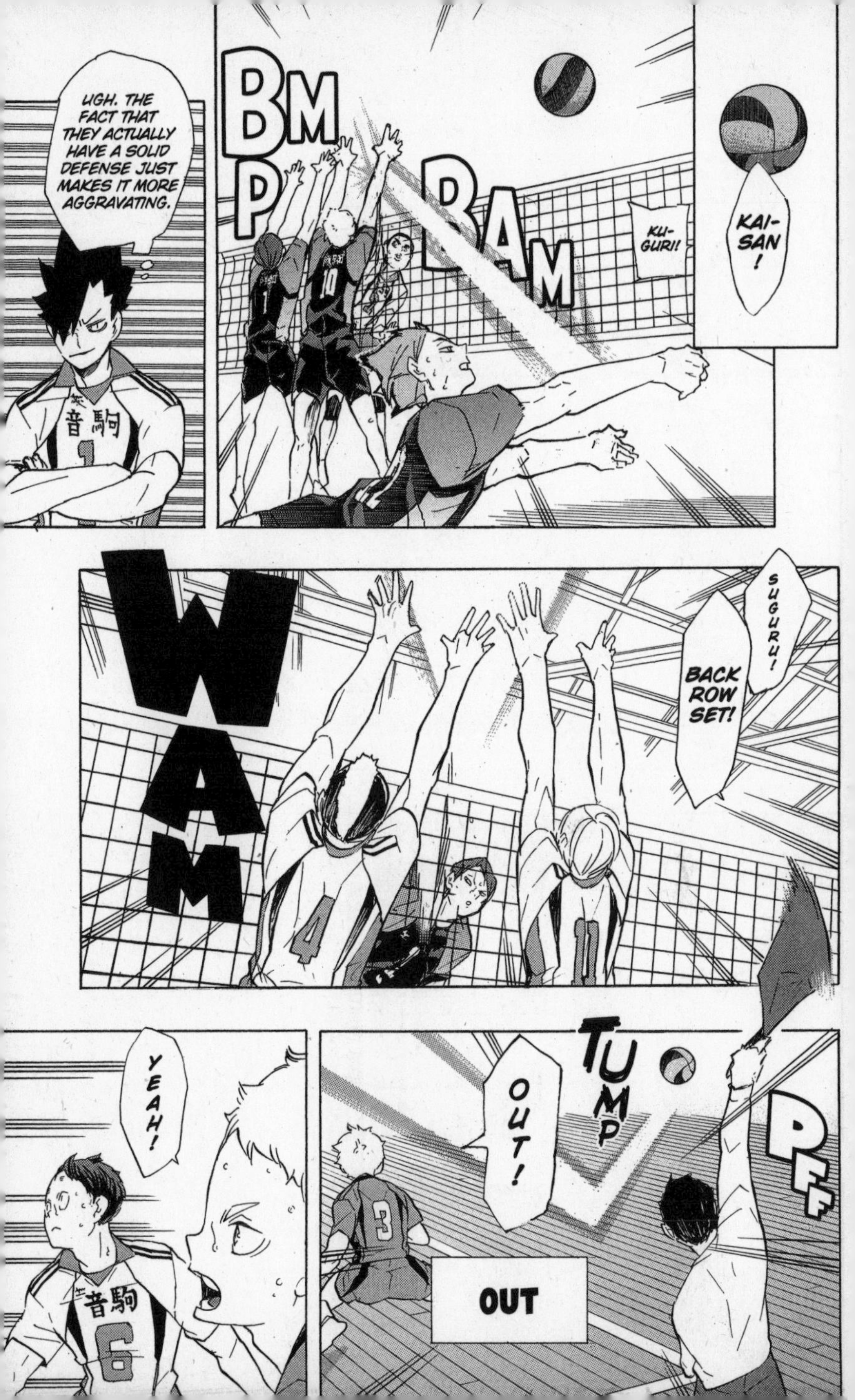
KAI-SAN!
KU-GURI!
BMP
BAM
UGH. THE FACT THAT THEY ACTUALLY HAVE A SOLID DEFENSE JUST MAKES IT MORE AGGRAVATING.
SUGURU!
BACK ROW SET!
WAM
PFF
TUMP
OUT!
OUT
YEAH!

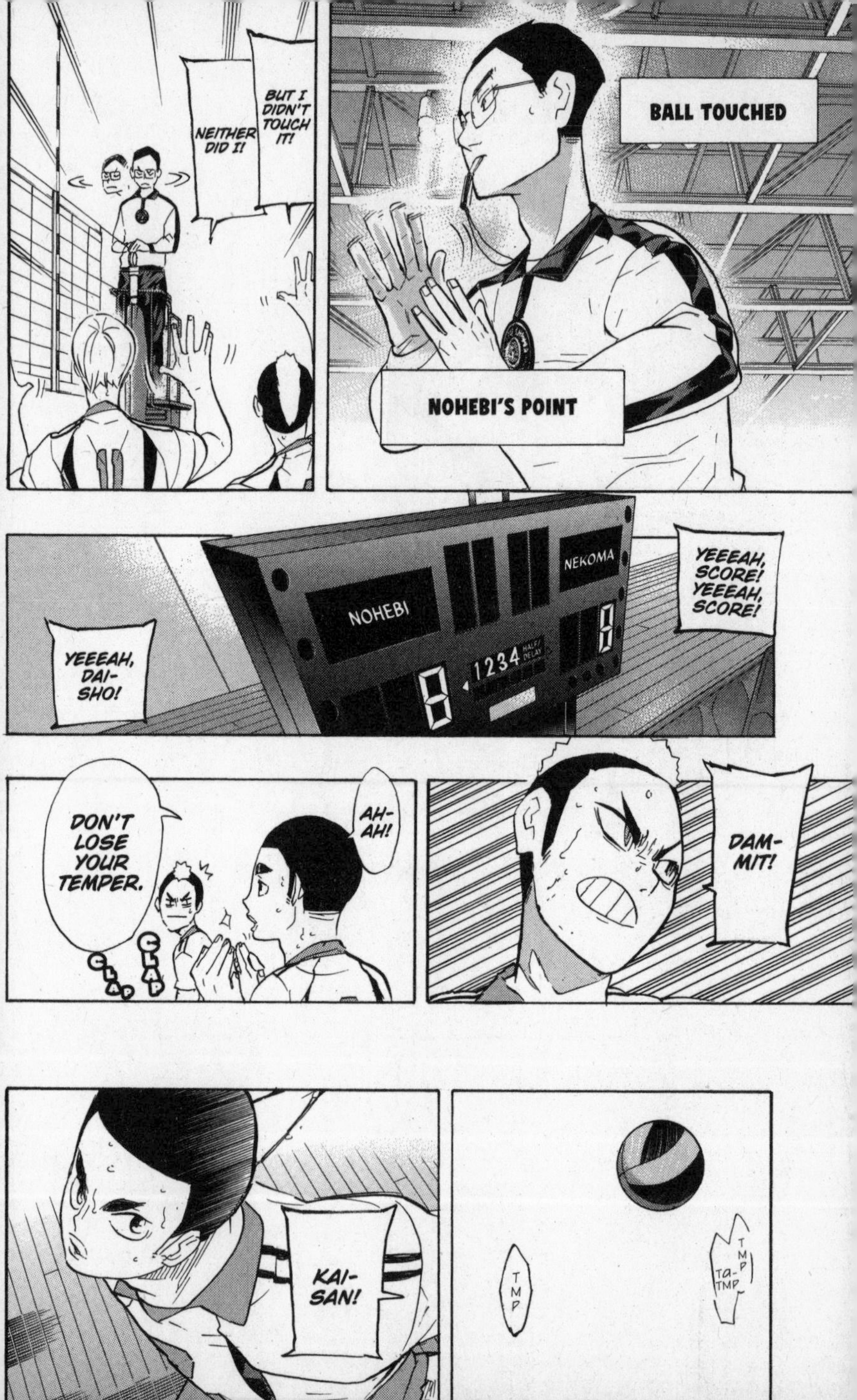
BALL TOUCHED
NOHEBI'S POINT
BUT I DIDN'T TOUCH IT!
NEITHER DID I!
YEEEAH, SCORE! YEEEAH, SCORE!
NEKOMA
NOHEBI
1234 HALF/DELAY
YEEEAH, DAI-SHO!
DAM-MIT!
AH-AH!
DON'T LOSE YOUR TEMPER.
CLAP
CLAP
Ta-TMP TMP
TMP
KAI-SAN!

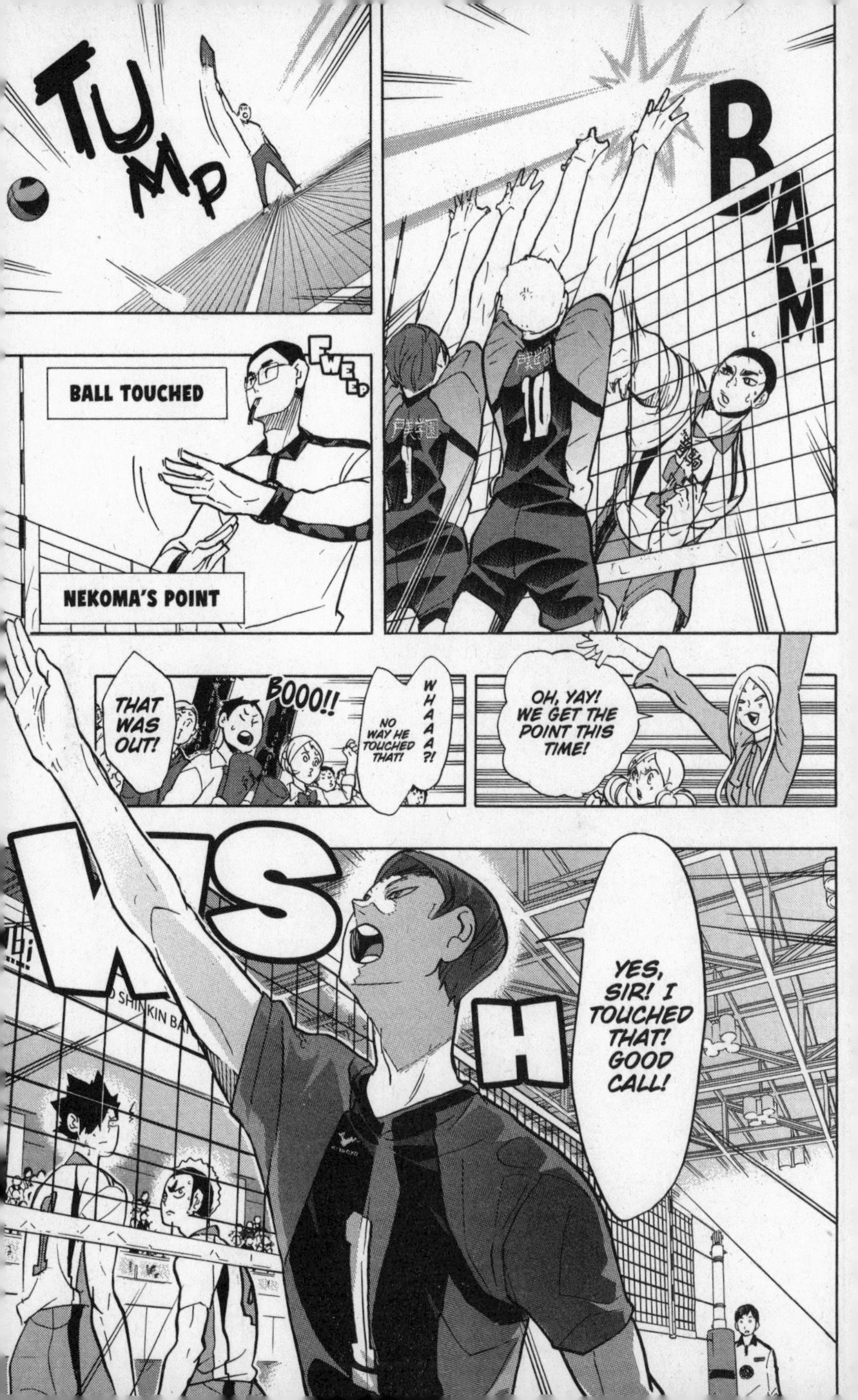
BAM
TUMP
FWEEP
BALL TOUCHED
NEKOMA'S POINT
OH, YAY! WE GET THE POINT THIS TIME!
WHAAAA?!
NO WAY HE TOUCHED THAT!
BOOO!!
THAT WAS OUT!
YES, SIR! I TOUCHED THAT! GOOD CALL!
WSH

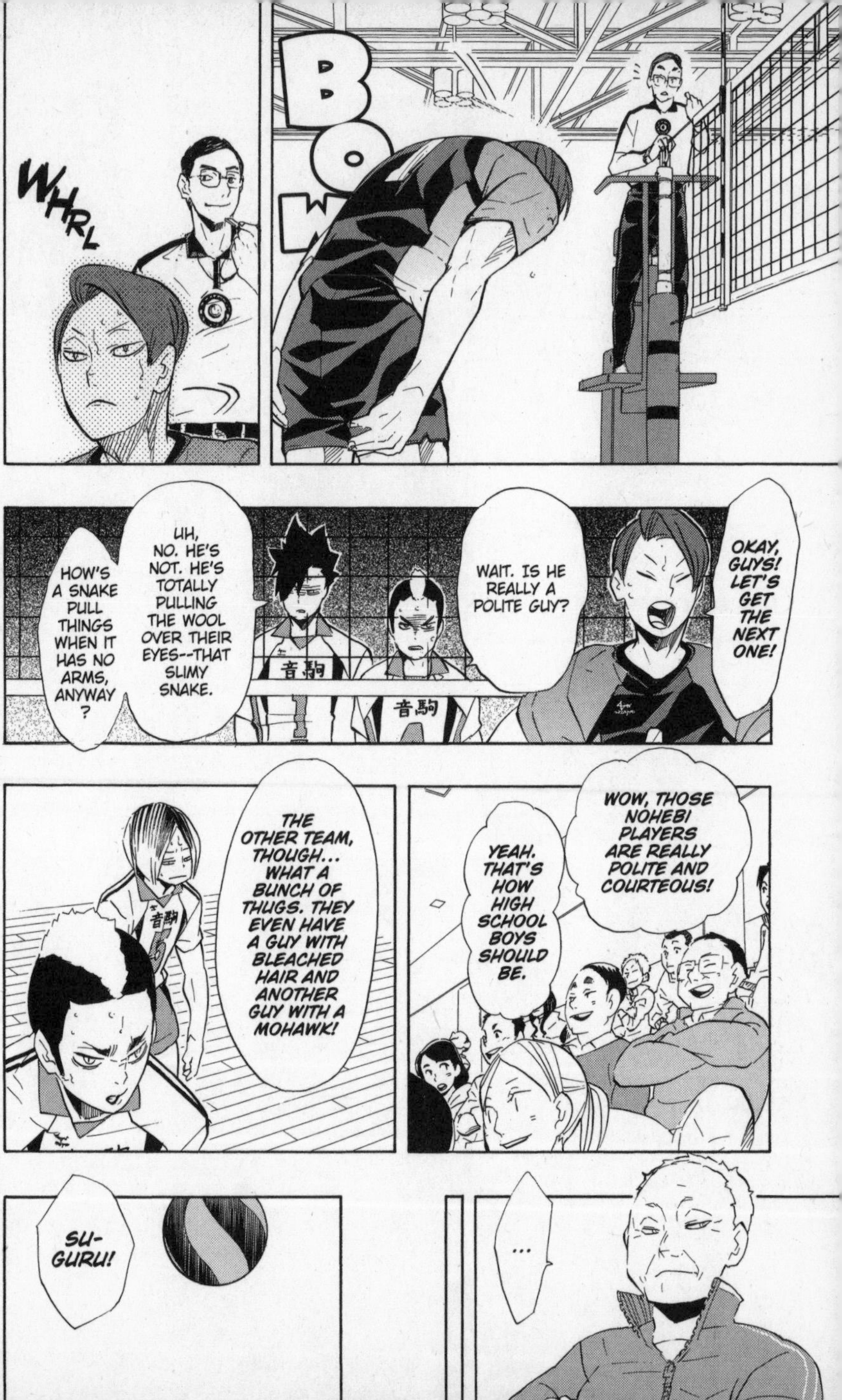
BOW
WHRL
OKAY, GUYS! LET'S GET THE NEXT ONE!
WAIT. IS HE REALLY A POLITE GUY?
UH, NO. HE'S NOT. HE'S TOTALLY PULLING THE WOOL OVER THEIR EYES--THAT SLIMY SNAKE.
HOW'S A SNAKE PULL THINGS WHEN IT HAS NO ARMS, ANYWAY?
音駒
WOW, THOSE NOHEBI PLAYERS ARE REALLY POLITE AND COURTEOUS!
YEAH. THAT'S HOW HIGH SCHOOL BOYS SHOULD BE.
THE OTHER TEAM, THOUGH... WHAT A BUNCH OF THUGS. THEY EVEN HAVE A GUY WITH BLEACHED HAIR AND ANOTHER GUY WITH A MOHAWK!
...
SU-GURU!

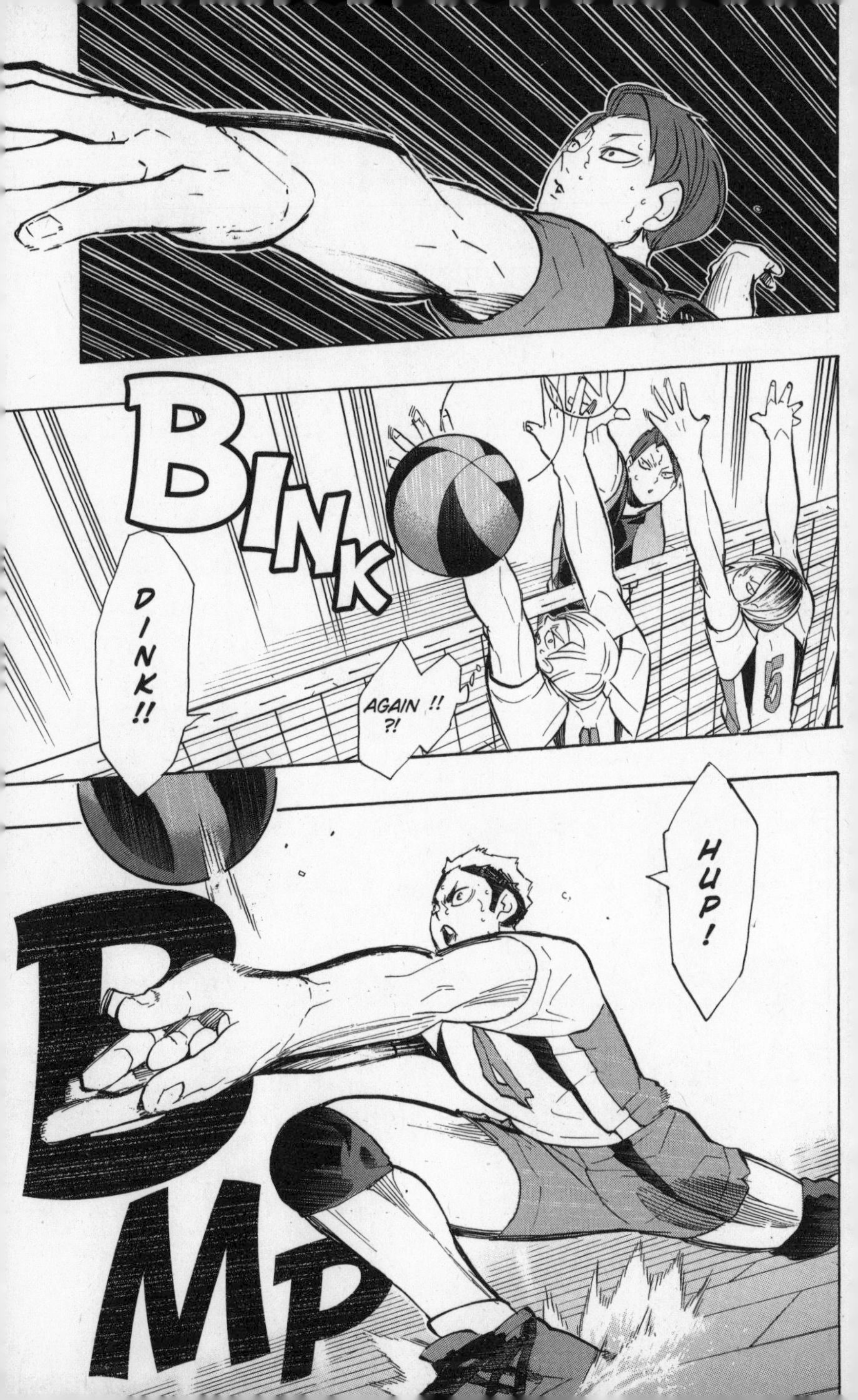
BINK
AGAIN!! ?!
DINK!!
HUP!
BUMP

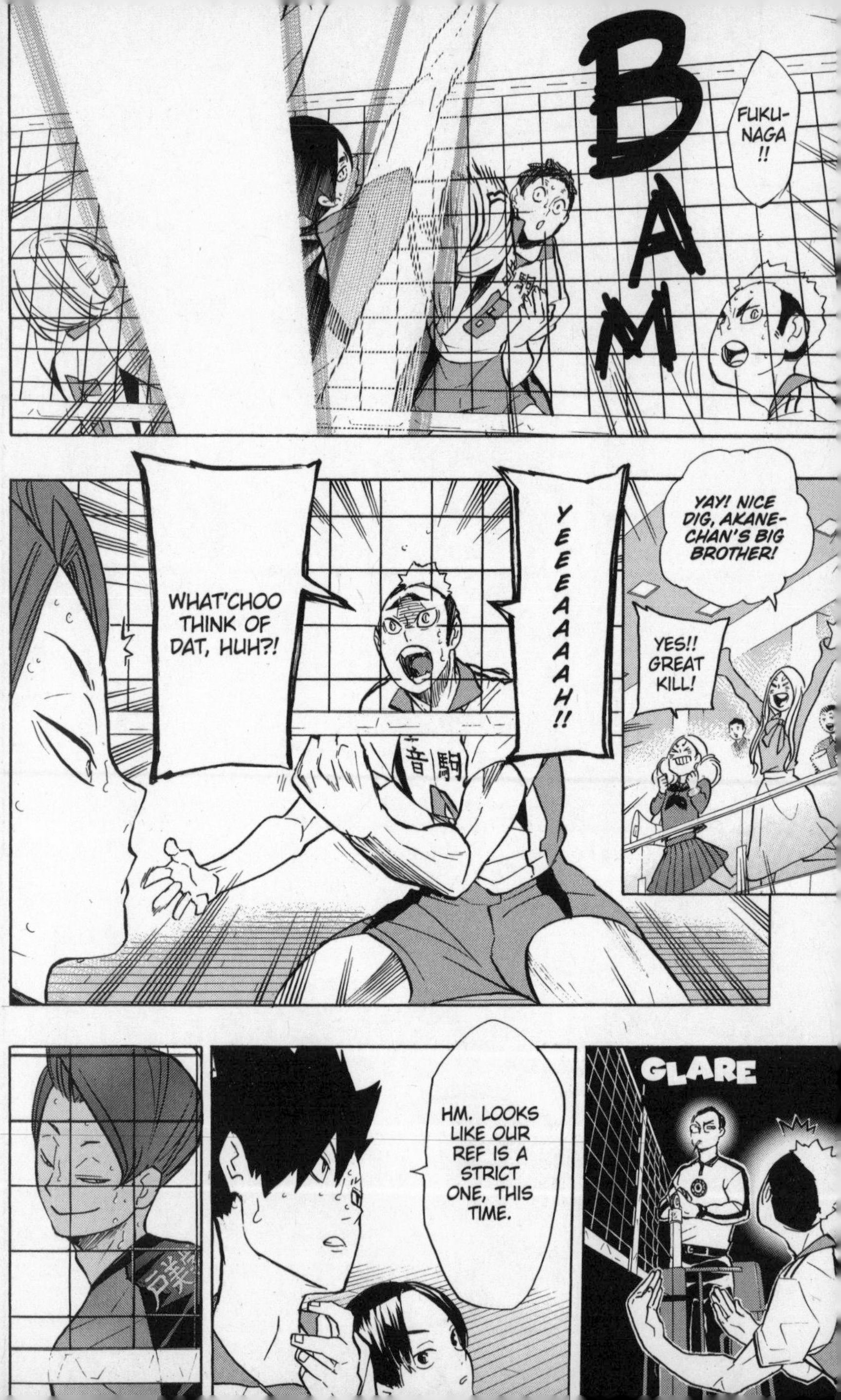
FUKU-NAGA!!
BAM
YAY! NICE DIG, AKANE-CHAN'S BIG BROTHER!
YES!! GREAT KILL!
YEEEAAAAAH!!
WHAT'CHOO THINK OF DAT, HUH?!
GLARE
HM. LOOKS LIKE OUR REF IS A STRICT ONE, THIS TIME.

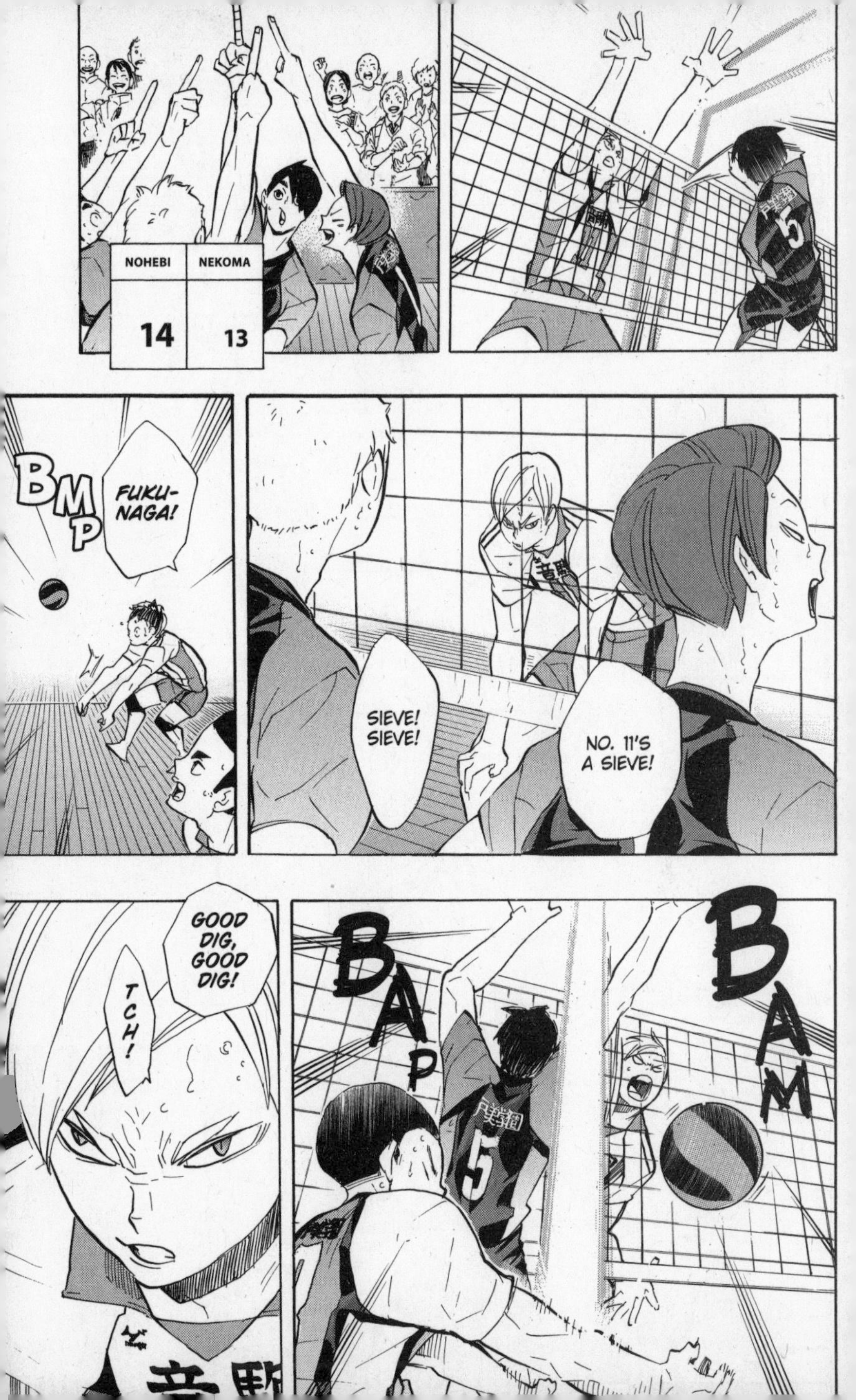
NOHEBI
NEKOMA
14
13
NO. 11'S A SIEVE!
SIEVE! SIEVE!
FUKU-NAGA!
BMP
BAM
BAP
GOOD DIG, GOOD DIG!
TCH!

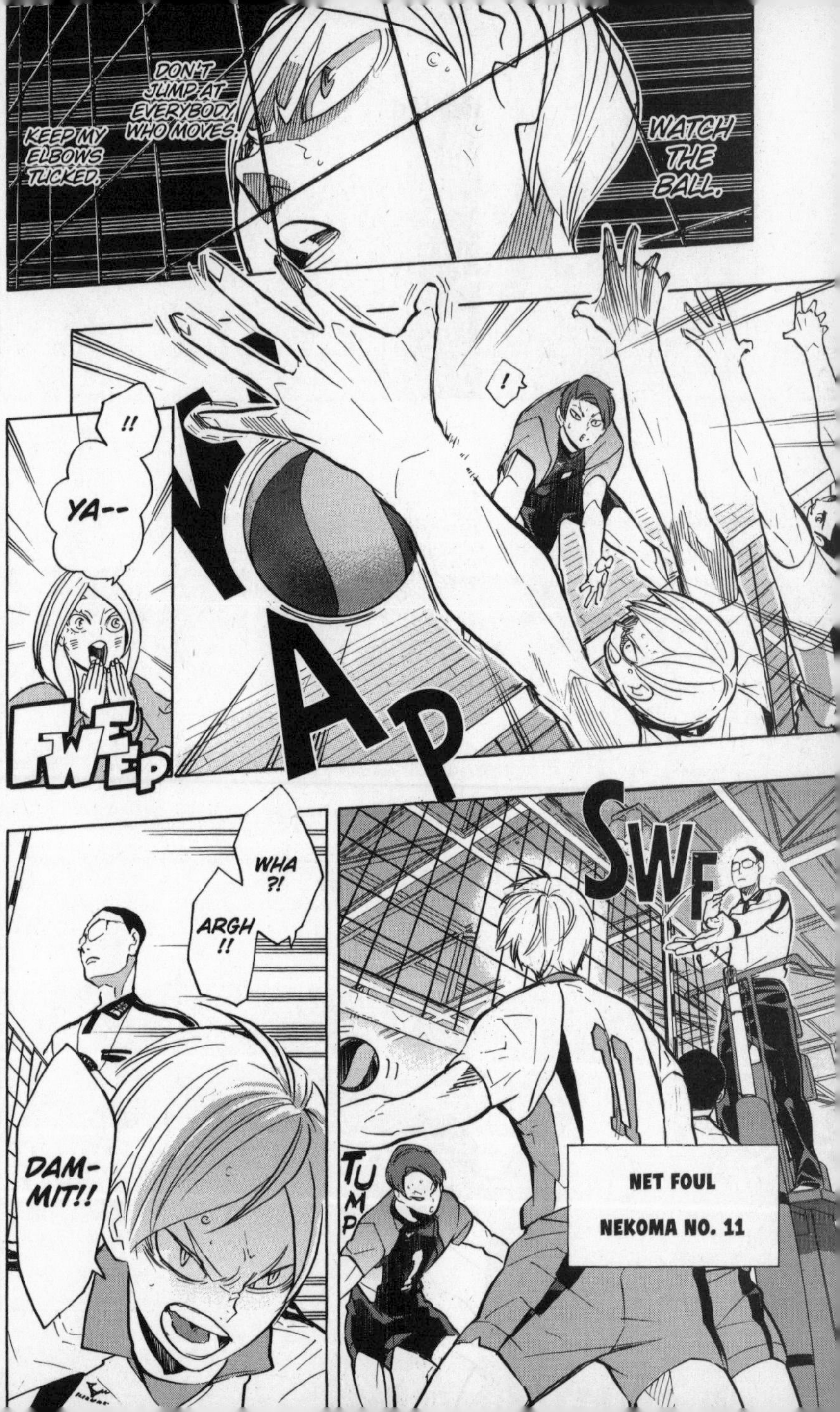
WATCH THE BALL.
DON'T JUMP AT EVERYBODY WHO MOVES.
KEEP MY ELBOWS TUCKED.
!
NYAP
!!
YA--
FWEEP
SWF
NET FOUL
NEKOMA NO. 11
TUMP
WHA ?!
ARGH !!
DAM-MIT!!

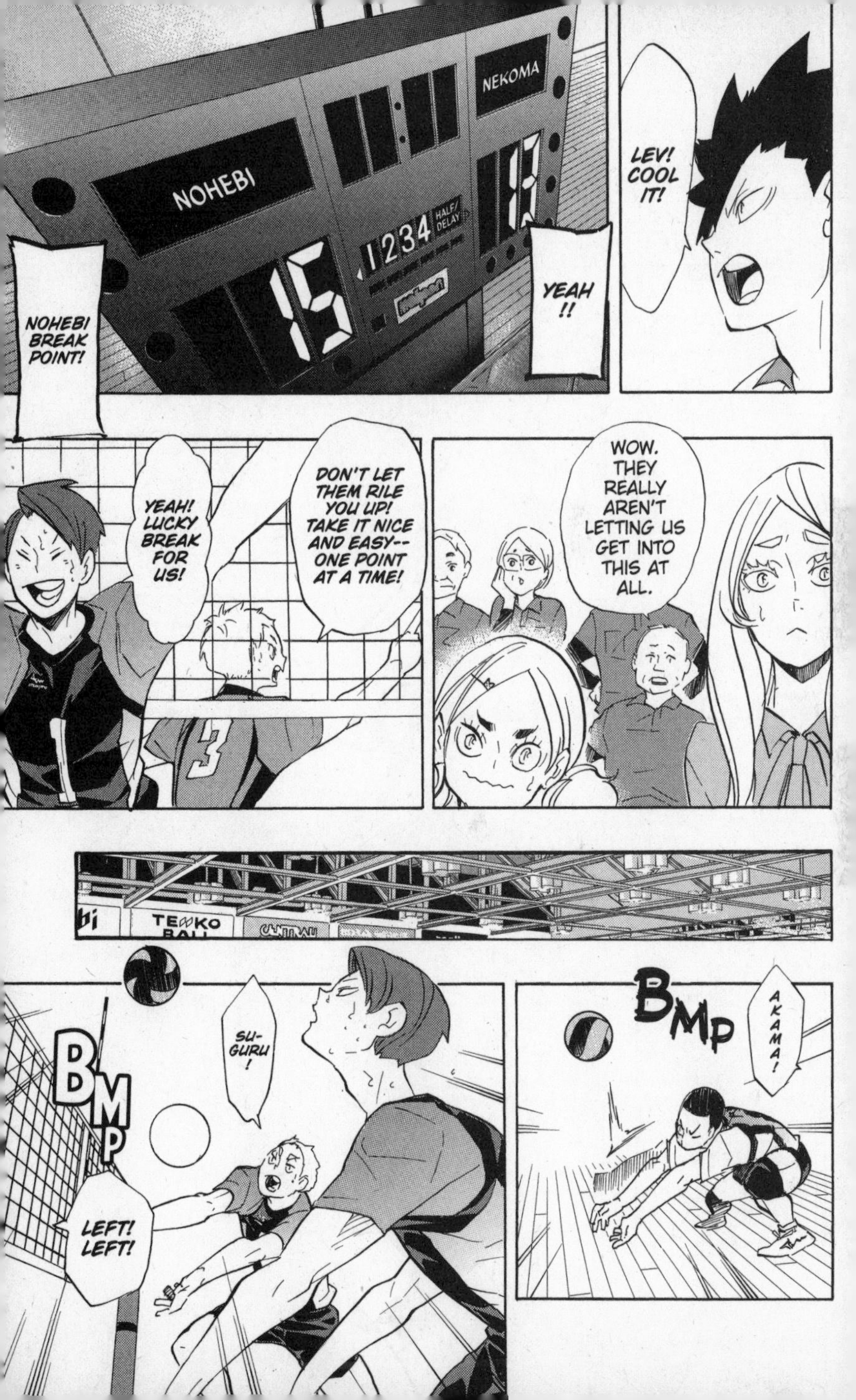
LEV! COOL IT!
NEKOMA
NOHEBI
YEAH!!
1234
HALF/ DELAY
NOHEBI BREAK POINT!
WOW. THEY REALLY AREN'T LETTING US GET INTO THIS AT ALL.
DON'T LET THEM RILE YOU UP! TAKE IT NICE AND EASY-- ONE POINT AT A TIME!
YEAH! LUCKY BREAK FOR US!
AKAMA!
BMP
SU-GURU!
BMP
LEFT! LEFT!

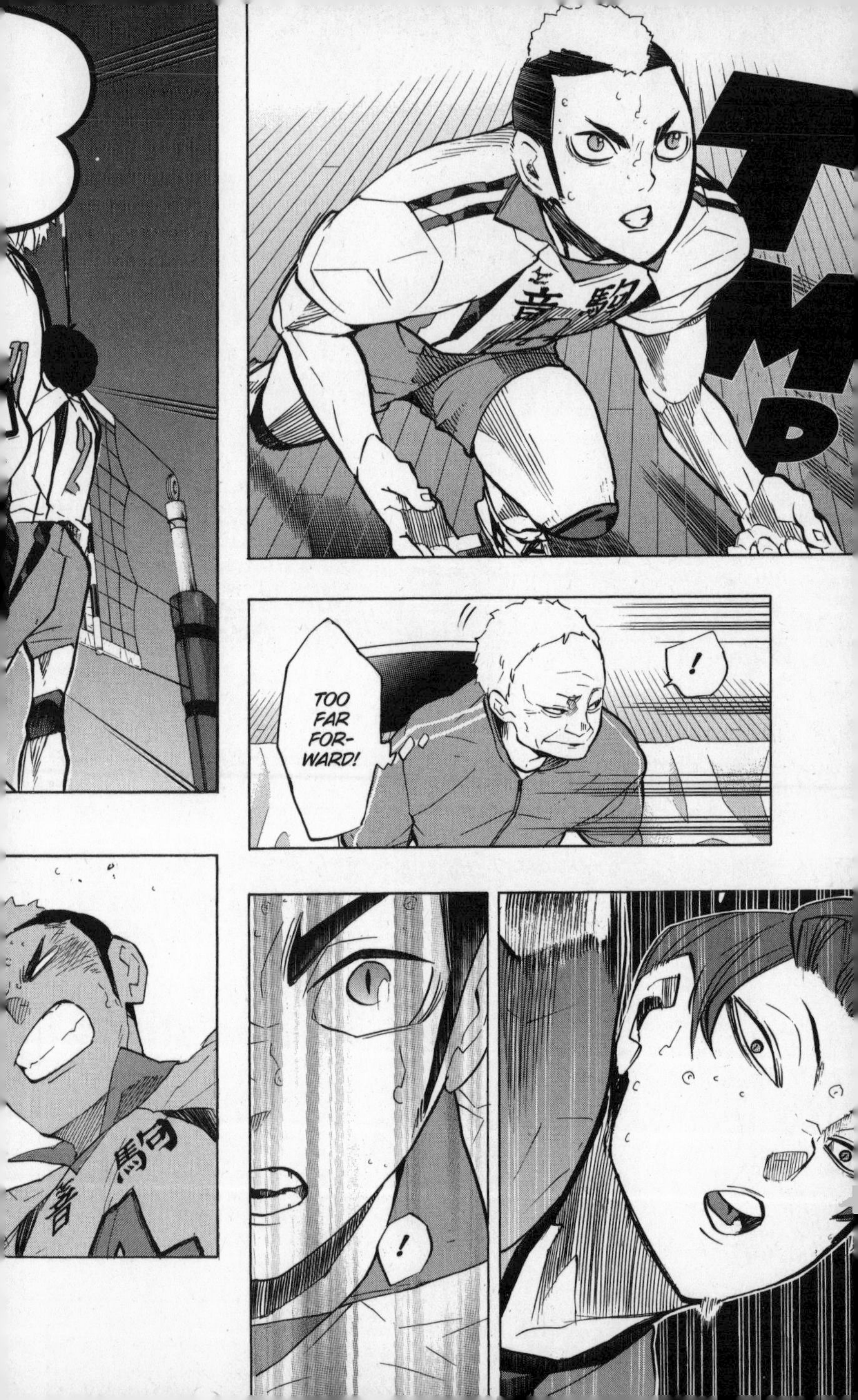
TMP
!
TOO FAR FOR-WARD!
!

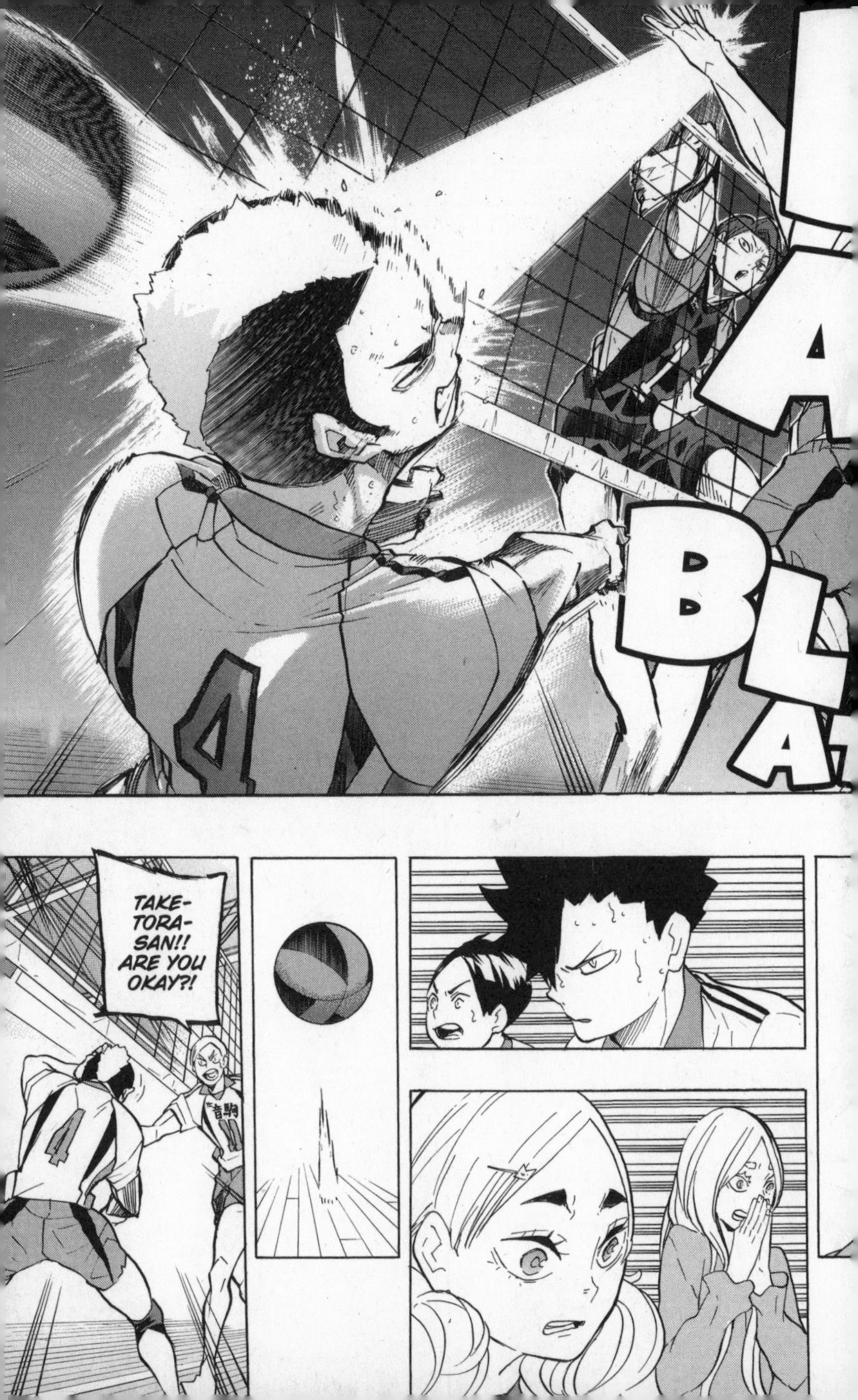
TAKE-TORA-SAN!! ARE YOU OKAY?!

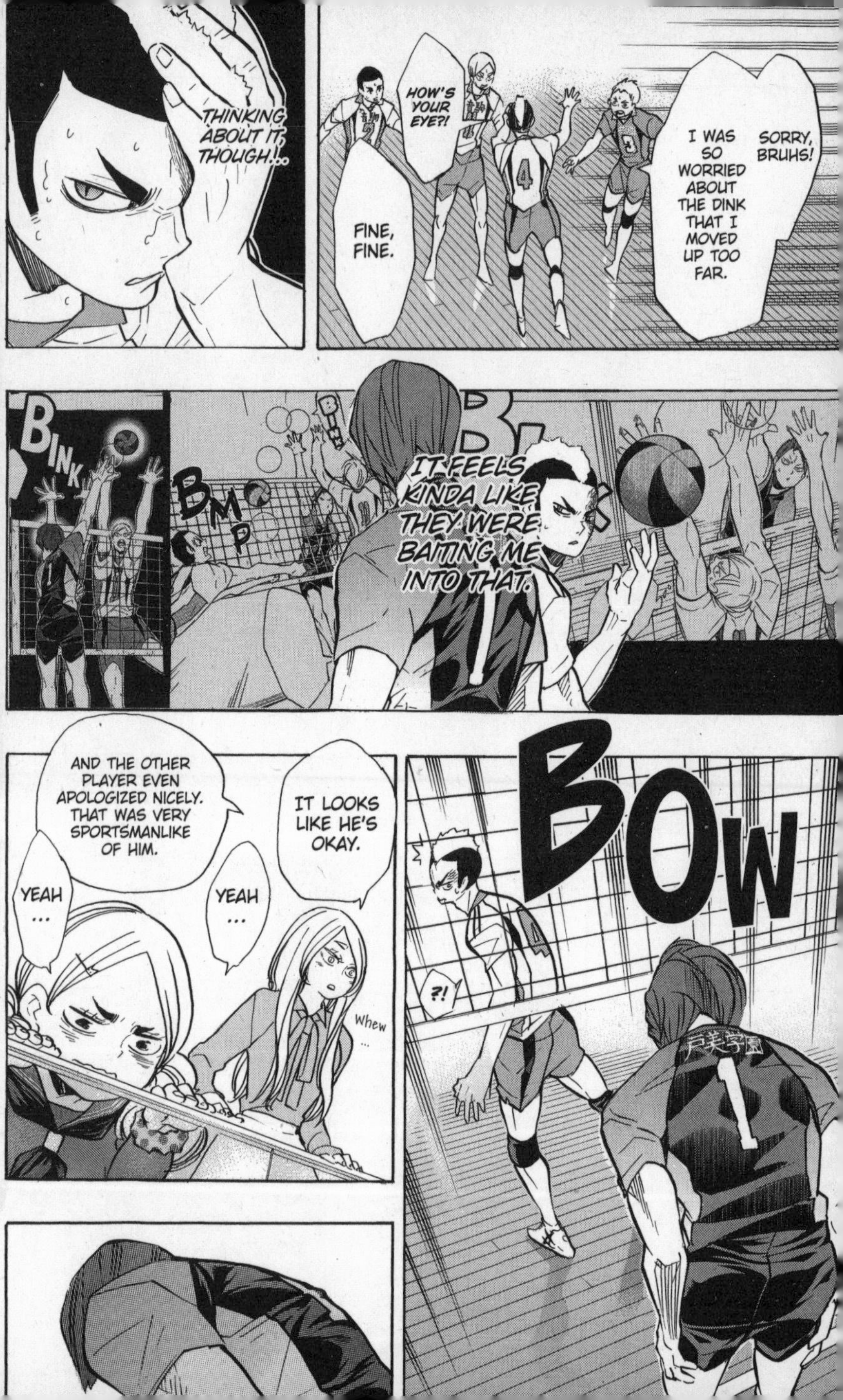
SORRY, BRUHS!
I WAS SO WORRIED ABOUT THE DINK THAT I MOVED UP TOO FAR.
HOW'S YOUR EYE?!
FINE, FINE.
THINKING ABOUT IT, THOUGH...
IT FEELS KINDA LIKE THEY WERE BAITING ME INTO THAT.
BMP
BINK
BOW
?!
IT LOOKS LIKE HE'S OKAY.
AND THE OTHER PLAYER EVEN APOLOGIZED NICELY. THAT WAS VERY SPORTSMANLIKE OF HIM.
YEAH...
YEAH...
Whew...

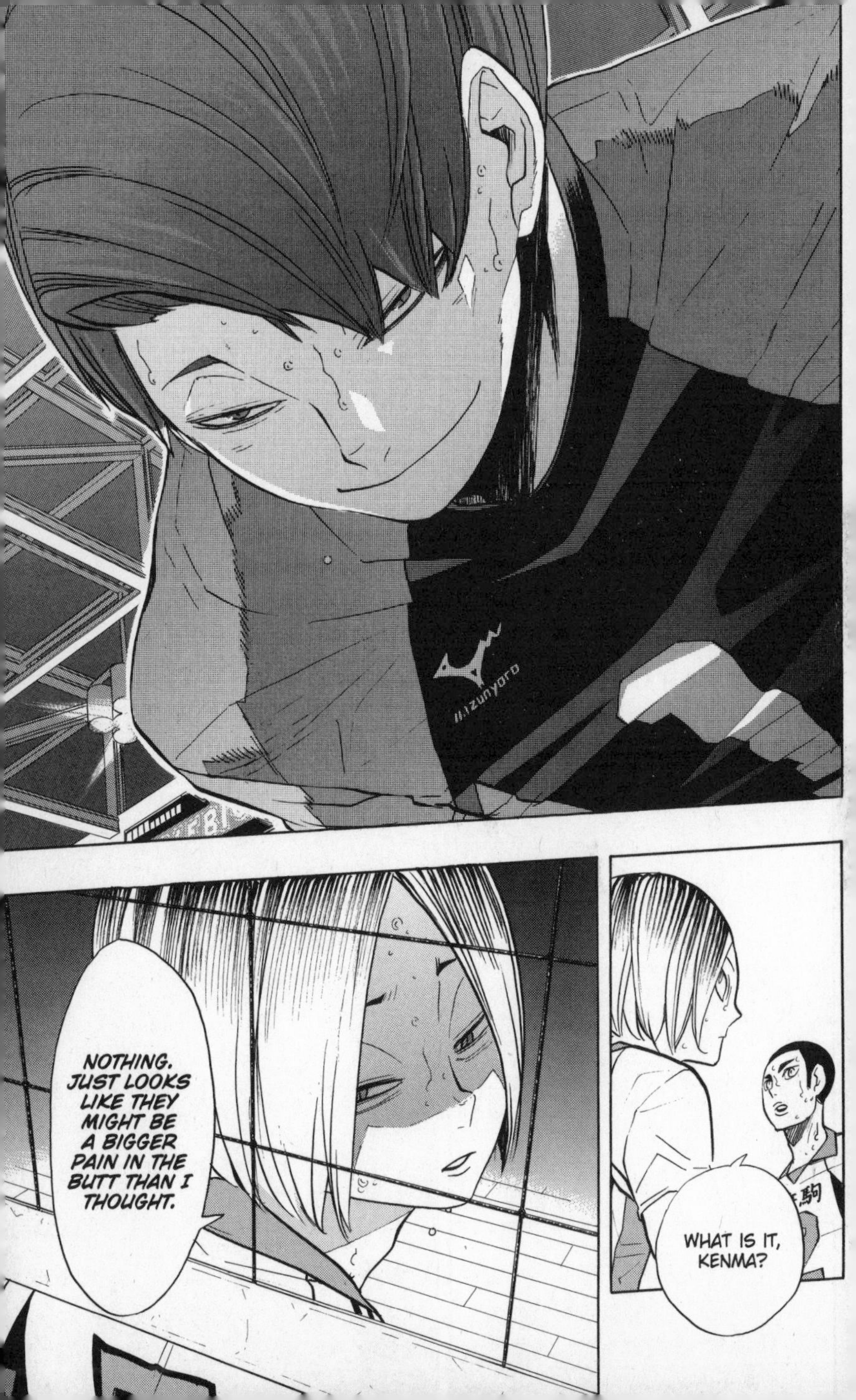
WHAT IS IT, KENMA?
NOTHING. JUST LOOKS LIKE THEY MIGHT BE A BIGGER PAIN IN THE BUTT THAN I THOUGHT.

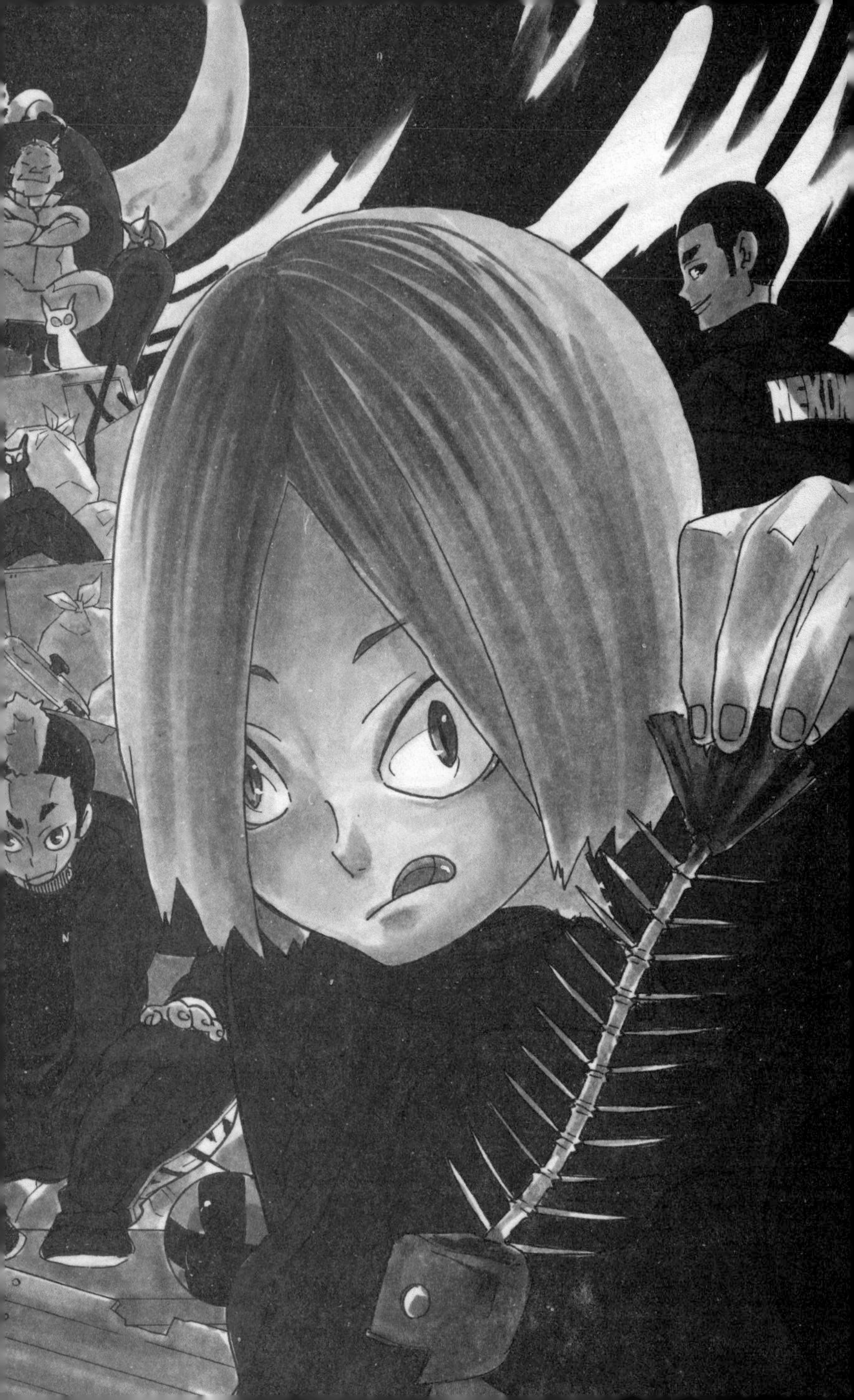
NEKO

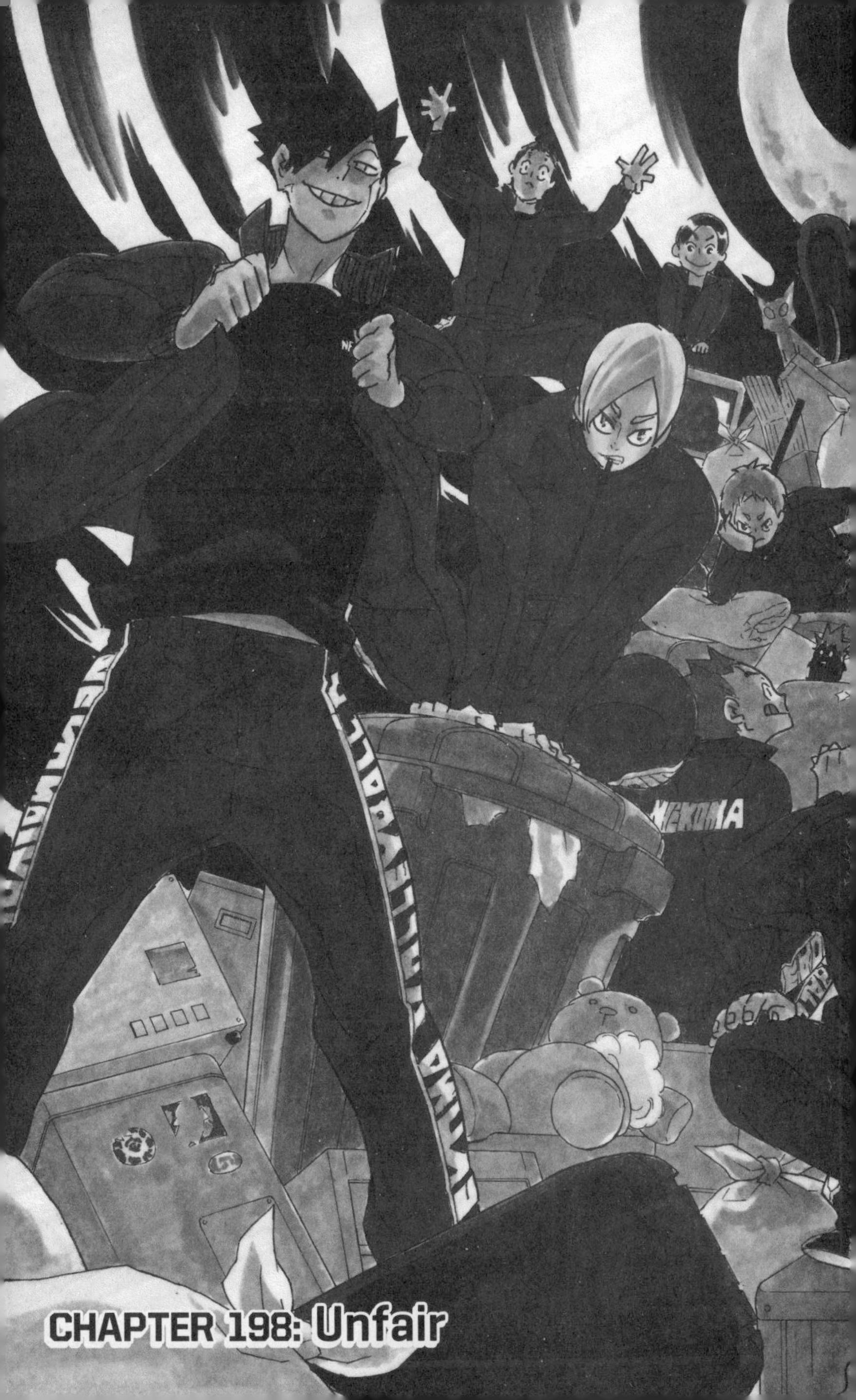
NEKOMA

CHAPTER 198: Unfair

HAIKYU!!

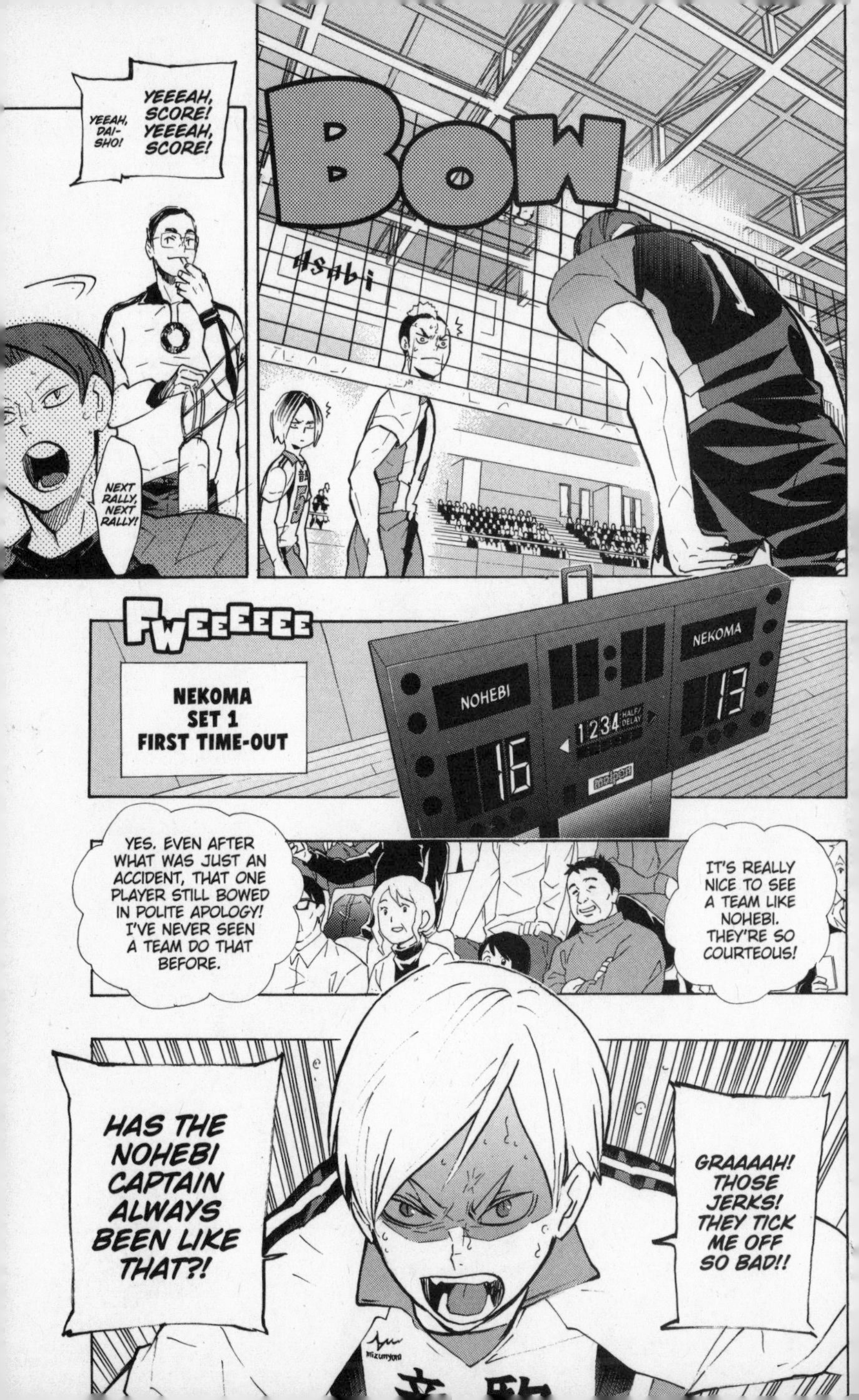
BOW
Asahi
YEEEAH, SCORE! YEEEAH, SCORE!
YEEAH, DAI-SHO!
NEXT RALLY, NEXT RALLY!
FWEEEEEE
NEKOMA SET 1 FIRST TIME-OUT
NEKOMA
NOHEBI
13
16
1234 HALF/DELAY
IT'S REALLY NICE TO SEE A TEAM LIKE NOHEBI. THEY'RE SO COURTEOUS!
YES. EVEN AFTER WHAT WAS JUST AN ACCIDENT, THAT ONE PLAYER STILL BOWED IN POLITE APOLOGY! I'VE NEVER SEEN A TEAM DO THAT BEFORE.
GRAAAAH! THOSE JERKS! THEY TICK ME OFF SO BAD!!
HAS THE NOHEBI CAPTAIN ALWAYS BEEN LIKE THAT?!

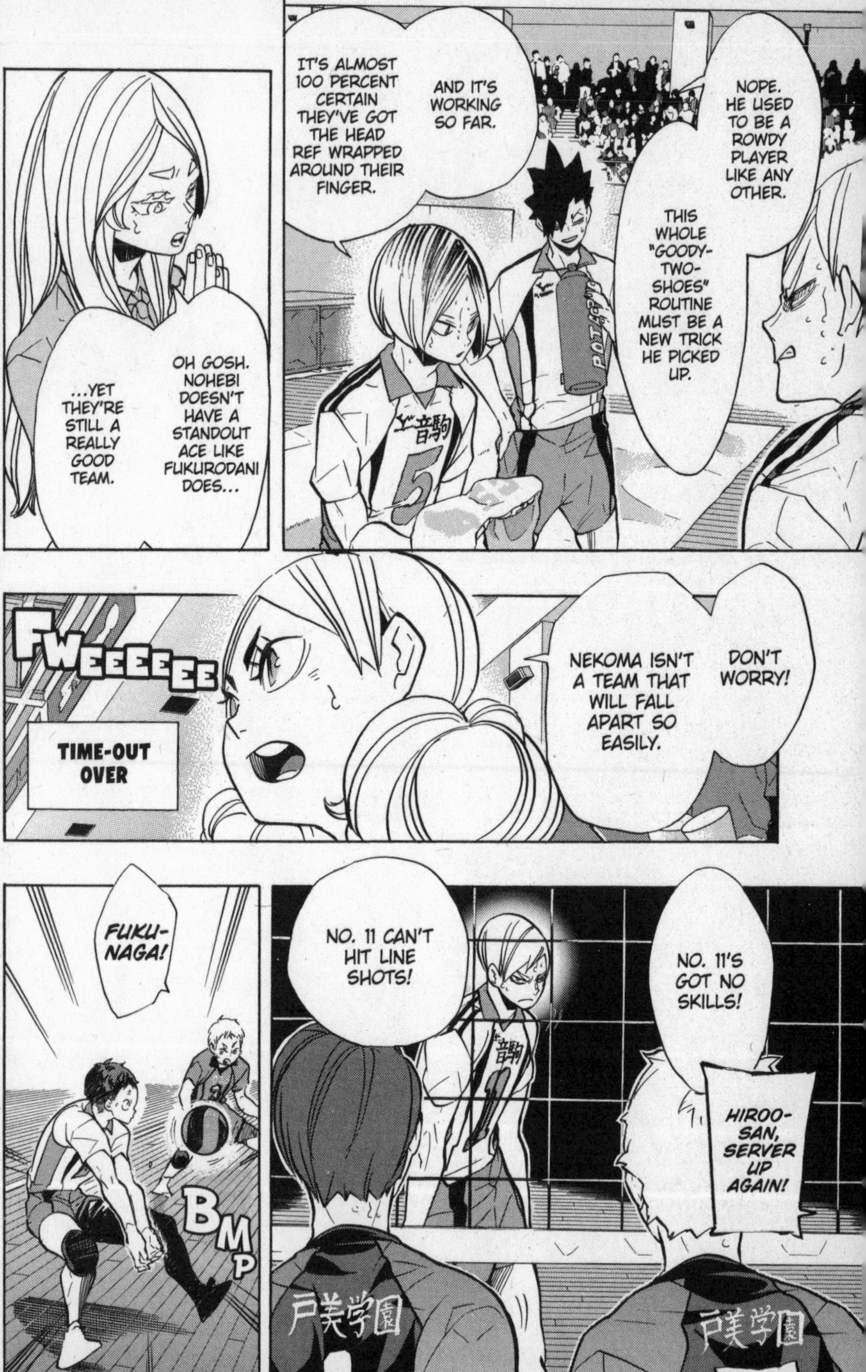
NOPE. HE USED TO BE A ROWDY PLAYER LIKE ANY OTHER.
THIS WHOLE "GOODY-TWO-SHOES" ROUTINE MUST BE A NEW TRICK HE PICKED UP.
IT'S ALMOST 100 PERCENT CERTAIN THEY'VE GOT THE HEAD REF WRAPPED AROUND THEIR FINGER.
AND IT'S WORKING SO FAR.
OH GOSH. NOHEBI DOESN'T HAVE A STANDOUT ACE LIKE FUKURODANI DOES...
...YET THEY'RE STILL A REALLY GOOD TEAM.
DON'T WORRY!
NEKOMA ISN'T A TEAM THAT WILL FALL APART SO EASILY.
FWEEEEEEE
TIME-OUT OVER
NO. 11'S GOT NO SKILLS!
NO. 11 CAN'T HIT LINE SHOTS!
HIROO-SAN, SERVER UP AGAIN!
FUKU-NAGA!
BMP

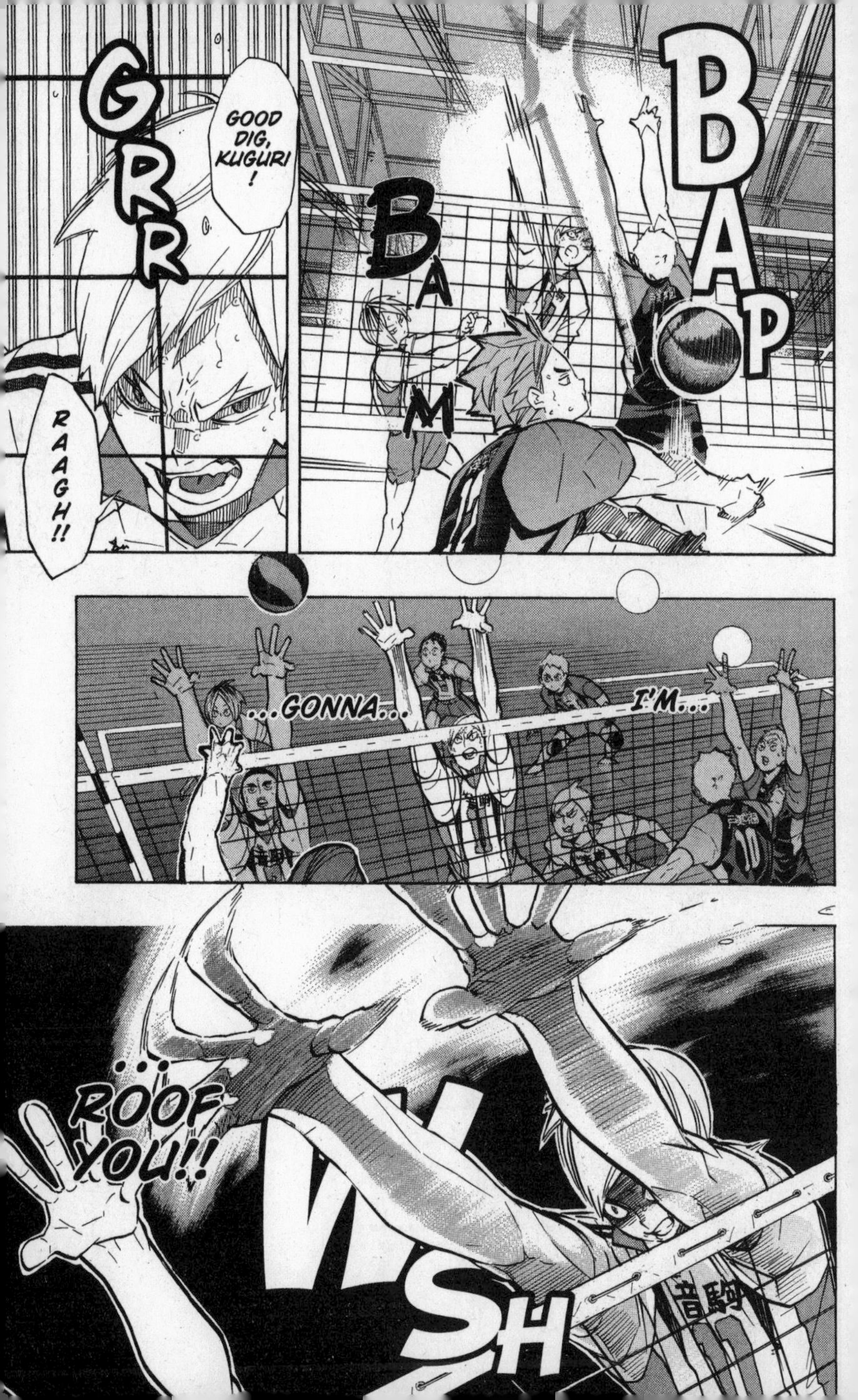
BAP
BAM
GRR
GOOD DIG, KUGURI!
RAAGH!!
I'M...
...GONNA...
...ROOF YOU!!
WSH
音駒

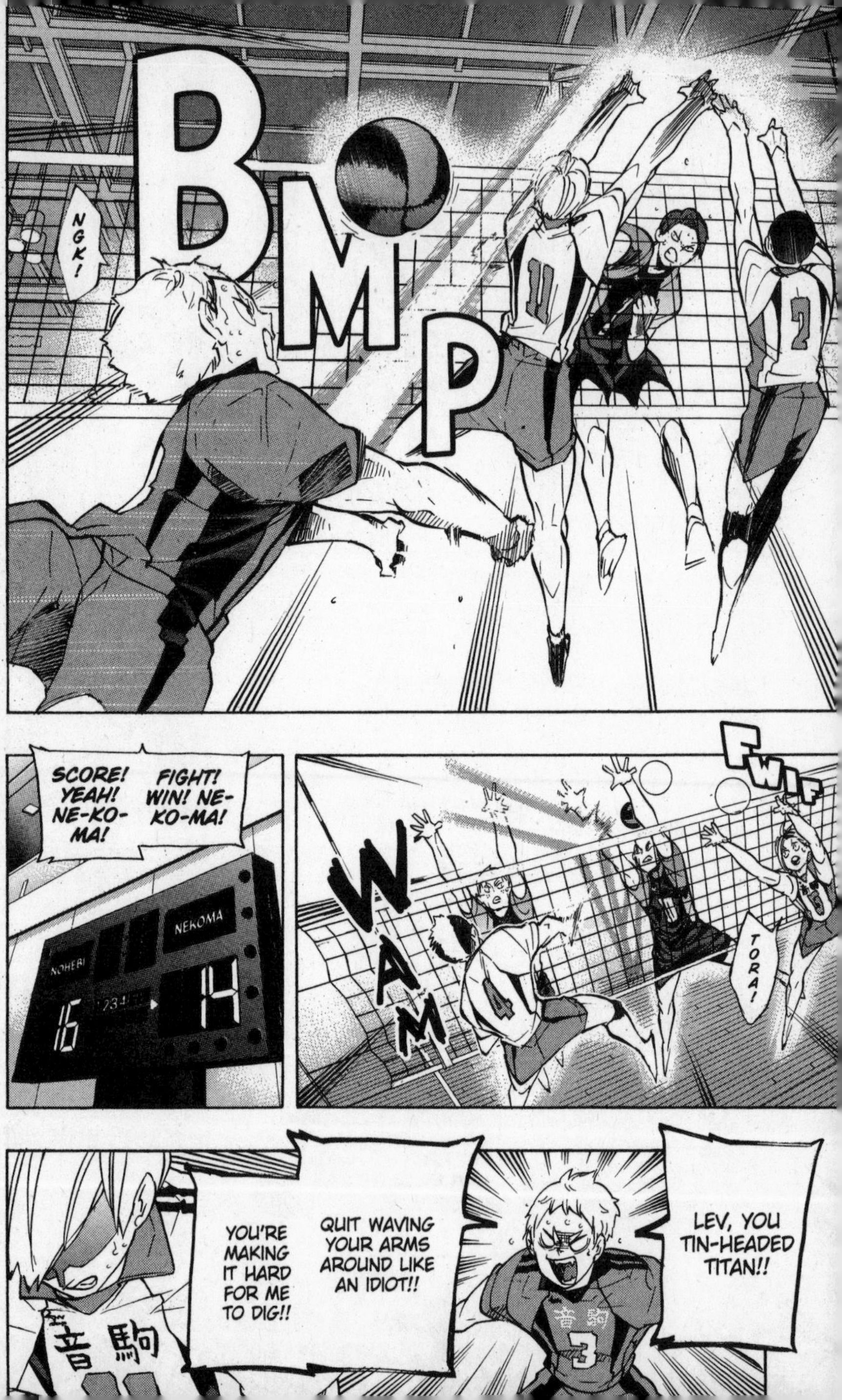
BMP
NGK!
FWIF
WAM
TORA!
FIGHT! WIN! NE-KO-MA!
SCORE! YEAH! NE-KO-MA!
NEKOMA
NOHEBI
16
14
LEV, YOU TIN-HEADED TITAN!!
音駒
3
QUIT WAVING YOUR ARMS AROUND LIKE AN IDIOT!!
YOU'RE MAKING IT HARD FOR ME TO DIG!!
音駒

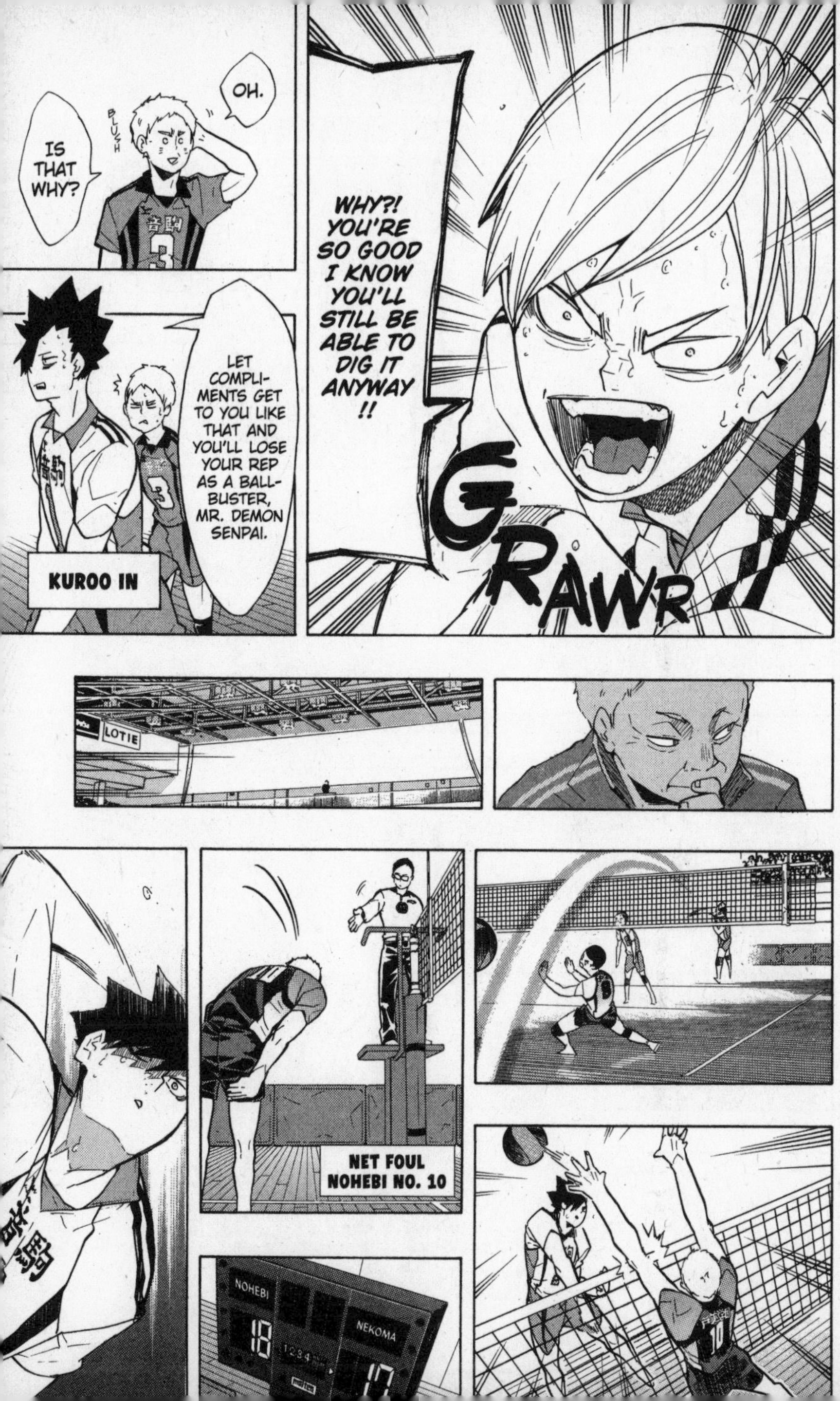
WHY?! YOU'RE SO GOOD I KNOW YOU'LL STILL BE ABLE TO DIG IT ANYWAY !!
GRAWR
OH.
BLUSH
IS THAT WHY?
LET COMPLIMENTS GET TO YOU LIKE THAT AND YOU'LL LOSE YOUR REP AS A BALL-BUSTER, MR. DEMON SENPAI.
KUROO IN
LOTIE
NET FOUL NOHEBI NO. 10
NOHEBI
18
NEKOMA
17

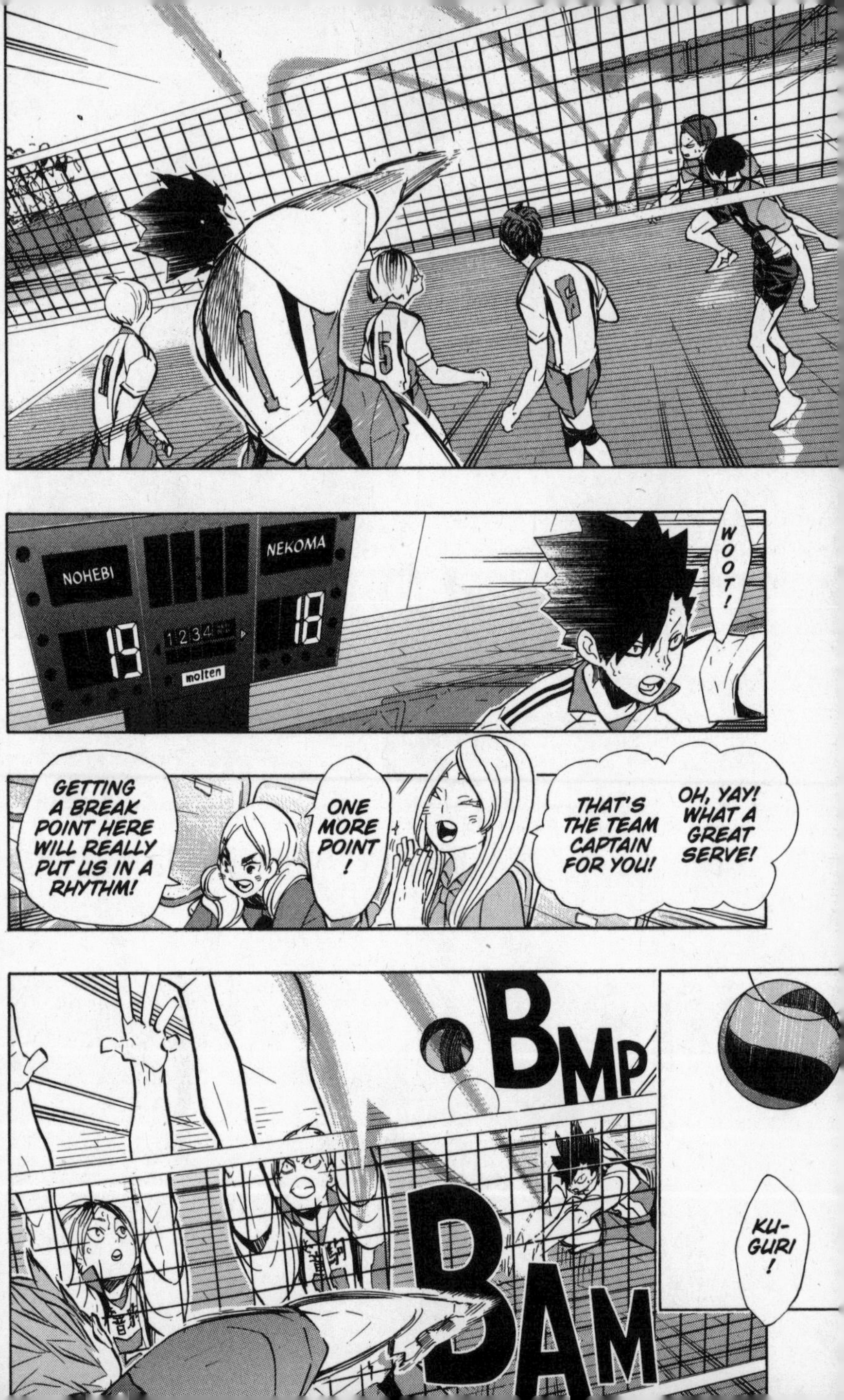

WOOT!
NEKOMA
18
NOHEBI
19
1234
molten
OH, YAY! WHAT A GREAT SERVE!
THAT'S THE TEAM CAPTAIN FOR YOU!
ONE MORE POINT!
GETTING A BREAK POINT HERE WILL REALLY PUT US IN A RHYTHM!
KU-GURI!
BMP
BAM

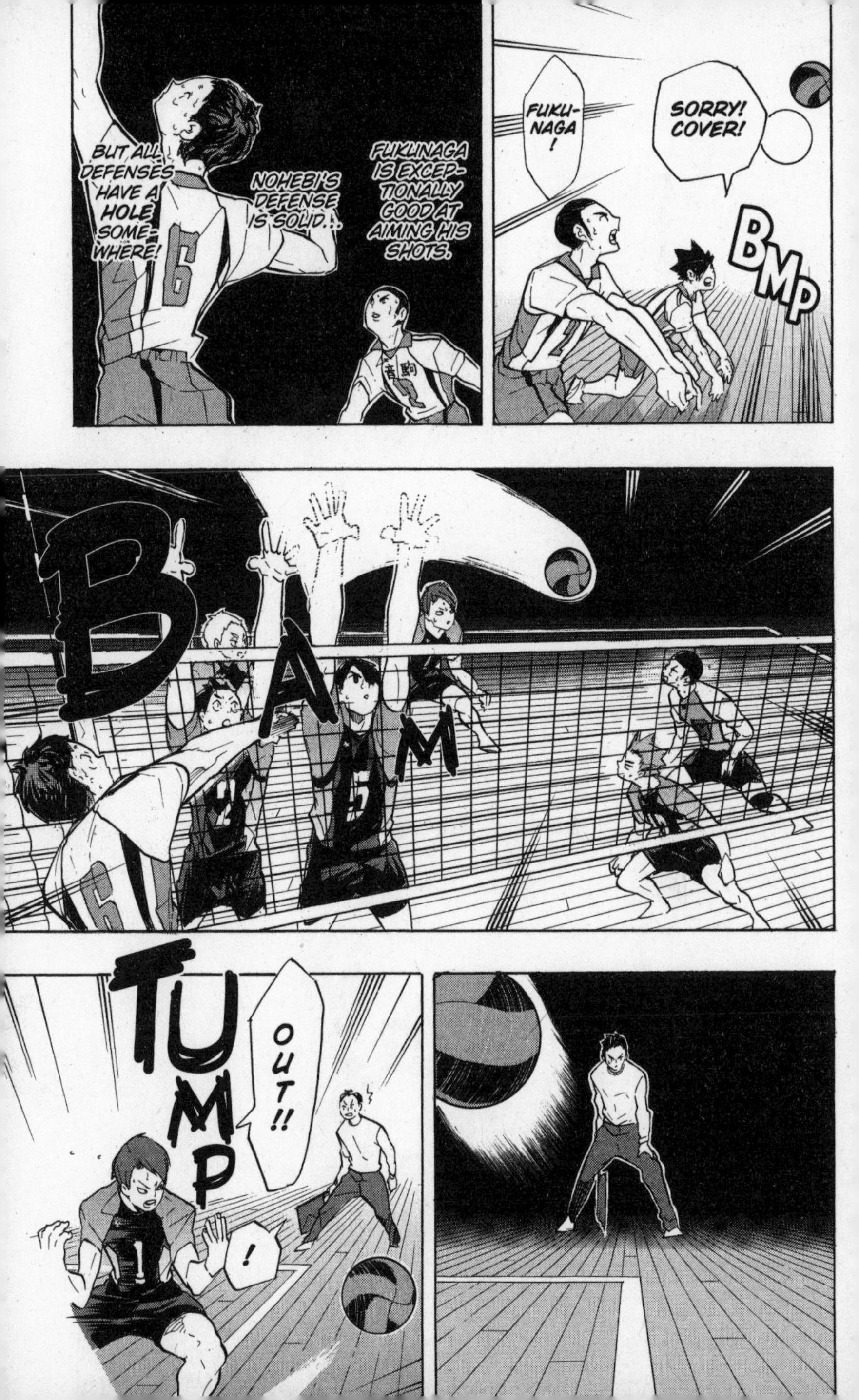
SORRY! COVER!
FUKUNAGA!
BMP
FUKUNAGA IS EXCEPTIONALLY GOOD AT AIMING HIS SHOTS.
NOHEBI'S DEFENSE IS SOLID...
BUT ALL DEFENSES HAVE A HOLE SOMEWHERE!
BAM
TUMP
OUT!!
!

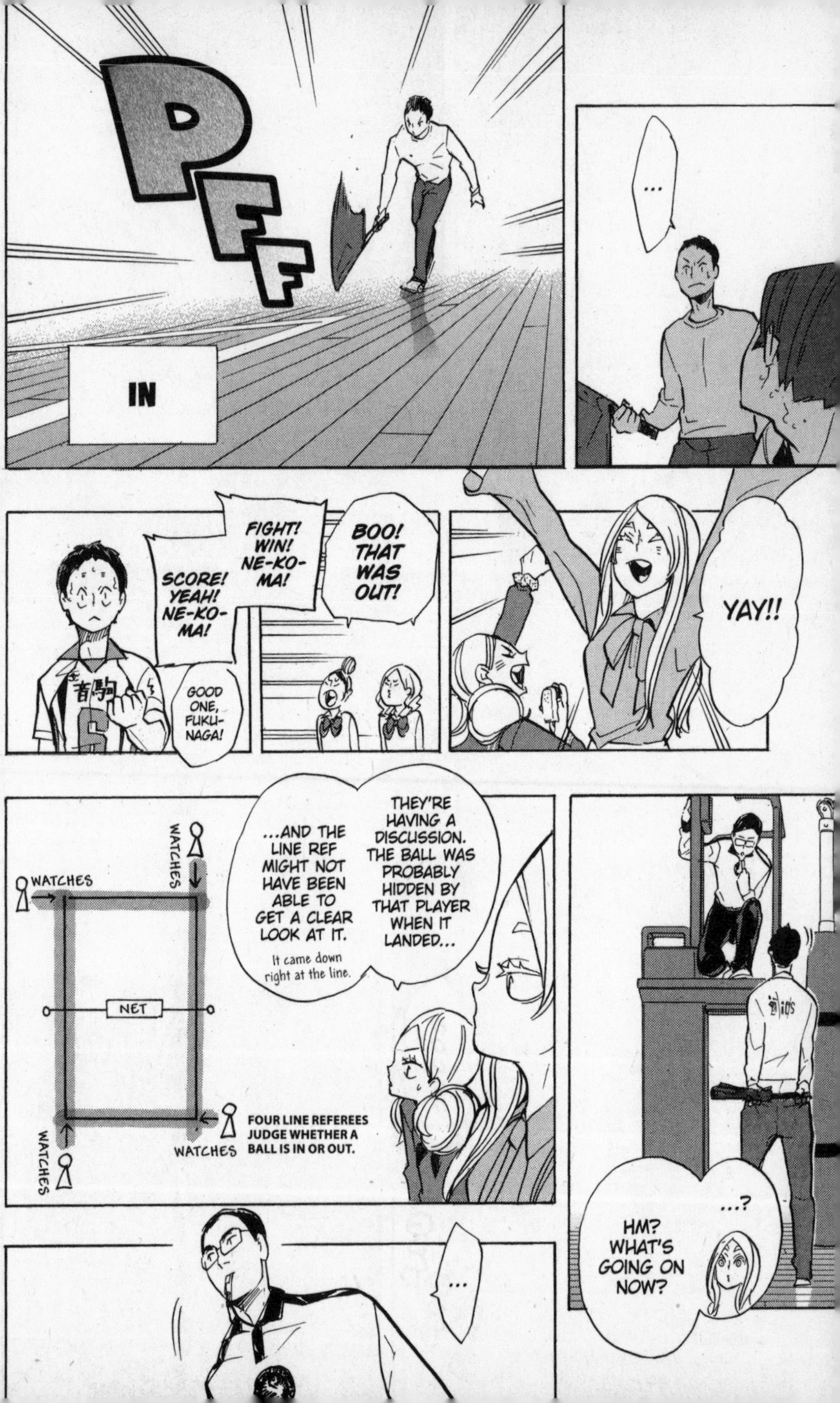
...
PFF
IN
YAY!!
BOO! THAT WAS OUT!
FIGHT! WIN! NE-KO-MA!
SCORE! YEAH! NE-KO-MA!
GOOD ONE, FUKUNAGA!
...?
HM? WHAT'S GOING ON NOW?
THEY'RE HAVING A DISCUSSION. THE BALL WAS PROBABLY HIDDEN BY THAT PLAYER WHEN IT LANDED...
...AND THE LINE REF MIGHT NOT HAVE BEEN ABLE TO GET A CLEAR LOOK AT IT.
It came down right at the line.
WATCHES
WATCHES
NET
WATCHES
WATCHES
FOUR LINE REFEREES JUDGE WHETHER A BALL IS IN OR OUT.
...

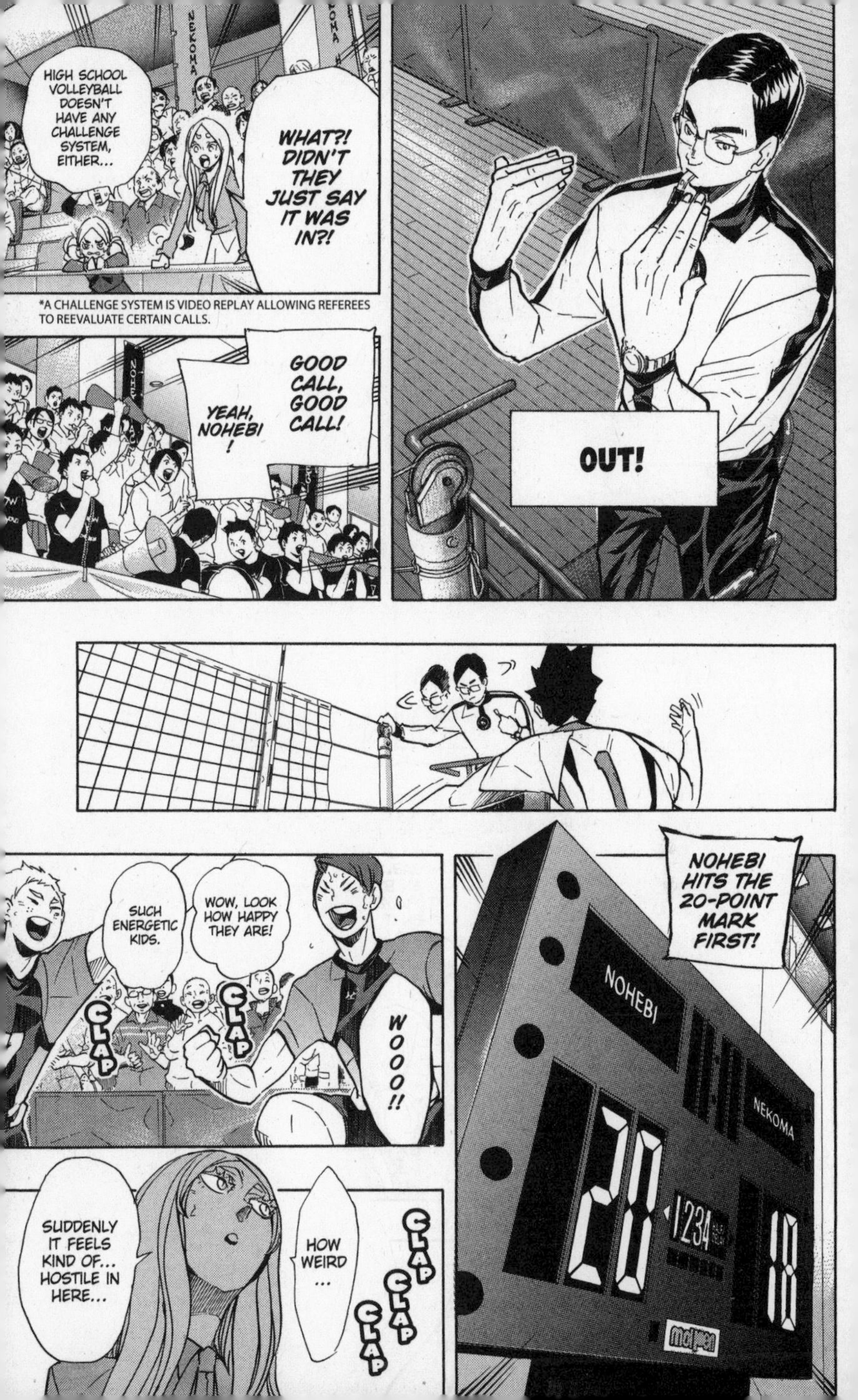
OUT!
WHAT?! DIDN'T THEY JUST SAY IT WAS IN?!
HIGH SCHOOL VOLLEYBALL DOESN'T HAVE ANY CHALLENGE SYSTEM, EITHER...
*A CHALLENGE SYSTEM IS VIDEO REPLAY ALLOWING REFEREES TO REEVALUATE CERTAIN CALLS.
GOOD CALL, GOOD CALL!
YEAH, NOHEBI!
NOHEBI HITS THE 20-POINT MARK FIRST!
NOHEBI
NEKOMA
20
18
WOOOO!!
WOW, LOOK HOW HAPPY THEY ARE!
SUCH ENERGETIC KIDS.
CLAP
CLAP
CLAP
CLAP
CLAP
HOW WEIRD...
SUDDENLY IT FEELS KIND OF... HOSTILE IN HERE...

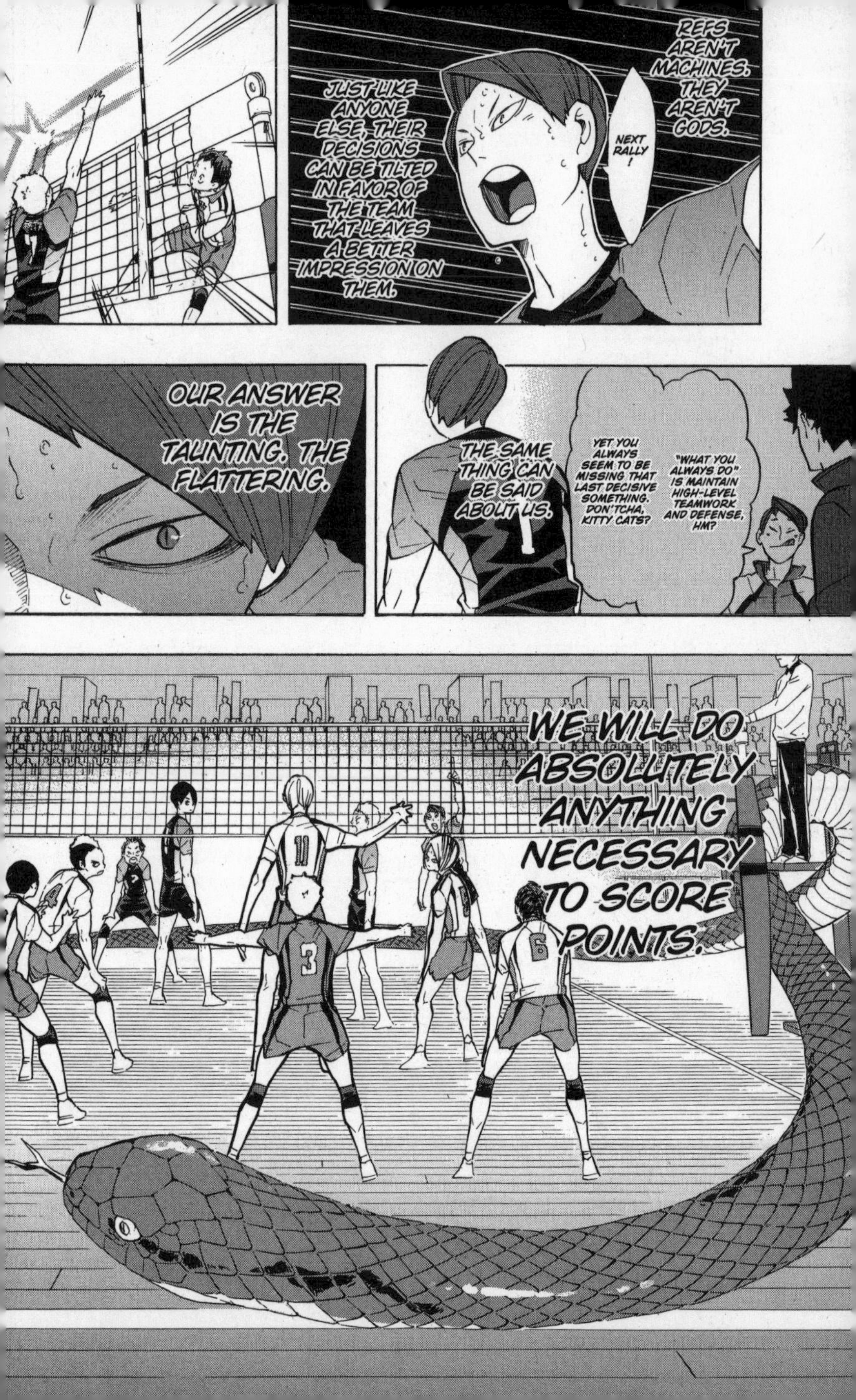
REFS AREN'T MACHINES. THEY AREN'T GODS.
NEXT RALLY!
JUST LIKE ANYONE ELSE, THEIR DECISIONS CAN BE TILTED IN FAVOR OF THE TEAM THAT LEAVES A BETTER IMPRESSION ON THEM.
"WHAT YOU ALWAYS DO" IS MAINTAIN HIGH-LEVEL TEAMWORK AND DEFENSE, HM?
YET YOU ALWAYS SEEM TO BE MISSING THAT LAST DECISIVE SOMETHING. DON'TCHA, KITTY CATS?
THE SAME THING CAN BE SAID ABOUT US.
OUR ANSWER IS THE TAUNTING. THE FLATTERING.
WE WILL DO ABSOLUTELY ANYTHING NECESSARY TO SCORE POINTS.

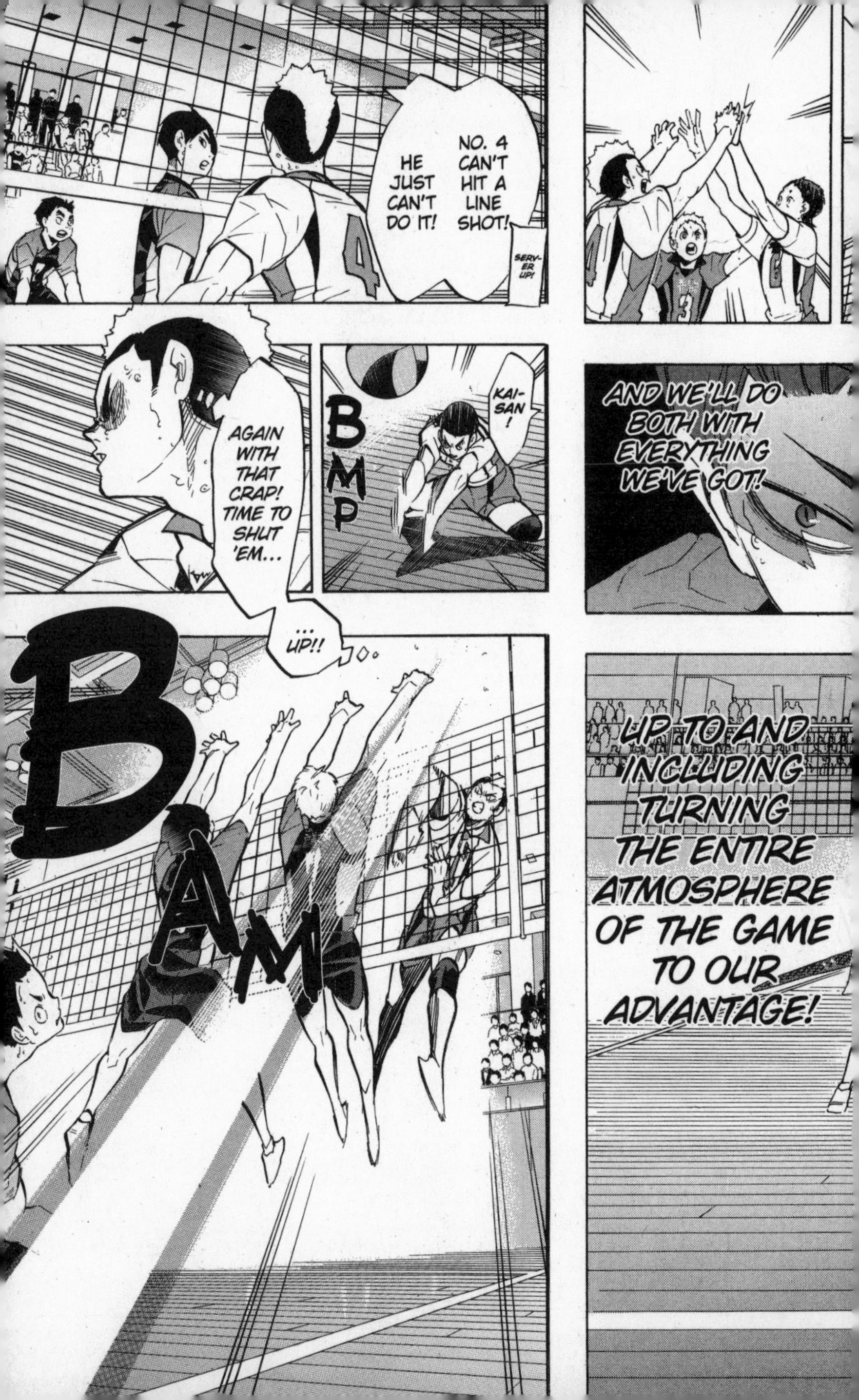
NO. 4 CAN'T HIT A LINE SHOT!
HE JUST CAN'T DO IT!
SERV-ER UP!
AND WE'LL DO BOTH WITH EVERYTHING WE'VE GOT!
KAI-SAN!
BMP
AGAIN WITH THAT CRAP! TIME TO SHUT 'EM...
UP TO AND INCLUDING TURNING THE ENTIRE ATMOSPHERE OF THE GAME TO OUR ADVANTAGE!
...UP!!
BAM

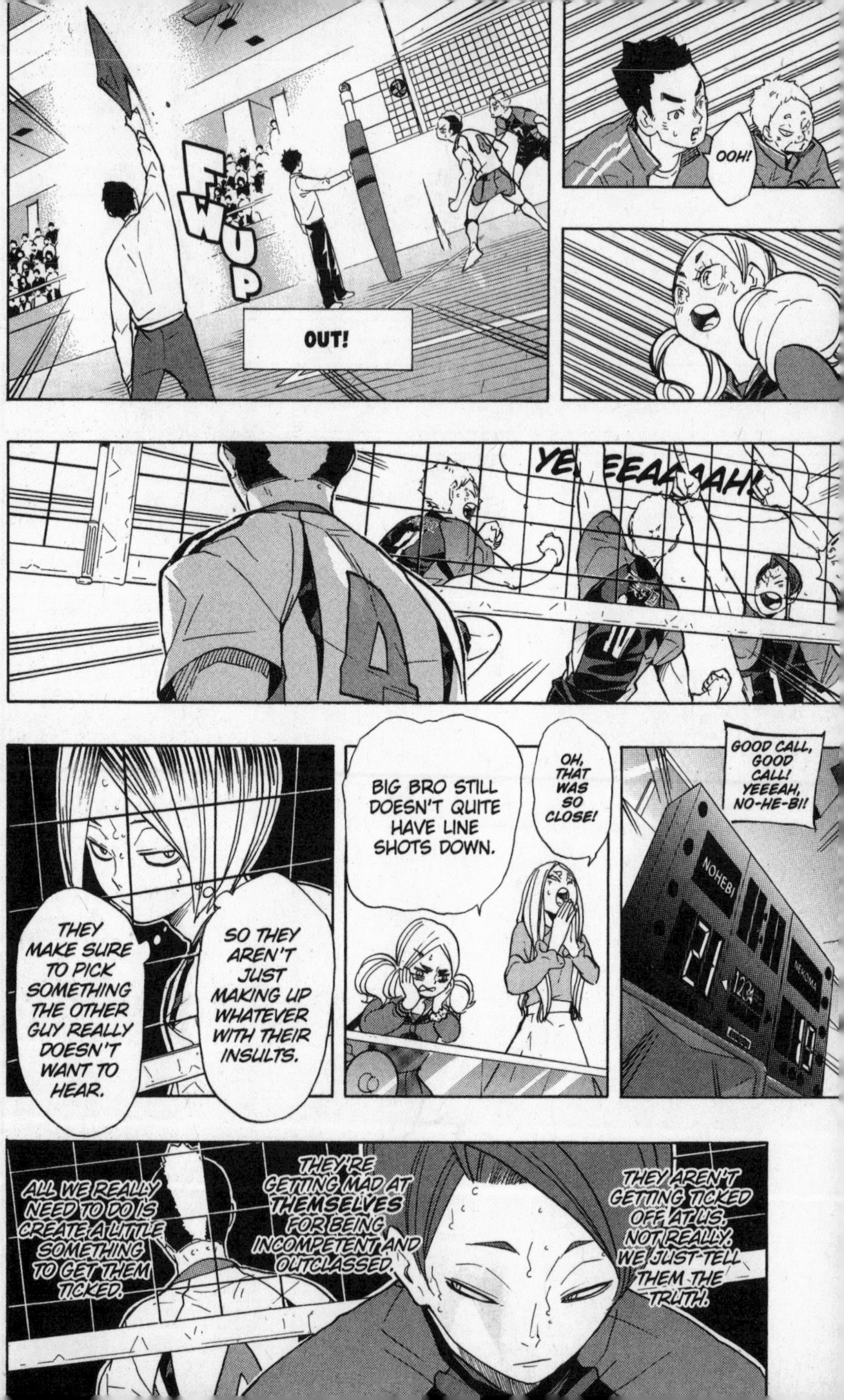
OOH!
FWUP
OUT!
YE EEAAAAH!
GOOD CALL, GOOD CALL! YEEEAH, NO-HE-BI!
NOHEBI
NEKOMA
OH, THAT WAS SO CLOSE!
BIG BRO STILL DOESN'T QUITE HAVE LINE SHOTS DOWN.
SO THEY AREN'T JUST MAKING UP WHATEVER WITH THEIR INSULTS.
THEY MAKE SURE TO PICK SOMETHING THE OTHER GUY REALLY DOESN'T WANT TO HEAR.
THEY AREN'T GETTING TICKED OFF AT US. NOT REALLY. WE JUST TELL THEM THE TRUTH.
THEY'RE GETTING MAD AT THEMSELVES FOR BEING INCOMPETENT AND OUTCLASSED.
ALL WE REALLY NEED TO DO IS CREATE A LITTLE SOMETHING TO GET THEM TICKED.

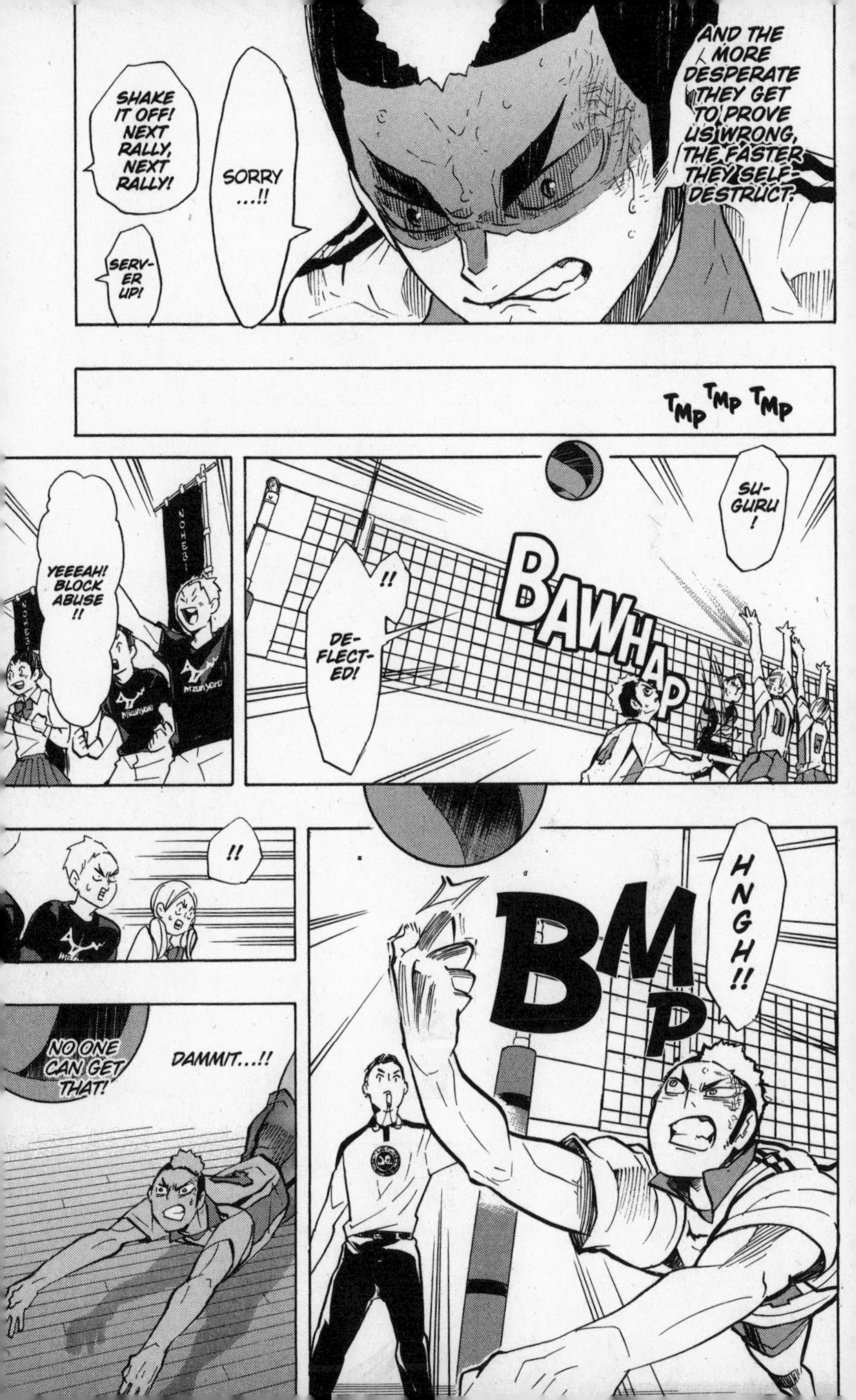
AND THE MORE DESPERATE THEY GET TO PROVE US WRONG, THE FASTER THEY SELF-DESTRUCT.
SORRY ...!!
SHAKE IT OFF! NEXT RALLY, NEXT RALLY!
SERV-ER UP!
TMP TMP TMP
SU-GURU!
BAWHAP
!! DE-FLECT-ED!
YEEEAH! BLOCK ABUSE!!
HNGH!!
BMP
!!
DAMMIT...!!
NO ONE CAN GET THAT!

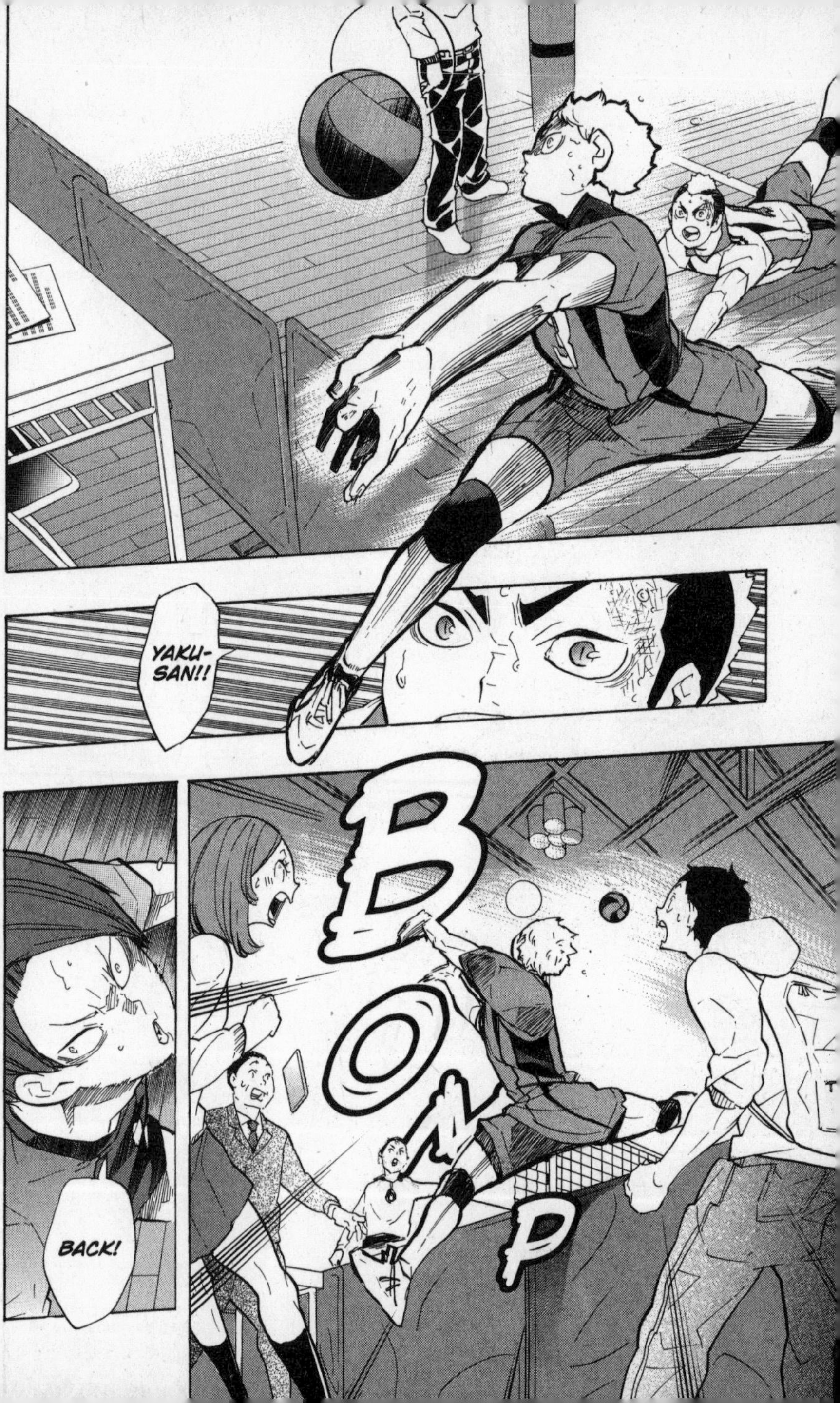
YAKU-SAN!!
BOMP
BACK!

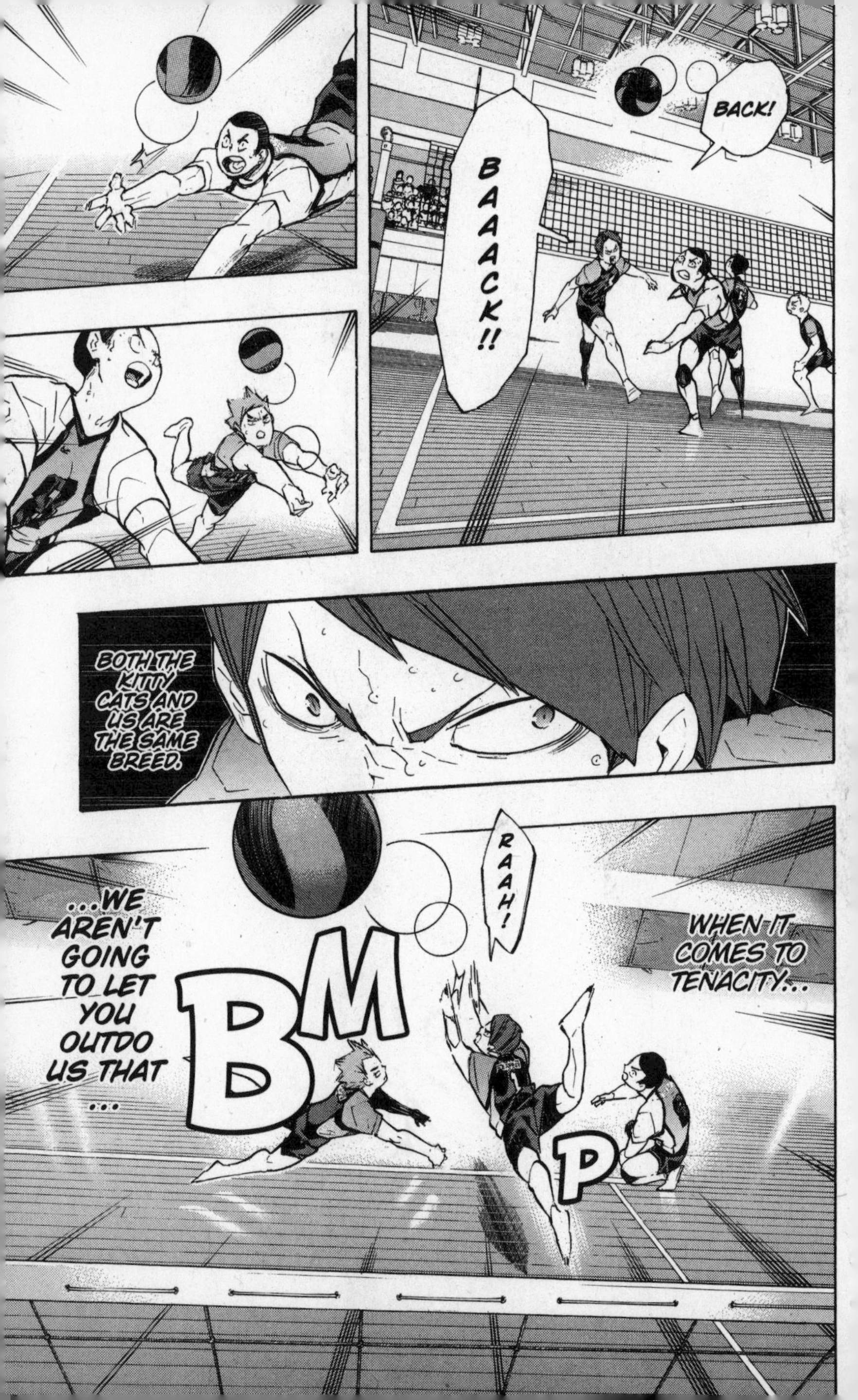

BACK!
BAAAACK!!
BOTH THE KITTY CATS AND US ARE THE SAME BREED.
WHEN IT COMES TO TENACITY...
RAAH!
BMP
...WE AREN'T GOING TO LET YOU OUTDO US THAT...

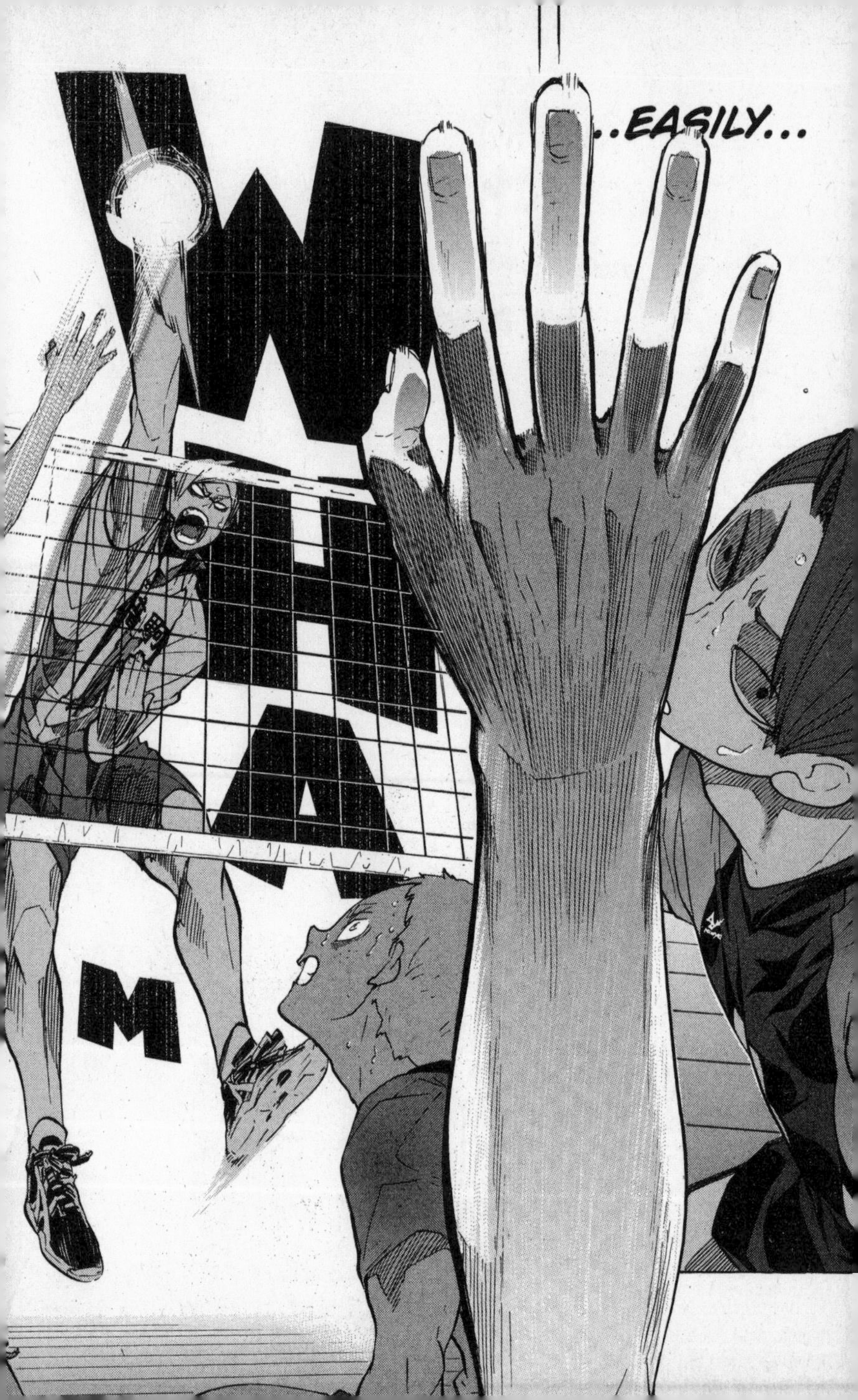
...EASILY...
WHAM

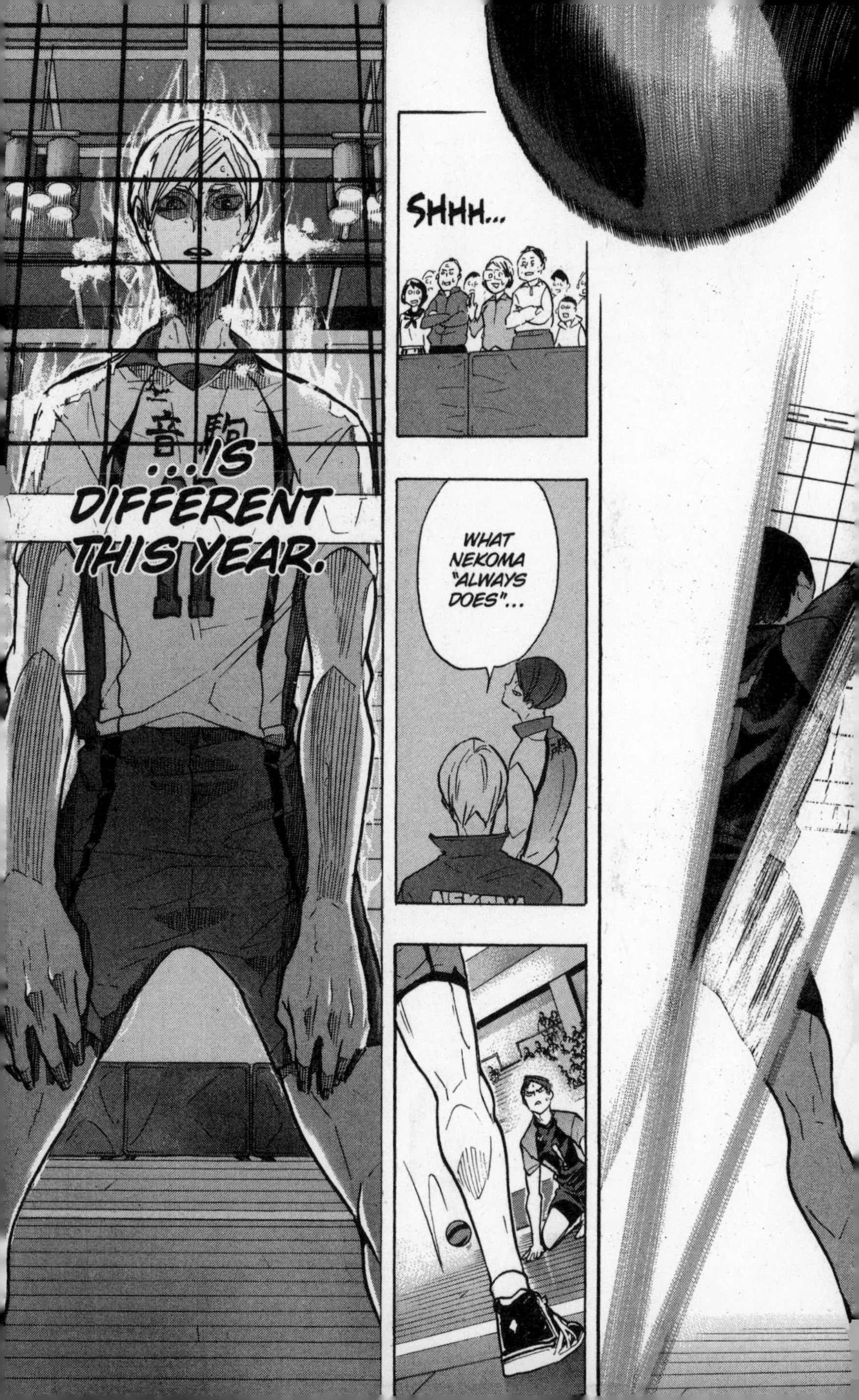
SHHH...
WHAT NEKOMA "ALWAYS DOES"...
音駒
...IS DIFFERENT THIS YEAR.

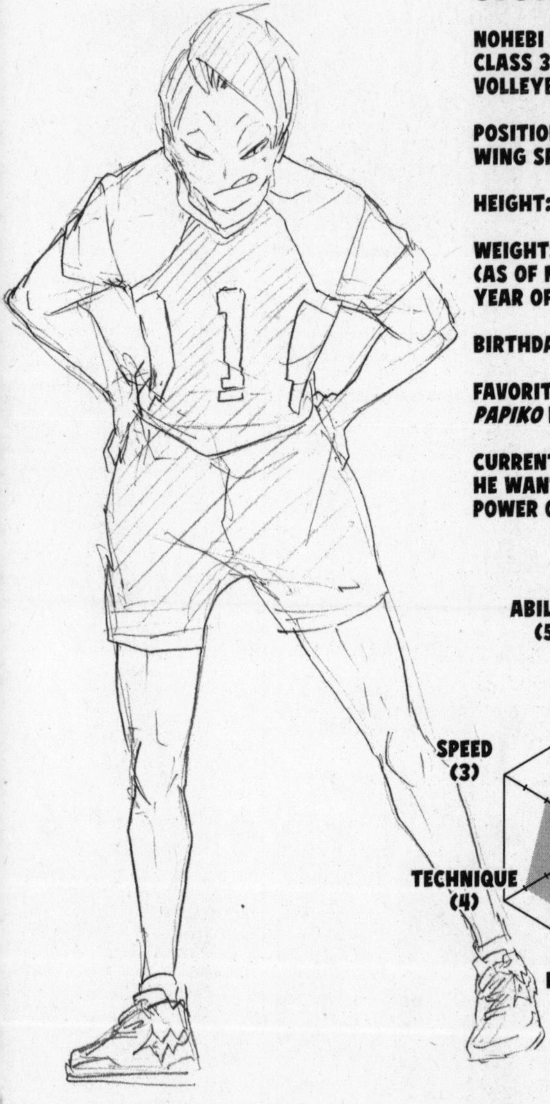

SUGURU DAISHO

NOHEBI ACADEMY
CLASS 3-6
VOLLEYBALL CLUB CAPTAIN

POSITION:
WING SPIKER

HEIGHT: 5'10"

WEIGHT: 147 LBS.
(AS OF NOVEMBER, 3RD YEAR OF HIGH SCHOOL)

BIRTHDAY: JULY 1

FAVORITE FOOD:
PAPIKO FROZEN DESSERTS

CURRENT WORRY:
HE WANTS TO BOOST THE POWER OF HIS SERVING.

ABILITY PARAMETERS
(5-POINT SCALE)

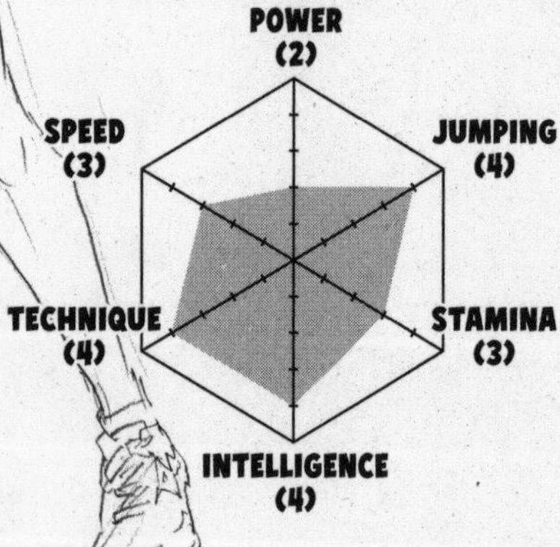
POWER (2)
JUMPING (4)
STAMINA (3)
INTELLIGENCE (4)
TECHNIQUE (4)
SPEED (3)

CHAPTER 199: Shaken

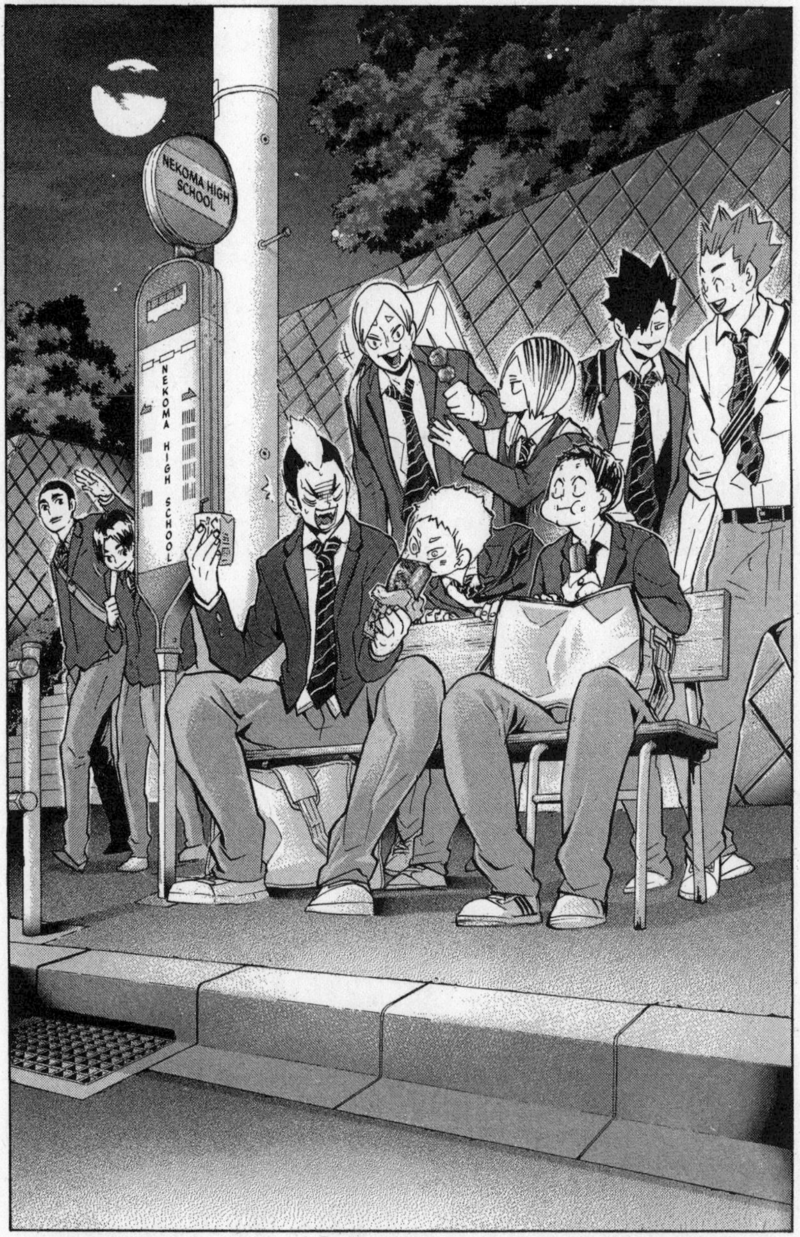
NEKOMA HIGH SCHOOL
NEKOMA HIGH SCHOOL

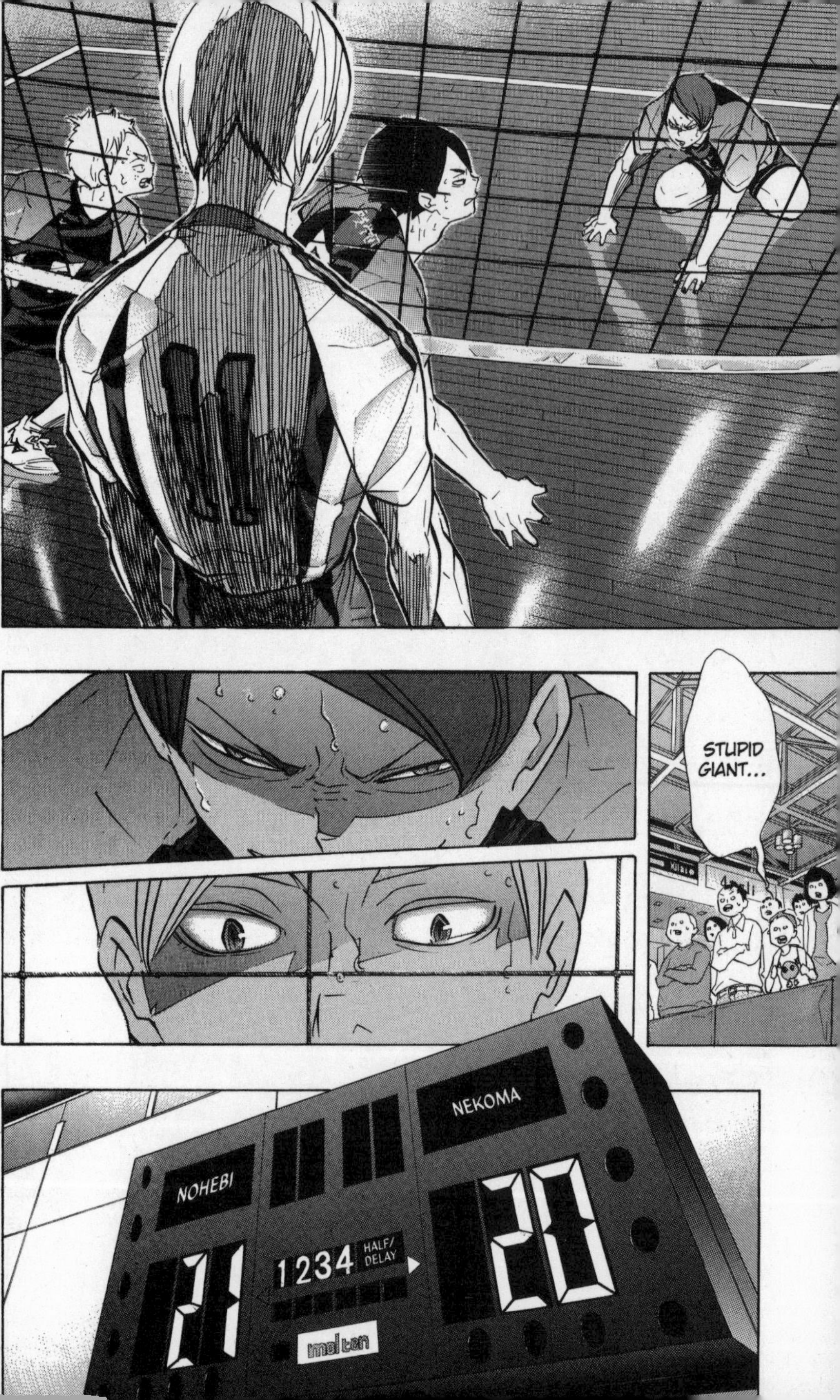
STUPID GIANT...
NEKOMA
NOHEBI
1234
HALF/ DELAY
molten

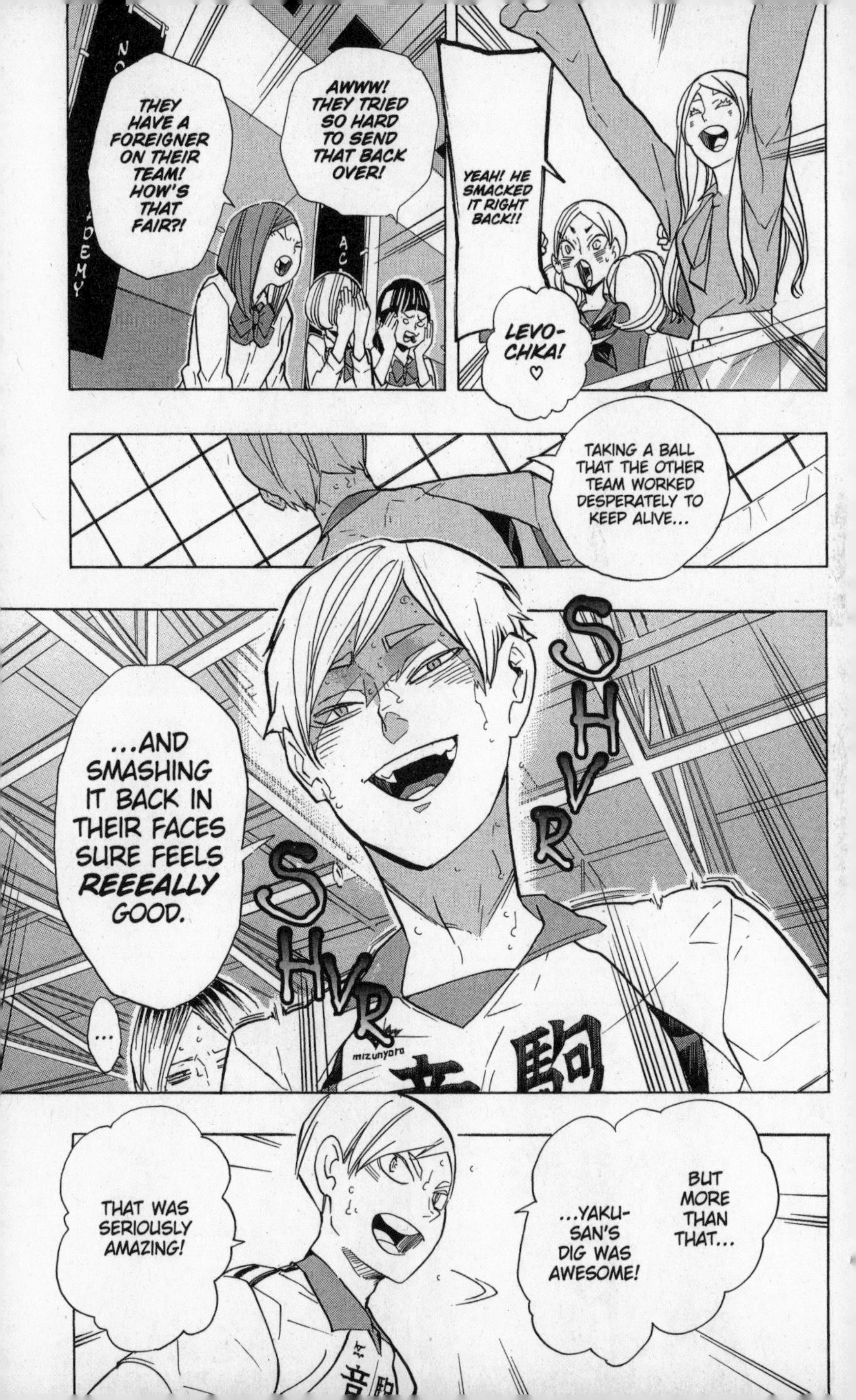
YEAH! HE SMACKED IT RIGHT BACK!!
LEVO-CHKA! ♡
AWWW! THEY TRIED SO HARD TO SEND THAT BACK OVER!
THEY HAVE A FOREIGNER ON THEIR TEAM! HOW'S THAT FAIR?!
TAKING A BALL THAT THE OTHER TEAM WORKED DESPERATELY TO KEEP ALIVE...
SHVR
...AND SMASHING IT BACK IN THEIR FACES SURE FEELS ***REEEALLY*** GOOD.
SHVR
...
BUT MORE THAN THAT...
...YAKU-SAN'S DIG WAS AWESOME!
THAT WAS SERIOUSLY AMAZING!

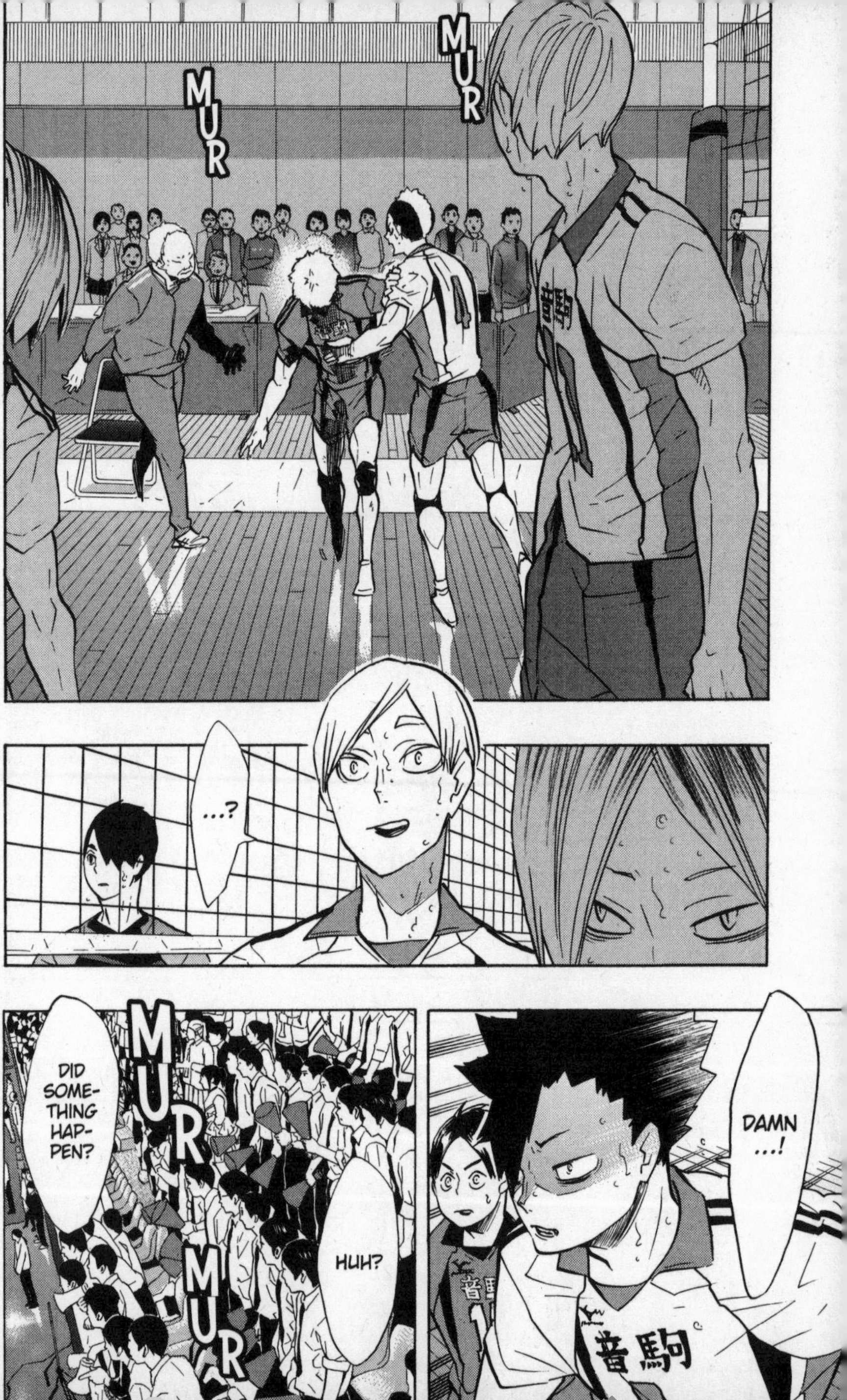
MUR
MUR
...?
DAMN ...!
MUR
DID SOMETHING HAPPEN?
HUH?
MUR
音駒

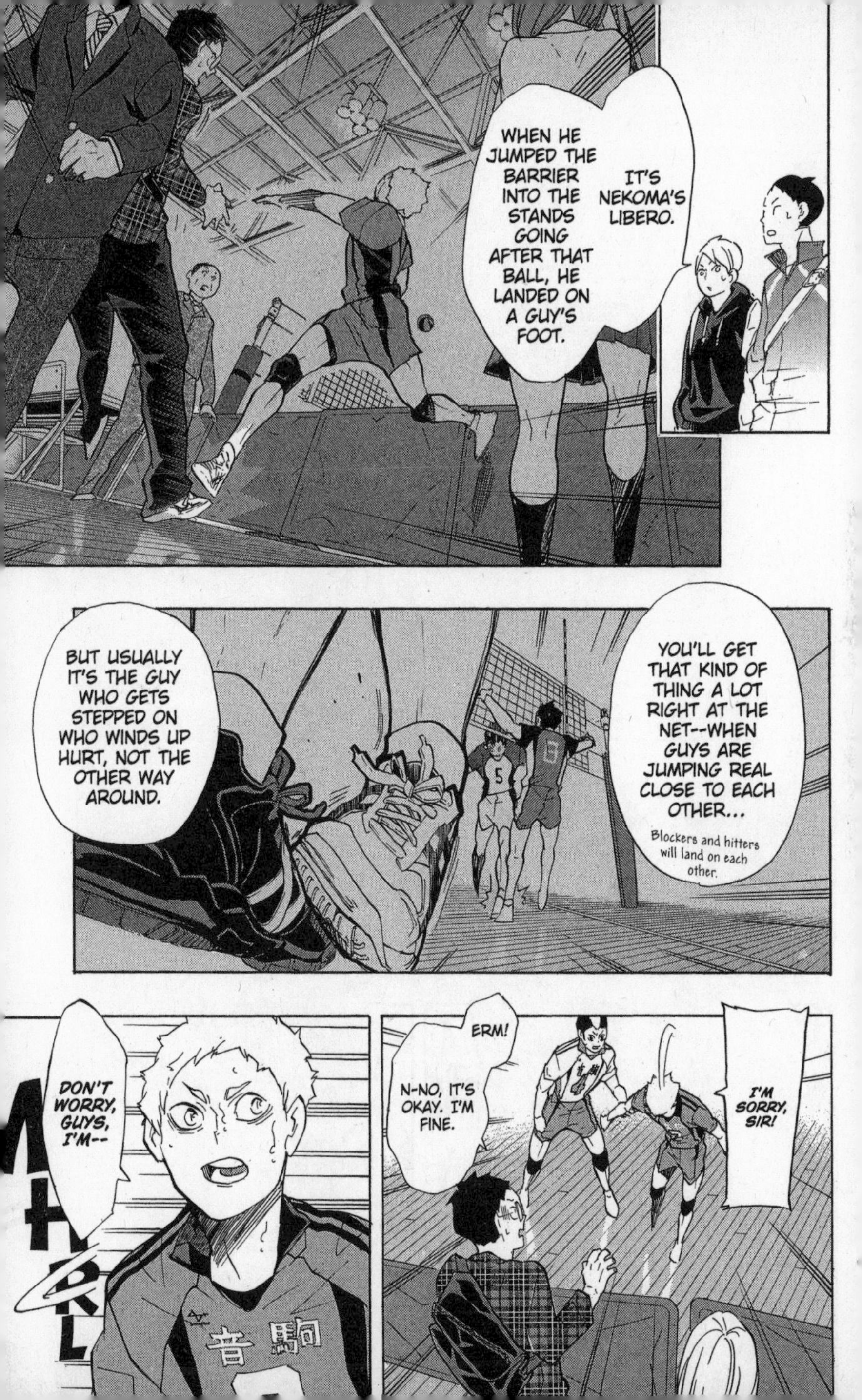
IT'S NEKOMA'S LIBERO.
WHEN HE JUMPED THE BARRIER INTO THE STANDS GOING AFTER THAT BALL, HE LANDED ON A GUY'S FOOT.
YOU'LL GET THAT KIND OF THING A LOT RIGHT AT THE NET--WHEN GUYS ARE JUMPING REAL CLOSE TO EACH OTHER...
Blockers and hitters will land on each other.
BUT USUALLY IT'S THE GUY WHO GETS STEPPED ON WHO WINDS UP HURT, NOT THE OTHER WAY AROUND.
I'M SORRY, SIR!
ERM!
N-NO, IT'S OKAY. I'M FINE.
DON'T WORRY, GUYS, I'M--

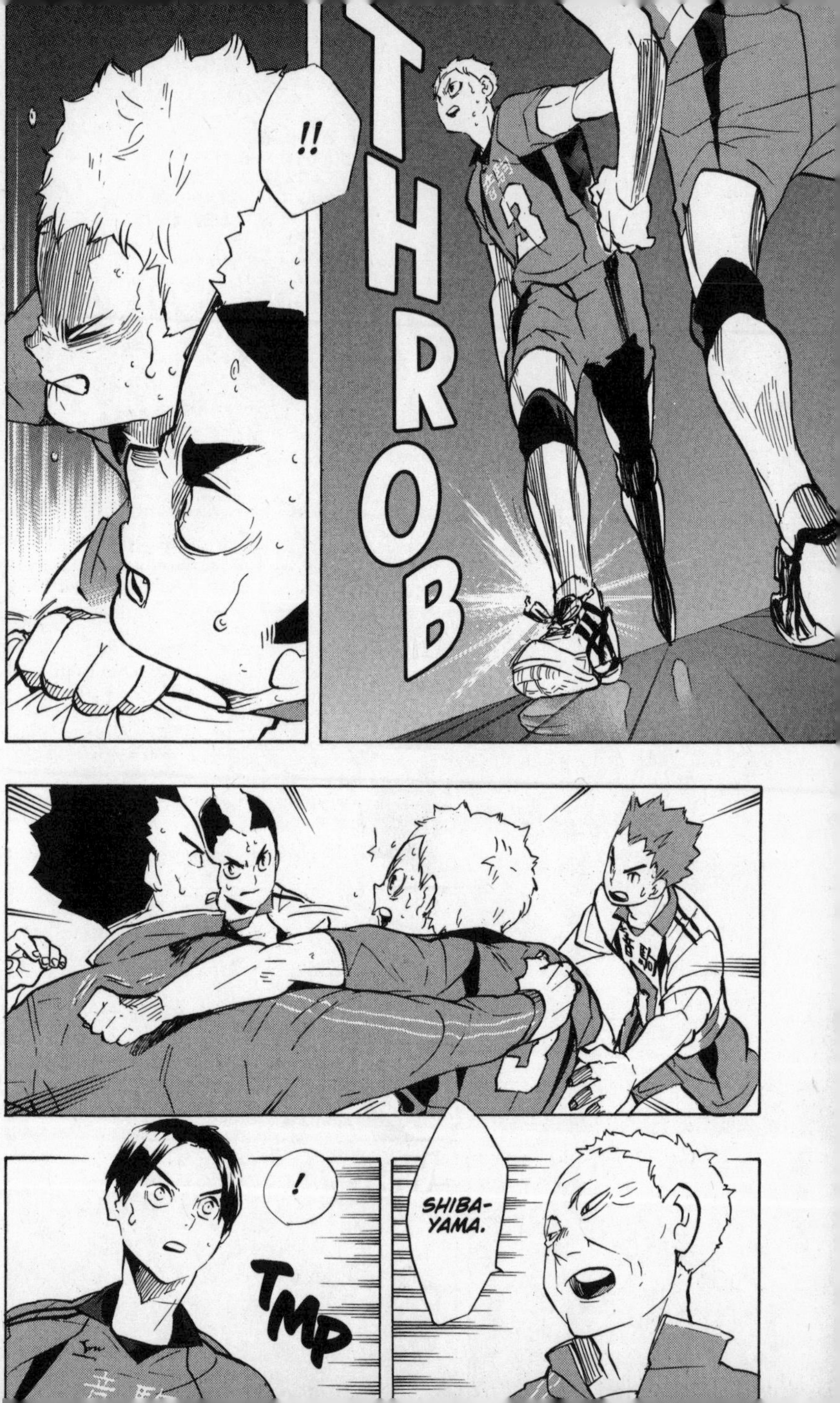
THROB
!!
SHIBA-YAMA.
!
TMP

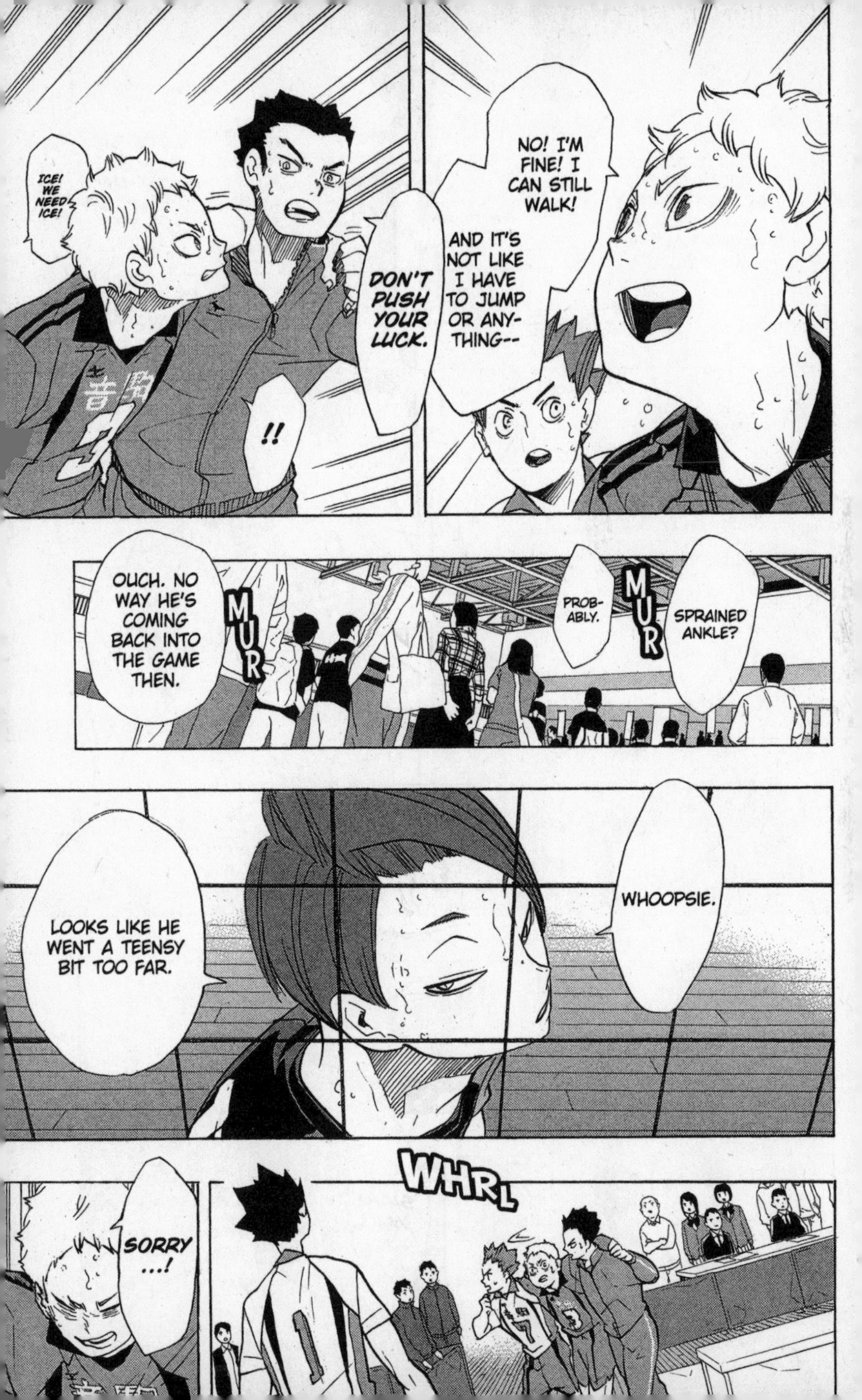
NO! I'M FINE! I CAN STILL WALK!
AND IT'S NOT LIKE I HAVE TO JUMP OR ANY-THING--
DON'T PUSH YOUR LUCK.
!!
ICE! WE NEED ICE!
SPRAINED ANKLE?
MUR
PROB-ABLY.
MUR
OUCH. NO WAY HE'S COMING BACK INTO THE GAME THEN.
WHOOPSIE.
LOOKS LIKE HE WENT A TEENSY BIT TOO FAR.
WHRL
SORRY ...!

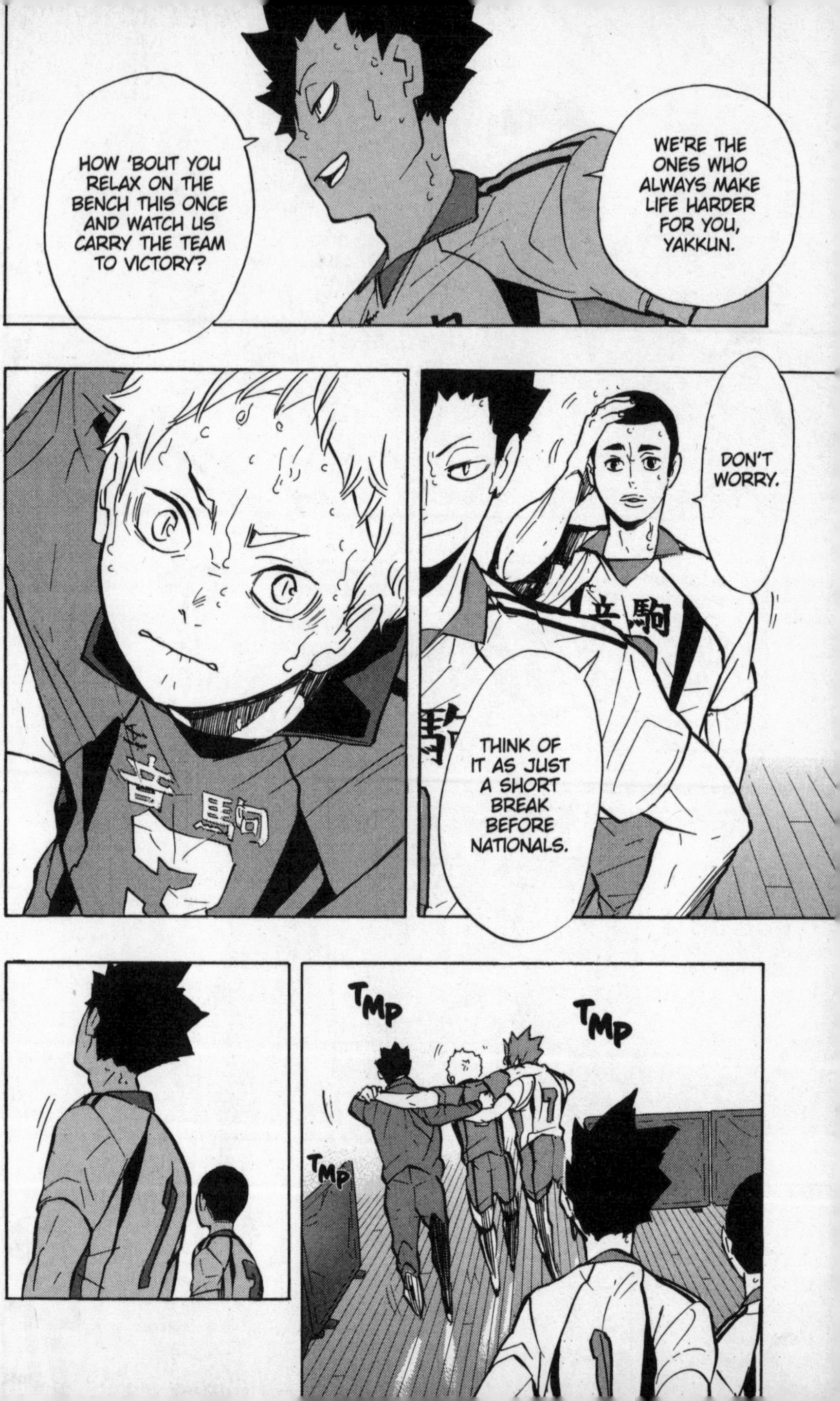
WE'RE THE ONES WHO ALWAYS MAKE LIFE HARDER FOR YOU, YAKKUN.
HOW 'BOUT YOU RELAX ON THE BENCH THIS ONCE AND WATCH US CARRY THE TEAM TO VICTORY?
DON'T WORRY.
THINK OF IT AS JUST A SHORT BREAK BEFORE NATIONALS.
TMP
TMP
TMP

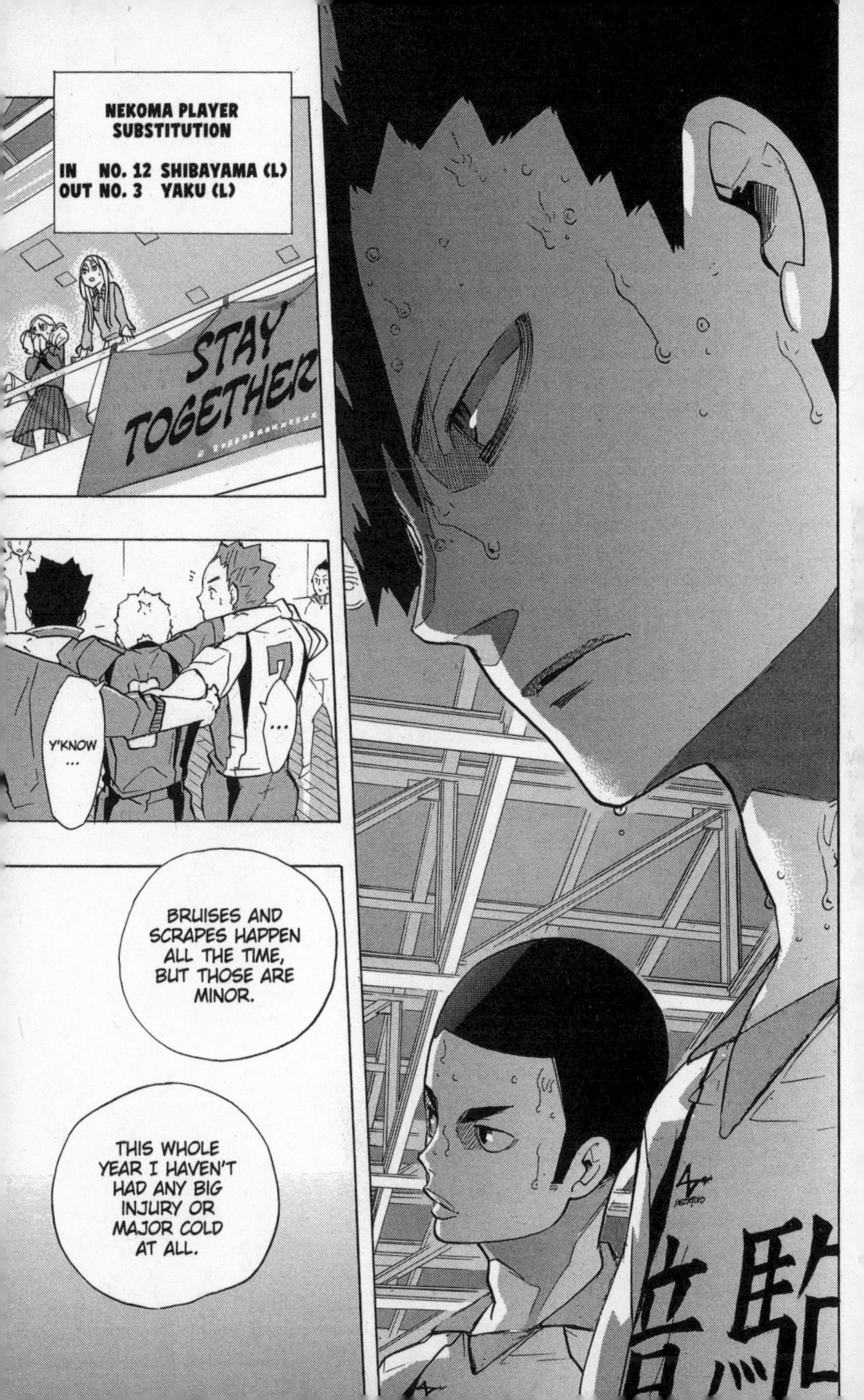
NEKOMA PLAYER SUBSTITUTION
IN NO. 12 SHIBAYAMA (L)
OUT NO. 3 YAKU (L)
STAY TOGETHER
...
Y'KNOW ...
BRUISES AND SCRAPES HAPPEN ALL THE TIME, BUT THOSE ARE MINOR.
THIS WHOLE YEAR I HAVEN'T HAD ANY BIG INJURY OR MAJOR COLD AT ALL.

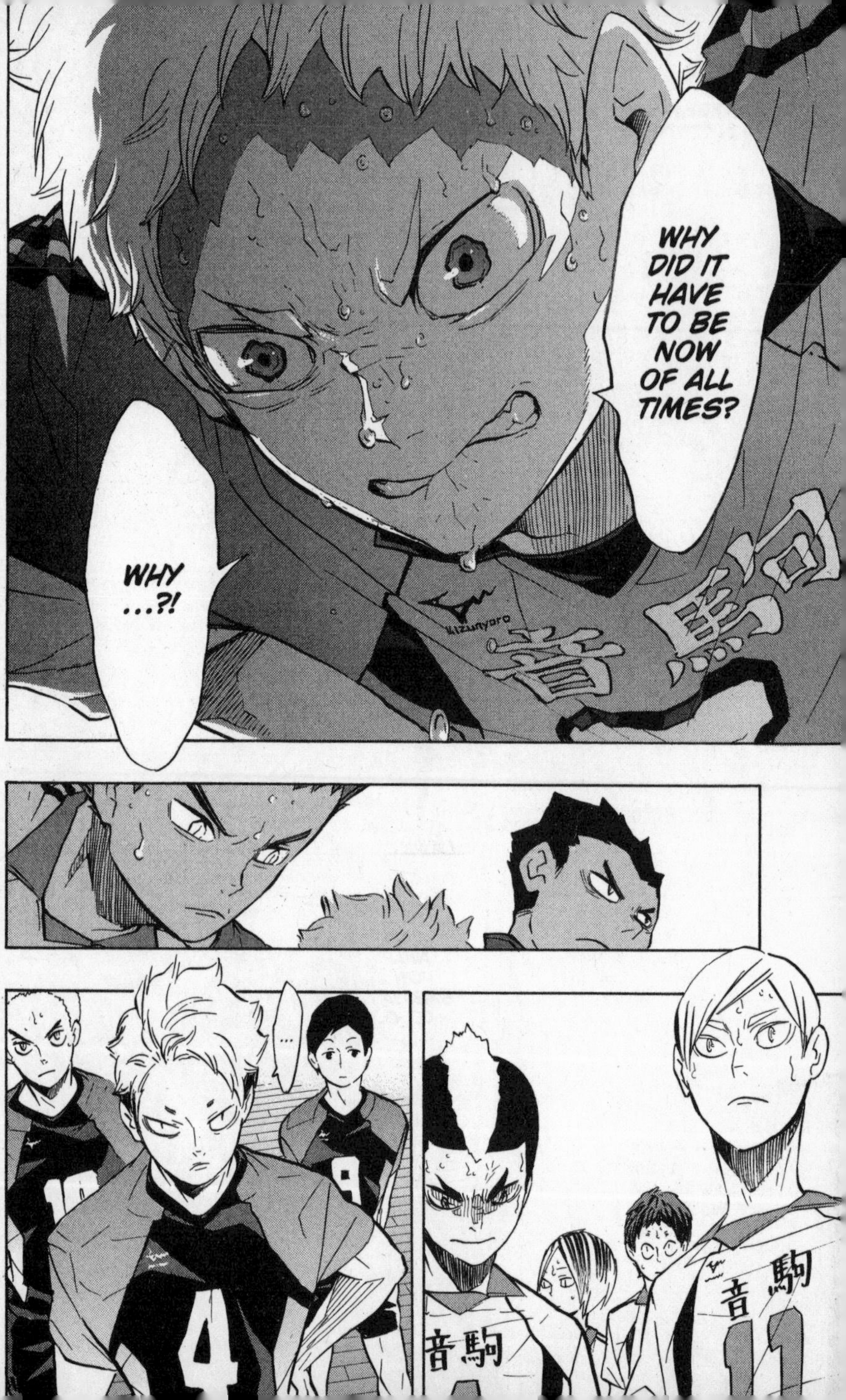
WHY DID IT HAVE TO BE NOW OF ALL TIMES?
WHY ...?!
...

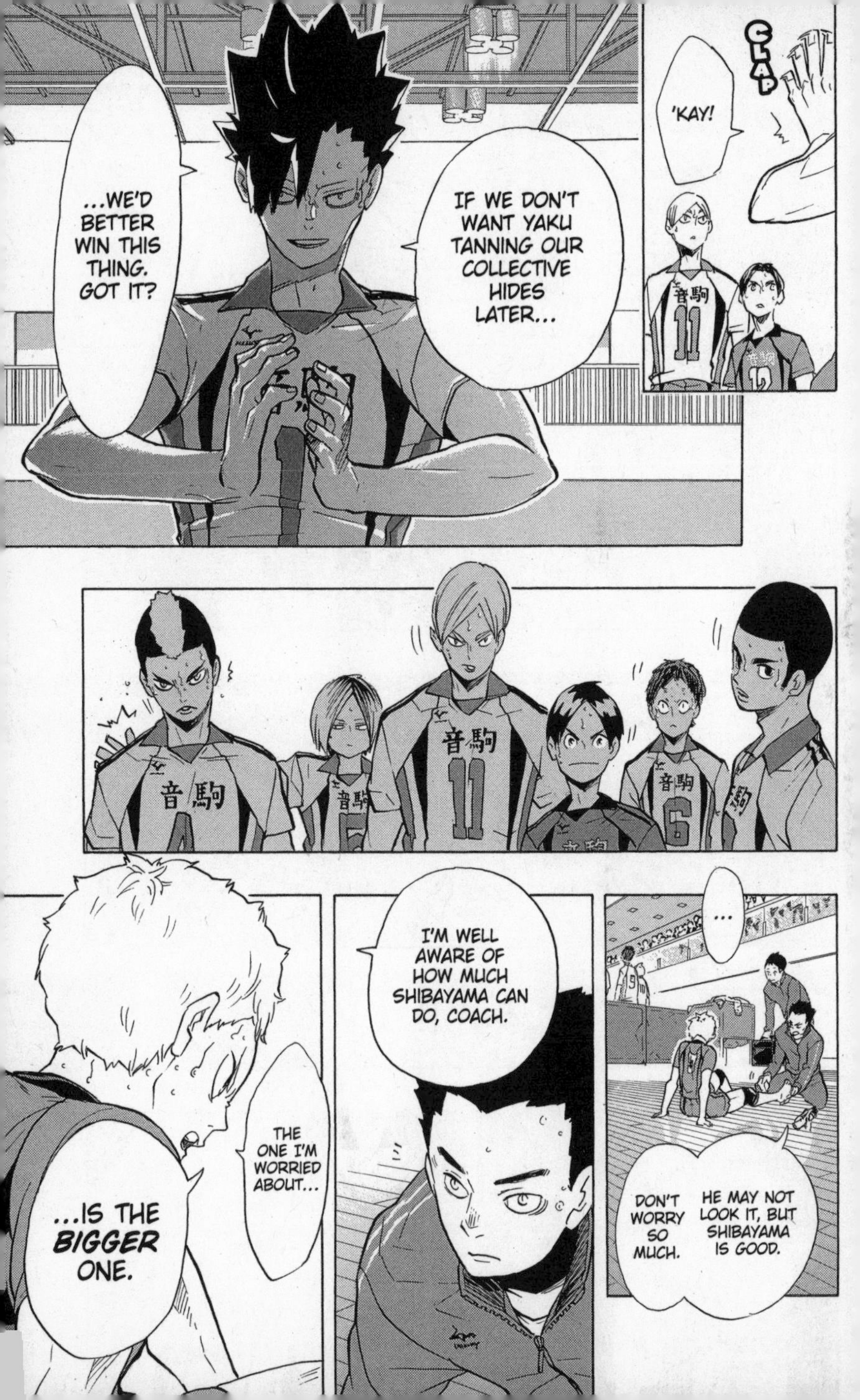
CLAP
'KAY!
IF WE DON'T WANT YAKU TANNING OUR COLLECTIVE HIDES LATER...
...WE'D BETTER WIN THIS THING. GOT IT?
...
HE MAY NOT LOOK IT, BUT SHIBAYAMA IS GOOD.
DON'T WORRY SO MUCH.
I'M WELL AWARE OF HOW MUCH SHIBAYAMA CAN DO, COACH.
THE ONE I'M WORRIED ABOUT...
...IS THE BIGGER ONE.

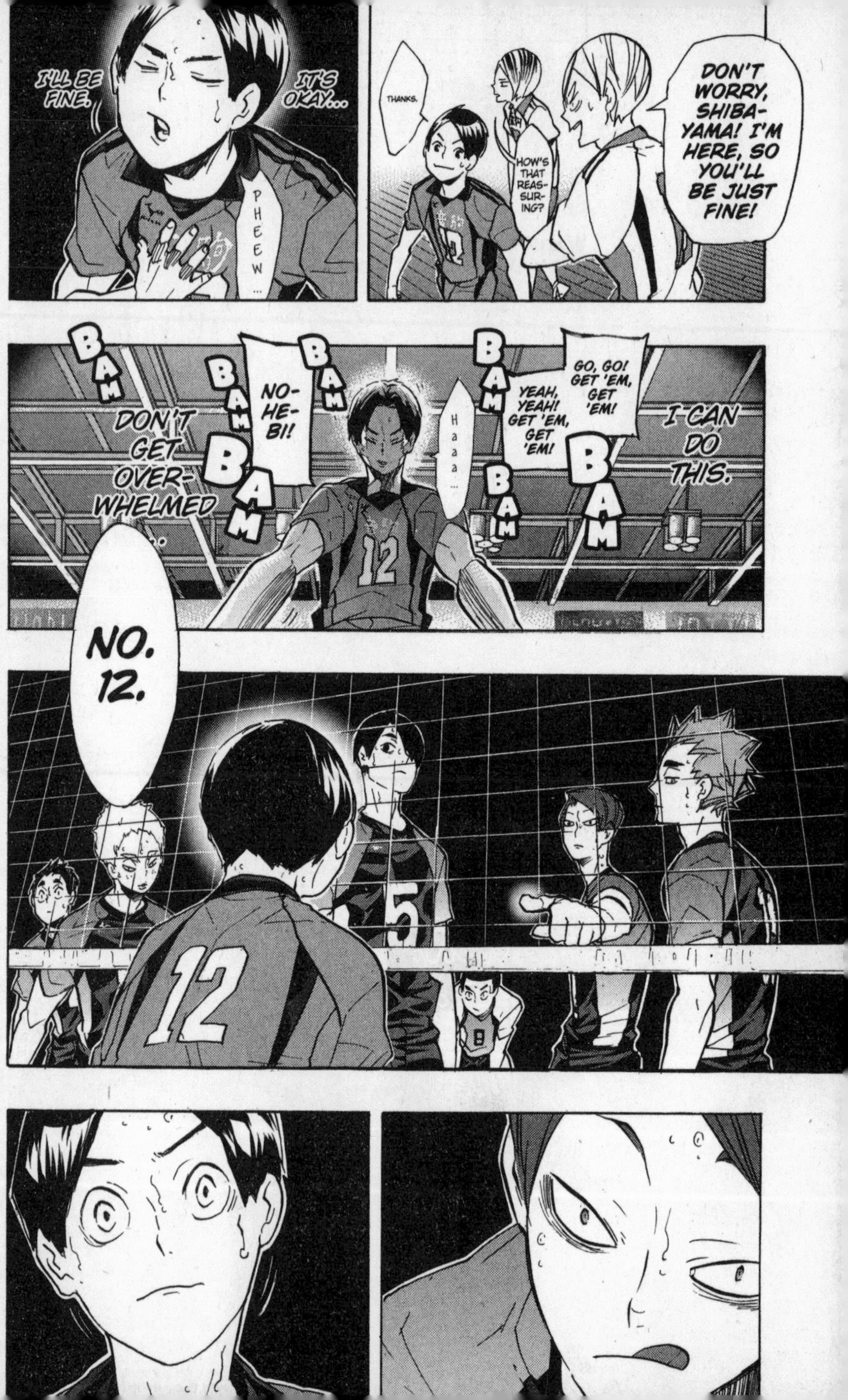
DON'T WORRY, SHIBAYAMA! I'M HERE, SO YOU'LL BE JUST FINE!
HOW'S THAT REASSURING?
THANKS.
IT'S OKAY...
I'LL BE FINE.
PHEEW...
I CAN DO THIS.
GO, GO! GET 'EM, GET 'EM!
BAM
YEAH, YEAH! GET 'EM, GET 'EM!
BAM
BAM
Haaa...
BAM
NO-HE-BI!
BAM
BAM
BAM
BAM
DON'T GET OVER-WHELMED...
NO. 12.

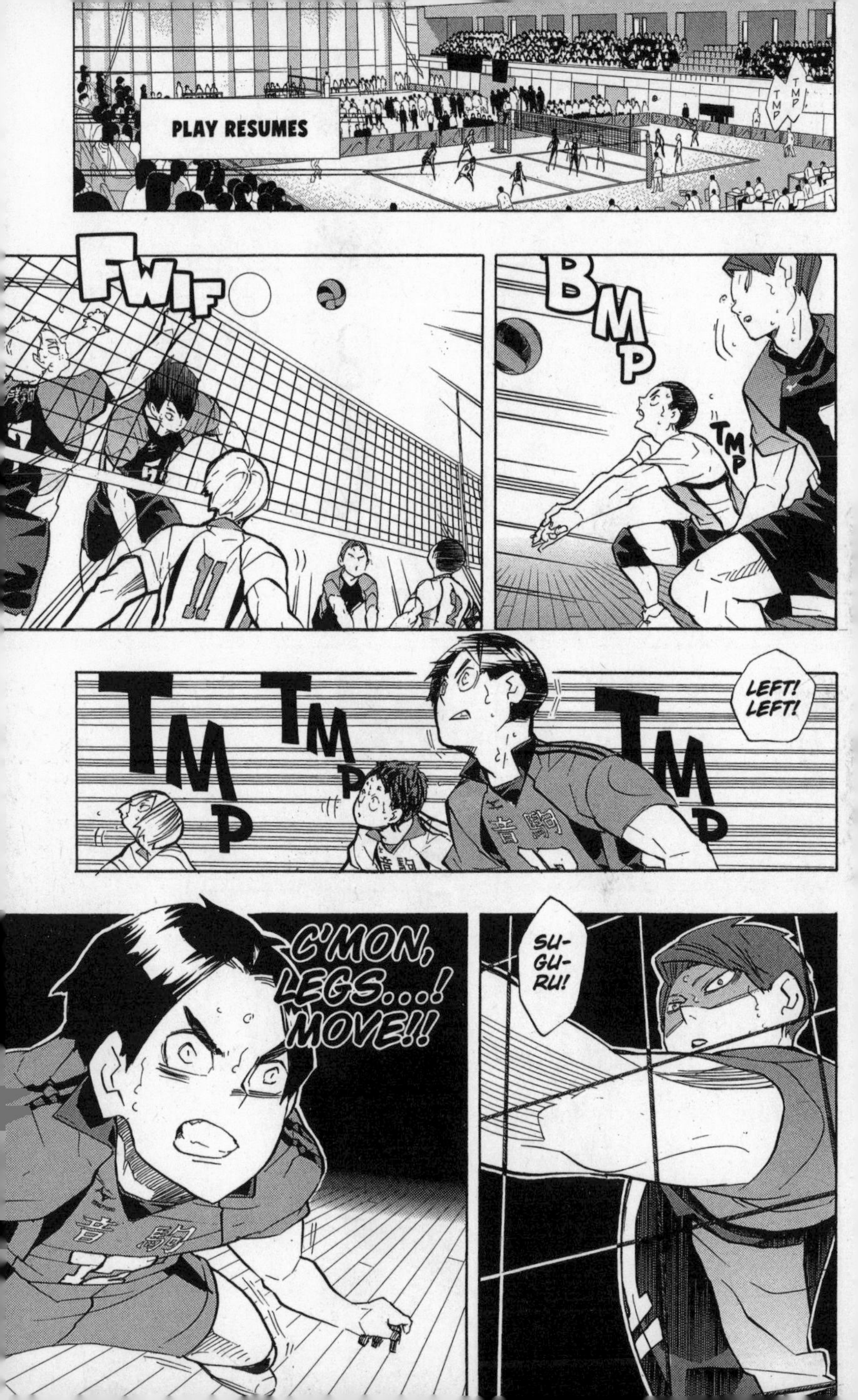
TMP TMP
PLAY RESUMES
BMP
TMP
FWIF
LEFT! LEFT!
TMP
TMP
TMP
SU-GU-RU!
C'MON, LEGS...! MOVE!!

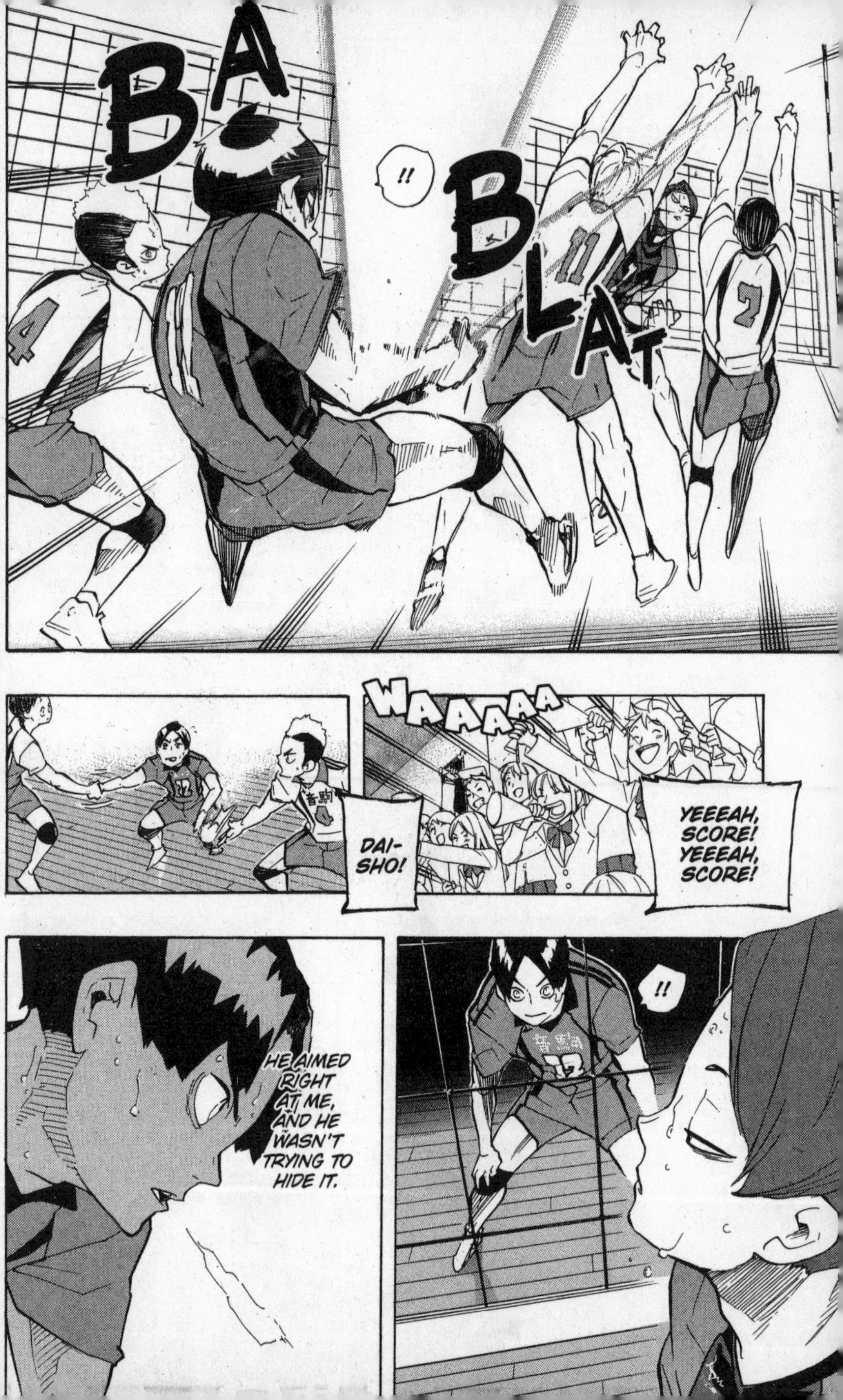
BLAT
!!
BA
WAAAAA
YEEEAH, SCORE! YEEEAH, SCORE!
DAI-SHO!
!!
HE AIMED RIGHT AT ME, AND HE WASN'T TRYING TO HIDE IT.

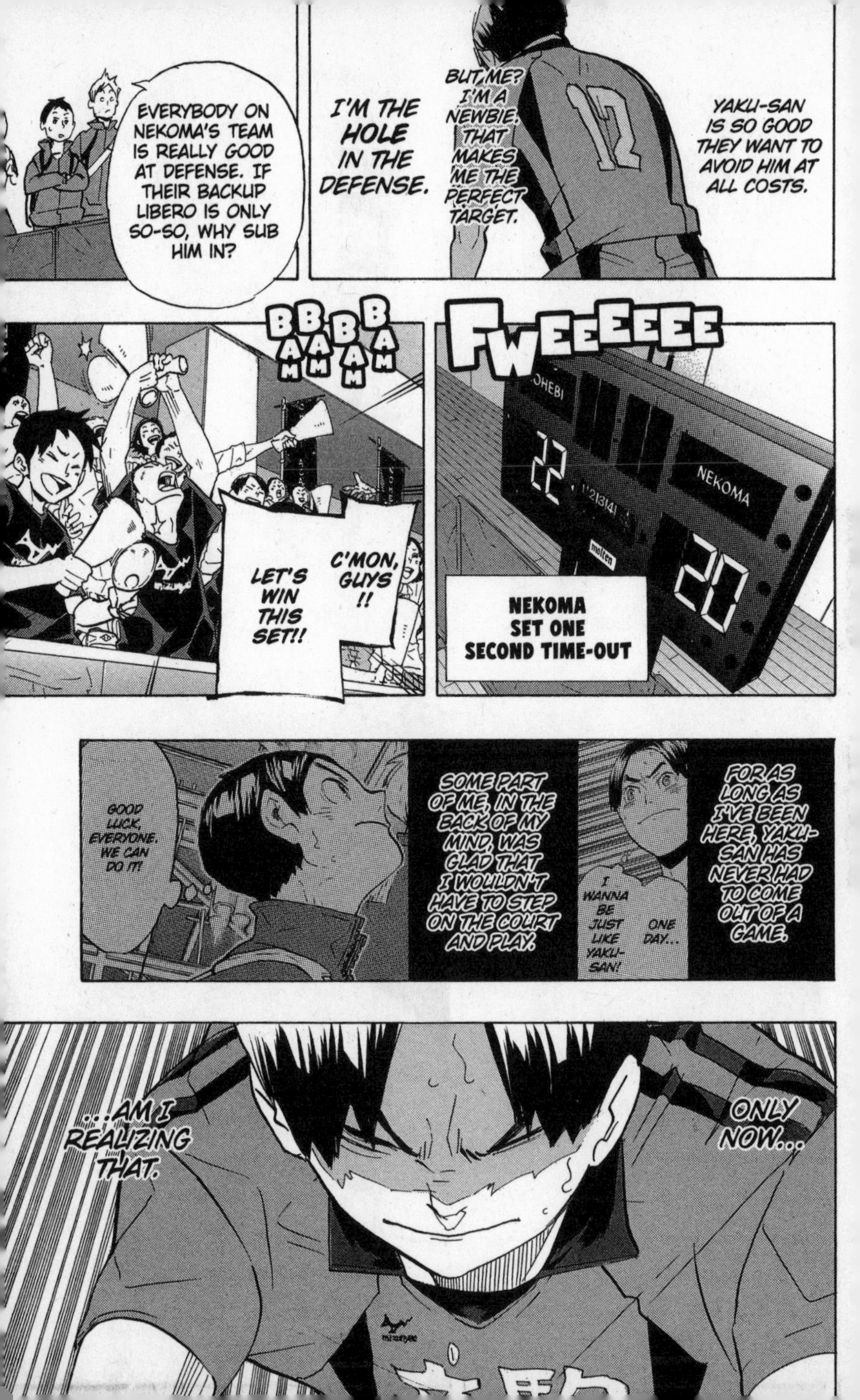

YAKU-SAN IS SO GOOD THEY WANT TO AVOID HIM AT ALL COSTS.
BUT ME? I'M A NEWBIE. THAT MAKES ME THE PERFECT TARGET.
I'M THE HOLE IN THE DEFENSE.
EVERYBODY ON NEKOMA'S TEAM IS REALLY GOOD AT DEFENSE. IF THEIR BACKUP LIBERO IS ONLY SO-SO, WHY SUB HIM IN?
FWEEEEEEE
OHEBI
NEKOMA
molten
NEKOMA SET ONE SECOND TIME-OUT
BBBBAAAAMMMM
C'MON, GUYS!!
LET'S WIN THIS SET!!
FOR AS LONG AS I'VE BEEN HERE, YAKU-SAN HAS NEVER HAD TO COME OUT OF A GAME.
ONE DAY...
I WANNA BE JUST LIKE YAKU-SAN!
SOME PART OF ME, IN THE BACK OF MY MIND, WAS GLAD THAT I WOULDN'T HAVE TO STEP ON THE COURT AND PLAY.
GOOD LUCK, EVERYONE. WE CAN DO IT!
ONLY NOW...
...AM I REALIZING THAT.

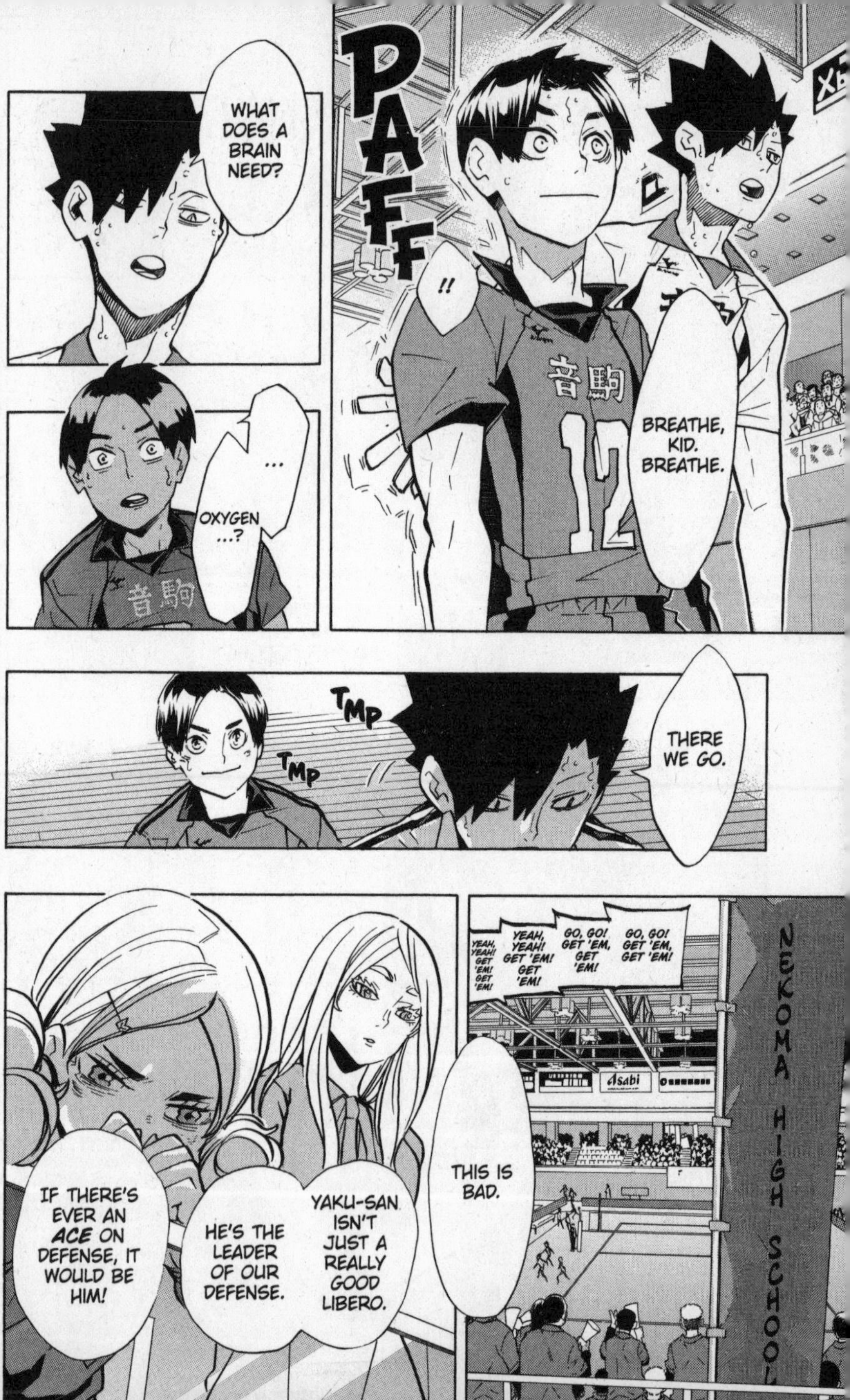
PAFF
!!
BREATHE, KID. BREATHE.
WHAT DOES A BRAIN NEED?
...
OXYGEN ...?
TMP
TMP
THERE WE GO.
GO, GO! GET 'EM, GET 'EM!
GO, GO! GET 'EM, GET 'EM!
YEAH, YEAH! GET 'EM! GET 'EM!
YEAH, YEAH! GET 'EM! GET 'EM!
Asabi
NEKOMA HIGH SCHOOL
THIS IS BAD.
YAKU-SAN ISN'T JUST A REALLY GOOD LIBERO.
HE'S THE LEADER OF OUR DEFENSE.
IF THERE'S EVER AN *ACE* ON DEFENSE, IT WOULD BE HIM!

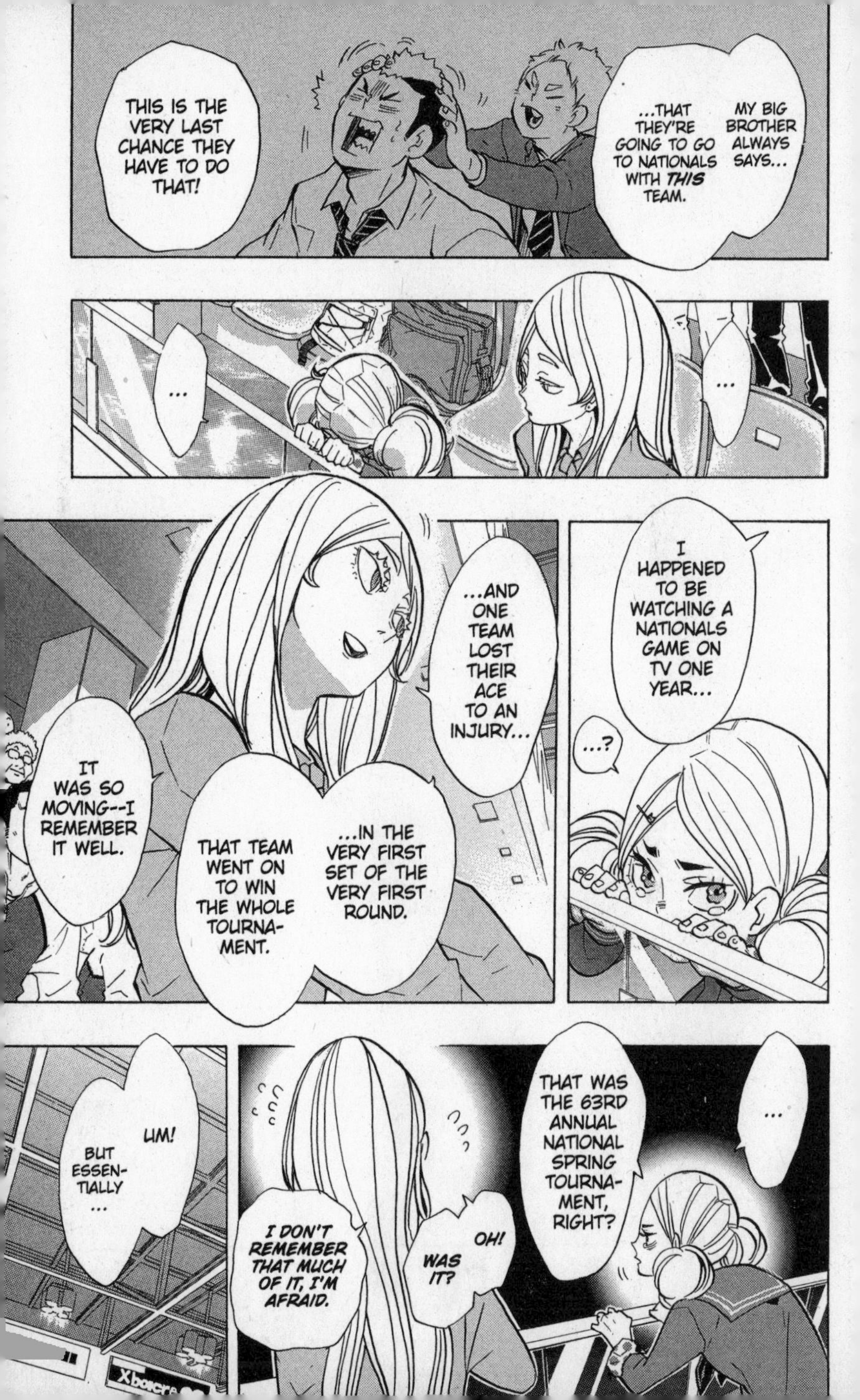
MY BIG BROTHER ALWAYS SAYS...
...THAT THEY'RE GOING TO GO TO NATIONALS WITH *THIS* TEAM.
THIS IS THE VERY LAST CHANCE THEY HAVE TO DO THAT!
...
...
I HAPPENED TO BE WATCHING A NATIONALS GAME ON TV ONE YEAR...
...?
...AND ONE TEAM LOST THEIR ACE TO AN INJURY...
...IN THE VERY FIRST SET OF THE VERY FIRST ROUND.
THAT TEAM WENT ON TO WIN THE WHOLE TOURNAMENT.
IT WAS SO MOVING--I REMEMBER IT WELL.
...
THAT WAS THE 63RD ANNUAL NATIONAL SPRING TOURNAMENT, RIGHT?
OH! WAS IT?
I DON'T REMEMBER THAT MUCH OF IT, I'M AFRAID.
UM!
BUT ESSENTIALLY...

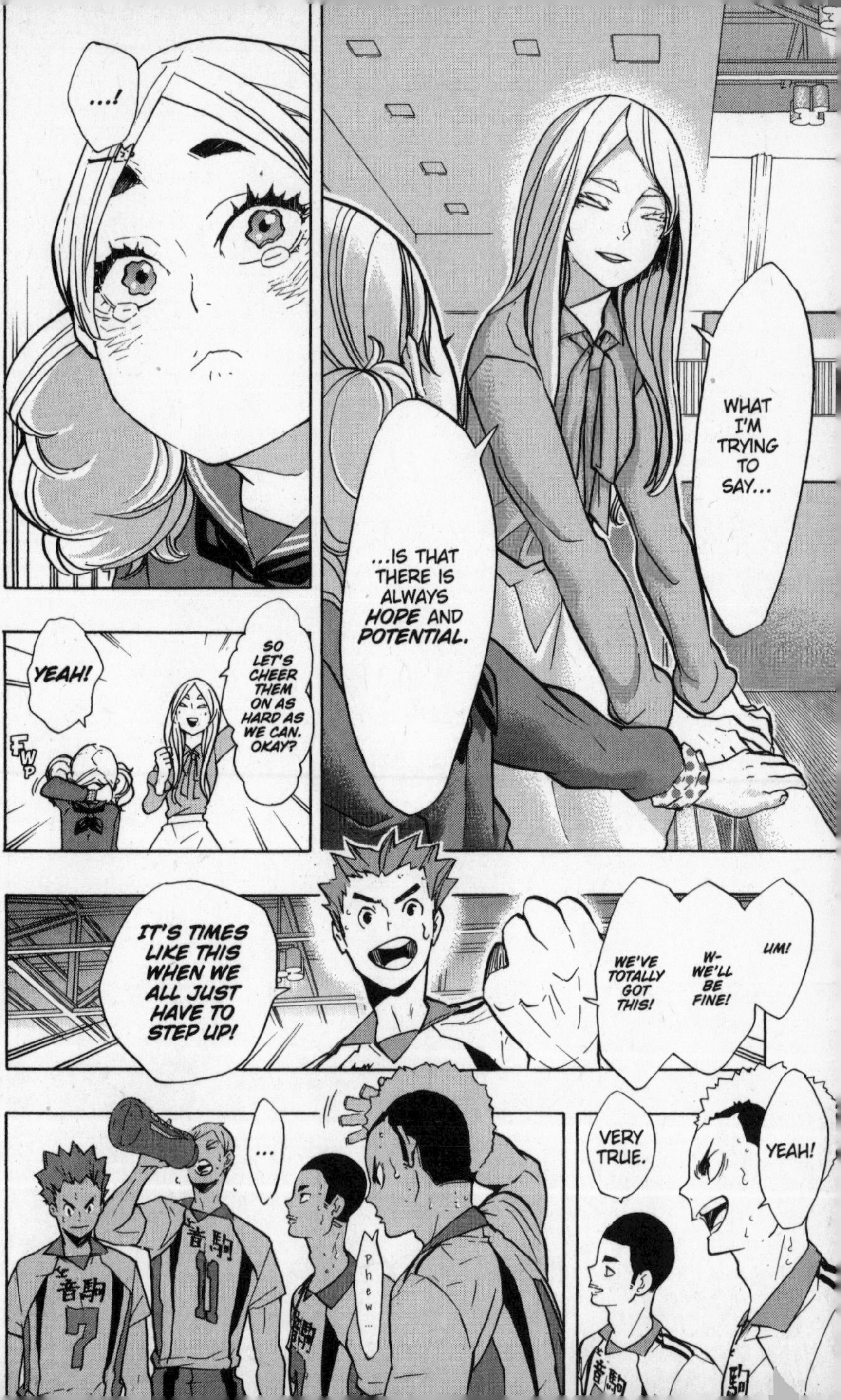
WHAT I'M TRYING TO SAY...
...IS THAT THERE IS ALWAYS HOPE AND POTENTIAL.
...!
SO LET'S CHEER THEM ON AS HARD AS WE CAN. OKAY?
YEAH!
FWP
UM!
W-WE'LL BE FINE!
WE'VE TOTALLY GOT THIS!
IT'S TIMES LIKE THIS WHEN WE ALL JUST HAVE TO STEP UP!
YEAH!
VERY TRUE.
...
Phew...

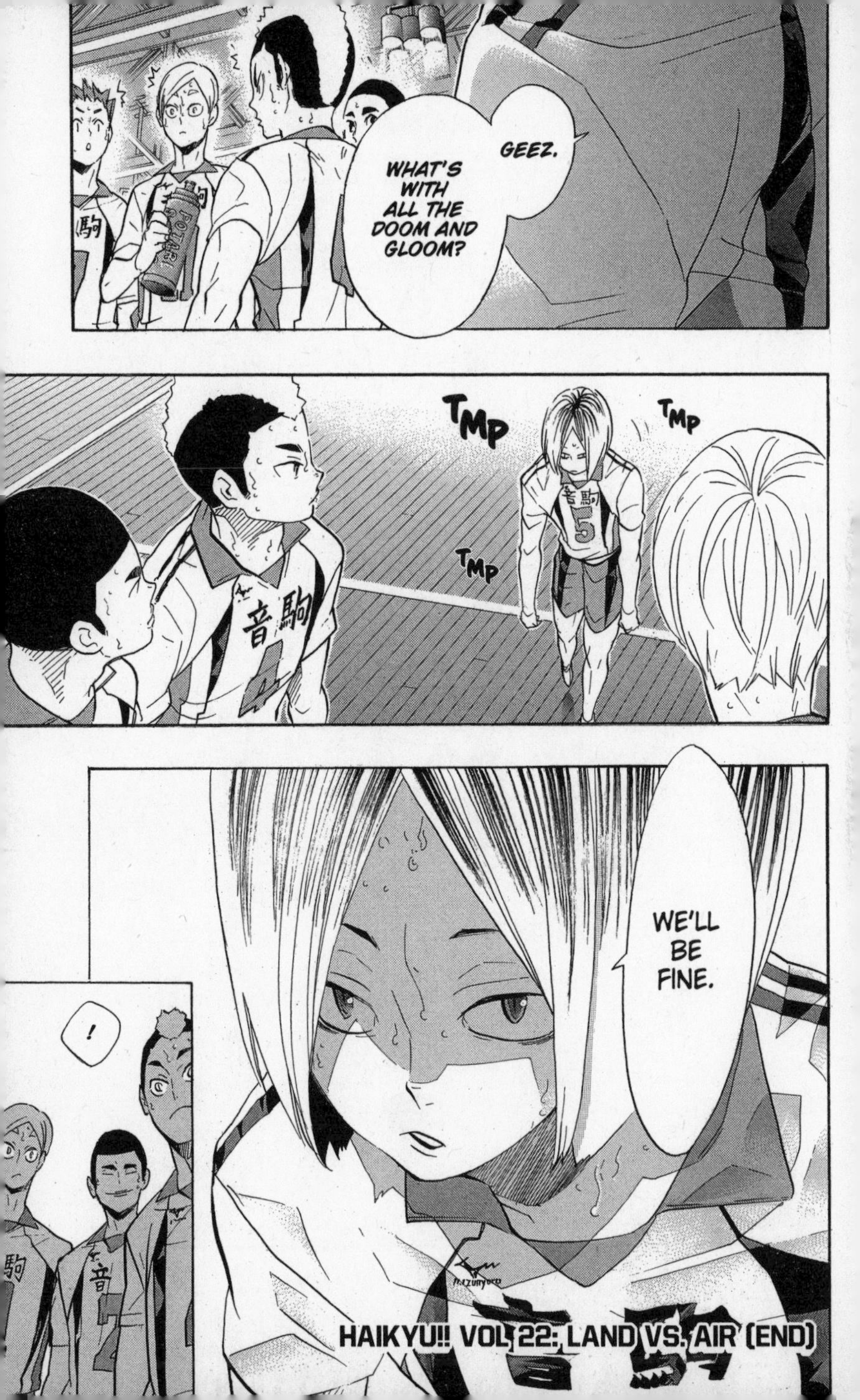
GEEZ.
WHAT'S WITH ALL THE DOOM AND GLOOM?
TMP
TMP
TMP
WE'LL BE FINE.
!
HAIKYU!! VOL 22: LAND VS. AIR (END)

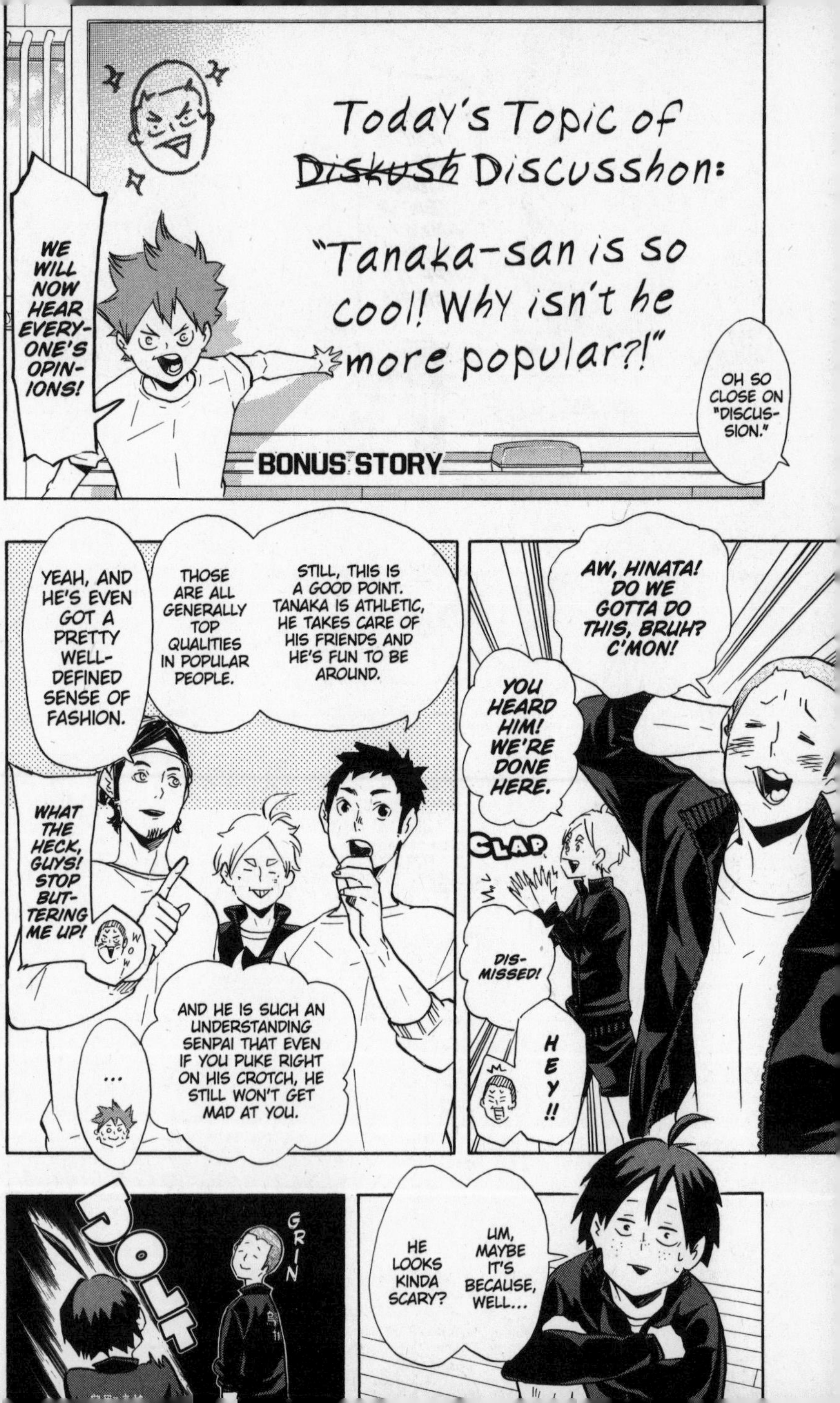
Today's Topic of ~~Diskush~~ Discusshon:
"Tanaka-san is so cool! Why isn't he more popular?!"
WE WILL NOW HEAR EVERYONE'S OPINIONS!
OH SO CLOSE ON "DISCUSSION."
BONUS STORY
AW, HINATA! DO WE GOTTA DO THIS, BRUH? C'MON!
YOU HEARD HIM! WE'RE DONE HERE.
CLAP
DISMISSED!
HEY!!
STILL, THIS IS A GOOD POINT. TANAKA IS ATHLETIC, HE TAKES CARE OF HIS FRIENDS AND HE'S FUN TO BE AROUND.
THOSE ARE ALL GENERALLY TOP QUALITIES IN POPULAR PEOPLE.
YEAH, AND HE'S EVEN GOT A PRETTY WELL-DEFINED SENSE OF FASHION.
WHAT THE HECK, GUYS! STOP BUTTERING ME UP!
WOW
AND HE IS SUCH AN UNDERSTANDING SENPAI THAT EVEN IF YOU PUKE RIGHT ON HIS CROTCH, HE STILL WON'T GET MAD AT YOU.
...
UM, MAYBE IT'S BECAUSE, WELL...
HE LOOKS KINDA SCARY?
JOLT
GRIN

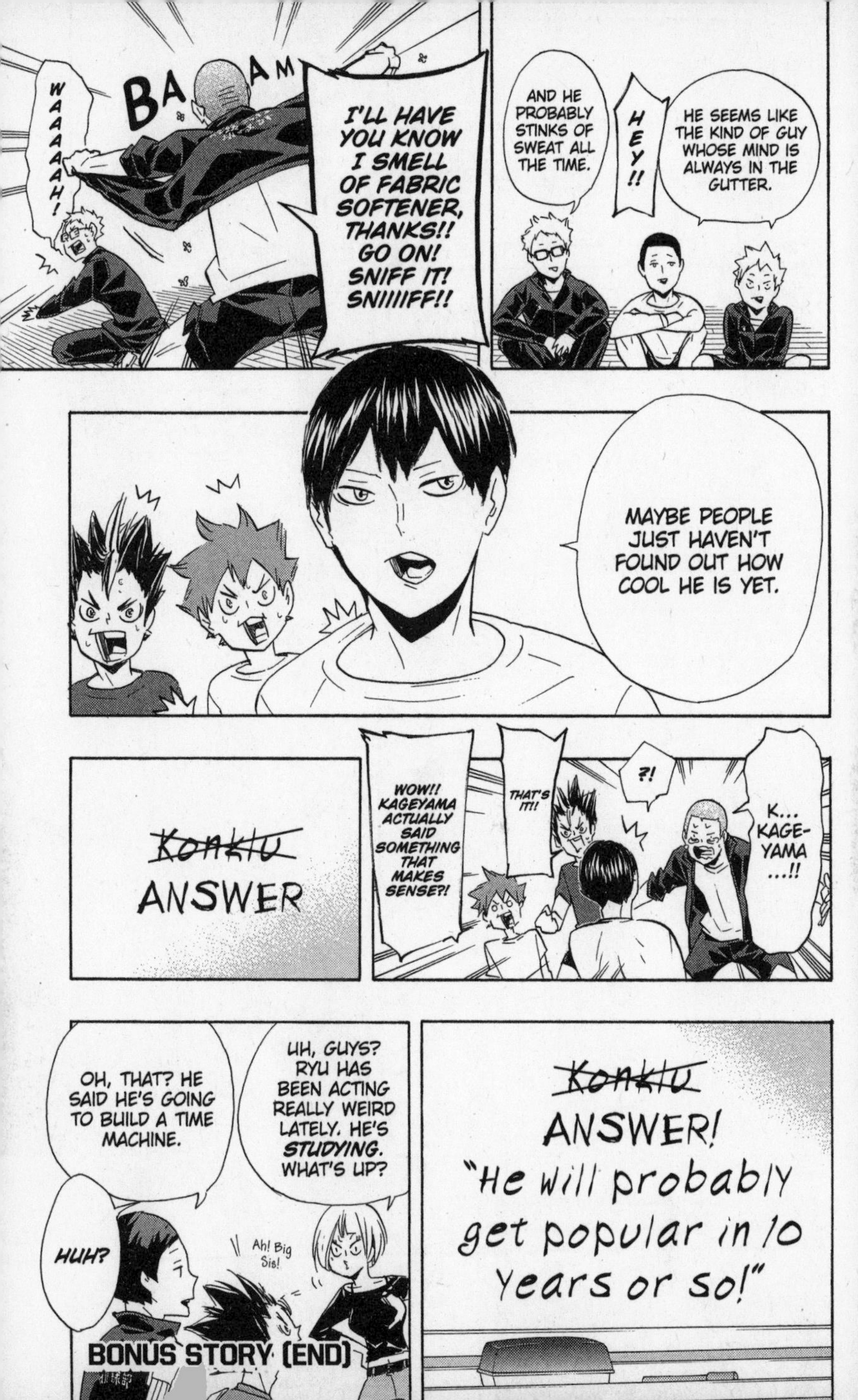

HE SEEMS LIKE THE KIND OF GUY WHOSE MIND IS ALWAYS IN THE GUTTER.
HEY!!
AND HE PROBABLY STINKS OF SWEAT ALL THE TIME.
BAAM
I'LL HAVE YOU KNOW I SMELL OF FABRIC SOFTENER, THANKS!! GO ON! SNIFF IT! SNIIIIFF!!
WAAAAAAH!
MAYBE PEOPLE JUST HAVEN'T FOUND OUT HOW COOL HE IS YET.
K... KAGE-YAMA ...!!
?!
THAT'S IT!!
WOW!! KAGEYAMA ACTUALLY SAID SOMETHING THAT MAKES SENSE?!
~~Konkiu~~
ANSWER
~~Konkiu~~
ANSWER!
"He will probably get popular in 10 years or so!"
UH, GUYS? RYU HAS BEEN ACTING REALLY WEIRD LATELY. HE'S STUDYING. WHAT'S UP?
OH, THAT? HE SAID HE'S GOING TO BUILD A TIME MACHINE.
Ah! Big Sis!
HUH?
BONUS STORY (END)

BONUS STORY 2

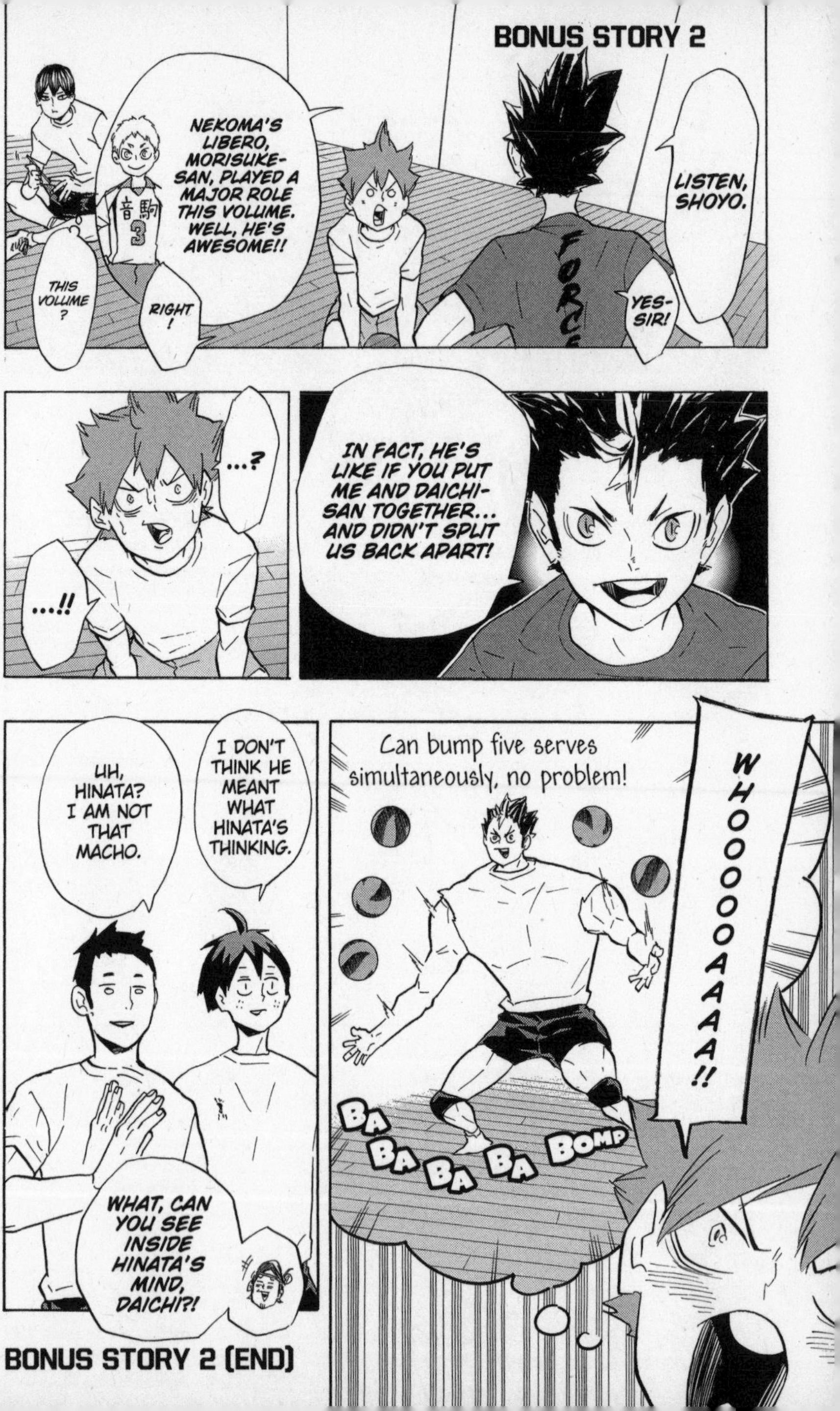
LISTEN, SHOYO.
YES-SIR!
NEKOMA'S LIBERO, MORISUKE-SAN, PLAYED A MAJOR ROLE THIS VOLUME. WELL, HE'S AWESOME!!
RIGHT!
THIS VOLUME?
IN FACT, HE'S LIKE IF YOU PUT ME AND DAICHI-SAN TOGETHER... AND DIDN'T SPLIT US BACK APART!
...?
...!!
WHOOOOOOAAAAA!!
Can bump five serves simultaneously, no problem!
BA BA BA BA BA BOMP
I DON'T THINK HE MEANT WHAT HINATA'S THINKING.
UH, HINATA? I AM NOT THAT MACHO.
WHAT, CAN YOU SEE INSIDE HINATA'S MIND, DAICHI?!

BONUS STORY 2 (END)

NEXT VOLUME:
The Tokyo Qualifiers wrap up! See you in **VOLUME 23!!**

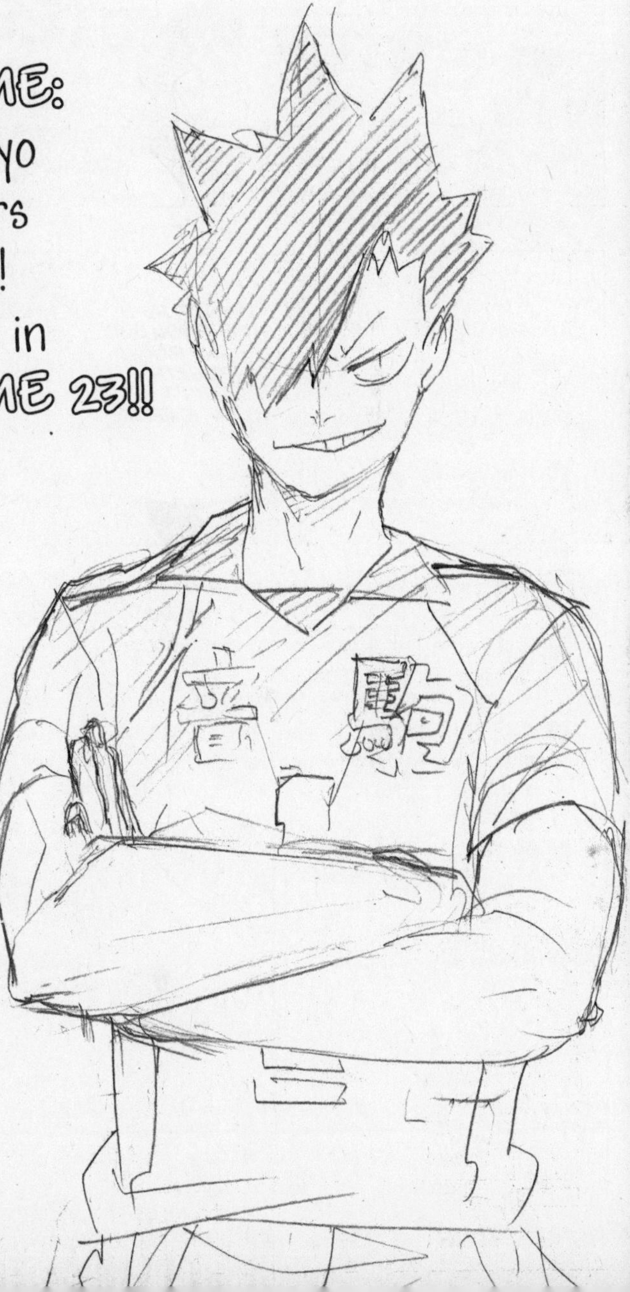
音駒

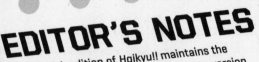

EDITOR'S NOTES

The English edition of *Haikyu!!* maintains the honorifics used in the original Japanese version. For those of you who are new to these terms, here's a brief explanation to help with your reading experience!

When saying someone's name in Japanese, a suffix is often attached to indicate how familiar the speaker is with the person. Some are more polite and respectful, while others are endearing.

1. **-kun** is often used for young men or boys, usually someone you are familiar with.

2. **-chan** is used for young children and can be used as a term of endearment.

3. **-san** is used for someone you respect or are not close to, or to be polite.

4. **Senpai** is used for someone who is older than you or in a higher position or grade in school.

5. **Kohai** is used for someone who is younger than you or in a lower position or grade in school.

6. **Sensei** means teacher.

Kuroko's BASKETBALL

TADATOSHI FUJIMAKI

When incoming first-year student Taiga Kagami joins the Seirin High basketball team, he meets Tetsuya Kuroko, a mysterious boy who's plain beyond words. But Kagami's in for the shock of his life when he learns that the practically invisible Kuroko was once a member of "the Miracle Generation"—the undefeated legendary team—and he wants Kagami's help taking down each of his old teammates!

viz media
www.viz.com

THE HIT SPORTS MANGA FROM *SHONEN JUMP* IN A 2-IN-1 EDITION!

KUROKO NO BASUKE © 2008 by Tadatoshi Fujimaki/SHUEISHA Inc.

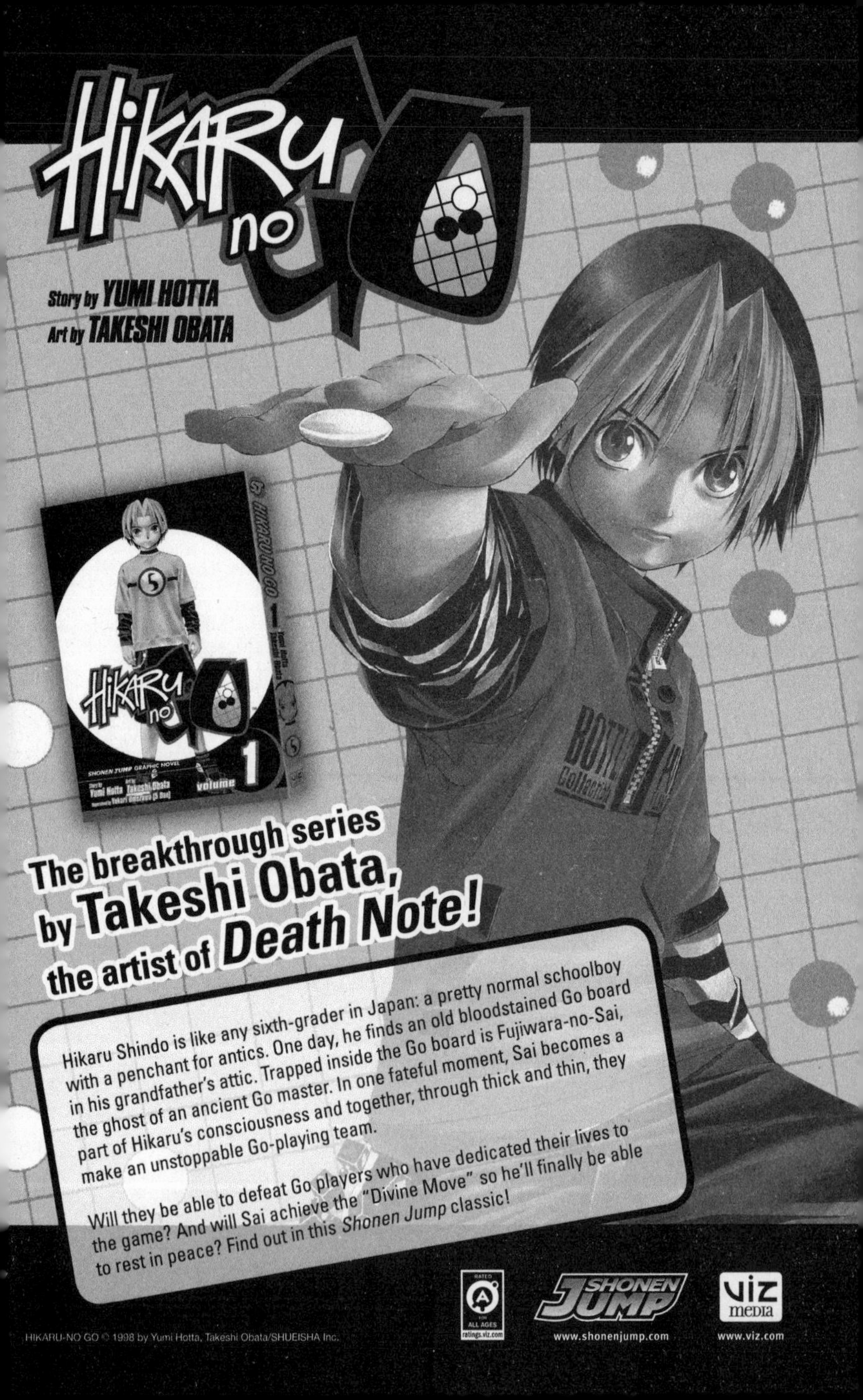
HIKARU no GO
Story by YUMI HOTTA
Art by TAKESHI OBATA
HIKARU no GO
SHONEN JUMP GRAPHIC NOVEL
volume 1
Story by Yumi Hotta
Art by Takeshi Obata
The breakthrough series by Takeshi Obata, the artist of Death Note!
Hikaru Shindo is like any sixth-grader in Japan: a pretty normal schoolboy with a penchant for antics. One day, he finds an old bloodstained Go board in his grandfather's attic. Trapped inside the Go board is Fujiwara-no-Sai, the ghost of an ancient Go master. In one fateful moment, Sai becomes a part of Hikaru's consciousness and together, through thick and thin, they make an unstoppable Go-playing team.
Will they be able to defeat Go players who have dedicated their lives to the game? And will Sai achieve the "Divine Move" so he'll finally be able to rest in peace? Find out in this Shonen Jump classic!
RATED A ALL AGES ratings.viz.com
SHONEN JUMP
VIZ media
HIKARU-NO GO © 1998 by Yumi Hotta, Takeshi Obata/SHUEISHA Inc.
www.shonenjump.com
www.viz.com

IN A SAVAGE WORLD RULED BY THE PURSUIT OF THE MOST DELICIOUS FOODS, IT'S EITHER EAT OR BE EATEN!

"The most bizarrely entertaining manga out there on comic shelves. *Toriko* is a great series. If you're looking for an weirdly fun book or a fighting manga with a bizarre take, this is the story for you to read."
—ComicAttack.com

TORIKO

Story and Art by Mitsutoshi Shimabukuro

In an era where the world's gone crazy for increasingly bizarre gourmet foods, only Gourmet Hunter Toriko can hunt down the ferocious ingredients that supply the world's best restaurants. Join Toriko as he tracks and defeats the tastiest and most dangerous animals with his bare hands.

TORIKO © 2008 by Mitsutoshi Shimabukuro/SHUEISHA Inc.

RATED T FOR TEEN
ratings.viz.com

www.shonenjump.com   www.viz.com

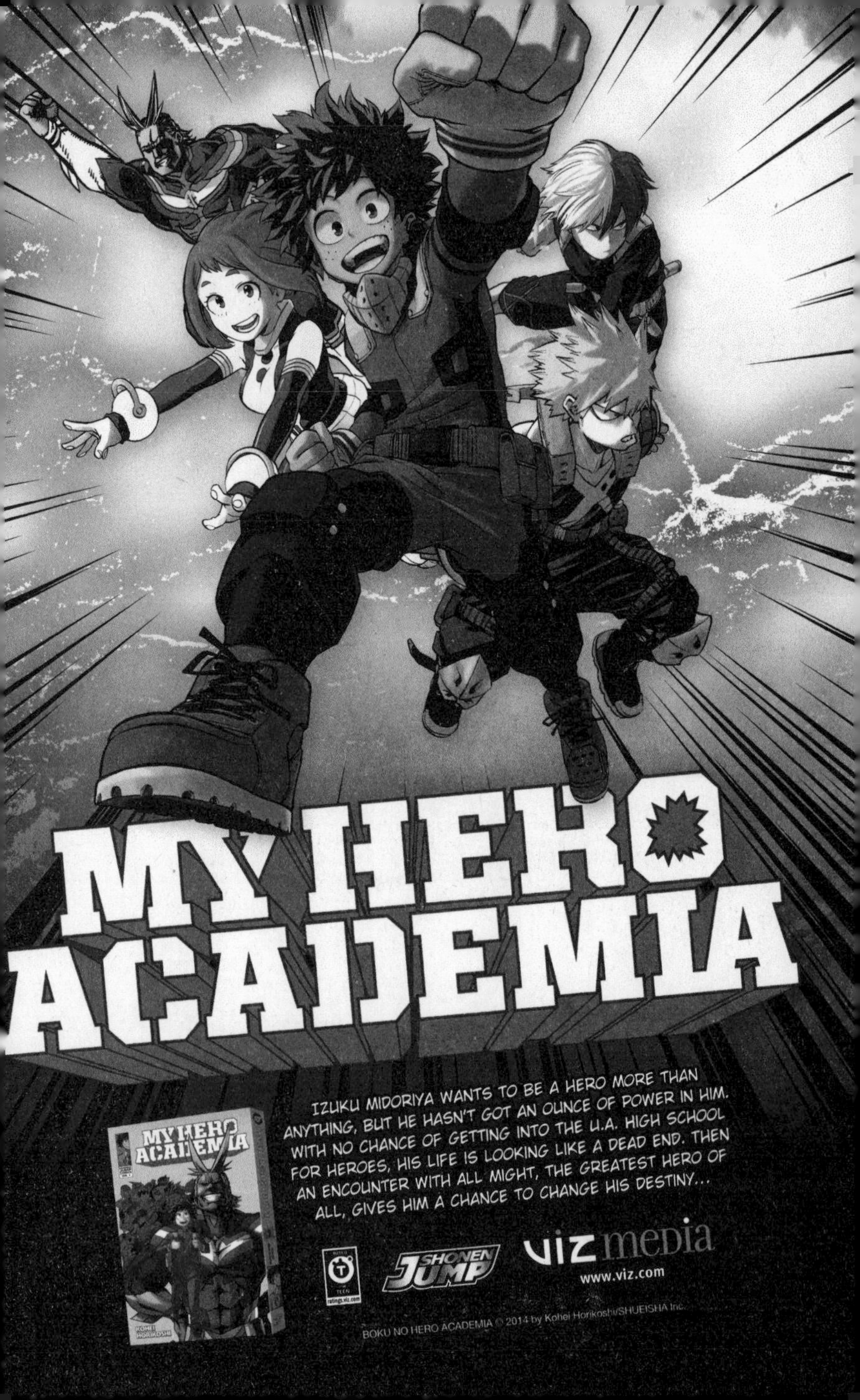
MY HERO ACADEMIA
IZUKU MIDORIYA WANTS TO BE A HERO MORE THAN ANYTHING, BUT HE HASN'T GOT AN OUNCE OF POWER IN HIM. WITH NO CHANCE OF GETTING INTO THE U.A. HIGH SCHOOL FOR HEROES, HIS LIFE IS LOOKING LIKE A DEAD END. THEN AN ENCOUNTER WITH ALL MIGHT, THE GREATEST HERO OF ALL, GIVES HIM A CHANCE TO CHANGE HIS DESTINY...
MY HERO ACADEMIA
KOHEI HORIKOSHI
TEEN
ratings.viz.com
SHONEN JUMP
viz media
www.viz.com
BOKU NO HERO ACADEMIA © 2014 by Kohei Horikoshi/SHUEISHA Inc.

A PREMIUM BOX SET OF THE FIRST TWO STORY ARCS OF ONE PIECE!

A PIRATE'S TREASURE FOR ANY MANGA FAN!

STORY AND ART BY EIICHIRO ODA

Comes with EXCLUSIVE POSTER and the ROMANCE DAWN mini-comic!

As a child, Monkey D. Luffy dreamed of becoming King of the Pirates. But his life changed when he accidentally gained the power to stretch like rubber...at the cost of never being able to swim again! Years later, Luffy sets off in search of the "One Piece," said to be the greatest treasure in the world...

This box set includes VOLUMES 1-23, which comprise the EAST BLUE and BAROQUE WORKS story arcs.

EXCLUSIVE PREMIUMS and GREAT SAVINGS
over buying the individual volumes!

WWW.SHONENJUMP.COM

RATED T FOR TEEN
ratings.viz.com

viz media
www.viz.com

ONE PIECE © 1997 by Eiichiro Oda/SHUEISHA Inc.

Love triangle!
Comedic antics!!
Gang warfare?!

A laugh-out-loud story that features a fake love relationship between two heirs of rival gangs!

Story and Art by
NAOSHI KOMI

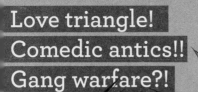

NISEKOI
False Love

It's hate at first sight...rather, a knee to the head at first sight when RAKU ICHIJO meets CHITOGE KIRISAKI! Unfortunately, Raku's gangster father arranges a false love match with their rival's daughter, who just so happens to be Chitoge! Raku's searching for his childhood sweetheart from ten years ago, however, with a pendant around his neck as a memento, but he can't even remember her name or face!

AVAILABLE NOW!

WWW.SHONENJUMP.COM

RATED
FOR
TEEN
ratings.viz.com

www.viz.com

NISEKOI © 2011 by Naoshi Komi/SHUEISHA Inc.

You're Reading the
WRONG WAY!

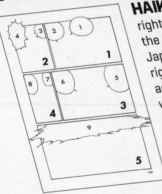

HAIKYU!! reads from right to left, starting in the upper-right corner. Japanese is read from right to left, meaning that action, sound effects and word-balloon order are completely reversed from English order.